THE CHINESE INFLATION

1937–1949

Studies of the East Asian Institute

SHUN-HSIN CHOU

The Chinese Inflation

1937-1949

New York and London

COLUMBIA UNIVERSITY PRESS

First printing 1963
Second printing, with supplementary tables, 1969
Library of Congress Catalog Card Number: 62-18260
Printed in the United States of America

The East Asian Institute of Columbia University

The East Asian Institute of Columbia University was established in 1949 to prepare graduate students for careers dealing with East Asia, and to aid research and publication on East Asia during the modern period. The faculty of the Institute are grateful to the Ford Foundation and the Rockefeller Foundation for their financial assistance.

The Studies of the East Asian Institute were inaugurated in 1962 to bring to a wider public the results of significant new research on modern and contemporary East Asia.

Studies of the East Asian Institute

The Ladder of Success in Imperial China by Ping-ti Ho. New York, Columbia University Press, 1962; reprint, John Wiley, 1964.

The Chinese Inflation, 1937–1949 by Shun-hsin Chou. New York, Columbia University Press, 1963.

Reformer in Modern China: Chang Chien, 1853–1926 by Samuel Chu. New York, Columbia University Press, 1965.

Research in Japanese Sources: A Guide by Herschel Webb with the assistance of Marleigh Ryan. New York, Columbia University Press, 1965.

Society and Education in Japan by Herbert Passin. New York, Bureau of Publications, Teachers College, Columbia University, 1965.

Agricultural Production and Economic Development in Japan, 1873–1922 by James I. Nakamura. Princeton, Princeton University Press, 1966.

The Korean Communist Movement and Kim Il-Song by Dae-Sook Suh. Princeton, Princeton University Press, 1967.

The First Vietnam Crisis by Melvin Gurtov. New York, Columbia University Press, 1967.

Japan's First Modern Novel: Ukigumo *of Futabatei Shimei* by Marleigh Grayer Ryan. New York, Columbia University Press, 1967.

Cadres, Bureaucracy, and Political Power in Communist China by A. Doak Barnett with a contribution by Ezra Vogel. New York, Columbia University Press, 1967.

The Japanese Imperial Institution in the Tokugawa Period by Herschel Webb. New York, Columbia University Press, 1968.

To Professor Carl S. Shoup

Foreword

This scholarly study of China's wartime and postwar inflation should be of great interest to economists, economic historians, and specialists on modern China. The purpose of the book is to analyze the process of the Chinese inflation with special emphasis on its economic and social effects. It also presents information on that part of China's recent economic history which is relevant to the inflation.

The analysis of the inflationary process involves the application of modern theories of inflation to the Chinese experience. Economists interested in the phenomenon may now, because of Professor Chou's work, add the Chinese experience to the list of classic cases which have been analyzed under rigorous and critical methodology.

As one interested in the history of modern China, I found this book highly illuminating. There seems little doubt that China's wartime and postwar inflation was one of the prime factors which caused the downfall of the Nationalist government and the conquest of the mainland by the Chinese Communist Party. The elucidation of this prime factor is one of Professor Chou's great contributions.

The book contains much revealing information concerning the operations of the Chinese government during the 1930s and 1940s, such as the government's fiscal system, proportions of all expenditures that were devoted to military purposes, note issues from 1937 to 1948, and the government's efforts to deal with the balance of payments problem. Professor Chou also deals at some length with the wartime and postwar American efforts to aid China and the frustrations attending these efforts. Most poignant are the sections dealing with the inflation's effects upon the Chinese social fabric, particularly effects upon Chinese intellectuals, salaried people, and the army. In any appraisal of the war years this story must not be forgotten. Professor Chou delivers his analysis as a professional economist interested in the phenomena of inflation, yet there is much meat here for the historian as well.

I should like to add one important point. Professor Chou's discussion of the several factors which contributed to the inflation, and of the devastating effects of the failure to control it, could be of great value to statesmen and economists directing the fiscal policies of underdeveloped countries in Asia, Africa, and Latin America.

The East Asian Institute feels greatly indebted to Professors Carl S. Shoup and Franklin L. Ho for the great assistance they rendered to Professor Chou while he was writing this book.

December, 1962

C. MARTIN WILBUR, *Director*
East Asian Institute
Columbia University

Preface and Acknowledgments

In his foreward to the English edition of C. Bresciani-Turroni's *The Economics of Inflation*, Professor Lionel Robbins comments on the German inflation:

> The depreciation of the mark of 1914–23 . . . is one of the outstanding episodes in the history of the twentieth century. Not only by reason of its magnitude but also by reason of its effects, it looms large on our horizon. . . . It must bear responsibility for many of the political and economic difficulties of our generation. It destroyed the wealth of the more solid elements in German society: and it left behind a moral and economic disequilibrium, apt breeding ground for the disasters which have followed. Hitler is the foster-child of the inflation. The financial convulsions of the Great Depression were, in part at least, the product of the distortions of the system of international borrowing and lending to which its ravages had given rise. If we are to understand correctly the present position of Europe, we must not neglect the study of the great German inflation. If we are to plan for greater stability in the future, we must learn to avoid the mistakes from which it sprang.

With a few modifications, Robbins's comment on the German inflation could equally well have introduced this study on the Chinese inflation of 1937–49. The inflation was a major cause of the downfall of the Nationalist government and the rise of Communism in mainland China, and it played an important role in shaping the history of Asia in the past decade. The Chinese inflation had also its social and economic significances. The inflation caused many inequitable redistributional effects which brought about important changes in the social system of the country. A study of the Chinese experience brought out many features of inflation which would have been unknown without a detailed knowledge of its processes. The blunders that the Chinese government committed in the course of its struggle against inflation can be a useful reference to the underdeveloped economies similarly plagued by inflation.

The purpose of this book is to analyze the processes of the Chinese inflation with a special emphasis on its economic and social effects and to study that part of China's economic history which is relevant to the inflation.

Originally, the first rather than the second was the main objective, but the lack of any comprehensive work providing the necessary historical background has made it imperative to study the related historical developments; for without a reliable historical background it would be extremely difficult to analyze the inflationary processes or to formulate any useful conclusions about the inflation. There is no pretense, however, of a comprehensive survey of China's economic history for the period under consideration; the present coverage is confined to topics related to the inflation.

The ground work of this study was laid during my association with the Central Bank of China under the governorship of Kiangau Chang and S. Y. Liu and with the Council for the United States Aid of the Chinese Government under the direction of Mr. H. J. Shen and Dr. Kan Lee. Chapter IV was benefited by discussions with K. P. Chen, formerly the chairman of the Chinese Foreign Exchange Committee and the Sino-American-British Stabilization Board.

The preliminary draft of this study was written at Columbia University during 1953–55 under a Rockefeller Foundation grant. Since then, the manuscript has been substantially revised and expanded.

The Center for East Asian Studies of Harvard University provided the financial assistance which enabled me to spend the summers of 1957, 1958, and 1959 revising the manuscript. I am grateful to Professors John K. Fairbank and Lien-sheng Yang for their advice. Professor Alexander Eckstein read the entire manuscript at different stages of its development. His suggestions led to substantial improvement of the manuscript. Professor William Vickery of Columbia, Drs. N. T. Wang and T. C. Chang of the United Nations, and Mr. Frank H. H. King of the World Bank also read parts of the manuscript.

I am grateful to Vice-Chancellor Charles Peake, Dean John P. Gillan, and Professor Asher Isaacs of the University of Pittsburgh. Their encouragement and consideration in planning my teaching program at the University facilitated greatly the progress of the study since 1957. I also benefited directly from discussions with many of my colleagues at Pittsburgh, particularly, I wish to mention Professors Raymond Richman, J. P. Watson, and James Witte, Jr.

Professor C. Martin Wilbur was instrumental in arranging the publication of this book. Publication was made possible by a grant from the East Asian Institute of Columbia University. This writer is grateful to Mr. Henry Wiggins of Columbia University Press for his advice and patience.

To Professor Franklin Ho, this writer is grateful for his continued interest in the study as well as his valuable comments on the manuscript. Without his unstinted support, this book would never have been published.

Professor Carl S. Shoup was the sponsor of this research project at Columbia in 1953–55. He read the entire manuscript several times and suggested numerous improvements. Without his sponsorship and his patient guidance, this book would never have been written. For these reasons, this volume is respectfully dedicated to him.

Thanks are also due to George Allen and Unwin Ltd. and Professor C. Bresciani-Turroni for their permission to quote from *The Economics of Inflation.*

Because of the high cost of production, many longer and more detailed tables from which the data were condensed into the tables used in this book were not published. Copies of these tables may be obtained at cost from the author.

University of Pittsburgh S. H. C.
January, 1961

Contents

	Introduction	1
I.	The Pattern of the Chinese Inflation	18
II.	Receipt and Expenditure: Inflationary Pressures in the Government Sector	40
III.	Consumption and Investment: Inflationary Pressures in the Private Sector	89
IV.	Foreign Exchange and Trade Policy: Inflationary Pressures in the International Sector	115
V.	Trade, Payment, and Foreign Aid: Inflationary Pressures in the International Sector	156
VI.	Bank Credit, Velocity, and Inflation	187
VII.	The Redistributional Effects of the Chinese Inflation	236
VIII.	A Comparison of the Chinese and Other Inflations	259
	Epilogue	272
	Appendixes	
	1. Mechanics of Inflationary Spiral	275
	2. Statistics of Chinese Government Revenue and Expenditure	286
	3. Effects of Inflation on Government Debt in Foreign Currencies	288
	4. Effects of Inflation on Income Tax	291
	5. Changes in Private Holdings in Foreign Assets	293
	6. Supplementary Tables	300
	Notes	314
	Index	331

Introduction

The Chinese inflation had many characteristics. Some of these were unique in the Chinese inflation, and some were similar to other cases of inflation. The characteristics, which will be explored in subsequent discussion, are the monetary areas, the stages, the dual economy, the question of demand-pull vs. cost-push, the effects of monetary factors on inflation, and the social implications of the inflation.

The monetary areas. A study of the Chinese inflation requires segregation of the inflationary process into several subprocesses. Each of these subprocesses, operating in a separate currency area, had its own characteristics. The most important among these currency areas were the fapi area, the Federal Reserve Bank (FRB) note area and the Central Reserve Bank (CRB) note area, Manchuria during the Japanese occupation, postwar Manchuria and Taiwan, and the Chinese communist area before 1950.

Fapi, the Chinese equivalent of legal tender, was the standard paper money used in the area under the control of the Nationalist government during 1935–48. The note was then displaced as legal tender by the gold yuan note in August, 1948. In July, 1949, the gold yuan was in turn superseded by the silver yuan note. For the sake of simplicity, the fapi area is used in this study to denote the currency area using these three Nationalist's notes in succession during the inflation (see Chapter IV for details of the Chinese currencies).

In the course of the war, Japan issued three major currencies in various parts of China which were under Japanese occupation. They were notes issued by the Central Bank of Manchou for circulation in Manchuria during 1933–45, by the Federal Reserve Banks in north China during 1938–45, and by the Central Reserve Banks in south and central China during 1940–45. The Manchurian currency was redeemable at par in Japanese yen and had a stability comparable to that of the Japanese currency. This is one of the few cases in history where the note issuance was used successfully as a major source of financing economic development. Taiwan also had a stable currency during most of the war years. However, the areas which used the CRB and FRB notes had a runaway inflation which at first was comparable to, and later became worse than, the inflation in the fapi area. After the war, the CRB and FRB notes were both redeemed by the fapi note; and all three currency areas became the fapi area.

When Manchuria and Taiwan were taken by the Nationalists after V-J Day, a separate regional currency was issued in each of these areas. The original intention in issuing these two regional currencies was to insulate, at least temporarily, the economies of these regions (then much more stable than those of other parts of China) from the plague of inflation. Both of these regional currencies had a flexible exchange rate against the fapi notes. Developments in Manchuria, however, ran entirely counter to expectation, the economic stability attained in the 1930s and the early 1940s, disappeared at the end of the war. The stability was disturbed first by the growing Japanese military expenditures in the country, and later by the Russian invasion and the issuance of a large amount of Russian military scrip to meet the occupation expenses. During 1946–48 chaos was further intensified by the civil war between the Nationalists and the Communists, with each side relying heavily upon its own regional paper money to finance their military expenses. On the eve of the Nationalist collapse in Manchuria, economic conditions were far worse than in any other part of mainland China.

In Taiwan, on the other hand, the regional currency system later proved to be a great asset. The flexible exchange rate between the Taiwan and fapi currencies reduced substantially the effects of the mainland inflation on the economy of the island. During 1945–49 the large-scale influx of private funds from the mainland and the heavy government expenditures resulted in some inflation on the island. These inflationary pressures, though much milder than those of the mainland, were not brought under control until 1952, when the United States aid programs began to take effect.

While the inflationary processes in various monetary areas had many features in common, they did not follow the same tempo or pattern throughout the years under consideration. This is shown by the wide variations in the rates of price increases and note expansions, the behaviors of price-note issue ratios, and the amplitudes of the fluctuations of these rates and ratios prevailing in various monetary areas of China.

The fapi area was the only monetary area where inflation prevailed during the entire period of 1937–49, and for which information is more complete than any of the others. Moreover, to cover in detail the economic developments in the other areas during those turbulent years would be a major undertaking in its own right. Therefore, the present study covers mainly the fapi area. Considerations of other areas is confined to the extent necessary for comparing with the fapi area and for studying the diffusion of inflationary pressure between the fapi and other areas.

The stages. Following Japan's occupation of Manchuria in 1931, there was much intermittent local warfare between the Japanese and Chinese military forces in Shanghai and north China. However, it was not until July, 1937, that the conflict finally emerged from limited local operations into a nation-wide war. A few months later north China and most of China's maritime provinces were occupied by the Japanese. The Nationalist government of China moved first from Nanking to Hankow in central China and later to Chungking in southwest China. Up to December, 1941, the foreign concessions in Shanghai and Tientsin, and the British colony of Hong Kong remained in the hands of the Western Powers. With their cooperation, the Nationalist government also maintained its financial centers in Hong Kong and Shanghai, despite the Japanese occupation of the areas surrounding these metropolises.

Following the attack on Pearl Harbor in December, 1941, Hong Kong and the foreign concessions in China were surrendered to the Japanese. The Chinese government agents operating in these places evacuated to interior China. Chungking became the financial as well as the political center of Free China (the part of China not under Japanese occupation). From then until the fall of Indochina in 1942, the land road through that country became the main artery of communication between Free China and the outside world. After the fall of Indochina, the Burma Road became the lifeline, and when Burma fell in the same year, the airlift over the Himalaya

Mountains was the contact between Free China and the outside world.

After V-J Day, the Chinese territories that had been occupied by the Japanese, including Manchuria, were returned to China. In addition, by the terms of the agreement at Yalta, Taiwan and the Pescadores (ceded to Japan by the Manchu Dynasty in the nineteenth century) were also restored to Chinese possession.

The power of the Nationalist regime, which reached its peak during 1945–46, began to wane. The decline resulted from a number of factors. First, the split between the Nationalists and the Chinese Communists, who had formed an united front to resist the Japanese aggression during the war, widened after 1945. Second, the Russians, who occupied Manchuria only a few days before the Japanese surrendered and remained to discharge a commitment to the Western Powers, exploited the situation to their advantage. They outfitted the Chinese Communists forces in Manchuria with Japanese military equipment and supplies and trained a new modern communist army. This later became the core of the Communist's might, which first annihilated the Nationalist army in Manchuria and then conquered the entire mainland of China in 1949–50. Third, corruption and incompetency permeated the officialdom of the Nationalist government because of the effects of inflation and war. This was particularly true among the military personnel, although signs of decadence were by no means uncommon among the civilian officials.

Although it has been generally agreed that China's inflation stemmed mainly from the continued fiscal deficit, the Nationalist government did little that was significant to reduce that deficit. On the other hand, it laid undue emphasis on its gold and foreign-exchange policies and on the premature monetary reforms as cure-alls for the inflation. During the brief span of thirteen years covered by the present study, two unsuccessful monetary reforms were attempted. One occurred in August, 1948, when the gold yuan notes were issued; the other in July, 1949, when the gold yuan notes were superseded by the silver yuan notes. The first of these reforms actually intensified the inflation. The second occurred only a few months before the Chinese mainland was overrun by the Communists, and was rather inconsequential.

The inflation in the fapi area had several different stages. The first stage covered from July, 1937, to December, 1941; the second, from the beginning of 1942 to V-J Day, 1945; the third, from V-J Day to the monetary reform of August, 1948; and the fourth, from the monetary reform to the occupation of Shanghai by the Communist in May, 1949. A fifth stage which would cover the developments in south and southwest China under the Nationalist's control after the government's evacuation from the Shanghai area could be included. But because of the paucity of data, the fifth stage is not amenable to a systematic study as the other four stages are.

The second stage covered the years when Free China was virtually isolated from the outside world because of the war and the blockade. In that sense, the Chinese economy in this stage may be conceived as a closed economy. If, on the other hand, a closed economy is construed to mean one where the international sector is inactive or nonexistent (an interpretation commonly used in economics), then such a condition might not even exist in the second stage, because there were in these years important payment transactions in China's international account. It is in this stage that the official foreign-exchange reserves reached an unprecedented height because of United States aid and military expenditures in China and that the Chinese government imported a large amount of gold for sales in the domestic market. In no case, should one conceive the entire Chinese inflation as a process which was developed under the condition of closed economy in view of the important roles played by international trade and payments in the stages other than the second.

The dual economy. Like other underdeveloped countries, the Chinese economy was dualistic in character. Agriculture dominated the largest part of the country; modern industry, mostly the urban areas of the coastal provinces.

Because of the wide differences between the economic structure of rural and urban communities, the impact of the inflation on these two sectors was accordingly different. First, while money economy was a standing feature of the urban economy, it had only a limited significance in rural communities. Thus, the runaway inflation caused much less disturbance in rural areas than in cities. Second, the agricultural production was the core of the rural economy and was more evenly distributed in various parts of the country; it did not cluster in a few areas as the industrial production did. The rural economy in China was generally more self-sustaining and less dependent on trade than the industrial. Thus, the effects of inflation and war were less pronounced in the agricultural than in the industrial sector of China.

However, odds were not invariably in favor of agriculture. An analysis of the statistics indicates that the prices of foodstuff and raw material, representing mainly the agricultural crops, did not rise so fast as the corresponding prices of manufactured products. A possible explanation for this unfavorable term of trade was the large imports of food supplies (such as rice and wheat) and raw materials (such as cotton) from abroad during the postwar years. These imports were made possible partly by the over-valuation of the Chinese currency in relation to foreign money and partly by foreign aid programs. The unfavorable terms of trade further discouraged the inflow of agricultural products into urban areas. This reduction in indigenous supply in turn required more imports from abroad, which further reduced the agricultural prices in relation to those of manufactured products in Chinese market.

While the Chinese farmers were not so fortunate as the manufacturers and traders, their position was certainly much better than that of government employees. The real income of farmers during the inflation dropped only slightly below the preinflation level; the real income of government employees was cut to only a small fraction of its preinflation magnitude.

Demand-pull vs. cost-push. Attempts have been made in recent writings to differentiate inflation of the demand-pull type from that of the cost-push type. To this writer, such differentiation has often been overemphasized. Instead of representing mutually exclusive processes, the mechanisms of demand-pull and cost-push are usually present in the same inflationary process. In fact, their simultaneous existence is almost a necessary condition for the self-propagation of an inflationary spiral. Excess demand causes high prices and living costs, leading to wage increases, which result in further increase in prices. This process can be started at any point of the cycle. This standard model may, however, be varied by the degree of importance of the role played by the excess demand and the rising cost in igniting or propagating the spiraling process. The Chinese inflation, like many other runaway inflations, was primarily a result of excess demand, with the cost-push mechanism playing a secondary role. It was a process consisting of "autonomous expansion of demand" (government spending and investment for ownership benefit) and "responsive price and wage increases."[1]

Excess demand or inflationary gap is defined by Hansen as the excess of "active attempt to purchase" or "optimum purchase" over available quantity of goods.[2] This inflationary gap, which is applicable to both the aggregate and the sectoral analyses, is then converted into either price increases, or unrealized (or ex post) inflationary potential, or both. The ex post inflationary potential represents the potential inflationary pressure which would be forthcoming had the normal expenditure been fully realized. If the demand or expenditure realized during inflation falls short of the "optimum" demand, then there exists an ex post inflationary potential which is repressed either by government controls or by some other restrictions imposed during inflation. This inflationary potential is likely to be converted into actual spending when these restrictions are removed. Of course, it is also conceivable for the realized expenditure rising above normal expenditure. In this sense, the excess of the actual over the normal expenditure represents the realized inflationary pressure arising from the abnormal expenditures due to inflationary conditions.

Changes in demand, however, are not the only source of inflationary pressure. A similar pressure may result from a reduction in supply even if the demand remains unchanged. In fact, it is the total effects arising from changes in both demand and supply that determine the magnitude of inflationary pressure under a given condition.

It may be argued that, since inflation usually implies full employment, changes on the supply side are not likely to be important. This argument is true only of a closed economy. As soon as international trade is allowed, the supply can no longer be constant even if the domestic economy is fully employed. Moreover, while the full employment does preclude the economy from further expansion, it does not necessarily prevent the economy from contraction. As later discussion will show, disturbances arising from inflation may at times result in reducing production to a level far below the full employment.

The excess demand may be studied with reference to a specific sector of the economy as well as the aggregate supply and demand. The sectoral approach, which has been used in several recent studies of inflation, is simpler and more susceptible to quantitative measurement than the aggregate studies. The study of a sector enables us to focus attention on selected strategic points and to avoid the generalities and vagueness, both of which are frequently the characteristics of the aggregate approach. The advantage of the sectoral study is particularly obvious in the case of China where the aggregate data are scarce and unreliable. Moreover, an equilibrium in aggregate demand and supply does not necessarily mean an equilibrium in all sectors. To confine this study to these aggregates precludes taking into account the important details arising from sectoral disequilibrium. The sector approach may also be instrumental in explaining the process by which inflationary pressures spread from one sector to another. In fact, a recent study by the United Nations shows that excess sectoral demand, rather than the excess aggregate demand, is the dominant feature of many of the recent inflations.[3]

In his generalized view of the inflationary gap, Lundberg[4] segregates the aggregate gap into a series of sectoral gaps referring to private consumption, private investment, government expenditure, and the balance of international payments. Each of these gaps represents the excess of planned expenditure over the actual expenditure within a particular sector. Lundberg's concept of the gap may be written algebraically: $Z = \Delta C + \Delta I + \Delta G + \Delta X - \Delta Y$, where Z represents the aggregate inflationary gap; ΔC is the excess of planned consumption over actual consumption; ΔI is the planned investment over actual investment; ΔG is the planned government expenditure over the actual expenditure; ΔX is the excess of planned export over actual export; and ΔY is the excess of planned import over actual import. In an inflationary situation, according to Lundberg, disparities may arise in any of these sectors, as well as in the aggregate demand and supply. Sectoral disparities, however, may not necessarily reflect the over-all condition of the aggregate economy.

Hansen,[5] on the other hand, divides the aggregate inflationary gap into only two categories: the commodity gap (or commodity market) and the factor gap (or factor market). Hansen uses the latter to refer primarily to the demand for and supply of labor, although it may also be applied to any other factor of production. Hansen's model is a simplified analysis which purposely ignores the disparities between supply and demand at all other points, but concentrates attention on the relation between the supply and demand for manpower (the most important factor of production) and the total output of finished goods for consumption and investment.[6]

It has been frequently argued that the inflationary gap should be defined with reference to ex ante expenditures or demand, rather than expenditures or demand realized.[7] Because expenditures ex post and supply ex post are always equal, the existence of inflationary gap invariably results in price increases which correct the disequilibrium and make expenditures ex post equal to supply ex post. It is therefore held that a comparison of demand ex post and supply ex post would be meaningless. Despite its wide acceptance, the proposition that the inflationary gap exists only in prospect but is always closed in retrospect may still be subject to the following criticisms.

(i) While rising prices might be able to equate momentarily the demand and the supply of goods and services ex post, as Keynes[8] observed, the inflationary pressure could remain and come into operation in the next "inning" when the recipients of the additional money income begin to exert their pressure on the economy.

(ii) The inflationary gap analysis is usually predicated upon the existence of full employment and upon any disequilibrium resulting from excess demand to be adjusted through the price mechanism rather than the quantity of supply. While this conclusion established on the basis of the P-approach[9] is true in a purely competitive market, it may not be applicable to oligopolistic markets where prices are administered. In the latter case, the shortage often manifests itself in large backlogs of unfilled orders and delivery delays rather than in price increases. The consideration of maximizing profits over time, of the fear of price wars, of the fear of the effects of public ill-will, etc., usually keeps oligopolist competitiors from meeting excess demand by raising prices to the short-run maximum.[10]

(iii) To confine the gap analysis to ex ante demand and supply tends unjustifiably to ignore the distinctive role that the study of ex post demand and supply may play in the gap analysis. The ex post quantities as recorded in the national income or other relevant statistics represent the result of the conflicts in various expenditure and production plans. One of the purposes of the inflationary gap analysis is to "explain the process of adaptation actually recorded."[11] Even if it is known that demand and supply ex post are always equal, it may still be of interest to know how the equilibrium was attained; for, within the general framework of equilibrium, there may exist useful information indicating how a given equilibrium may have derived from a prior position of disequilibrium. If, for instance, the study of the ex post record indicates that the equilibrium between saving and investment is attained by a drain on the nation's gold or foreign exchange reserve, then it will be obvious that this equilibrium is more apparent than real. There would exist an excess demand if it had not been offset by the drain on gold or foreign exchange reserves.[12] The existence of unduly large backlogs of unfilled orders or an undue delay in product delivery is another possible symptom of disequilibrium, although prima facie the ex post quantities are at equilibrium.[13] A sharp increase of the ratio of private savings to disposable personal income in association with the rationing of consumer goods is usually indicative of the possible existence of pent-up demand and of the inflation potential in the event of the abolition of the rationing system.[14] Even if the saving is voluntary, there still is a difference in terms of the inflation potential between the case where the saving is made available to government expenditure and the case where the saving is absorbed by private investment. For instance, savings that are used for investment of ownership benefit usually result in heavy drains on official gold and foreign exchange reserves. While maintaining the apparent equilibrium between savings and investment, this type of saving-investment process results merely in shifting inflationary pressure from one economic sector to another, without reducing the pressure on the economy as a whole.

The model, on which this study is based, is an adaptation of the analyses of Lundberg and Hansen. It divides the economy into the government sector where inflationary pressures are measured by comparing government revenues with government expenditures; the private sector where behavior is gauged in terms of consumption and investment spendings; and the international sector where conditions are determined by the international trade and payments. In this study, the question of excess demand is examined with reference to each of the economic sectors. The examination covers not only the process by which the inflationary pressures rose in each of these sectors, but also the processes by which such pressures were diffused from one sector to another in the course of the Chinese inflation.

The prime mover of the Chinese inflation is found in the government sector. The expenditures of the Chinese government consisted of two parts: those in local currency and those in foreign currency. During the inflation, the local-currency expenditures dwindled in real terms. The reduction was necessitated by the loss in the real revenue of the government. During the war, the loss of real revenue was due partly to the loss of taxes derived from the coastal areas under Japanese occupation. As the tempo of the inflation accentuated, the loss was intensified by the erosive effects resulting from the lag in the adjustment of tax structure and in tax collection. The government expenditures in foreign currencies, on the other hand, rose sharply during the inflation. The increase was partially to offset the decrease in the local-currency expenditures. The additional outlays were met by drains on the official reserves in foreign assets rather than by new receipts from abroad. In short, during the Chinese inflation, there was a strong ex post inflation potential in the local-currency part of the government sector and realized inflationary pressure in the foreign-currency part of the same sector. The realization of the inflationary pressure in the foreign-currency part was made possible by drains on the international sector of the Chinese economy.

While the inflationary pressure in the government sector was the prime force motivating the inflation, the fiscal policies pursued by the government to cope with the situation were mostly ineffectual. Instead of reducing the budgetary deficit or curtailing nongovernment spending to offset the government deficit, the government merely transferred the pressure to the international sector by expanding its outlays in foreign currencies. The failure on the part of the government's fiscal policies was in fact one of the major factors responsible for the rampage of inflation.

In China, consumption consisted mainly of food, clothing, and fuel. For government employees, teachers, and the recipients of fixed interest and rent, the inflation resulted in some reduction in consumption because of the shrinkage of their real income. By comparison, the real income of farmers and factory workers, and their consumption expenditure were less vulnerable to the erosive effects of inflation. Business profits were generally improved, since the Chinese inflation was basically of the demand-pull type. Accordingly, the consumption expenditures of the recipients of entrepreneurial incomes were not so seriously affected as those of others. For the economy as a whole, the consumption expenditures during the war were probably lower than their prewar norms. An ex post inflation potential thus resulted.

The amount of investment expenditures during the Chinese inflation was substantial. These expenditures were divided into investments for use benefit and for ownership benefit.[15]

Investments for use benefit refer to those for trade and production in China. During the war, there were substantial investments for use benefit in both Free China and the Japanese-occupied areas for expanding essential productions. Most of such expansions, occurring in industries supplying producer goods, were undertaken by government or pseudo-government agencies, and were financed mainly by government appropriations and by loans from government banks rather than by equity investments. This does not mean that private investments and loans from ordinary banks were entirely nonexistent, but their amounts were inconsequential compared with the funds from the government and from government banks. As a whole, the expenditures on investment for use benefit did contribute to accentuating the inflationary pressure with the government and pseudo-government investments chiefly accounting for such pressure. This was particularly true during the war years.

Investments for ownership benefit consisted mainly of converting resources in China into holdings in gold, foreign currencies, and assets in foreign countries. Because of the magnitude of these investments and the resulting substantial drains on the foreign-exchange reserves of China, their effects on the economy were much more significant than those of investments for use benefit.

During the prewar years, China's trade balances were usually in deficit, and the inward remittances from overseas Chinese contributed substantially toward bridging the gap. After the war, these remittances were sharply curtailed. Exports were hampered by the faulty trade and foreign-exchange policies of the Chinese government and by unfavorable market conditions abroad. The growing government expenditures in foreign currencies, the speculative investments in gold and foreign assets, the purchases of food and industrial supplies from abroad added to the payment deficit. The deficit was met by heavy drains on China's own official reserves, by foreign aid, and by foreign loans. In addition, there were substantial reductions in nongovernment imports, rendering unfilled many needs normally met by supplies from abroad, and thereby accentuating the potential inflationary pressure on the economy.

Much of the trouble in the international sector resulted from the attempt on the part of the government to maintain the external value of the Chinese currency at a high level; whereas, domestic prices continued to rise. The absurdity of this foreign-exchange policy was particularly obvious during the early stages of the inflation, when the Chinese government tried to maintain the external value of its currency by draining on its meager exchange reserve without the help of effective trade and exchange controls.

In short, there was ex post inflation potential in the consumption sector and in the local-currency part of the government sector and realized inflationary pressures in the investment sector and in the foreign-currency part of the government sector. By comparison, the pressures arising from the investment and government expenditures were much more serious than those from the consumption sector. Relieving these pressures resulted in heavy drains on the foreign-exchange reserves of China. The gravity of these drains was further complicated by dwindling trade and nontrade receipts in China's international account during the course of the inflation and by the failure on the part of the Chinese government to avail itself of effective measures to reduce these inflationary pressures. Consequently, the compensatory effects that the international sector was then in a position to provide were far from adequate to relieve the pressures in the other three sectors of the economy.

Effects of monetary factors on inflation. In all the monetary areas under consideration, inflation was usually accompanied by substantial (in some cases phenomenal) expansion in money supply. The real value of money stock, however, generally declined with the intensification of inflation. One of the possible explanations for the shrinkage in the real value of money supply was the increase in the velocity of money circulation. The high velocity made, at least in part, the prices rise faster than the expansion of money supply. The only exceptions were the experience of Manchuria from 1936 through 1944 and that of the fapi and of the Central Reserve Bank note areas during early stages of the inflation. In all these exceptional cases, the rate of price increase lagged behind that of note expansion. Thus controlling the velocity of money circulation became a major, if not the most important, problem of combating inflation.

Another problem confronting authorities of virtually all the monetary areas was how to keep the rate of expansion of bank credit below the corresponding rate of the currency expansion, and how to channel available bank credit from nongovernment to government uses. These are the necessary conditions for maximizing the contribution of currency expansion to government revenue. As a whole, the Chinese monetary authorities were more successful in expanding the note issue faster than bank credit, than they were in controlling the velocity. In virtually all the monetary areas for which necessary statistics are available, the rate of credit expansion lagged behind the corresponding rate for the note issue. With the government printing press spear-heading the inflationary process, the ratio of the volume of bank credit to that of note issue, which had been low in China, declined steadily with the intensification of inflation. On the other hand, the authorities were far less successful in their attempts of diverting bank credit to government uses.

To offset the undesirable effects of these monetary considerations, the Nationalist government used a host of monetary policies. Among these policies, the Central Bank's operations in gold market and its credit policies deserves special attention. The gold operation, as later discussion will show, was undoubtedly the most significant (though not necessarily the most rational) undertaking among all the monetary measures pursued by the Nationalist government. The credit policies used during the Chinese inflation consisted mainly of those relating to the interest rates on the loans from government banks, to the screening of bank loans, and to the control of government deposits with banks. Because of differences in the institutional background, most of the standard monetary measures used in advanced economies are not applicable to China. A different set of measure had therefore to be developed to cope with the Chinese situation.

Social implications of the inflation. Besides its economic effects, the Chinese inflation had also important social implications which were reflected mainly in the redistributional effects of inflation. Being primarily a demand-pull type, the Chinese inflation brought about windfall gains to entrepreneurs, which resulted from the lag of rise of factor costs behind that of products prices. The absence of effective progressive taxation made it possible for these entrepreneurs to become rightful owners of such windfalls instead of being merely tax-collecting agents of government. The latter would have been the case, if there had been effective progressive taxation on income and profits. On the other hand, the real incomes of the helpless fixed-income recipients eroded with the intensification of inflation, and so were the real incomes of government employees. While the meagre incomes and possessions of millions of the Chinese people dissipated under the impact of inflation, the process facilitated the accumulation of wealth (often in the form of gold and foreign assets) by a small group of the privileged. The fortune of this minority group was due not so much to the helplessness of the Chinese populace as to the incompetence of the fiscal and monetary policies of the government, and frequently to the group's special position derived from the family or other relationship with high government officials. In fact, many of those who suffered during the inflation have now been the victims of the Communist despotism in mainland China, whereas, many of those inflation profiteers are now living comfortably outside the country. The social injustice bred by the inflation has outlasted the process itself.

The book begins with a study of the price behavior of the fapi area and an analysis of the relationship between the fapi prices and those of other monetary areas in Chapter I. The behavior of various economic sectors of the fapi area with particular emphasis on analysing the factors giving rise to inflationary pressure in each of these sectors, the diffusion of such pressure from one sector to another, and the government policies for coping with the inflation are taken up in Chapters II to V. The monetary aspects of inflation and the monetary policies of the Nationalist government are examined in Chapter VI. Chapter VII is devoted to the study of redistributional effects of the Chinese inflation. The Chinese experience is compared with other hyperinflations in Chapter VIII. The purpose of this comparison is to measure the intensity of the Chinese inflation in relation to that of other hyperinflations, and to find out if there are features common to all runaway inflations.

Throughout this book there is a substantial reliance on statistics. Almost any study involving Chinese statistics is confronted with the following questions: Are these statistics reliable? Are they representative of the actual conditions? In my opinion, the Chinese statistics in the present study fall into three categories. The first category consists of statistics which are reliable, or at least whose margin of error is within a tolerable limit. Included in this category are the statistics on note issues and other banking statistics, quotations of financial markets, trade statistics, railway statistics, statistics of gold and foreign-exchange holdings of the Central Bank, government expenditures in foreign currencies, and to a lesser extent the price indices compiled by the Central Bank and the Bureau of Statistics of the Chinese government. The second category consists of the statistics which are estimates and guesses subject to a wide margin of error. Estimates of China's national product and income, and most of the production statistics (particularly those of agricultural productions) are examples. Between these two extremes is the third category consisting of statistics, which when properly used requires careful selection and adjustment on the part of an investigator and a thorough knowledge of the sources and methods used in compiling the statistics. A good example of such a series is the statistics of government receipts and expenditures in local currency (see Appendix 2).

Because of these complications, any study involving the use of Chinese statistics should be done with extreme caution. Conclusions reached on the basis of the statistics of the second category, for instance, can at best be used as indicators of trend and direction of changes rather than as measures of exact magnitude of such changes. The only justification for the use of some of the Chinese statistics is the unavailability of a better alternative. On the other hand, observations derived from the data of the first and third categories can be treated with confidence. By and large the statistics measuring the behavior of individual economic sectors are more reliable than those measuring the aggregate behavior of the Chinese economy. The use of the sectoral analysis in the present study reduces greatly the reliance upon the unreliable statistics of the aggregate. A sweeping statement that the Chinese statistics are invariably unreliable and that the studies based thereon are necessarily valueless, however, is as unjustifiable as an uncritical use of the statistics. It is on the basis of these understandings that statistical data are used in this study. Speculations and generalizations without a proper knowledge of facts and figures would be more objectionable than the approach used in this study, however imperfect the latter may be.

Because of my association and work with the Central Bank of China during 1946–49, the Economic Council of Northeastern Provinces (Manchuria) during 1946–47, and the Council for the United States Aid of the Chinese government during 1948–49, I was able to assemble during these years a large collection of data which otherwise would not have been available. In addition, my work in these offices also provided me with a background concerning the *modus operandi* of the Chinese government. Both the background and the data collected have been extremely useful to this study. However, the use of unpublished data or "inside" information is not necessarily an asset for scientific research. It has been my policy in this study to use published materials whenever they are available and authentic; the unpublished materials are used only to fill in gaps. To an extent the problem of statistics has been simplified by several recent publications in mainland China, providing many important statistical series which had been available only in fragments or in the unpublished files of the Central Bank.

CHAPTER I

The Pattern of the Chinese Inflation

PATTERN OF THE INFLATION IN THE FAPI AREA

This section studies the movements of China's commodity prices and note circulations in the course of inflation and the interrelations between the changes of these two economic series. It is designed to provide an over-all view of the Chinese inflation prior to exploring its relationship with the various segments of the economy. Because of the peculiarity of the Chinese statistics, it is desirable to make a few observations concerning the nature of the data on note issues and prices used in the present study and the problem of their selection.

For the statistics of fapi note issue, there is no question of selection; the data compiled by the Department of Issue of the Central Bank of China are the only such series available. These data, which were taken from unpublished records of the Central Bank, are used in the present study. While fragmentary information about the Chinese notes issued during 1937–49 did appear occasionally in publications, complete statistics for the entire period have never been officially released by the Nationalist government.[1] The statistics of the Department of Issue give only the total amount of notes outstanding at specific dates as recorded by the department; they do not show the average circulation for each period or the amount of notes in the Bank's vaults other than those of the Department of Issue.[2] Information on average circulation is essential for a close comparison of the note-issue statistics with those of commodity prices, which are usually given in monthly averages. Information on the note holdings in the Bank's vault is important for a correct estimate of the currency actually in circulation outside the Central Bank. Consequently the result of the present study can represent only a crude approximation of actual conditions.

The multiplicity of such Chinese price indices as are in existence makes the choice of price data slightly complicated. This study uses those compiled by the Research Department of the Central Bank. The choice is for these reasons: First, the Bank's series are the only ones which cover from 1937 to 1949. The price series compiled by the Ministry of Audit, Accounts, and Statistics are in many respects superior to those of the Bank, but they are not available for the latter part of 1948 and the early months of 1949. Second, the coverage of the Bank series is among the most comprehensive of China's price indices. Geographically, the Bank's series cover Shanghai, Chungking, Canton, and Kunming. While this coverage is rather incomplete compared with the ministry's, which compiled separate price series for twenty-five major cities,[3] the Bank's statistics provide a geographical basis sufficiently comprehensive for the present study. Third, in addition to the wholesale price indices for various classes of commodities grouped in broad categories (such as foodstuffs, textile products, fuels, metal and metal products, structural materials, sundries), there are also price indices for products at different stages of production (such as raw materials, semimanufactured products, and manufactured products), which are not found in any other price series and are useful for this study.

There are, however, two important defects in the indices compiled by the Bank. First, the indices were compiled on the basis of the prices of twenty-two commodities in the case of Chungking and Canton and twenty-three commodities in the case of Shanghai and Kunming. The indices would be more representative if a larger number of items were included. Second, they are unduly weighted by the prices of food. The formula was constructed on the basis of the estimated transaction values of the commodities included in the index in a prewar year. This gave a weight of 38.6 percent for the price of rice and 40.3 percent for the price of other foodstuffs. Out of a total of twenty-two or twenty-three items included in the indices, eleven represented foodstuffs; whereas, some of the other group indices were compiled on the basis of two or three items.[4] It is essential that the results attained in this study be interpreted in the light of these limitations.

The indices of the wholesale prices and note issues are studied under four separate periods: July, 1937, to December, 1941;

TABLE 1.1. AVERAGE, VARIABILITY, AND TREND OF MONTHLY LINK-RELATIVES OF NOTE ISSUES AND PRICE INDICES, 1937–49

	1937–41	*1942–45*	*1945–48*	*1948–49*
Note issue				
Mean	1.0393	1.0864	1.2077	3.1499
Standard deviation	.0310	.0439	.1663	1.7095
Rates of standard deviation to mean	.0823	1.4428	.2756	.8616
Regression coefficient[a]	1.006[b]	1.003[b]	1.032[b]	1.086[b]
Shanghai price index				
Mean	1.0473	1.2597	1.3370	3.9975
Standard deviation	.0862	1.8179	.3665	3.4464
Ratio of standard deviation to mean	.0823	1.4428	.2756	.8616
Regression coefficient[a]	1.004[c]	1.010[c]	1.032[d]	1.116[b]
Chungking price index				
Mean	1.0681	1.1000	1.2631	2.9775
Standard deviation	.0925	.1185	.3917	1.7675
Ratio of standard deviation to mean	.0866	.1077	.3109	.5936
Regression coefficient[a]	1.000[e]	1.008[c]	1.004[b]	1.232[d]

[a] Refers to the coefficient b, derived by fitting the equation $y = ab^t$ to the relevant link relatives of the period t; b minus 1 gives the annual rate of growth.

[b] Indicates the lack of significant difference from one at the 10 percent probable error level.

[c], [d], and [e] indicate that a regression coefficient is significantly different from 1, 5, and 10 percent probable error level.

TABLE 1.2. RATIO OF LINK-RELATIVE OF PRICE INDEX TO NOTE ISSUE, 1937–49

	1937–41	*1942–45*	*1945–48*	*1948–49*
Shanghai prices				
Mean	1.0081		1.1000	1.6325
Standard deviation	.0061		.1010	2.8209
Ratio of standard deviation to mean	.0061		.0918	1.7070
Regression coefficient[a]	1.012[b]		1.000[b]	1.073[e]
Chungking prices				
Mean	1.0519	1.0170	1.0343	1.1250
Standard deviation	.0104	.0120	.0447	.2694
Ratio of standard deviation to mean	.0099	.0120	.0432	.2395
Regression coefficient[a]	1.002[c]	.999[b]	1.012[c]	1.183[c]

See notes for Table 1.1.

Shanghai ratios for 1942–45 were not computed.

January, 1942, to July, 1945; August, 1945, to July, 1948; and August, 1948, to April, 1949. The breakdown of the indices are not identical with the stages mentioned in the Introduction because the indices were compiled on a monthly basis and the stages do not always fall at the beginning or end of a month. Furthermore, no indices were compiled for the months after April, 1949; therefore, the statistical analysis does not cover the entire fourth and fifth stages.

For each of these periods, the link relatives showing month-to-month percentage changes in commodity prices and note issues were studied with particular reference to their central tendency and variability measured in terms of mean, standard deviation, and coefficient of variation. For each period, the value of b was also computed by fitting an exponential curve, $y = ab^t$ (y denotes the link relative, a, the constant, b, the regression coefficient, and t, the period), to each set of these link relatives with a view to determine whether or not there was any significant trend in the rate of change during each of the periods. Besides application to the link relatives of prices and note issues, the procedure was also used to study the relationship between these two types of link relatives. This was done by computing the ratios of the link relative of price to the corresponding relative of note issue. The results are presented in Tables 1.1 and 1.2.

The transitional period (July, 1937–December, 1941)

This period began with the outbreak of the Sino-Japanese War in 1937 and extended to the attack on Pearl Harbor in December, 1941. Military reverses compelled the Chinese government to withdraw its seat from Nanking to Hankow and then to Chungking in interior China; however, Hong Kong and the foreign settlements in Shanghai continued to be the *de facto* financial centers of Free China. During this period, the circulation of the fapi notes expanded at an average rate of 3.9 percent a month[6], and the wholesale prices rose at the rate of 4.7 percent in Shanghai and 6.8 percent in Chungking. These percentages show the lead of Chungking prices over Shanghai prices, and the lead of both these prices over the fapi note issues in the early years of the war. During 1937–38 most of the ratios of prices to note issues fell short of the unity level, showing that note issues expanded at a rate faster than that of price rises. From 1939 to 1941 the reverse became true. This change was particularly evident in the case of Chungking, where nine of the thirty-five price note issue ratios for this three-year period had a value less than unity. In the case of Shanghai, thirteen of its thirty-five ratios for the same period fell below the unity level. The over-all averages of the price-note issue ratios for the entire period of 1937–41 were 1.0081 for Shanghai and 1.0519 for Chungking (see Table 1.2). The *b* coefficients indicate that there were significant trends in the rates of change in the Shanghai price, the Chungking price, and the price-note issue of Chungking. The trends for the note issues and the ratio of Shanghai are insignificant even at the 10 percent level.

The high average rate of increase of Chungking prices and the significant positive trend for Chungking's price-currency ratio are indicative of the high inflationary pressure during the early years of the Sino-Japanese War. This pressure was a result of large-scale migrations from the maritime provinces to interior China and the decrease of the usual flow of manufactured products from the seaports to the interior because of the war. The low ratio of Shanghai's prices to note issues and the lack of any significant positive trend of the ratio indicate that as a whole the expansion of the fapi circulation did not result in any disproportional increase in the price of Shanghai. In fact, during 1937 and 1938 the note issues increased faster than the Shanghai prices—a relationship which did not exist in any other period of the Chinese inflation. If the expansion of note issues were considered as a deliberate policy of the Chinese government for meeting fiscal needs, then these two years would be the only ones in which that policy was successful.

The fapi regime in Free China (January, 1942–July, 1945)

After Japan joined the war against the Allies in 1941, Hong Kong and the foreign settlements in China (formerly under the control of the British, the French, and the Americans) were occupied by the Japanese. Chungking became the financial and political center of Free China. During this period, the fapi circulation expanded at an average rate of 8.6 percent per month, with no significant trend in the rate of change. The monthly increase of Chungking prices averaged 10 percent, with a small negative trend. Out of Chungking's forty-four price-note issue ratios for this entire period, twenty-one had a value of less than unity, and their average dropped from 1.0519 in the previous period to 1.0170. No significant trend was found in the ratios.

The mildness of the inflationary pressure in Free China during these years relative to the pressure of other periods may be attributed to the following developments. First, the Pearl Harbor attack resulted in the United States participation in the war with a substantial increase in aid to China. There was also sharp reduction in the flow of refugees from the occupied areas to Free China. Second, during the months immediately preceding V-J Day, the anticipation of victory brought an abrupt slump in commodity prices in Free China. This slump was mainly responsible for the negative trend in the rate of change of Chungking prices.

After December, 1941, the notes of the Japanese-sponsored Central Reserve Bank became the main currency for the Shanghai area. To compare the fapi circulation with the price index of Shanghai would be meaningless. However, it should be noted that from 1942 to August, 1945, Shanghai prices increased at an average rate of 26.0 percent per month, as against a monthly average rise of 10 percent for Chungking prices. The rapid rise of Shanghai prices was due to the reckless expansion of the CRB notes to meet the financial needs of the Japanese and their puppet government operating in the area.

The fapi regime after the war (August, 1945–July, 1948)

At the end of World War II, the price slump which had started before V-J Day continued in both Free China and the Japanese occupied areas. The anticipation of the resumption of international trade and the flow of fresh supplies from coastal provinces into interior China resulted not only in a reduction in the buying pressure on the market, but also in a large-scale dishoarding of commodities by speculators; thus, a nation-wide fall in prices. This bearish trend was further augmented by an unique optimism on the part of the public toward the postwar political developments in China under the Nationalist government.

The immediate problem that confronted the Nationalist government, following its victorious return to the formerly occupied areas, was to fix a proper fapi exchange rate at which the Central Reserve Bank notes and other puppet currencies then circulating were to be redeemed. A comparison of the price indices of Chungking and Shanghai shows that the parities were approximately 48.1 in August, 56.4 in September, 62.2 in October, and 145.6 in November, 1945, of the CRB note to one fapi yuan.[6] The Japanese surrendered in August; the redemption of the CRB and allied currencies did not start until early November. All the price parities therefore should have had an important bearing upon the choice of a redemption rate. Based on this consideration, the rate should have been in the neighborhood of a hundred CRB notes to one fapi. Because of the undue optimism then prevailing throughout the country and because of the temporary shortage of notes in the formerly occupied areas which were caused by a lag in shipments from Free China, the fapi notes were quoted in the Shanghai open market at about two hundred CRB notes to one fapi at the time the redemption rate was being studied. The ultimate decision, unfortunately, was made on the basis of that market rate.

The overvaluation of the fapi currency resulted in a great increase in the purchasing power of the currency, making everything in the occupied areas unusually cheap to those which came from the fapi area. This led to a rapid large-scale influx of fapi into the former occupied areas and to an explosive rise in commodity prices in such areas.

Because of the two hundred-to-one redemption rate, the price index in Shanghai when converted from CRB notes into fapi units dropped from its record peak to a level below that of Chungking in the months immediately following V-J Day. But in the early months of 1946 the Shanghai index surpassed that of Chungking. By the end of 1947 the fapi index of Shanghai once more reached the height attained during the last few months of the war when prices were based on CRB notes.

To a limited extent, this rising tide was slowed down by the large-scale sales of gold, by a liberal supply of foreign exchange by the Central Bank during 1946, and by the arrival of foreign-aid supplies during 1947 and 1948 (see Chapters IV and V). Despite these compensatory operations, the average monthly rate of increase for 1945–48 was 20.8 percent for note issue, 33.7 percent for Shanghai prices, and 26.3 percent for Chungking prices. Besides, the rate of change of Shanghai prices showed a significant positive trend.

The average price-currency ratio in Shanghai reached an unprecedented high of 2.36 in November, 1945, and 1.73 in February, 1946. The average ratio of prices to note issues for 1945–48 was 1.10 for Shanghai and 1.03 for Chungking. The trend was positive and significant in the case of the Chungking ratio. The fact that the average of the Shanghai ratio was higher than that of Chungking clearly indicates a greater intensity of inflation in the former Japanese-occupied areas than in Free China during the postwar period. The lack of any significant trend in the Shanghai ratio was due to the high price-currency ratios during 1945 and 1946, as previously mentioned; for these high ratios greatly reduced the significance of developments toward the end of the period. On the other hand, because of the low price-currency ratios for the early months, the increasingly high ratio of Chungking became especially conspicuous in the latter months of the period.

The gold yuan regime (August, 1948–April, 1949)

In August, 1948, the Chinese government in a futile attempt to check the inflation introduced a monetary reform of the following measures:

1. The fapi note, the old legal tender, was displaced by the new gold yuan note at the rate of 3 million fapi to one gold yaun.
2. All gold and foreign exchange held by individuals, banks, and institutions was to be surrendered to the Central Bank of China.
3. To offset the expansion of note issue, which resulted from the large-scale purchases of gold and foreign currencies and also to minimize its budgetary deficit, the government offered for sale some state-owned enterprises and real estate (primarily those properties seized from the Japanese and their collaborationists after V-J Day).
4. Rigid price controls were imposed on several major cities.
5. The issuance of the new bank notes was limited strictly in amount and was supervised by a special committee consisting of representatives of various government departments and public institutions.

6. General Chiang Ching Kuo, the eldest son of President Chiang Kai-shek, was appointed to supervise the enforcement of price controls and other restrictive measures and was to check clandestine dealings and market speculations.

The improvements in fiscal and economic conditions as contemplated in the reform, however, were never realized. The price control and other economic restrictions, though quite rigidly enforced in Shanghai, were never extended beyond the orbit of a few major cities and in many cases scarcely beyond the city limits of Shanghai where General Chiang's headquarter was located.

The monetary reform did not in itself offer a cure for the Chinese inflation. Its success or failure had to be predicated upon the effectiveness of the measures for correcting the economic maladjustments adopted after the monetary reform. It did not take long for the people, and later for the government, to ascertain the fate of the reform. At the beginning of November, about six weeks after the announcement of the reform, price controls were abandoned, and the Central Bank reverted to the old gold sales policy (see Chapter VI). In the meantime, military conditions in Manchuria and north China gradually slipped from the control of the Nationalist government.

The price index of Shanghai was held at almost a constant level in September and October, 1948. In November, however, following the abolition of price control at the end of October, the index multiplied by 11.53 times. This explosive trend continued, though at a somewhat slackened tempo. During February and March, 1949, the price index rose by 6.97 and 4.51 times respectively.[7] If the cumulative price-index curve of 1948–49 is compared with earlier years, the results show that within a brief span of eight months following the monetary reform (from the end of August, 1948, to the end of April, 1949), the price index of Shanghai increased by 135,742 times, which is comparable to the rise in the Chungking price index from the first half of 1937 to March, 1948, or the rise in the Shanghai price index from 1937 to November, 1945. In Chungking, where the postreform price control was not so effectively enforced as in Shanghai, the rise in prices from August, 1948, to April, 1949, was steadier but less phenomenal than in Shanghai. During this period the average price increase was 198 percent per month for Chungking as against 300 percent per month for Shanghai (see Table 1.1).

The expansion of note issue during the postreform months was also spectacular. During the eight-month period ending April 23, 1949, the volume of currency circulation was multiplied by 4,524 times, an expansion comparable to that of the fapi notes from June, 1937, to April, 1947. The average rate of increase in note circulation in this postreform period was 215 percent per month.

In November, 1948, the price-note issue ratio rose to 5.77, the highest ever attained during the entire inflation. The average price-currency ratios for the entire period were 1.6525 for Shanghai and 1.1250 Chungking.

Month-to-month link relatives of both the price and price-currency series of Shanghai and Chungking had a significant positive trend. This means that during this period not only were there rapid increases in note issues and in prices, but also there was a rise in the rates of price increase and the price-currency ratios. Because of the unusually rapid expansion of note issues during the early stages of the monetary reform, there was no significant trend in the rate of the expansion of note issues.

The period after the fall of Shanghai (May, 1949–October, 1949)

In the weeks immediately before the Communist occupation of Shanghai in May, 1949, the gold yuan notes began to show signs of collapse under a double-barreled pressure from mounting commodity prices and an acute shortage of note supply. The shortage was caused mainly by the lag in the adjustment of the denominations of the note to match the rapid depreciation in the value of the currency. After the fall of Shanghai, the gold yuan notes were rejected by the public first in Kwangtung and then gradually in all the other provinces held by the Nationalist government. Until the issuance of the silver yuan notes in July, 1949, Hong Kong dollar notes, silver dollars, and gold bars were the chief media of circulation in the non-Communist area. Gold yuan notes were used only occasionally, although in name they were still the standard money.

In July, 1949, the silver yuan notes were formally issued to displace the gold yuan notes. A main feature of the silver yuan note was that it was freely redeemable in silver or silver coins. In fact some 17 million pieces of the silver dollar with the specified contents of the Chinese currency were coined by the Philadelphia mint before the silver yuan notes were issued. Because of their redeemability, the use of the silver notes became nominal, for only under very rare circumstances would the public accept the notes for payment rather than the silver dollar.

During this period the entire Nationalist government was in a state of confusion. The compilation of price indices was suspended. Even the data for the note issue and the specie and foreign-exchange reserves of the Central Bank became fragmentary. For this reason, it is impossible to make any quantitative study of developments in this period.

COMPARISON OF THE INFLATION IN THE FAPI, CRB, AND FRB CURRENCY AREAS

The expansion of the CRB note issues was generally faster than the FRB notes and the fapi notes (see Table 1.3). On the other hand, prices rose faster in the fapi area (as represented by Chungking prices) than they did in the occupied areas (as represented by Shanghai and Tientsin) during 1940–41. From 1943 to the middle of 1945, however, the trend was reversed because the tempo of inflation was intensified in the Japanese occupied areas. Because of the divergencies in the changes in prices and in note issues, the behavior of the ratio of price changes to note-issue changes naturally

TABLE 1.3. COMPARISON OF THE AVERAGES OF THE LINK RELATIVES FOR FRB, CRB, AND FAPI AREAS, 1940–44

	1940		*1941*		
	FRB	*Fapi*	*FRB*	*CRB*	*Fapi*
Note issue					
Mean	1.04	1.05	1.04	1.27	1.05
Standard deviation	.04	.03	.05	.08	.02
Ratio of standard deviation to mean	.04	.03	.05	.06	.02
Price					
Mean	1.05	1.10	1.01	1.07	1.09
Standard deviation	.08	.10	.02	.07	.12
Ratio of standard deviation to mean	.08	.09	.02	.06	.11
Price-currency ratio					
Mean	1.01	1.10	1.00	.85	1.05
Standard deviation	.10	.12	.05	.09	.16
Ratio of standard deviation to mean	.10	.11	.05	.10	.15

became quite different from the behavior of either prices or note issues. From 1941 through 1943 the average price to note-issue ratios for the CRB currency area were invariably below the unity level; whereas, the ratios for 1944 and 1945 were far in excess of unity. The price-currency ratios of the fapi area (as represented by the ratio of the Chungking price and the fapi note issues) were high during 1940 and 1941 in comparison with the corresponding ratios of the occupied areas. From 1941 through 1945 the ratio fluctuated between 1.0 and 1.05; whereas, the ratios for the occupied areas rose in 1944 and 1945 to the vicinity of 1.10.

If the less-than-unity ratio is indicative of the effectiveness of note issuance as a source of government revenue, then the authority of the CRB currency area was more successful in raising revenue by printing press, at least during the years 1941–43, than the governments of either the fapi area or the FRB note area. The price-note-issue ratios of the CRB currency area for these three years were the only ones which fall below the unity level.

COMPARISON OF THE INFLATION IN MANCHURIA AND CHINA PROPER

Because of the limitations of data on note issues and prices, a comparison between the inflation in postwar Manchuria and in

TABLE 1.3. (continued)

	1942			*1943*			*1944*	
FRB	*CRB*	*Fapi*	*FRB*	*CRB*	*Fapi*	*FRB*	*CRB*	*Fapi*
1.04	1.26	1.07	1.09	1.16	1.06	1.13	1.18	1.08
.06	.17	.06	.05	.11	.03	.07	.05	.01
.06	.14	.06	.05	.10	.03	.06	.04	.01
1.07	1.10	1.06	1.09	1.12	1.11	1.19	1.26	1.09
.05	.10	.07	.08	.18	.09	.12	.20	.11
.05	.09	.07	.07	.16	.08	.10	.16	.10
1.03	.89	1.00	1.02	.97	1.04	1.09	1.07	1.01
.06	.12	.08	.09	.19	.10	.07	.14	.14
.06	.12	.08	.07	.19	.10	.06	.14	.14

There are no data for 1940 in CRB area.

TABLE 1.4. COMPARISON OF AVERAGES OF LINK RELATIVES FOR MANCHURIA AND FAPI AREAS, 1946–48

	July–Dec. 1946		*Jan.–June 1947*		*July–Dec. 1947*		*Jan.–May 1948*	
	Manchuria	*Fapi*	*Manchuria*	*Fapi*	*Manchuria*	*Fapi*	*Manchuria*	*Fapi*
Note issue								
Mean	1.36	1.10	1.17	1.18	1.25	1.22	1.35	1.33
Standard deviation	.19	.04	.08	.05	.11	.04	.16	.06
Ratio of standard deviation to mean	.14	.04	.01	.04	.09	.03	.12	.05
Price								
Mean	1.17	1.07	1.37	1.32	1.48	1.17	1.58	1.43
Standard deviation	.21	.06	.91	.23	.14	.16	.46	.15
Ratio of standard deviation to mean	.18	.06	.67	.18	.09	.14	.29	.11
Price-currrency ratio								
Mean	.90	.97	1.33	1.16	1.50	.97	1.56	1.08
Standard deviation	.06	.06	.19	.20	.33	.12	.30	.16
Ratio of standard deviation to mean	.07	.06	.14	.17	.22	.12	.19	.15

China proper is possible only for July, 1946, through May, 1948 (see Table 1.4).

The rate of expansion of the note issues in Manchuria was comparable to that of China proper. The only exception was in the early months of 1946 when the initial demand for the new Manchurian notes, resulting from the expansion of the area then under the control of the Nationalist government, made that note far exceed the fapi note in expansion. The rate of price increases in Manchuria was generally much higher than the corresponding rate for the fapi area. This is shown by the fact that all the semi-annual averages of the month-to-month link relatives of the Manchurian price indices were higher than the corresponding averages of the price indices of Shanghai, which represented the general price conditions in China proper. This situation was particularly evident during the second half of 1947 and the early months of 1948. The relatively high rate of increase in Manchurian prices resulted from the high ratio of prices to note issues, indicating the rapidity of money circulation. The high velocity was indicative of the declining public confidence in the Manchurian currency—a position to be expected in view of the deterioration of the military situation in Manchuria after the middle of 1947.

Since the exchange between the fapi and the Manchurian notes was rigidly pegged at the rate of thirteen to one fapi yuan, the difference in the pace by which the prices in Manchuria and in China proper rose naturally resulted in a substantial disparity between the official exchange rate and the corresponding price parity. Chaos thus resulted which finally forced the Nationalist government in the middle of 1948 to displace the Manchurian notes with fapi currency after having experimented unsuccessfully with exchange control over remittances from Manchuria to China proper.[8]

COMPARISON OF THE INFLATION IN TAIWAN AND MAINLAND CHINA

A comparison between the inflation in Taiwan and mainland China for January, 1947, through April, 1949 shows several important differences (see Table 1.5).

During 1947 and 1948 the rates of note expansion in the two areas were quite similar, although the rate for the mainland was slightly

TABLE 1.5. COMPARISON OF AVERAGES OF LINK RELATIVES FOR TAIWAN AND FAPI AREAS, 1947–49

	Jan.–June 1947		*July–Dec. 1947*		*Jan.–June 1948*		*July–Dec. 1948*		*Jan.–Apr. 1949*	
Note issue	*Taipi*	*Fapi*	*Taipi*	*Fapi*	*Taipi*	*Fapi*	*Taipi*	*Fapi*	*Taipi*	*Fapi*
Mean	.94	1.18	1.08	1.22	1.25	1.33	1.27	1.29	1.29	8.80
Standard deviation	.18	.05	.04	.04	.23	.05	.16	.04	.04	2.16
Ratio of standard deviation to mean	.19	.04	.04	.03	.18	.19	.13	.03	.03	.56
Price										
Mean	1.20	1.32	1.19	1.17	1.07	1.49	1.42	3.49	1.52	10.43
Standard deviation	.16	.23	.09	.16	.10	.20	.42	4.02	.16	9.46
Ratio of standard deviation to mean	.13	.18	.07	.14	.09	.13	.30	1.15	.11	.91
Price-currency ratio										
Mean	1.08	1.16	1.11	.97	.89	1.11	1.14	1.63	1.18	1.55
Standard deviation	.14	.20	.07	.12	.18	.16	.04	1.91	.11	1.06
Ratio of standard deviation to mean	.13	.17	.07	.12	.20	.15	.32	1.17	.09	.46

higher than for Taiwan. In 1949, however, not only was the average link relative for the mainland (indicating the average rate of growth of fapi notes) more than six times as high as that of taipi notes, but the coefficient of variation of the former was also much higher than of the latter. In the case of the link relatives of prices, the similarity between the rates of change in these two areas was confined only to 1947 and the first half of 1948. In the second half of 1948 and early 1949, however, the difference between the two rates of change became substantial, reflecting the increasing effectiveness of the multiple regional currency system as a means for preventing the spread of inflation from one region to another. There was an obvious tendency for the velocity of money circulation (as measured by the ratio of price change to the corresponding change of note issue) to increase with the intensification of inflation. This upward trend was much more obvious on the mainland than on Taiwan.

THE EFFICACY OF REGIONAL CURRENCY SYSTEMS FOR CONTAINING INFLATION

The main purpose in using separate regional currency systems in Manchuria and Taiwan during the postwar years was to insulate these areas (where the economic conditions had been more stable than in other parts of China) from the epidemic of inflation rampant in the fapi and the formerly occupied areas. It was hoped that by using different currencies, the discrepancies among the tempos of inflation prevailing in the various monetary areas might be compensated for by properly adjusting the rate of exchange between the relevant currencies. The principle underlying this policy was obviously not without basis. The application of the principle to actual practice, however, was by no means simple. Political and administrative considerations frequently called for such deviations of practice from the basic principle that the system of separate monetary areas was often deprived of all the functions originally conceived for it.

The experience of Taiwan will be examined first. In the thirty-five months from May, 1946, through March, 1949, the fapi was overvalued in terms of the Shanghai-Taipei price parity in twenty three months, and the taipi was overvalued in only thirteen months (see Table 1.6). Adjustment of the fapi-taipi exchange rate was a

TABLE 1.6. TAIPI-FAPI EXCHANGE RATES AND PRICE PARITIES, 1946–49

	Index of taipi-fapi exchange rate	*Wholesale price index*		*Price parity*	*Exchange rate-parity ratio*
		Shanghai	*Taipei*		
	1	2	3	4(2 ÷ 3)	5(1 ÷ 4)
1946					
May	1.00	1.00	1.00	1.00	1.00
June	1.00	.98	1.08	.91	1.10
July	1.00	1.07	1.12	.96	1.04
Aug.	1.13	1.13	1.16	.97	1.16
Sept.	1.28	1.34	1.10	1.22	1.05
Oct.	1.17	1.41	1.14	1.24	.94
Nov.	1.17	1.40	1.21	1.16	1.01
Dec.	1.17	1.50	1.36	1.10	1.06
1947					
Jan.	1.17	1.80	1.75	1.03	1.14
Feb.	1.17	2.80	2.64	1.06	1.10
March	1.17	2.94	2.96	.99	1.18
April	1.21	4.85	3.15	1.54	.79
May	1.40	7.47	3.52	2.12	.66
June	1.69	8.79	3.79	2.32	.73
July	2.14	8.19	4.14	1.98	1.08
Aug.	2.17	8.66	4.73	1.83	1.19
Sept.	2.40	11.36	5.60	2.03	1.18
Oct.	2.40	15.73	7.71	2.04	1.18
Nov.	2.65	17.49	9.21	1.90	1.39
Dec.	2.97	22.01	10.55	2.09	1.42
1948					
Jan.	3.16	34.08	10.34	3.30	.96
Feb.	3.69	47.95	11.64	4.12	.90
March	6.19	77.50	14.25	5.44	1.14
April	7.60	89.84	15.47	5.81	1.31
May	10.65	129.13	15.13	8.53	1.25
June	13.93	232.40	15.68	14.82	.94
July	33.90	684.22	16.00	42.76	.79
Aug.	51.04	1,240	16.79	73.84	.68
Sept.	54.50	1,576	20.73	76.02	.72
Oct.	54.50	1,991	24.91	79.93	.68
Nov.	270.27	20,307	30.88	657.62	.41
Dec.	450.47	48,313	64.11	753.60	.60

TABLE 1.6 (continued)

	Index of taipi-fapi exchange rate 1	*Wholesale price index Shanghai* 2	*Taipei* 3	*Price parity* 4(2 ÷ 3)	*Exchange rate-parity ratio* 5(1 ÷ 4)
1949					
Jan.	1,250	126,075	164.57	766.09	1.63
Feb.	7,143	1,225,293	244.68	5,008	1.43
March	25,000	7,476,520	327.50	22,829	1.10

All indices use May, 1946, as the base period. The wholesale price indices of Shanghai are computed on the basis of those of the Central Bank. The price indices of Taipei are derived from the wholesale price indices compiled by the Provincial Government of Taiwan. The average taipi-fapi exchange rate for May, 1946, was thirty fapi yuan to one taipi. The excess of the ratio of the taipi-fapi exchange rate to the price parity (column 5) over the unity level indicates the overevaluation of fapi in terms of the price parity. Conversely, if the ratio is less than one, taipi is overvalued, because, if we have

$$\frac{\text{the current taipi-fapi rate (in the fapi equivalent of one taipi)}}{\text{the taipi-fapi rate of the base period}} < (\text{or} >) \frac{\text{price index of Shanghai}}{\text{price index of Taipei}},$$

then the value of fapi will be too high (or too low) in relation to the price parity.

Sources: *Chung-yang yin-hang yueh-pao* (The Central Bank Monthly) (Shanghai, 1946–49), Vols I–IV; *Tai-wan yin-hang chi-k'an* (The Bank of Taiwan Quarterly); *Tai-wan wu-shih-i-nien-lai tung-chi t'so-yao* (The 51-Year Statistical Abstract of Taiwan) (Taiwan, 1946), p. 90.

hotly disputed issue between the provincial government of Taiwan and the central government authorities despite the original intention of instituting the multiple-currency system in the country. While the provincial authority pressed for adjustments in the exchange rate in accordance with the depreciation of the fapi currency which occurred during the postwar months, the central government often felt hesitant and frowned upon too frequent adjustments reflecting the depreciation of fapi. The central government considered that such *de jure* depreciation could impair the public confidence in the fapi note. Consequently the fapi-taipi exchange rate remained fairly stable during the period from May, 1946, to March, 1947, despite the rapid price increases in the fapi area. After March, 1947, the adjustment of the exchange rate became more frequent than before. With the rapid depreciation after November, 1947, the alteration in the exchange rate, following closely the Shanghai-Taipei price parity,

TABLE 1.7. INTER-PROVINCIAL REMITTANCE OF TAIWAN, 1947–49

	Outward remittances	*Inward remittances*	*Excess inward (+) or excess outward (−) remittances*	*Increase of note issues*
1947	48,556	46,810	−1,740	11,802.6
Jan.	383	343	−40	358
Feb.	509	388	−121	730
March	763	792	+27	538
April	2,295	2,090	−205	539
May	2,287	1,860	−427	1,385
June	1,790	1,662	−128	1,370
July	4,243	3,834	−406	774
Aug.	3,315	3,327	+12	294
Sept.	3,771	3,480	−291	1,244
Oct.	7,731	7,690	−41	1,620
Nov.	10,007	9,650	−257	452
Dec.	11,462	11,693	+331	2,495
1948	188,880	470,098	+281,218	124,907.6
Jan.	6,189	5,907	−282	769
Feb.	4,975	6,544	+1,569	3,141
March	9,266	5,365	−3,901	1,883
April	8,173	5,569	−2,606	2,045
May	10,318	6,097	−4,221	4,071
June	5,850	9,342	+3,492	6,708
July	15,806	9,940	−5,864	4,805
Aug.	9,467	15,301	+5,834	9,450
Sept.	8,480	44,304	+36,824	9,699
Oct.	8,062	68,219	+60,157	19,579
Nov.	70,659	47,382	−23,277	9,476
Dec.	31,635	246,130	+214,495	53,284
1949	48.508	47.821	−.687	194.077
Jan.	5.234	5.814	+.580	1.242
Feb.	2.660	2.350	−.310	1.059
March	6.501	6.677	+.176	.838
April	9.811	9.242	−.569	2.913
May	.203	.212	+.009	3.130
June		.080	+.080	19.163
July	4.590	6.821	+2.231	44.980
Aug.	8.870	6.393	−2.477	16.618
Sept.	9.269	10.011	+.742	18.106
Oct.	1.366	.211	−1.155	9.333
Nov.				22.659
Dec.	.004		−.004	54.036

All figures for 1947 and 1948 are in millions of old taipi and for 1949 are in millions of new Taiwan dollars.

There are no data for spaces left blank in the table.

became virtually a daily routine. As a result of these shifts in policy, the value of the taipi was raised above the corresponding price parity during the second quarter of 1947 and in January, February, June, and July, 1948. In August, September, and October, 1948, the stringent price controls then in effect in Shanghai kept the price index there at an artificially low level. Consequently, the value of taipi became inordinately high in relation to the price parity, even though the official taipi-fapi rate remained virtually unchanged during these months. Frequent and prompt adjustments during November and December of the year continued to keep the value of taipi high in comparison with the price parity. After the turn of the year, the exchange rate once more lagged behind the rising price parity, due primarily to the unprecedentedly rapid deterioration of economic conditions on the mainland. This discrepancy was reduced in February and March when the exchange rate-price parity ratio dropped to 1.43 and 1.10 respectively from the February ratio of 1.63.

An examination of the statistics of remittances between Taiwan and the mainland (see Table 1.7) reveals that in both 1947 and 1949 the remittances from Taiwan to the mainland were in excess of those to Taiwan, and that the months which should really have caused concern to the provincial authority of Taiwan were those immediately after the monetary reform of August, 1948. In 1948 the amount of excess inward remittances to Taiwan was more than twice as large as that of the Taiwan notes issued in that year, and the bulk of such remittances occurred in September, October, and December of the year when the taipi was overvalued in comparison with the price parity. It is thus apparent that the primary cause for the flow of funds to Taiwan was the worsening of economic conditions on the mainland, not the lucrativeness of the taipi exchange rate. Thus while the flexible exchange rate failed to prevent the large-scale exodus of funds from the mainland to Taiwan, it did, however, succeed in reducing the taipi value of these inward remittances, and therefore their inflationary effect on the island's economy, by maintaining the exchange rate of taipi at a high level.

Besides adjusting the exchange rate, Taiwan also instituted an elaborate system to control the interregional flow of funds. In fact, during the period under consideration, it was the control of remittances rather than the flexible exchange rate that was the main bulwark for preventing the spread of economic chaos from the mainland to Taiwan, although the control system itself was by no means a watertight one.

The story of Manchuria is entirely different from that of Taiwan. The original purpose of setting up a separate monetary system in the area was to prevent the spread of inflation from China proper to Manchuria. The rapid deterioration of the military situation in Manchuria during 1947 and 1948 made the economic conditions there much more chaotic than in China proper. The actual problem in this case thus became to prevent Manchuria's chaos from spreading to other parts of the country rather than to save Manchuria from the fapi inflation.

The exchange rate for the Manchurian currency was first set at 13 fapi yuan to one Manchurian yuan and later was changed to 11.50 to one unit of the Manchurian money. But the rapid depreciation of the latter currency after October, 1947, proved that the official exchange rate was entirely out of line with the parities between the prices of north China and Manchuria. As a result of the overvaluation of the Manchurian currency at the official rate, an avalanche of funds flowed from Manchuria to the fapi area. Efforts on the part of the Central Bank to slow down this avalanche by restricting remittances from Manchuria to China proper proved fruitless. In the middle of 1948 the complete loss of public confidence in the Manchurian yuan made necessary both its abolition and the use of fapi notes as the standard money of Manchuria.

While the separate regional monetary system failed entirely in the case of Manchuria, it did help to a certain extent in slowing down the spread of inflation from the mainland to Taiwan. The usefulness of such a system was particularly obvious when Taiwan was politically separated from the mainland in 1949. Had there not been a separate currency in Taiwan, the stability of the island's economy could have been adversely affected by the large-scale influx of fapi notes from the Communist-controlled mainland. The fact that a different currency had been used in Taiwan in 1949 virtually eliminated the possibility of such an avalanche.

The reluctance on the part of the Nationalist government to keep the exchange rate between the various regional currencies flexible, however, did make the regional currency system lose some of its effectiveness in preventing the spread of inflation from one area to another. Whatever results the government regulations then in force might have attained in curtailing interregional remittances, these cumbersome and restrictive regulations provided no substitute to a policy of flexible exchange rates.

SUMMARY

The rates of increase in prices and note issues, the amplitudes of the fluctuation of these rates, and the ratios of price increase to that of note issues all varied directly with the intensification of inflation. The increasing rates of growth reflect the ability of the inflationary spiral to self perpetuate once the process is started. The increasing amplitudes of fluctuation are indicative of the inherent instability of the Chinese inflationary process. The rising ratios of price change to the increasing of note issues show the role which the velocity of money circulation played in intensifying the Chinese inflation. The increase in the velocity makes the prices rise faster than the expansion of note issue. It is a major force making the inflationary process self-perpetuating and unstable. The role of the velocity is further discussed in Chapter VI. The theoretical models depicting various types of inflationary processes, including the one applicable to the pattern described in this chapter, is found in Appendix 1.

CHAPTER II

Receipt and Expenditure: Inflationary Pressures in the Government Sector

THE FISCAL SYSTEM BEFORE 1937

A chief characteristic of China's fiscal system before the war was a continuing deficit. During 1928–35 taxes and other current revenues covered on the average only 79.57 percent of the government's total expenditures.[1] The remainder was met by borrowing. In the fiscal year 1935–36 smuggling became rampant in north China under the *de facto* control of the Japanese, and as a consequence, the customs revenue registered a sharp decrease. The ratio of the government's total current revenue (excluding borrowing) in its total receipts (including borrowing) or expenditure dropped to 40.0 percent. In the fiscal year 1936–37, however, the current revenue rose to cover 65.81 percent of the total expenditures, because of a substantial reduction in smuggling and of improvement in the customs revenue.

In these prewar years, the bulk of current revenue was derived from the customs revenue, the salt tax, and the commodity tax. These contributed 68.52 percent of government's total receipts, or 86.08 percent of the total revenue.

During 1928–35 customs revenue consisted mainly of import duties and contributed on an average 42.23 percent of the government's total receipts (including borrowing) or 53.03 percent of its current revenue (excluding borrowing). And, except for the fiscal year 1935–36, it was invariably the most important tax revenue of the Nationalist government.

The salt tax was an excise tax, usually collected at the producing center at the time the salt was shipped out. During 1928–35 the salt tax yielded 17.13 percent of the government's total receipts, or 21.41 percent of its current revenue.

The commodity tax was also an excise tax mostly collected at the manufacturer's level. The commodity tax system was instituted in 1928 by the Nationalist government as a consolidated tax to displace the multifarious transit levies on indigenous products imposed by various local governments. Because of the limitations imposed by its treaties with foreign powers, the Chinese government was not free at that time to impose any tax or customs duty on imports without prior approval of the governments dominating China's international trade. These transit levies were therefore imposed only on indigenous products and often hampered their competition with imported commodities in domestic markets. It was hoped that the integration of these unorganized and ill-planned local levies would not only increase the government's revenue, but would also minimize unfair and multiple taxation on the native products. For this reason, the tax during its early stage was commonly known as the "consolidated tax." The principle of consolidated taxation was first applied to rolled tobacco (i.e., cigars and cigarettes), but was later extended to other commodities. The scope of the tax, as will be seen in later discussion, was subject to frequent changes. During 1928–35 the commodity tax contributed 9.16 percent of the total government receipts and 11.64 percent of its current revenue.

The high yield of the customs duties and the salt tax was due primarily to the simplicity of their administration. The commodity tax, imposed only upon a few selected commodities produced in the urban areas of the coastal provinces, was also simple to operate. Up to 1936 there was no progressive taxation with reference to either personal income or property. Several attempts were made during the early years of this century to introduce such taxes into China, but none were successful. It was not until 1936 that the income tax was finally instituted and became an integral part of the Chinese tax system. Because of administrative difficulties, however, it never played a significant role in the tax system of the Nationalist government.

From 1928 to 1937 the outlays for defense and debt service invariably dominated the expenditure side of the government budget. From 1929 to 1935 military expenditure accounted for 40.3 to 48.4

percent of the total annual expenditure; but during the fiscal years 1935 and 1936, the percentage was reduced to 30.23 and 34.65 respectively (see Table 2.6), because of the expansion of other expenditures. During 1928–36 the percentage of debt service (including both amortization and interest) to total government expenditure ranged from 25.18 to 37.46 percent. In the fiscal year 1928–29 outlays on defense and debt service accounted for 85.41 percent of the total expenditure. This percentage then declined steadily and reached an unprecedented low of 56.05 percent in the year 1935–36 before the trend turned upward again in the following year as a result of the war.

During 1931–36 the expenditure of the central government ranged from 2.12 to 4.90 percent; that of local governments, from 0.64 to 1.10 percent; and the total government expenditure from 3.22 to 6.00 percent of the corresponding gross national product (see Table 2.7).

In the sections that follow, the effects of inflation on China's fiscal system will be examined, particularly the revenue system, the public expenditure, and the debt policy of the government.

GOVERNMENT REVENUES UNDER INFLATION

During the war numerous attempts were made by the Chinese government to strengthen its current revenue. They included tax collection in kind, government monopoly, and ad valorem taxation in lieu of specific levies. A large number of tax rates were increased, and rate progression was steepened. New taxes, including an excess profit tax, were introduced. The base of the commodity tax was broadened to include a host of new products previously not subject to the tax (such as sugar, leather, and woolen products, and paper products for religious purposes). Attempts were also made to raise revenue from the sale of government properties. Some of these efforts did yield significant results, but most of them were futile. As a whole, their contribution to improving the nation's revenue system was too limited to turn the tide of inflation.

In the discussions that follow, the effects of inflation on taxation and the experiments to improve government revenue will be examined with particular reference to the custom duties, the salt tax, the commodity taxes, the income tax, the land tax, and the sales of government properties.

Customs revenue

During the prewar years the customs revenue was the most important tax source of the Chinese government, but during the war it proved to be the most unreliable of all revenues. Its unreliability was partly because the tax revenue depended on international trade, which was disrupted during a war, and partly because the bulk of the revenue was derived from a few seaports which were rendered

TABLE 2.1. PERCENT DISTRIBUTION OF CUSTOMS REVENUE COLLECTED AT PRINCIPAL PORTS, 1932–36

	1932	*1933*	*1934*	*1935*	*1936*
Shanghai	46.1	51.9	52.4	47.3	45.9
Tientsin	12.5	12.3	12.3	12.9	10.9
Bingtao	7.8	6.6	6.0	7.1	6.3
Hankow	4.1	6.0	5.8	7.1	7.3
Canton	4.6	3.2	2.4	3.0	3.4
Kowloon	2.8	2.5	2.2	2.3	2.8
Swatow	2.8	2.4	1.7	1.5	2.1
Amoy	2.1	1.5	1.7	1.9	1.7
Other Ports	17.2	13.6	15.5	16.9	19.6
Total	100.0	100.0	100.0	100.0	100.0

Source: *Yin-hang nien-chien* (The Chinese Bank Yearbook) (Shanghai, 1937), p. 400.

vulnerable to enemy attack by the inadequacy of China's military defense. During 1923–36 about 60 percent of the customs revenue was collected at three seaports, Shanghai, Tientsin, and Tsingtao. These were occupied by the Japanese during the first few months after the outbreak of the Sino-Japanese War in 1937. Within a year, when all China's maritime provinces were occupied, the stream of customs revenue was reduced to a trickle. In fact, no other tax revenue of the Chinese government suffered so much during the war. The loss of this important revenue during the initial stage of the war and the increasing military expenditures were two of the fundamental factors leading to the ultimate runaway inflation.

After V-J Day, the customs revenue regained importance and constituted one of three major tax sources of the Nationalist government. But because of import restrictions and unrealistic official rates of foreign exchange—both of which substantially reduced the yield of customs revenue—its position in government finance was no longer comparable to the prewar days.

Among the developments affecting customs administration during the inflation, two are worthy of special note. One is the effect of inflation on the system of the Customs Gold Unit; the other is the effect of the trade and foreign exchange policies pursued by the Chinese government upon the customs revenue.

The customs gold unit. Because of the depreciation of silver in terms of gold in 1930, the Chinese government adopted the Customs Gold Unit (C.G.U.) as the basis for payment of import duties; that is to say, if on the basis of the yuan-C.G.U. exchange rate prevailing in 1930 a specific duty amounted to ten C.G.U. per physical unit, then the tax in subsequent years remained at that amount, although the value of the yuan changed in terms of C.G.U. The purpose of using the C.G.U. as the basis of duty payment, according to the official explanation, was to minimize in the course of the depreciation of silver the loss of China's customs revenue in terms of gold-standard currencies on which most of the foreign debts serviced by the customs revenue was based.

The C.G.U. was a unit of account which was not actually coined, and had a theoretical content of 60.1866 grams of fine gold. Based on the official gold price of the United States dollar and of the pound sterling in 1930 (both currencies were then on gold standard) the C.G.U. was worth seventy cents or 19.7265 *d.* in sterling. The yuan value of the C.G.U. was derived on the basis of these conversion rates and the yuan-dollar or yuan-sterling exchange rates in the market. After the United Kingdom abandoned the gold standard in September, 1931, the yuan-dollar rate became the main factor in the yuan-C.G.U. quotation. After the American devaluation in 1933, the Chinese government used the sterling price of gold in the London market and the current yuan-sterling exchange rate to determine the yuan-C.G.U. quotation in Shanghai. To facilitate duty payment, the Central Bank of China also issued C.G.U. notes, which could be purchased at any time from the bank at its prevailing quotation, so that the exchange risks stemming from fluctuations of the yuan-C.G.U. rate would be minimized.

In April, 1942, the official yuan-C.G.U. rate was fixed at twenty to one C.G.U., a ratio identical to the official yuan-dollar rate then prevailing. In the meantime, the theoretical gold content was raised from 60.1866 fine grams to 88.8671 fine grams (i.e., the gold content of the current U.S. dollar) in order to rationalize the identity between the yuan-C.G.U. and the yuan-dollar rates. After these changes, the C.G.U. became in fact a twenty-yuan fapi note, having no longer any special relation to duty payment.

That the use of the C.G.U. for duty collection could reduce the government's loss in customs revenue in real terms was true only when the tax had been a specific duty collectible in Chinese currency. When the price of silver depreciated in terms of gold, so did the value of the Chinese currency unit, which until 1935 was on a silver standard. A specific duty of a fixed amount in Chinese currency would then result in reducing government revenue in terms of not only gold-based foreign currencies, but also the effective rate of China's import duty. For when the Chinese currency depreciated in terms of gold currency, the price of imported goods from gold-standard countries would necessarily rise in the Chinese market, and an import duty specified in a fixed sum of Chinese currency would represent a lower effective tax rate. On the other hand, if the duty were an ad valorem tax and if conversion were made on the basis of a realistic exchange rate, changes in the gold price of silver or the external value of the yuan would not likely affect either the effective rate of import duty or the tax revenue in terms of foreign currency.

If the above line of reasoning is correct, the C.G.U. could be useful in the cases where the specific duties are used. To make the unit useful, its price in yuan must be realistic. It follows, therefore, that the actual contribution of the C.G.U. system was reduced when the external value of the yuan, upon which the yuan-C.G.U. exchange rate was based, became overvalued during 1938–40. Upon the substitution of ad valorem customs rates for specific duties in 1941 and upon pegging of the yuan-C.G.U. rate at twenty to one yuan in April, 1942, the significance of the C.G.U. was entirely lost.

Effect of China's trade and foreign-exchange policies on the customs revenue. Before the war, some of the Chinese customs duties were imposed on an ad valorem basis and some, on a specific basis. When the price of taxable commodities rose after the outbreak of the war, the specific rates declined in effectiveness. To avoid possible inequalities in taxation and losses in government revenue that might result from price fluctuations, the Chinese government decided in 1941 to levy all customs duties on the ad valorem basis.

As long as the ad valorem duties are collected on the basis of realistic prices, the effects of price changes are allowed under ad valorem taxation. But in actual administration, the practical difficulties involved usually required the collection of duties on imports into China on the basis of their c. and f. cost, which was usually quoted in foreign currency. This basis of valuation involved the conversion of the foreign-currency cost into Chinese currency units, in which the duties were paid. Under such circumstances, both a proper estimate of the foreign-currency cost and a proper exchange rate for converting the cost into Chinese currency would have been essential to the tax collection. During the inflation the Chinese currency was often overvalued in terms of foreign currency. This was particularly true of the official exchange rate, which was usually the rate used for the above-mentioned conversion. To that extent, therefore, ad valorem taxation failed to provide a satisfactory solution to the problem of tax assessment.

Revenue from salt and other commodity taxes

The word "revenue" rather than "tax" is used here, because the present discussion covers not only the taxes on salt and other commodities but also the "profits" for a certain period (1941–48) from government monopolies. In most of the works on government finance of China, the salt revenue and the taxes (or monopoly revenues) from other commodities are usually treated as two separate groups, but because of the similar nature of these taxes and monopoly profits—a point which will be further explored presently—the subsequent discussion will treat them as members of the same revenue group.

During the inflation, the Nationalist government attempted many times to improve the yield from this group of revenues. These measures fall into four broad categories: widening of the tax base; adjustment of tax-rate structure; experimentation in government monopoly; and collection in kind of commodity taxes.

Widening of the tax base. There were fifteen commodities subject to tax in 1941; sixteen, in November, 1946, against only ten in the fiscal year 1935–36.

Adjustment of the tax-rate structure. Up to 1941 practically all these salt and commodity taxes were on a specific basis which had been in use because of its simplicity in administration. In September, 1941, all these specific taxes were replaced by ad valorem levies.

In theory, an ad valorem tax should be more rational and effective than a specific levy under conditions of inflation. But in its actual application to China's commodity taxation, this difference was often more apparent than real. For the convenience of administration and for the avoidance of irregularities in tax collection, the commodity prices upon which the ad valorem taxes were based were not the prices actually prevailing in the market at the time of assessment. They were prices specified by the government and based usually on quotation averages from previous periods. For most of the commodity taxes, such specified prices were adjusted only once every three months. This procedure was used as late as 1949. Under the circumstances, the ad valorem taxes were in fact tantamount to specific levies subject to adjustment once every three months.

The statutory rates of the commodity taxes were raised in the course of the inflation. It is difficult to compare the specific tax rates used before 1941 with the ad valorem rates used after 1941. But a comparison of the ad valorem rates of 1941 with those of 1946 (see Table 2.2) shows a definite increase. The higher tax rates, however, were not higher tax burdens. On the contrary, there is good reason to believe that these upward adjustments in statutory rates were inadequate to offset the loss of government revenue, which resulted from the lag in the price adjustment for tax assessment. To this extent, the real burden of the commodity taxes was reduced rather than increased in the course of inflation.

Experimentation in government monopolies. In March, 1941, the government approved in principle the institution of government monopoly in the distribution of salt, tea, rolled tobacco, matches, and sugar in lieu of the commodity taxes then in force, but the decision was not actually implemented until the following year.

The difference between the government monopoly and the early taxes on these five commodities must not be exaggerated. In order to minimize the outflow of government funds, the products whose distribution were monopolized by the government were not actually purchased by it for resale. Instead, after production the commodities were directed to government-controlled warehouses; and when sold, the government merely collected its "monopoly profit" as a percentage of the price realized through the usual commercial channel. In some cases, such as salt, the monopoly profit was collected on a specific rather than on an ad valorem basis.

The establishment of these government monopolies, however, contributed to a certain extent to improving government revenue. The improvement was due partly to the fact that the rates for monopoly-profit collections were higher than the corresponding rates used for the previous commodity taxes and partly to the use of more realistic price bases for assessment. It is obvious that these objectives could have been attained under an ordinary commodity tax, if it had been effectively administered. The institution of government monopolies brought into existence a number of special monopoly administrations and thereby greatly complicated the administrative mechanism of the government.

In January, 1945, the government reversed its policy and replaced all its monopolies with the commodity taxes.

Collection of commodity taxes in kind. Inspired by the results of collection in kind of the land tax (see Land Tax), the Chinese government attempted to apply a similar method to commodity taxes. The objective of this measure was not only to increase revenue but also to strengthen the government's control over the supply, and thereby the prices, of some of the essential commodities. The collection in kind procedure was first applied in 1942 to the commodity taxes on cotton yarn and wheat flour. In 1944 this method was also used for the sugar tax, which was then in force as a substitute for the system of government monopoly previously used. These in-kind collection systems remained in force until September, 1945, when they were abolished and were replaced by ordinary commodity taxes. For, as it was then believed, the expanded supply of cotton yarn, wheat flour, and sugar resulting from the restoration of industries in formerly Japanese-occupied areas, and also of imports from abroad, made the clumsy in-kind collections uneconomical and unnecessary.

At the end of the war, therefore, the salt and commodity tax system reverted to that of prewar days. The salt tax became a specific levy. However, the rate was raised to about 7,000 yuan a picul[3] in 1946 from 6.10 yuan in 1936–37, representing approximately a 1,200-fold increase against a 2,688-fold rise in the price index from 1937 to the end of 1946. In the case of the taxes on commodities other than salt, the principle of ad valorem taxation was continued after the war. But the intermittent, rather than the continuous, adjustment of the price base on which the ad valorem taxes were

TABLE 2.2. COVERAGE AND RATE OF COMMODITY TAX, 1941 AND 46
(in percent)

	1941	*1946*
Rolled tobacco	80	100
Flue-cured tobacco	25	30
Beer and foreign wine	60	100
Matches	20	20
Cotton yarn	3.5	5
Wheat flour	2.5	2.5
Cement	15	15
Sugar	15	25
Tea		10
Fur, leather, and woolen products		15
Joss paper		60
Aerated water	20	20
Cosmetics		45
Alcohol: Ordinary	20	
Refined	10	
Fuel	5	
Native tobacco leaf	30	50
Native pipe tobacco	15	30
Native wine	40	80

Source; P. T. Chen, "Recent Financial Developments in China, 1934–36," *The Chinese Yearbook*, 1937 ed., pp. 702–03; *Ts'ai-cheng nien-chien* (The Public Finance Yearbook) (Nanking, 1948), Part VIII, p. 65; Council of International Affairs, Chungking, *The Chinese Yearbook* (Bombay, 1943), p. 399.

computed impaired their effectiveness. Because of the unavailability of the relevant price data, it is impossible to compare the rates of the postwar ad valorem commodity taxes with the specific taxes used before the war. However, there is evidence that, in real terms, the postwar rates of the commodity taxes were lower than the prewar rates—a situation similar to that of the salt tax.

Such devices as government monopolies and tax collection in kind made some contribution to strengthening the financial position of the government. But the contribution was more in the nature of preventing government revenue from being further reduced in real terms rather than of actually expanding the real revenue.

Income tax

Income taxation is brought into this discussion not because of its importance to the revenue system of the Chinese government, but rather for the purpose of examining why it could not be effectively enforced during the Chinese inflation. Particular interest is in studying the effect of inflation on such a tax, and whether or not the Chinese government followed a rational policy in coping with the anomalous situation arising from a protracted inflation. In the paragraphs that follow, the discussion will fall into the following broad categories: adjustment of the income-tax base during the inflation; adjustment of tax rates; effects of changing prices on taxable income; and effects of lag in tax assessment and collection on real value of government revenue.

Several attempts were made by the predecessors of the Chinese Nationalist government to introduce the income tax in China, but none succeeded in reaching a stage comparable to that of the income-tax administration under the Nationalists. The first income-tax law of the Nationalist government was promulgated in October, 1936. It was redrafted in February, 1943, and further revised in April, 1946. It is on these versions of the income-tax law that this discussion will be based.

Adjustment of the tax base during inflation. Under the law of 1936, only three classes of income were subject to tax: business profits (of both incorporated and unincorporated enterprises), salaries and professional fees, and interest or dividends derived from bank deposits, securities, or loans. No tax was imposed with respect to the aggregate income of an individual taxpayer.

In the revised versions of 1943 and 1946 many important changes were introduced. First, taxable income was extended to include rental receipts derived from leased property (including land, building, equipment, etc.). Second, a progressive surtax was imposed on an individual's total personal income exceeding a specified exemption level. To avoid double taxation, some of the taxes levied on the classified incomes of an individual taxpayer were deductible from his surtax liability.

In many respects, such as, the division of taxable incomes into schedules and the deductions at source, the Chinese income-tax system resembled the income tax of the United Kingdom.

Adjustment of tax rates. With the exception of a proportional rate for the tax on interest and dividends, all the other income-tax rates were progressive. For the tax on business profits in all three versions of the tax law, the rate was progressive with respect to the ratio of profit to invested capital. For the cases in which the amount of invested capital could not be readily ascertained, the rate of the profits tax progressed simply with respect to the total net profit. Generally, the first method was used for taxing incorporated enterprises; the second, for unincorporated firms when the amount of invested capital was not known. For the other income taxes—including those on salary, professional fees, rental receipts, and aggregate personal income—the rates progressed by bracket of income.

In the course of inflation, the rate structures of the income tax were also adjusted, while the tax base was widened. The rate adjustments consisted of steepening the progression of statutory rates and of revaluing exemption levels and limits of various income brackets to allow for changes in the purchasing power of money.

In the case of the tax based on the profit-capital ratio, a comparison of the degree of progression of the successive rate schedules is easy, for the inflation did not affect the basis of progression. It is merely a matter of comparing the rates applicable to a common tax base under the various rate schedules. Such a comparison is made in Chart 2.1. In the 1943 revision, only the tax rates applicable to high profit-capital ratios were raised. In the 1946 revision, all the tax rates were raised, but the increases in the upper-bracket rates were greater than those in the lower-bracket rates.

The tax based on the profit-capital ratio, however, gave rise to one of the main difficulties encountered in the administration of the Chinese income tax. Such a tax requires an accurate estimate not only of a taxpayer's current earnings but also of his capital investment, yet both had to be estimated in terms of a currency whose value itself was in a state of flux. To allow for changes in the purchasing power of money, the income-tax law of 1946 permitted an adjustment in the value of paid-up capital used in computing the income-capital ratio for the tax. Such adjustment for a given tax year, however, was limited to a maximum of 50 percent of the change in the price index during the second twelve-month period prior to that tax year.[4] An adjustment of this nature was evidently inadequate to offset the currency depreciation which occurred during the Chinese inflation. The result was an undue undervaluation of capital investment, an exaggeration of the income-capital ratio which determined the tax rate, and therefore a great

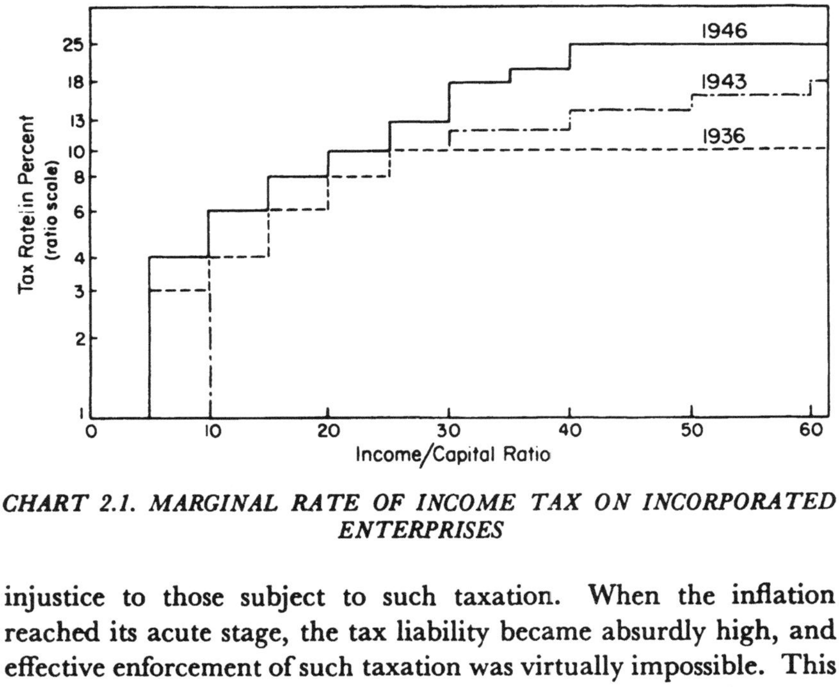

CHART 2.1. MARGINAL RATE OF INCOME TAX ON INCORPORATED ENTERPRISES

injustice to those subject to such taxation. When the inflation reached its acute stage, the tax liability became absurdly high, and effective enforcement of such taxation was virtually impossible. This evident defect of the income-tax system was not corrected, however, until the tax law was revised in 1951 after the removal of the Nationalist government from the mainland to Taiwan.

To compare successive tax-rate schedules which are graduated with respect to an absolute amount of taxable income is a much more complex problem; for in these comparisons the tax base, being in absolute value and thus subject to the distortions arising from price changes, is no longer a constant under inflation. The exemption level and the income brackets set up in a tax law will mean one thing in one year, but an entirely different thing in another year. To eliminate this distortion, the exemption levels and income brackets as provided in various versions of the Chinese tax law are here adjusted and expressed in terms of the 1936 yuan. The adjustments are made by dividing the exemption and the upper- and lower-bracket limits by the wholesale price index of the month in which the revised income-tax laws were promulgated. The result obtained in this manner is shown in Chart 2.2 with respect to the schedule tax on profits of unincorporated enterprises.

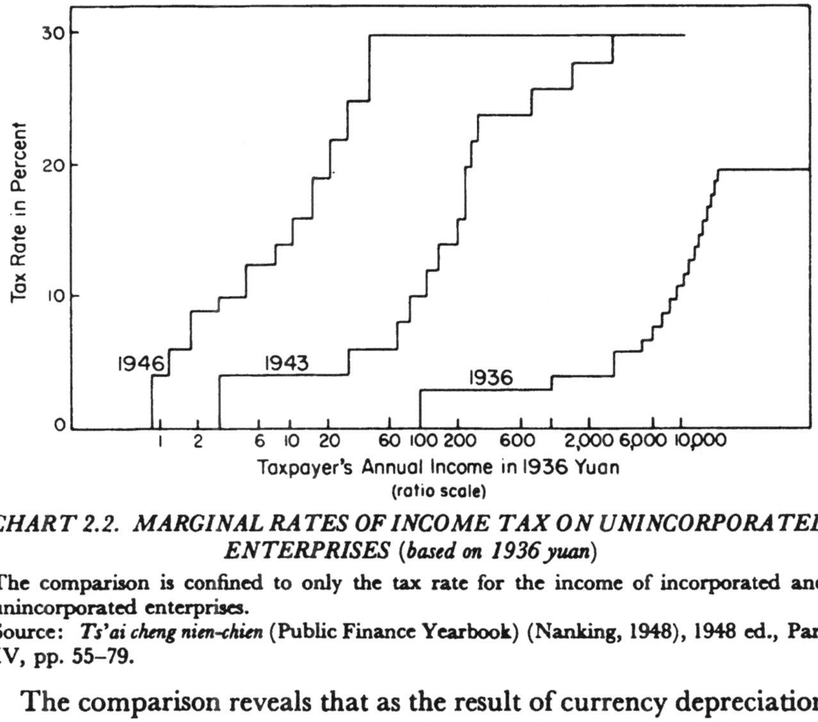

CHART 2.2. MARGINAL RATES OF INCOME TAX ON UNINCORPORATED ENTERPRISES (based on 1936 yuan)

The comparison is confined to only the tax rate for the income of incorporated and unincorporated enterprises.
Source: *Ts'ai cheng nien-chien* (Public Finance Yearbook) (Nanking, 1948), 1948 ed., Part IV, pp. 55–79.

The comparison reveals that as the result of currency depreciation and changes in tax law, the exemption level in the terms of the 1936 yuan was greatly reduced from 100 yuan in 1936 to 2.76 yuan in 1943 and to 0.84 yuan in 1946. Similarly, in the terms of the 1936 yuan, the progressive rates were applicable only to the incomes ranging from 2.76 to 2,757 yuan under the 1943 schedule, and to those ranging from 0.84 to 39.43 yuan under the 1946 schedule. Both to an annual income exceeding 39.43 yuan (of 1936) in the case of the 1946 schedule, and to an income exceeding 2,757 yuan (of 1936) under the 1943 schedule, a proportional tax rate of 30 percent was applicable. Therefore, in terms of the 1936 yuan, the

Chinese income tax during the later part of the inflation became a progressive tax on incomes of low brackets and a proportional tax on moderate and high incomes.[5] Despite the government's attempts to adjust exemption levels, bracket limits, and tax rates, inflation resulted in a substantial reduction not only in the progressivity in China's income-tax rates but also in the range within which such progressive taxation could be effective.

Effects of changing prices upon taxable income. Despite the protracted inflation, the Chinese income-tax law did not make adequate provision for the effects of changing prices upon income.

For depreciation charges on fixed assets, the law of 1946[6] permitted the use of either the straight-line method or the declining-balance method; both based on historical cost. Under the first method, the annual depreciation charge was determined by dividing the years of expected life of the asset into its historical cost. Under the second method, the annual depreciation charge was determined by applying a constant depreciation rate to the declining net asset (i.e., the historical cost minus accumulated depreciation charges). The rate at which the depreciation was charged for an asset with a given expected life varied inversely as the length of its expected life, and was accordingly specified in the tax law.[7] However, neither the straight-line method nor the declining-balance method, when based on historical cost, adequately allowed for the effects of changing prices on income. The absence of such an allowance naturally resulted in understating the business or manufacturing cost of a taxpayer and in overstating his taxable income.[8]

For the valuation of inventory, the income-tax law of 1946 had the following provisions:[9] First, a security dealer might value his security inventory on the basis of the average price for the last month of his fiscal year. Second, a taxpayer, in the case of a commodity inventory, might use for his valuation the "weighted average"[10] of the cost of inventory brought forward from the previous year and the prices at which the new supplies were procured during the current year. In short, the valuation was based on the historical costs of the inventory. Both of the provisions, like those of depreciation charges, tend to exaggerate business profit in the course of an inflation.

Effects of lag in tax assessment and collection on the real value of government revenue. Another important difficulty which hampers income taxation in the course of inflation is the time lag between making the tax assessment and collection. The effect of such a lag is particularly important where the tax is paid by the taxpayer on the basis of the income of the previous year instead of that of the current year. Consider the case in which the tax return is filed three months after the conclusion of the tax year and in which the tax is collected immediately after the return is filed; assume further that during these fifteen months commodity prices double every month; then the amount of tax collected, in terms of real purchasing power, will be about $\frac{1}{2{,}730}$ of what would have been received if there had been no change in prices (see appendix 4). The bulk of China's income tax was assessed on the basis of the income of the previous year. Moreover, during the later stages of the Chinese inflation, the currency actually depreciated much faster than what is assumed here. Under the circumstances, it is apparent why an income tax like the one in force in China failed under hyperinflation.

Land tax

The land tax, represented mainly by the tax on agricultural land, was the core of the Chinese tax system of early dynasties and became the main revenue of the provincial governments during the early years of the Nationalist regime. The most important reform in the land tax introduced during the war was the institution of a collection in kind procedure in 1941 and the transfer in the same year of the land-tax administration from the provincial governments to the central government. The use of collection in kind in lieu of money payment was designed to augment the tax revenue and to strengthen the government's control over food supply, for which the nation's need, both civilian and military, was mounting with the extension of war. In view of the complexity of problems involved in implementing the in-kind collections, most of which were apparently beyond the power and competency of local authorities to handle, the administration of the land tax was transferred to the central government.

The collection in kind program had these basic features:

1. The tax in kind was applicable only to agricultural land, not to urban land.

2. The tax liability in kind of a taxpayer was at first derived by converting the money value of his prewar tax at a rate of 2 *tou*[11] of unhusked rice per yuan. If, for instance, the prewar levy was one thousand yuan, then the tax liability in kind would be 2,000 tou of unhusked rice, or some other approved agricultural product with a current market value comparable to that of the unhusked rice. In 1942 the conversion rates were modified to increase the amount of tax and to make a prewar yuan equivalent to 4 *tou* of unhusked rice, 2.8 *tou* of wheat, or 5 *shih chin*[12] of cotton.

3. The tax in kind was payable in cotton, rice, wheat, or other types of grains, depending upon the product of the land subject to tax. The basic principle was that the tax liability should be met directly with the product of the land upon which the tax was imposed. For areas where the crop yields were insufficient to meet local need, payment in cash on the basis of prevailing prices of the agricultural products concerned was also permitted.

4. In areas whose production in rice, wheat, cotton, or other essential crops had exceeded local needs, landowners were also obligated to sell and/or lend their products to the government up to the amount specified by the latter, in addition to their tax payment. In some provinces, the amount of such sales and lending for which a landowner was responsible varied in direct proportion with his tax liability. In other provinces, these obligations to sell or lend were imposed only on those whose holdings of agricultural product exceeded a certain limit. A person with an inventory falling short of the limit was not obligated to sell or to lend.

5. The lending to government was effected by requiring the sale of the crop to the government against government bonds, most of which were not redeemable in cash but might be used by the holder after a stipulated period to meet his in-kind tax liability. The purchases, on the other hand, were usually made with a cash payment. The collection-in-kind method was used for the land tax not only during the war but also to a lesser extent during the postwar years.

The use of collecting the land tax in kind, whose statistics are shown in Table 2.3, had the following results:

1. The collection of the land tax and government borrowing in kind was more effectively enforced in rice-producing than in wheat-producing provinces in terms of total production. This difference

apparently stemmed from the fact that rice was produced mainly in the central and southern parts of China over which the Nationalist government had a more direct control during the war than it did over the wheat-producing provinces in the north.

2. The revision of the rate at which the prewar tax liability in money terms was converted into the liability in kind in 1942 and the introduction of the system of forced loans in the fiscal year 1943–44 substantially increased the government's collection in both rice and wheat. But the spurt was only temporary. During the fiscal years 1945–46 and 1946–47 the percentages of government collection (including both the tax and the loan) to the total production of rice and wheat fell back to the 1941–42 level, before the force-loan system was introduced. One explanation for this decrease was the exemption in 1945–46 of the tax on agricultural land in the areas formerly occupied by the Japanese, and the similar tax exemption in 1946–47 for the provinces in Free China. These exemptions were decreed by the Nationalist government as a measure to compensate for the undue burden imposed upon the people during the war.

3. During 1943–45 the rice collections (including both the tax and the loans) were in the order of 7 to 9 percent of the rice production in Free China. These tax-production ratios were actually higher than any of the ratios that the total government expenditure bore to the national product during the period of 1931–36 (see Table 2.7). The success of collecting the land tax in kind, however, was often exaggerated. One estimate placed the tax-production ratio in China between 15 and 20 percent.[13] This, in the light of our statistics, is apparently too high.

Revenue from the sales of government properties

During the postwar years, receipts from the sales of government properties became one of the major government revenues. It accounted for 33.3 percent of the government's current revenue in 1946, 21.6 percent in 1947, 17.4 percent during the first seven months of 1948, and 6.4 percent during the last five months. In terms of the total government expenditures of these years, the revenue from sales of government property was 8.8 percent, 7.0 percent, 5.4 percent, and 1.4 percent respectively (see Appendix Table 2.1). In 1946, this source contributed more than any other current revenue. In 1947

TABLE 2.3. LAND TAX COLLECTION, 1941–47

Fiscal year	Crop	Collection in kind (thousand shih piculs[b]): Tax	Purchase	Loan	Total	Production[a] (thousand shih piculs)	Collection (percent of production)
1941–42	Rice	22,002.8			22,002.8	643,519	3.42
	Wheat	3,162.1			3,162.1	165,120	1.91
1942–43	Rice	29,022.9			29,022.9	635,229	4.57
	Wheat	5,825.9			5,825.9	209,729	2.78
1943–44	Rice	28,749.1	11,000.1	13,787.2	53,536.4	609,488	8.78
	Wheat	7,154.3	1,991.7	2,514.3	11,660.3	199,196	5.85
1944–45	Rice	23,182.8		24,355.5	47,538.3	674,715	7.05
	Wheat	6,239.3		3,676.3	9,915.6	248,264	3.99
1945–46	Rice	12,242.4		13,298.9	25,541.3	588,205	4.05
	Wheat	3,178.0		1,207.4	4,385.4	219,481	2.00
1946–47	Rice	24,075.8		12,614.9	36,690.7	889,770	4.08
	Wheat	2,902.4		1,965.3	4,867.7	467,762	1.04

[a] The production figures represent the crops produced during each of the years 1941–45 in fifteen provinces of Free China and twenty-two provinces for 1946.

[b] One *shih picul* equals $\frac{1}{20}$ metric ton.

There are no data for spaces left blank in table.

Source: *Chung-hua min-kuo tung-ch'i t'so-yao* (The Statistical Abstract of the Republic of China) (Nanking, 1947), pp. 13 and 63; *The Public Finance Yearbook*, 1948 ed., Part 5, pp. 32–33.

it was surpassed only by the commodity tax, and in the first seven months of 1948 only by the commodity tax and the custom duties.

The properties sold included mainly war surplus supplies in the Pacific islands bought by the Chinese government from the United States; the German, Italian, and Japanese properties in China; and properties of convicted Chinese traitors confiscated by the Chinese government.

The American surplus properties were taken over by the Chinese government primarily for meeting China's military and industrial requirements and for possible resale at a profit. To what extent these surplus properties benefited the Chinese military machinery and industries is not exactly known. If one considers the military and industrial organizations of China as they were during the post-war years and considers the practical difficulties involved in surplus property administration, it would be difficult to understand how either the military forces or the industries could have benefited as originally expected. The anti-inflationary aspects of the program failed miserably. With the exception of a small fraction of the consumption goods (e.g., canned food, textile products, etc.) whose handling did not involve unduly high expenses and which could readily be disposed of in domestic markets, the bulk of the surplus properties was not or could not be utilized as had originally been planned. In many cases, handling and transportation were so expensive that the surplus properties could only be resold in bulk as scrap to commercial firms after a long delay and often at a price lower than that originally paid by the government. Although the sale of these properties did make some contribution to the meagre revenue of the Chinese government in the postwar years, the results would have been much better had the program been efficiently administered.

The bulk of the enemy properties and those of collaborators consisted of factories, wharves, godowns, real estate, and commodities. As originally planned, they were either to be sold to the public or operated as government enterprises. It was hoped that the sales of these properties would help to combat inflation by withdrawing surplus funds from the market, that the products of such government enterprises would contribute to increasing the supply of consumption goods in the domestic market, and that the operating profits from these undertakings would augment the revenue of the government. Administrative complications, however, made the liquidation of the properties too slow and the revenue realized too small to be of much assistance in combating inflation. Moreover, there was usually a tendency among government departments to keep too large a part of the properties for government enterprises, which were not efficiently managed. Often, the properties that the public wished to purchase were also the ones which the government offices wished to keep for their own operations; whereas, those put on sale were not the ones attractive to the public. Worst of all was the unauthorized occupation of real estate by military and other government officials. This manifestation of maladministration and corruption was particularly common in Shanghai and other metropolitan areas where housing was in acute shortage and real estate was at a premium.

Following the monetary reform in August, 1948, under which the gold yuan was issued, the government also made an attempt to issue and sell shares of stock in the China Textile Industries, Inc., a government concern in charge of operating most of the former Japanese textile mills in China; the China Merchant Steamship Navigation Co.; the Taiwan Sugar Company; the Taiwan Paper Mill; and other leading enterprises owned by the government. At that time there was a plethora of new paper notes in the market because of the sales of private gold and foreign-exchange holdings to the Central Bank as required by the financial regulations then in force. There was an acute shortage of commodity supplies in the urban market (particularly in Shanghai). Holders of commodities were unwilling to sell their stocks at the unrealistically controlled prices for paper notes, in which they had no confidence. The usual flow of agricultural products from rural sources dwindled. Stocks in these government enterprises, appearing to be a better store of value than paper money, did have some attraction for the public, when the hoarding of commodities, gold, or foreign currency was liable to criminal prosecution and when there was practically nothing else in the market worthy of purchase. But the attraction was in no way a lasting one. First, most of the government offices managing these enterprises were reluctant to relinquish their control; whereas, private investors were prejudiced against government management or even government participation. Second, some of the enterprises for sale[14] were not those especially attractive to private investors. Moreover, when the control over prices and the restrictions on speculation and hoarding were relaxed, market interest in the stocks of those government enterprises was accordingly reduced, and the demand shifted to other, more lucrative investments.

Effects of price change on government revenue

The discussion in this section will be classified in two groups: effects on the real value of the revenue, and effects on the pattern of the revenue.

Effects on the real value of the revenue. During 1928–37 there was a steady expansion in the real value of government revenue (see Table 2.4). The only exception to this upward trend occurred in 1935–36, when the index of revenue dipped because of the unusually large loss in the customs revenue. The decline was a result of the prevalence of smuggling in north China, then under Japanese dominance. In terms of 1936–37 yuan, the revenue of the fiscal year 1936–37 was the largest ever collected by the Nationalist government during its reign over the Chinese mainland from 1928 to 1949. As the inflation intensified, the index for the real value of revenue declined steadily from 0.50 (1936–37 = 100) in the fiscal year 1937–38, to 0.44 in 1938–39, and to 0.30 in 1939–40. From 1940–41 through 1945–46, the index fluctuated between 0.03 and 0.05. Restoration of tax collections in the areas formerly under Japanese occupation and the decline in the tempo of the Chinese inflation during the months immediately after V-J Day resulted in a substantial improvement in the real value of government revenue. The index rose to 3.9 percent in 1946. The recovery, however, was only a temporary phenomenon, with the index of real revenue (in annual rate) dropping to 35 percent in 1947, 24 percent in the first seven months of 1948, and to 12 percent in the remaining five months of 1948. The sharp decline of the index after August, 1948, clearly indicates the detrimental effects of the monetary reform of 1948 on government revenue.

Effects on the pattern of the revenue. During 1928–42 the customs revenue, the salt tax, and the commodity taxes contributed from 62 to 92 percent of the current revenue of the Nationalist government.

TABLE 2.4. TOTAL EXPENDITURES AND REVENUES OF THE NATIONALIST GOVERNMENT, 1929–48

	EXPENDITURES				REVENUES[a]	
	Index[b]		*U.S. $ equivalent*[c]		*Index*[b]	
	current yuan	*1936–37 yuan*	*current dollars*	*1948 dollars*	*current yuan*	*1936–37 yuan*
Fiscal year						
1929–30	31	36	205.8	367.5	37	43
1930–31	41	42	198.7	415.7	43	44
1931–32	40	43	159.1	385.2	48	51
1932–33	37	42	168.4	441.9	47	53
1933–34	44	53	251.4	576.5	55	66
1934–35	50	59	329.5	698.1	62	73
1935–36	71	78	438.6	904.4	41	45
1936–37	100	100	553.4	1,080.6	100	100
1937–38	111	111	582.1	1,165.6	50	50
1938–39	124	112	188.5	402.9	48	44
1939–40	149	81	200.6	422.2	56	30
1940–41	202	20			45	5
1941–42	429	15			92	3
1942–43	1,331	10			524	4
1943–44	2,767	11			898	4
1944–45	9,704	12			3,086	4
1945–46	67,221	41			10,890	8
Calendar year						
1946	295,504	78	1,717.4	2,343.0	146,303	39
1947	1,901,581	66	1,258.4[d]	1,366.4	1,064,439	35
1948			695.1[e]	695.1		
Jan.–July	36,580,389[f]	51[f]			17,274,079[f]	24[f]
Aug.–Dec.	1,587,821,476[f]	38[f]			501,582,876[f]	12[f]

Expenditures and receipts for 1938–39 are for the six-month period ending June, 1939; the indices are compiled on the basis of annual expenditure and revenue rates. The indices of expenditures and revenues in 1936–37 yuan are obtained by deflating the index for the expenditures and revenues in current yuan by the Chungking wholesale price index (1936–37 = 1) of the corresponding year. The dollar equivalents for the fiscal years 1941–46 are not computed because of the unavailability of realistic exchange rate between yuan and the dollar.

Source: For figures for 1929–35, *The Public Finance Yearbook*, 1943 ed., Part III, Chapter 4; and 1948 ed., Part III, Chapters 2 and 4. For 1946–48, unpublished records of the Central Bank of China.

[a] Excludes borrowing. [b] 1936–37 = 100. [c] Unit: 1 million.
[d] Includes 172.4 expenditures in foreign currency.
[e] Includes 176.4 expenditures in foreign currency.
[f] Indices for the annual rate.

With the exception of the fiscal year 1935–36, the customs revenue, contributing 36.7 to 58.4 percent of the current revenue, was the most important of all the tax revenues. The salt tax usually ranked second to the customs revenue, and the commodity taxes, third (see Table 2.5).

The occupation of the Chinese maritime customs from 1942 to 1945 by the Japanese reduced the collection of customs revenue to a negligible quantity. Consequently, the salt tax, the commodity tax, the land tax, and business taxes became the mainstays of the Chinese tax system. During 1942–43 the revenue from the land tax rose to 46 percent of the total current revenue, and boosted the total revenue to 25.7 percent of the government's aggregate expenditure as against 11.2 percent in the preceding year. This position of the land tax was, however, only a temporary phenomenon. In the following year, the commodity tax, the land tax, the business taxes, and the salt tax accounted for 22.8, 20.3, 15.9, and 14.2 percent of the current revenue respectively. In the years 1944–45 and 1945–46, the salt tax became the leading revenue as a result of its rate adjustment. The percentage of yield from direct taxes (including income, inheritance, and excess profits taxes) also increased during the war, although insignificantly.

After the war, the customs revenue, the salt tax, and the commodity tax regained their usual importance in the Chinese tax system. The leading role, however, was shifted from the customs revenue to the commodity tax. The shift was due more to the adverse effects on the customs revenue of the restrictive trade policy and the unrealistic foreign-exchange rate than to an expansion of the commodity-tax yield.

Another important postwar development was the increased importance of the yield from sales of government properties. It became the most important single source of current revenue in 1946 and ranked next only to the salt tax in 1945–46 and to the commodity tax in 1947.

The current revenue of the Chinese government, expressed as a percentage of government expenditure, dwindled steadily following the outbreak of the Sino-Japanese War in 1937, and reached its first trough in 1941–42 (see Table 2.5). The drastic loss in customs revenue was the main factor in this decline. A recovery during the

TABLE 2.5. PATTERN OF CHINA'S GOVERNMENT REVENUE, 1928–1948

Fiscal year	*Total revenue*		*Customs revenue*		*Salt tax and revenue*		*Commodity tax and revenue*	
	1	2	1	2	1	2	1	2
1928–29	76.1	100	41.4	53.9	3.0	3.8	6.9	8.9
1929–30	82.7	100	47.1	57.0	20.9	25.2	6.9	8.4
1930–31	72.1	100	40.3	55.8	19.4	26.8	6.9	9.5
1931–32	83.0	100	48.5	58.4	18.9	22.8	11.6	14.0
1932–33	84.5	100	44.8	53.0	21.8	25.7	11.0	13.0
1933–34	79.9	100	39.3	40.2	19.8	24.8	11.7	14.7
1934–35	78.1	100	34.3	43.9	16.2	20.8	10.1	13.0
1935–36	40.0	100	1.8	4.5	13.7	34.5	12.2	30.7
1936–37	65.8	100	32.0	48.6	12.5	18.9	7.5	11.4
1937–38	31.0	100	11.4	36.7	6.7	21.6	2.1	6.8
1938–39	26.2	100	10.8	41.4	4.2	16.2	2.1	7.8
1939–40	23.8	100	11.3	47.5	2.0	8.4	1.4	5.8
1940–41	13.5	100	5.9	44.0	2.3	17.4	1.4	10.3
1941–42	11.2	100	6.2	55.2	1.1	10.0	1.6	14.4
1942–43	25.7	100	.6	2.3	5.1	20.0	1.1	4.1
1943–44	20.8	100	.6	2.7	3.0	14.2	4.7	22.8
1944–45	22.1	100	.3	1.1	10.0	45.3	3.7	16.9
1945–46	11.4	100	.2	1.1	5.0	34.8	1.9	16.6
1946	26.7	100	4.4	16.5	3.3	12.4	6.5	24.4
1947	32.4	100	5.4	16.8	4.5	14.0	11.1	34.1
1948								
Jan.–July	30.9	100	8.3	26.9	3.1	9.9	10.3	33.4
Aug.–Dec.	21.9	100	4.2	19.2	1.8	8.4	7.8	35.7

latter part of the war was due to the government's effort in improving the salt, the commodity, and the land tax collections (including the use of the collection-in-kind procedure, and the institution of government monopolies in some of the commodity distributions). Then in 1945–46 came another decline in this percentage, caused primarily by the abrupt expansion of government outlay during the months immediately following V-J Day, while tax collections failed to keep pace. In 1946 and 1947, current revenue improved somewhat in relation to total government expenditure. This upward trend however was interrupted in 1948, particularly during the months following the monetary reform in August.

Defects of the revenue system

The experience during the war and the inflation proved that the Chinese tax system had many defects. First, the base of the system

TABLE 2.5 (continued)

	DIRECT TAX													
	Income tax		*Inheritance tax*		*Excess profits tax*		*Subtotal*		*Land tax*		*Business tax*		*Sales of government properties*	
	1	2	1	2	1	2	1	2	1	2	1	2	1	2
	.9	2.9					.9	2.9						
	.7	2.7					.7	2.7						
	.9	3.8			.6	2.6	1.5	6.4						
	1.1	7.4			.3	2.0	1.4	9.4						
	.8	6.8	.001	.01	.7	5.9	1.5	12.7						
	.7	2.6			1.0	3.9	2.4	6.6	11.8	46.0	2.2	8.6		
	1.0	4.5	.023	.10	1.2	5.1	2.2	9.6	4.2	20.3	3.3	15.9		
	.7	3.2	.310	.14	.7	3.3	1.7	7.9	1.8	8.3	2.1	9.5		
	.1	1.3	.008	.07	.1	1.2	.2	2.5	.3	2.1	.4	3.6	2.4	20.9
	.4	1.5	.02	.08	.2	.8	.6	2.4	.2	.7	.9	3.3	8.8	33.3
	1.7	5.3	.04	.12	.4	1.2	2.1	6.6	.2	.6	.2	.5	7.0	21.6
	1.6	5.2	.02	.06	.03	1.7	1.7	5.4	.04	.4	.4	.1	5.4	17.4
	1.1	5.0	.01	.05			1.1	5.1	.02	.1	.1	.4	1.4	6.4

1 The ratio in percent of total government expenditures or total government receipts (including borrowing).

2 The ratio in percent of total government revenue (excluding borrowing).

There are no data for spaces left blank in the table.

Source: For the fiscal years, *The Public Finance Yearbook*, 1943 and 1948 eds., Part III; and for the calendar years, unpublished records of the Central Bank of China.

was too narrow and too unstable to cope with any emergency. Its yield depended too much upon collections from metropolitan areas in maritime provinces. With the occupation of the maritime provinces by the Japanese, virtually all the customs revenue was lost. Since most of the industries were located in coastal cities, their occupation accordingly deprived the Nationalist government of a major portion of the commodity tax revenue. The effect of the war on the salt tax, though also substantial, was not so serious as that on the other two taxes because China's salt-producing centers, where the tax was usually collected, were widely scattered in different parts of the country. While the fields in Manchuria, north China, and the maritime provinces fell under the control of the Japanese, those in Szechuan and other southwestern provinces continued to yield a substantial tax revenue to the Chinese government. In fact, in the fiscal years 1944–45 and 1945–46 the salt tax became the most important tax revenue although the absolute amount of receipts was insignificant in comparison with the magnitude of the government outlay (see Table 2.5).

A second important defect in the Chinese tax system was that, like the systems in many other countries, it had been designed on the premise of a stable national currency in which taxes were assessed and collected. There was no adequate provision in these tax laws to cope with complications caused by inflation. In the income, inheritance, and excess-profits tax laws, for instance, no provision was made to avoid or minimize the possible government losses which rose under inflation because of the time lag involved in the assessment and collection of these taxes; nor were the procedures used in determining the value of taxable income or property adequate to ensure an equitable taxation under the conditions of changing prices. There were also losses due to the time lag in the assessment and collection of the customs duties, the salt tax, and the commodity taxes, but the effect was not so serious as that on the direct taxes. Moreover, in the case of the salt tax and some of the commodity taxes, the use of collection in kind, the institution of a government monopoly, and the substitution of ad valorem taxation for specific levies contributed to offset, at least in part, the adverse effects of inflation upon tax revenue.

A third defect was that the Chinese government relied too heavily upon excise taxes and taxes on business turnover for its revenue. Some of these taxes were in the form of a sales tax at the manufacturer's or wholesaler's level, some in the form of taxes on gross business receipts, known as the business tax. In addition, there was also a stamp duty on invoices and receipts, assessed in accordance with the amount of the transaction or payment involved.

A chief advantage of such excise and business taxes is to make it possible to tax low-income groups and those who successfully evade income tax. To that extent, therefore, the excise and turnover taxes may be considered as useful channels for taxing current income that an income tax cannot normally reach.[15] Moreover, an excise tax can usually be collected on a current basis and does not involve so much time lag as the income tax does. These arguments for excise and turnover taxes, however, do not justify the unusually important role that this group of taxes played in the Chinese tax system.

The excise and turnover tax system itself, as it was administered in China, was not satisfactory. First, China's system of excise taxes (including the salt and commodity taxes) was regressive because it taxed salt, wheat flour, and cotton yarn of low counts, all of which were necessities for ordinary people, and taxed a few consumption goods of the rich. A comparison between the commodity taxes in Japan and China is revealing. Instead of being confined to a few commodities, the Japanese commodity tax covered a wide range of articles, with luxury goods subjected to heavier taxes than general consumption goods.[16] Second, in China the salt and commodity taxes were collected at the manufacturer's or wholesaler's level, and could therefore have had undesirable pyramiding effect. Third, some of China's turnover taxes (such as the business tax) were levied on the basis of gross sales.[17] This tax, as the Shoup Mission on Japanese taxation points out in its report

> is the least refined member of the sales tax family. It favors the vertically combined firm, which starts with its own raw materials and also produces and sells the finished product. A competing group of independent firms comprising raw materials producers, manufacturers, wholesalers and retailers is at a disadvantage under a transactions tax, for there is a tax to pay at each turnover, while the vertically integrated firm pays the tax only once.

This discrimination in favor of vertical integration was further aggravated by the existence of the stamp duty on invoices and receipts, which, as previously indicated, was merely another form of a tax on gross turnover.

GOVERNMENT EXPENDITURE UNDER INFLATION

The real and dollar value of the expenditure

The real value of government expenditures at the beginning of the Sino-Japanese War, 1937–38 and 1938–39, were about the same as the expenditure of 1936–37 (see Table 2.4). This situation, however, was only a temporary phenomenon. The index of expenditures in real value dropped sharply to a range of from 10 to 20 percent (1936–37 = 100) during the period 1940–45 despite the astronomical expansion of expenditures in money values. During the months immediately following V-J Day, commodity prices in China dropped precipitously, and the tempo of inflation temporarily slackened. In the meantime, the restoration after V-J Day of the areas previously occupied by the Japanese resulted in a great expansion in both the activity and outlay of the Nationalist government. The real value of expenditures for the fiscal year 1945–46 was raised to 47 percent of the 1936–37 level. After 1946, only the statistics based on calendar years, instead of those for fiscal years, are available. These data show that in 1946 and 1947, the real expenditure indices were 78 and 66 percent respectively. These were the highest percentages attained since 1939 and 1940. In 1948 when the economic condition of the country turned from bad to worse, the real value of government expenditures again receded and the index dropped to 51 percent during the first seven months of the year and to 38 percent during the five-month period following the monetary reform in August.

The reduction in real value of government expenditures during the inflation was made possible by drastically curtailing the real wage and salary of civil and military government employees. Toward the end of the war and during the postwar years, their remuneration, fixed in terms of monetary units subject to only an occasional adjustment, were so low that the consequent demoralizing effects upon these employees later constituted one of the major causes leading to the collapse of the Nationalist government on the mainland (see Chapter VII).

As a whole, the real expenditure decreased more slowly than the real revenue. The relative sluggishness of expenditures in its downward adjustment after 1936–37 may be ascribed to the following causes: First, because of the absence of drastic and fruitful tax reforms, the real value of the government revenue was determined mainly by the changes in commodity prices and by the responsiveness of various taxes to such change. Expenditures, on the other hand, consisted mainly of wages and salaries of government employees, and reductions in these outlays could not have gone much below what was needed for maintaining a minimum subsistence for these employees. Second, when the area under the control of the Nationalist government shrank, the revenue contracted accordingly; but government expenditures could not have been similarly curtailed so long as the size of the army and the magnitude of the military outlays remained, as they did, unaffected.

To facilitate comparison, expenditures of the Chinese government in the prewar and postwar years are converted into United States dollars of 1948. The conversion is made on the basis of the wholesale price index of the United States Department of Labor and the annual average dollar-yuan exchange free-market rate for the prewar years. For postwar years, the monthly average of this exchange rate rather than its annual average is used in order to avoid the bias introduced by the rapid depreciation of the Chinese currency. When the relevant data are available, government expenditures in foreign currency are added to the amount derived from the local currency account. The Chinese government expenditures in terms of United States dollars of 1948 thus obtained for various years are shown in Table 2.4.

The expenditures of the postwar years in terms of a stable United States dollar were higher than those of the prewar years. The only exception to this was the expenditures of 1948, which even after including government outlays in foreign currency were lower than 1935–36. This comparison between prewar and postwar expenditures is apparently at variance with that of the expenditures expressed in terms of a stable Chinese currency; the latter shows that the outlays in such a currency were much lower in the postwar than the prewar years. The discrepancy is due primarily to the overvaluation, even in the open market, of the Chinese yuan in terms of the United States dollar during most of the war and the postwar years—a point discussed at length in Chapter IV. The overvaluation tends to exaggerate the amount of the government expenditures when converted into United States dollars. The inclusion of government expenditures in foreign currencies in 1947 and 1948 also contributed to raise the dollar value of the total annual expenditures.

The pattern of government expenditures

Besides the shrinkage in the real and dollar value, important changes also occurred in the pattern of government expenditures in the course of inflation. During 1929–35 military expenditure accounted for 40.3 to 45.9 percent of the total expenditures (see Table 2.6). After the outbreak of the Sino-Japanese War in 1937, the percentage accounted for by military expenditure rose sharply. From then until 1942–43, it fluctuated within a range of 63.5 to 83.2 percent. During the fiscal years 1943–44 and 1944–45, it dropped to 50.6 and 43.7 percent because of the relative expansion of civil

TABLE 2.6. PATTERN OF CHINA'S GOVERNMENT EXPENDITURES, 1928–46

Fiscal year	*Military expenditure* (*total exp.* = 100) *percent*	*Service expenditure debt* (*total exp.* = 100) *percent*	(*borrowing of current year* = 100) *percent*
1928–29	48.43	36.98	160
1929–30	42.27	34.36	199
1930–31	40.31	37.46	134
1931–32	40.58	36.04	208
1932–33	45.92	30.04	187
1933–34	44.61	29.18	136
1934–35	41.23	25.18	105
1935–36	30.23	26.82	94
1936–37	34.65	44.30	123
1937–38	69.07	17.88	26
1938–39	76.61	20.71	28
1939–40	63.45	19.52	23
1940–41	83.21	5.78	6
1941–42	70.86	15.63	13
1942–43	70.14	7.00	9
1943–44	50.55	2.96	3
1944–45	43.67	3.11	
1945–46	96.62	.55	

There are no data for spaces left blank in table.

Source: *The Public Finance Yearbook*, 1943 and 1948 eds. and unpublished records of the Central Bank of China.

and other expenditures. After V-J Day military expenditure again increased because of the revival of full-fledged civil strife between the Nationalists and the Communists. Despite these high percentages, the military expenditure reported in the local-currency budget usually did not reflect the entire resources at the disposal of the Chinese military authorities. For these figures did not include all the military supplies acquired under foreign-aid programs; and these figures were undervalued in the budget because practically all such supplies were budgeted in Chinese currency on the basis of the unrealistic official foreign-exchange rate.

Thus far the discussion has been confined to the expenditures of the central government. Information about local government finance is too fragmentary to warrant any comprehensive study. There is, however, one point which should be noted: in the course of inflation, the importance of the expenditures of local government declined in comparison with that of the central government (see Table 2.7). A possible explanation for this relative change in national and local expenditures was the Japanese military expansion in China during the war, which reduced the number of local governments under the Nationalist's control. This however could not be the only answer, for never in the course of the war did the government of Free China control less than one half of the nation's provinces. Even in the provinces under occupation, Japanese control was confined only to cities and areas near main arteries of communication, the countryside and the less accessible areas remained under Chinese administrators who were loyal to, and financially supported by, the Nationalist government. The loss of territory alone, therefore, does not account for the almost uninterrupted decline of local government expenditures from 51.67 percent of the central-government expenditures in the fiscal year 1931–32 to 4.71 percent in 1945–46 (see Table 2.7). During the latter year, the expenditures of local governments were even lower than in previous years, despite the restoration to the Chinese government of the formerly occupied areas. To reduce the expenditures of local governments to an extent exceeding the corresponding reduction in national government expenditures meant a greater curtailment in wages and salaries of the employees of local governments in relation to similar payments in the central government, although the latter payments were already unbelievably low.

Estimates for China's national income, even in rudimentary form, are available only for 1931–36. In Table 2.7 these estimates and the corresponding expenditures are compared. During these years, the expenditures of the central government ranged only from 2.12 to 4.90 percent, of local governments from 0.64 to 1.10 percent, and the total expenditures from 3.22 to 6.00 percent of the corresponding gross national product. These percentages are extremely low in

TABLE 2.7. RELATION BETWEEN GOVERNMENT EXPENDITURES AND NATIONAL INCOME, 1931–46

	EXPENDITURE IN MILLION YUAN			EXPENDITURE IN PERCENT OF GROSS NATIONAL PRODUCT			
Fiscal year	*Central government* 1	*Local government* 2	3(2 ÷ 1 × 100)	*Gross national product in billion yuan* 4	*Central government* 5(1 ÷ 4 × 100)	*Local government* 6(2 ÷ 4 × 100)	*Total* 7(5 + 6)
1931–32	749.0	387.0	51.67	35.31	2.12	1.10	3.22
1932–33	699.0	295.5	42.27	29.20	4.18	1.01	5.19
1933–34	836.0	232.8	27.85	25.08	3.33	.93	4.26
1934–35	941.0	241.5	25.66	24.79	3.80	.64	4.44
1935–36	1,336.9	290.3	21.71	27.29	4.90	1.10	6.00
1936–37	1.884.0						
1937–38	2,091.3	369.9	17.69				
1938–39	1,168.7	217.4	18.60				
1939–40	2,797.1	375.3	13.42				
1940–41	3,796.8	492.5	12.97				
1941–42	8,076.1	1,077.0	13.34				
1942–43	23,237.7[a]	1,914.1	8.24				
1943–44	48,733.1[a]	4,186.5	8.59				
1944–45	176,529.9[a]	9,240.2	5.23				
1945–46	1,236,417.1[a]	58,266.1	4.71				

[a] Figures are adjusted to exclude local expenditures in the accounts of the central government.

In comparison with some of the recent findings, the estimate for China's gross national product given in the United Nations' publication (based primarily on Ou Pao San's study) is low. If so, then the percentages in the gross national product should be further reduced.

There are no data for spaces left blank in the table.

Source: For the central government, see Table 2.4. For local government expenditures, 1931–36, see *The Chinese Yearbook*, 1937 ed., pp. 702–03; and for 1937–46, *The Statistical Abstract of the Rebublic of China*, 1947 ed., pp. 65–66 and *Chung-hua min-kuo t'ung-chi nien-chien* (The Statistical Yearbook of the Republic of China) (Nanking, 1948), pp. 273–38. For the G.N.P., United Nations, *National Income Statistics of Various Countries, 1937–47* (New York, 1948), pp. 45–46.

comparison with corresponding ratios of other countries. For example, in the United States, the ratio of the total government expenditures (including those of the federal, state, and local governments) to the gross national product was 8.2 percent in 1929, 19.1 percent in 1933, 22.9 percent in 1941, 48 percent in 1943 and 1944, and well over 20 percent in the 1950s. From 1955 through 1958 the ratio of the expenditures of national (or central) government to gross national product ranged from 13.1 to 16.9 percent in Japan, from 20.9 to 24.7 percent in Ceylon, from 27.8 to 28.6 percent in the United Kingdom, and from 13.2 to 23.3 percent in South Korea.[19]

China's low government expenditures relative to her gross national product during the prewar years was mainly due to the inability of the government to raise revenue which was required to meet the expansion. Two main factors impaired the government's ability to raise revenue. First, the base of the Chinese national tax system was too narrow, and progressive direct taxes were never effectively enforced. Second, China was not a highly industrialized country. Data for other countries indicate that the ratio between government expenditures and national income is usually lower for an underdeveloped country than for an industrially developed country. One possible reason for such a difference is the lack of modern enterprises organized on a corporative basis which not only have been the core of a highly industrialized economy but have also borne a large share of government expenditures in such countries.

Government expenditures in foreign currencies

If the foreign exchange required for financing government procurements aboard was purchased on the open market at a realistic exchange rate, and if the local currency required for such purchases was fully allowed for in the government's budget, a study of the local currency expenses would be comprehensive enough to cover all expenditures of the government at home and abroad. This was generally the situation before 1937 and during the early years of the Sino-Japanese conflict. Toward the end of the war and during the postwar period, most of the foreign exchange required for government purchases abroad was provided by the Central Bank either at the official rate, which usually undervalued foreign currency in terms of the local money, or as an intragovernment advance by the Bank, for which no counterpart payment in local currency was involved. In neither case, therefore, was the foreign-currency expenditure fully reflected in the government's local-currency account. It is therefore necessary, for these years, to study foreign-currency expenses separately from those in local currency, if our analysis is to be comprehensive.

The data for Chinese government expenditures in foreign currencies, however, are even more fragmentary than those for local-currency disbursements, for there is neither an annual budget nor a published report for such expenditures. Not until 1947 were comprehensive statistics for such expenditures compiled. The compilation, done under my supervision, was based on the accounting records of the Central Bank and was designed primarily to provide a convenient reference for the Bank's administration. A summary statement of the compilation for 1947 and 1948 is shown in Table 2.8. The following general comments may be made about the facts in this table.

1. Foreign-currency expenditures of the government amounted to an equivalent of U.S. $172.38 million in 1947 and U.S. $176.38 million in 1948. These expenditures compared with China's exports, which amounted to U.S. $230.1 million in 1947 and U.S. $170.4 million in 1948 indicate the seriousness of the situation. The magnitude of government expenditures meant not only substantial curtailment in private imports but also continued deficit in China's international account during the postwar years.

2. Expenditures for military supplies, debt service, and the printing of bank notes, amounting to 61.96 percent of total foreign-currency expenditures in 1947 and 64.35 percent in 1948, were by far the most important outlays. Another important group of foreign-currency expenditures consisted of payments for government imports (including cereal, fertilizers, coal, and coke) used for various rationing programs instituted in Taiwan and major cities on the mainland. These payments accounted for 12.16 percent in 1947 and 17.94 percent in 1948. Foreign services (including expenses of the Chinese embassies and consular services in foreign countries, membership dues in international organizations, expenses for international conferences, etc.) and purchases of nonmilitary and industrial supplies were the items of next importance. Education expenses

for Chinese students studying abroad constituted only 1.64 percent of the total in 1947 and 1.54 percent in 1948.

3. In the case of military expenditure, about 50 percent of the outlay in 1947 and about 30 percent in 1948 were for the purchase of petroleum fuels for military use. The foreign-currency requirements of the military forces would have been much higher than they were had it not been for the supplies provided by United States aid during and after the war. It is therefore evident that, under the circumstances then prevailing, even to maintain a fighting force of a size and quality comparable to the one in existence was well beyond China's means.

4. Even including the prewar foreign debts, the services on which had been suspended in 1939 and never restored, China's debt burden remained staggering in 1946, 1947, and 1948. Total payments of the debt during this two-year period amounted to about 22 percent of the value of exports or about 25 percent of the total foreign-currency expenditure incurred during the period. This question of the public debt will be further explored in the next section of this chapter.

5. Expenditure on note issue was a characteristic outgrowth of the protracted inflation. In 1947 and 1948, payment for the printing of bank notes abroad amounted to U.S. $31.8 million (or 18.44 percent of the total government expenditure in foreign currency of 1947) and U.S. $29.3 million (or 16.60 percent of the total expenditure of 1948). In addition to these two payments, U.S. $55 million of the U.S. $500 million U.S. Treasury Credit of 1942 were spent for the purchase of bank notes in the United States.[20] The records of these three payments, amounting to U.S. $116 million, are the only ones this writer has. While these payments may not include all that the Chinese government spent on purchasing bank notes from abroad, it should cover the bulk of such payments during and after the war. The high cost of bank notes was due primarily to the lag in adjusting the denominations of notes in relation to the rate of their expansion. During these years an issue of new large-denomination notes was usually considered as a sign of further currency depreciation and as a possible factor in aggravating inflation. For this reason, the Chinese government usually hesitated to make an upward adjustment in the denomination of its notes until the shortage of money supply became

TABLE 2.8. FOREIGN CURRENCY EXPENDITURES OF THE CHINESE GOVERNMENT, 1947 AND 1948

	1947		*1948*	
	U.S. $ million	*percent*	*U.S. $ million*	*percent*
Military import	37.61	21.82	33.42	18.95
Munitions	(17.56)	(10.19)	(22.95)	(13.01)
Petroleum products	(20.05)	(11.63)	(10.47)	(5.94)
Supplies and equipment for government enterprises	18.19	10.55	13.84	7.84
Petroleum products	(3.86)	(2.24)	(3.80)	(2.15)
Other supplies	(14.33)	(8.31)	(10.04)	(5.69)
Diplomatic service	23.59	13.68	14.68	8.32
Education	2.83	1.64	2.71	1.54
Bank notes	31.78	18.44	29.28	16.60
Debt service	37.40	21.70	50.80	28.80
Cereals	20.97	12.16	21.48	12.18
Fertilizers			7.20	4.08
Coal and coke			2.97	1.68
Total	172.38	100.00	176.38	100.00

Individual items may not add up to the total because of rounding.
Source: Unpublished accounts of the Central Bank of China.

unbearable. Strange as it may appear in retrospect, this consideration did play an important role in determining the "programming" of note production by the Chinese government. Heavy purchases of notes from abroad were necessary during the war because of the limited production capacity of printing presses in Free China. A large part of the payment made in 1947 and 1948 was for purchases contracted for during the war. A comparison of the cost of producing the notes paid in foreign currency (not including the costs of the notes printed in China) with their market value in terms of United States dollars (see Table 2.9), indicates that after the middle of 1948, the former was for most of the time higher than the latter. This is true even if we confine the cost to the three payments previously mentioned (amounting to U.S. $116.2 million).

6. Expenditures on industrial and communication supplies consisted mainly of those needed for maintaining the nation's industrial and transportation equipment and for importing fuels for government-owned river transportation, civil aviation, and other public utilities. There was virtually no outlay for new industrial development. All these government enterprises depended upon imported

TABLE 2.9. DOLLAR VALUE OF YUAN NOTE ISSUES, 1937–49
(U.S. $ million)

1937		1946	
March	402.44	March	646.92
June	414.19	June	792.68
Sept.	453.38	Sept.	755.20
Dec.	479.70	Dec.	614.56
1938		1947	
March	480.70	March	410.29
June	320.31	June	269.78
Sept.	311.77	Sept.	336.51
Dec.	360.94	Dec.	221.83
1939		1948	
March	376.56	March	154.98
June	345.94	June	85.03
Sept.	217.55	Aug.	74.20
Dec.	296.50	Sept.	212.61
1940		Oct.	106.36
March	294.91	Nov.	76.29
June	332.99	Dec.	60.64
Sept.	347.70	1949	
Dec.	443.30	Jan.	29.75
1941		Feb.	20.20
March	488.06	March	10.03
June	567.64	Apr. 25	2.55
Sept.	668.02		
Dec.	797.47		

The yuan note issues include only those issued by the Central Bank of China.
Source: Unpublished records of the Central Bank of China.

supplies for their maintenance and operation but did not have enough earnings in foreign currency to meet their own requirements. To the extent that the Central Bank financed these imports at a cost lower than market value, these disbursements may also be considered as a government subsidy to such enterprises.

7. The food and coal imports were used primarily to relieve shortages in China's major cities and thereby to stabilize the cost of living in these urban areas. The fertilizers were primarily for distribution in Taiwan. In all these cases, the sales or distributions were made at a nominal price, which usually did not adequately cover the actual cost involved. For this reason the foreign-currency outlays involved in financing these imports may be considered as a government expenditure for effecting its food and other subsidy programs.

8. Diplomatic service, which amounted to an equivalent of U.S. $23.6 million in 1947 and of U.S. $14.7 in 1948, was much more costly than in prewar days. The increase was partly due to the high cost of living abroad, and partly to the multiplicity of international conferences and organizations after World War II.

It is clear from this analysis that inflation and war greatly expanded the amount of foreign-currency expenditure. Even with the American aid programs, the foreign-currency resources of the Chinese government fell far short of its needs. Had mainland China not been overrun by the Communists in 1949, the Nationalist government would have had either to curtail drastically its foreign-currency expenditures, or to reduce further nongovernment imports. The present analysis also shows the difficulties that may confront an underdeveloped country which, lacking natural resources and industrial capacity of its own, attempts to develop a modern industry and military force with supplies from abroad.

THE PUBLIC DEBT UNDER INFLATION

Before 1937 the proceeds received from borrowing usually fell far short of the outlays for debt services, including both interest and amortization. This phenomenon persisted throughout 1928–35 and the fiscal year 1936–37. The year 1935–36 was the only prewar year in which the Nationalist government borrowed more than it paid out for debt services; in this year there was a sharp rise in the amount of government borrowing (see the last column of Table 2.10).

The high debt-service cost in relation to the receipts from borrowing during most of the prewar years was for several reasons. First, the Nationalist government took over large numbers of its predecessor's debts and continued to service them in addition to the loans it raised itself. Second, the effective rates of interest (i.e., including discounts) of the internal loans, often amounting to more than 10 percent per annum, were unusually high. While the high yield was necessary to induce public subscription of the government bonds, it greatly increased the financial burden of the government. Third, virtually all foreign loans had to be serviced and repaid in foreign currencies. The continued depreciation of the Chinese currency in terms of foreign money during the period from 1929 to

1943, undoubtedly contributed to increasing the nation's burden in debt service during these years.

After the outbreak of the Sino-Japanese War in 1937, as far as internal loans were concerned, government borrowing consisted almost entirely of advances which were financed by note issue from the Central Bank. Hence, there was no question of debt service involved. In the meantime, because of the protracted inflation, old obligations in domestic currency were gradually wiped out in real terms. For these reasons, the service charge for these debts at the end of World War II and in the postwar years became negligible. It was reduced in terms of the current borrowing of the government and annual government expenditures, although the ratio of government borrowing to total expenditures increased substantially each year in the course of the inflation.

With respect to foreign loans, the situation was somewhat different. Up to 1938, all foreign obligations of the Chinese government were met in full despite the strain on the nation's economy. After January, 1939, however, the Nationalist government suspended the interest and amortization payments of all foreign loans secured by the customs duties and the salt taxes collected in the areas under Japanese occupation. This moratorium undoubtedly accounted for the sharp reduction in the debt-service expenditure in terms of foreign currencies in 1939 and 1940 (see Table 2.10). The moratorium, however, provided only a partial and temporary relief to the Chinese government, for the suspension of payment was not applicable to the loans contracted by the Nationalist government during the early 1930s, nor to those accumulated after 1939. The fact that the costs of servicing foreign loans listed in the government budget were based on the official exchange rate was also responsible for the low local-currency costs of debt services in the early 1940s. The official exchange rate was then pegged at the level of twenty yuan to one dollar, an unduly low rate in comparison with the rate then prevailing in the free market.

The debt service suspended in 1939 was never restored after World War II. Nevertheless, the dollar cost of China's foreign-debt service in 1946 and 1947 was almost equal to—and that of 1948 was even heavier than—the corresponding cost of the prewar years (see Table 2.10). The unusually heavy service charge on foreign loans

TABLE 2.10. AMOUNT OF DEBT SERVICE FOR CHINA'S FOREIGN DEBTS, 1933–48 (U.S. $ million)

1933	26.6	1937	32.0	1946	31.3
1934	38.4	1938	25.0	1947	37.4
1935	39.3	1939	.5	1948	50.8
1936	38.0	1940	1.5		

All the dollar-yuan conversions are on the basis of the dollar-yuan exchange rate at annual average of noon quotations in New York.

Source: For year 1933–36, Bank of China, *Annual Reports*; (Shanghai, 1933–36); for 1937–40, Frank M. Tamagana, *Banking and Finance in China* (New York, 1942), Table 41 and 41A; for years 1946–48, International Monetary Fund, *Balance of Payment Yearbook, 1948 and 1949* (Washington, D.C., 1950), pp. 113–18.

TABLE 2.11. REPAYMENT AND INTEREST OF CHINA'S FOREIGN DEBT, 1946–1948 (U.S. $ million)

	1946	*1947*	*1948*		
Name of loan	*Repayment and interest*	*Repayment and interest*	*Repayment*	*Interest*	*Total*
U.S. Export-Import Bank loans					
Tin loan	3.5	4.2	3.7	.3	4.0
Other metals loan	7.8	13.0	17.3	.3	17.6
Cotton loan			12.1	.8	12.9
Coal-mining, railway and other equipment		.2	.1	.8	.9
U.S. maintenance commodities credit			.4	.4	.8
U.S. surplus property credit			.1		.1
U.S. Lend-Lease loan		2.8	1.7	1.1	2.8
Total U.S. credit	*11.3*	*20.2*	*35.4*	*3.7*	*39.1*
U.K. 1939 and 1941 export credit	1.7	2.9	2.2	1.0	3.2
Canadian credit			2.7	.1	2.8
USSR barter credit	18.3	14.3	5.5	.2	5.7
Total	31.3	37.4	45.8	5.0	50.8

Source: International Monetary Fund, *Balance of Payment Yearbook, 1948–1949* p. 115.

during the postwar period was due in part to the large amount of such debts raised after 1937 (see Table 2.11). Up to August, 1937, the amount of foreign loans secured on customs, salt, and other government revenues amounted to only £59,059,000; U.S. $30,400,000; 3,330,000 yen; and a small amount in other currencies. The new foreign loans contracted during the period from August, 1937, to the end of 1947 alone amounted to U.S. $541.5 million and £58,047,000.[21] These amounts did not include the U.S. Treasury Credit of 1942, amounting to U.S. $500 million,[22] for which no service has yet been made Another factor which made the debt burden staggering was that virtually all the wartime loans were used for purchasing military supplies and none were self-liquidating. This was true not only of the barter credits of the USSR granted during 1938 and 1939, but also of other loans. The proceeds of the Sino-American wood-oil and metals loans contracted during 1939–42, for instance, were used primarily for purchasing war supplies rather than for improving production of the commodities whose exports were to be used for the loan services. Nor did United States loans, granted after the war for rehabilitating China's shipping, railway, and other industries, result in any substantial improvement in China's exports. The United States cotton loan of 1945, which was used for financing imports of American cotton to China, did contribute substantially to increasing textile production and exports. But the resulting improvement was far from sufficient to make the heavy annual amortization of this short-term loan painless to the Chinese economy.

As the service cost of the internal debt decreased during the inflation, the importance of domestic-loan receipts other than the advances from the Central Bank accordingly decreased with the accentuation of the inflation. Many attempts were made and many schemes were considered by the Nationalist government during and after the war to reconstitute the domestic market for government bonds. In the discussion that follows, however, only five experiments are examined because of their prime importance to debt administration under a runaway inflation. They include bonds subscribable and redeemable in gold or foreign currency; bonds subscribable in local currency and redeemable in gold or foreign currency; bonds subscribable and redeemable in local currency with a face value in foreign currency; short-term notes with a variable interest rate; and bonds with repayment and/or interest service based on a price index.

Bonds subscribable and redeemable in gold or foreign currency

The administration of bonds subscribable and repayable in gold or foreign currency is simple. It differs, however, from that of the ordinary government bond (i.e., subscribable and payable in local currency) in several respects. The market for a gold or foreign-currency bond depends mainly on the investor's confidence in the government's willingness and ability to repay the debt. This ability depends upon the position of the nation's international accounts rather than upon the capacity of its printing press as is the case of the local-currency bond. Since the bond is both subscribable and serviceable in gold or foreign currency, its attraction to investors depends upon its yield in relation to that of an alternative investment in foreign market. For this reason, the nominal yield of the U.S. Dollar Bond of 1947 was set at 6 percent per annum—a rate comparable to that prevailing in the foreign market, but low in comparison with that of China's local-currency bond issued during the inflation.

Because of frequent changes in the financial policy of the Nationalist government and because of the chronic deficit in the nation's balance-of-payment accounts, the gold or foreign-currency bonds issued during and after the war were not in a position to meet the criteria; therefore, the sale of the bonds in this category was unsuccessful. For instance, only U.S. $21.35 million of an authorized U.S. $100 million of the United States dollar bonds of 1947 was subscribed in the twelve-month period following the issuance of these bonds. Of this amount, U.S. $16.7 million represented subscriptions of the government banks (excluding the Central Bank) and U.S. $2.82 million[23] was subscriptions of leading textile-mill owners in China. The former represented merely an account transfer among government agencies; the latter, a result of government pressure exerted through the Central Bank.

Bonds subscribable in local currency and redeemable in gold or foreign currency

The attraction of a bond subscribable in local currency and redeemable in gold or foreign currency depends primarily upon the conversion rate which these bonds are sold in local currency. If this conversion rate is favorable in comparison with the market valuation of gold or foreign exchange, the bond is likely to be in good demand. However, the relation between the official conversion rate and the corresponding market rate also determines the cost involved in floating such bonds and its efficiency as a deflationary measure. The higher the official conversion rate is in relation to the market rate, the lower will be the cost of such government borrowing and the greater will be its deflationary effect.

The U.S. Dollar Victory Bond and the U.S. Dollar Savings Certificate, both issued by the Chinese government in 1942, belong to this category of borrowing. The Victory Bond had an authorized amount of U.S. $100 million, bore an interest of 6 percent per annum, and was repayable in twenty equal, semiannual installments. While the bond was subscribable in local currency on the basis of the official exchange rate then prevailing, both its principal and interest were payable in U.S. dollars provided by the U.S. Treasury credit of 1942. In 1942 the official quotation for the U.S. dollar was twenty yuan to one dollar, while the market rate was well above that level. Because of such favorable terms, the bond was one of the few issues of the Chinese government which was fully subscribed.[24]

The U.S. Dollar Savings Certificate of 1942 was not a government bond in its usual sense. It was rather a form of time deposit with a few designated banks which were obligated to redeposit the proceeds with the Central Bank. The deposit, with fixed maturity dates ranging from one to three years, was repayable in gold also provided by the U.S. Treasury credit of 1942, although the original deposit was in local currency on the basis of the unrealistic official exchange rate. Like the U.S. Dollar Bond of 1942, the Savings Certificate was in great demand, and the entire amount of its authorized issue (U.S. $100 million) was subscribed not very long after its issuance. In fact, the Certificate was even more popular than the Bond because of its short maturity.

The low local-currency prices at which the Bond and the Certificate were sold greatly increased the cost of government borrowing, gave undue profit to their subscribers, and reduced substantially the deflationary effects of the government borrowings.

Bonds subscribable and redeemable in local currency with a face value in foreign currency

The administration of a foreign-currency bond, which has a face value in foreign currency and is subscribable and redeemable in local currency on the basis of the prevailing rate exchange, is probably the most complicated, for it involves foreign-exchange conversion both at the time of subscription and at the time of repayment. Because of these conversions, it is possible in the course of a hyperinflation for debt charges payable in a given period to exceed not only the local-currency receipts realized from sales of the bonds during that period, but also the cumulative total of all the past receipts derived from that bond in that and earlier periods. Such an anomaly may occur either when the amount of amortization is unduly large in comparison with the sale proceeds received during the period of payment, or when the local currency depreciates so sharply that the exchange rate at which the debt is serviced becomes inordinately high in comparison with the early rates at which the bonds were subscribed or when both of these conditions exist (see Appendix 3). For instance, in the case of the U.S. Dollar Short-Term Treasury Notes of 1947, when the first amortization amounting to $\frac{1}{6}$ of the debt subscribed and its first interest payment amounting to $\frac{1}{10}$ of the subscription fell due on September 30, 1947, the Chinese government paid out 252.8 billion yuan in local currency. In comparison 24.4 billion yuan were received during the month of September and 514.2 billion yuan received from the subscription of the Treasury Notes since their issuance in April, 1947. At the end of March, 1948, the debt-service charge amounted to 1516.4 billion yuan as against 2841.3 billion yuan received from the sales of the Treasury Notes during the month of March, and a cumulative receipt of 3398.1 billion yuan for all months. Had this trend not been interrupted by the monetary reform in August, 1948, which temporarily reinstituted a foreign-exchange policy of pegged rate, the current debt-service payment at the end of September would have easily exceeded the cumulative receipts.[25] Under conditions of hyperinflation, this type of borrowing can become too costly to be of any real assistance to government finance.

The attraction of such a bond to the investor depends primarily upon the extent to which the official exchange rate realistically reflects the market valuation of the currency. So long as the debt service is based on an official exchange rate in line with the market rate, this type of bond, as the experience of the Short-term Treasury Notes of 1947 testified, will be in demand despite inflation. The opposite will be true if the official rate becomes unrealistic.

Short-term notes with a variable interest rate

An example of government debt with a variable interest rate is the Short-term Treasury Notes of 1948 issued in April. These Notes, with maturities ranging from one to three months, were subscribable at a discounted price as quoted in the Shanghai Security Exchange, where the Notes were traded. The amount of discount was set by the Central Bank from time to time so that the discount, together with a stipulated rate of interest of 5 percent per month, gave an actual yield which fluctuated according to the market conditions.

The 1948 Notes were originally intended to serve as a big stick for the control of the Shanghai money market in the place of, or as a supplement to, gold sales and other open-market operations of the Central Bank, but never aroused much interest among the public. Favorable though their terms were, they were still not in a position to compete with other investment or speculation opportunities in the market. In the later stages of the inflation, particularly in the early months of 1949, the market rate of interest in Shanghai ranged from 300 to 400 percent per month as against the actual yield of about 30 percent per month for Treasury Notes.

Bonds with repayment and interest based on price index

Another form of government borrowing, which may prove useful during inflation, is the issue of the price-index bond. The maturity value and interest payments of such a bond are based not on monetary units but on real purchasing power whose money value increases in proportion to a specially compiled or selected commodity-price index. This scheme, though extensively discussed in China during the inflation, was never put into practical use by the Nationalist government. It was adopted by the Communist government, however, in 1949.[26]

The price-index bond and the various types of gold and foreign-currency bonds belong to the family of the so-called "guaranteed-purchasing-power bonds."[27] The principles underlying such bonds have been extensively discussed in the United States and in the United Kingdom.[28] On the basis of these discussions, the following observations may be made in connection with government borrowing under the conditions of hyperinflation:

1. The Chinese government erred by selling most of the gold and foreign-currency bonds involving foreign-exchange conversions at a rate too favorable to bond subscribers, and by making their terms of repayment too generous in relation to the subscription prices.

2. The Chinese experience with the U.S. Dollar Short-term Treasury Notes of 1947 seems to indicate that under a hyperinflation it is not necessary to have currency depreciation fully allowed in the debt service in order to attract buyers. An allowance equivalent to 65–70 percent of the currency depreciation would be sufficient to make the bond attractive. But even at that percentage, the borrowing cost was already prohibitive.

3. The maturities of the Chinese bonds with escalator adjustments were mostly too short. The U.S. Dollar Savings Certificate of 1942 had maturity dates ranging from one to three years from the date of issuance. The U.S. Dollar Treasury Notes of 1947 were repayable in six semiannual installments. The cost of borrowing during the initial years following the bond issue could have been substantially reduced, had the period of amortization payment been lengthened. Under the terms of these Notes, the cash payments for amortization and interest (see Appendix 3) could exceed the cumulative cash receipts from the bond sales under the condition of hyperinflation.

4. In virtually all the guaranteed purchasing-power bonds issued by the Nationalist government, the escalator clause was usually applicable not only to their principal but also to the interest payments. The effect of applying such a clause to interest payments, as is shown in Appendix 3, is substantial when depreciation of currency is as rapid as that of the Chinese yuan. Thus in these bond issues the Chinese government tended to burden itself unduly. In the opinion of this writer, the attraction of the bonds would not likely have been substantially affected, even if the interest payments had been excluded from the escalator clause.

The analysis up to this point seems to show that during an inflation the government can borrow from the public only at a cost which tends to make borrowing very uneconomical. This conclusion applies to virtually all forms of government borrowing covered in this analysis. There is, however, another type of government borrowing which has not been tried in China, but which was adopted in several of the Middle East countries in the course of their inflation during World War II. This is the issuance of government bonds bearing lottery prizes.[29] The basic idea behind this type of borrowing is that, in addition to the remuneration accruing from regular debt service, an investor has also a chance to win a highly attractive prize. By offering prizes to a few bondholders, the government may reduce substantially interest payments to all the bondholders without impairing the attraction of the bond to the prize-minded investors. While the game of chance may not necessarily appeal to every investor, it does offer an inducement to those having a high valuation for such a chance. It seems that this is probably the most promising arrangement under which a government may economically borrow from its people under a runaway inflation.

SUMMARY

The fiscal system of the Nationalist government was too inefficient and too rigid to be able to cope with the changing conditions that developed during the inflation. The loss of major tax revenues and the expanding war expenditures resulted in a substantial expansion in the fiscal deficit during the early years of the Sino-Japanese War. Instead of strengthening its tax system and other sources of revenue, the government relied almost solely upon note issues to cover the deficit. The excess demand in the government sector, through the expansion of note issue, thus sparked the inflationary process which plagued the country in the subsequent decade.

Attempts on the part of the government to transmit the excess demand to other sectors of the economy were abortive. Despite the introduction of new taxes and the revision of old taxes the government revenue in real terms shrunk abruptly. Accordingly, the government had to curtail sharply its expenditures in real terms, particularly the real incomes of its employees. This was probably the only substantial inroad that the government made upon the private sector of the economy toward sharing the fiscal deficits. Instead of sharing the war cost of the government, the business sector, with its swelling profits and shrinking tax burdens, throve during the inflation.

Because of its incapacity to tap domestic resources, the government came in the course of inflation to rely increasingly upon the foreign sector to absorb the government deficit. Expenditures in foreign currencies were increased in order to offset the loss in outlays in the domestic economy. The receipts from sales of gold and of bonds redeemable in gold or foreign currencies became increasingly important as sources of government income for meeting its excessive expenditures. The resources of the foreign sector, however, were not limitless. During the war, the foreign sector, having benefited from foreign aid, from the dollar receipts resulting from United States military expenditures in China, and from the lack of imports because of the wartime blockade, was in a favorable position to absorb at least part of the government deficit. After the war, however, the unfavorable balance of trade, the stringent restrictions on the use of foreign-aid funds, and the wasteful government operations in gold and foreign-exchange markets soon exhausted the available resources in the foreign sector. In 1949 the Nationalist government was at the end of its rope, economically and militarily: a situation which culminated in its total retreat from the mainland.

CHAPTER III

Consumption and Investment: Inflationary Pressures in the Private Sector

The purpose of this chapter is to study the inflationary pressure arising from the nongovernment sectors in terms of consumption and investment expenditures. It is hoped that the study of consumption expenditures will demonstrate the behavior of the household sector, and the study of investment expenditures will show the behavior of the business sector during the Chinese inflation. The business sector refers to the activities of both government and nongovernment business enterprises.[1]

INFLATIONARY PRESSURE FROM PRIVATE CONSUMPTION

In the following discussion of Chinese consumption, several facts should be noted. First the private consumption of the Chinese economy will be studied only in terms of a few essential consumer goods, rather than on the basis of comprehensive social accounts, because of the unavailability of necessary statistics of China's national income and of products for the years under consideration. Any decrease in the supply during the inflation compared with the prewar supply will be construed to reflect the inflationary pressure on the economy arising from the household sector. This assumes that the demand for consumer goods during the Chinese inflation was about the same as the prewar demand. This approach admittedly is a very crude way of studying consumption. It however should be noted that in view of the absence of an effective progressive taxation, the nonexistence of any significant rationing system, and the immunity of the business, industrial, and agricultural incomes from the erosive effects of inflation, the real income and effective demand for consumption of a large part of the Chinese populace were not likely to have been substantially curtailed. To the populace whose consumption was confined only to maintaining minimum subsistence, it is not likely that the inflation could have significantly reduced the consumption, even if their real income shrank because of rising prices. For this reason, the assumption that the consumption expenditures remained more or less unchanged during the inflation and the years preceding is probably not so absurd as it might appear to be at first consideration.

Second, consumer expenditures are normally broken down into those for durable consumer's goods, those for nondurable consumer's goods, and those for services. In order to adapt this analysis to the data in China, however, consumer expenditures will be grouped with those on agricultural products, manufactured products, and imported products.

Because of the low standard of living, an unusually high proportion of China's household expenditures went for food, clothing, and fuel. Expenditures for other goods often were considered luxuries and were of minor importance. The proportionate expenditure for food on the part of the rural population was on the average much higher than for the urban inhabitants.[2] Accordingly, consumption supplies will be confined to items relevant to these major consumption outlays. These supplies consisted of cereals, wheat and wheat flour, cotton yarn, cotton piece goods, kerosene, and tobacco. In each case, the aggregate supply came from domestic production and imports.

Third, the comparison will be divided into two parts because of the changes in territory under the control of the Chinese government during the Sino-Japanese War. The first part compares the conditions of the early 1930s with those of the immediate postwar years, 1946–49. This comparison applies to the entire country. The second part compares year-to-year changes in Free China and Japanese-occupied areas during the period from 1938 through 1944, or 1945 depending on the availability of data.

Comparison between free and occupied China

Free China: consumer goods produced by agriculture. In studies of China's agricultural production during the 1940s, it has been a common practice to use the production in twenty-two provinces on the Chinese mainland to represent that of the entire nation (excluding Manchuria and Taiwan), and the production in the fifteen provinces in central, south, and southwest China to denote that of Free China. The fifteen provinces usually include Chekiang, Kiangsi, Hupei, Hunan, Szechuan, Honan, Shensi, Kansu, Chinghai, Fukien, Kwantung, Kwangsi, Yunnan, Kweichow, and Ningsia.[3] These, together with Hopei, Shangtung, Shansi, Chahar, Suiyuan, Kiangsu, and Anhwei, constitute the twenty-two provinces. It is clear that this definition of Free China does not include Sinkiang, Tibet, and Sikang; data relating to the agricultural production of these provinces are not available. While this definition of China and Free China may not be entirely satisfactory,[4] it does provide a good approximation for the present discussion.

Based on the 1931–37 averages, the ratio of the acreage of land used for cultivating various crops in the fifteen provinces to the corresponding average in the twenty-two provinces ranged from 26.7 to 78.0 percent (see Table 3.1). Similar ratios for various crop productions ranged from 14.6 to 78.1 percent (see Table 3.2). Based on the official statistics, the fifteen provinces had altogether about 74.2 percent of the land area and 61.0 percent of the cultivated land of the twenty-two provinces. China's agricultural production was more evenly distributed over the country than was her mining and manufacturing production. Agricultural production in the maritime provinces was not of such great importance to the nation's economy as was the industrial production in these provinces.

From 1931 to 1937 average rice production for the fifteen provinces amounted to 77.0 percent of the corresponding production for the twenty-two provinces; whereas, the population of the fifteen provinces amounted to only 54.2 percent of the twenty-two. The percentages for rice production declined substantially during the war; but even after allowing for the decreases, these percentages were still high in comparison with the percentage of population. In fact the per capita production of rice in Free China was actually higher than the corresponding production for the entire twenty-two provinces before the war, that is to say, so far as rice production is concerned, the situation in Free China was even better than that of prewar

TABLE 3.1. ACREAGE INDEX OF PRINCIPAL CROPS, 1931–49
(averages of 1931–37 for twenty-two provinces = 100)

	ACREAGE IN FIFTEEN PROVINCES						
	1931–37	*1937*	*1938*	*1939*	*1940*	*1941*	*1942*
Wheat	47.6	36.6	36.7	38.0	39.3	41.4	44.1
Barley	61.3	51.5	50.7	55.7	49.8	51.0	53.1
Rapseed	78.0	74.3	73.5	77.9	91.5	94.9	94.1
Oats	15.5	17.0	14.7	15.4	14.9	15.2	15.3
Rice	77.0	67.1	69.6	69.8	67.0	66.9	68.3
Kaoliang (or sorghum)	32.1	22.0	20.9	20.4	20.3	20.3	20.4
Millet	26.7	16.5	15.5	14.6	13.8	13.7	13.9
Corn	51.0	45.8	46.5	46.8	48.0	49.8	50.8
Soy beans	41.1	29.2	28.5	28.6	29.7	29.1	28.8
Sweet potatoes	71.1	74.5	71.6	72.8	78.1	82.3	84.7
Cotton (lint)		45.1	39.3	40.3	48.0	47.4	45.3
Peanuts	50.0	41.8	40.1	41.4	44.1	44.6	44.9
Sesame	56.1	43.9	41.7	44.9	48.3	46.8	45.1

There are no data for spaces left blank in table.

Source: *Chung-hua min-kuo t'ung-chi nien-chien* (The Statistical Yearbook of the Republic of China) (Nanking, 1948), pp. 74–77.

TABLE 3.2. PRODUCTION INDEX OF PRINCIPAL CROPS, 1931–49
(averages of 1931–37 for twenty-two provinces = 100)

	PRODUCTION IN FIFTEEN PROVINCES						
	1931–37	*1937*	*1938*	*1939*	*1940*	*1941*	*1942*
Wheat	50.0	30.2	46.7	45.6	46.2	40.0	48.2
Barley	62.7	45.8	57.4	58.2	54.5	46.9	56.8
Rapseed	78.5	65.6	72.5	87.2	77.9	92.3	89.2
Oats	14.6	13.9	15.1	16.3	14.7	13.9	15.0
Rice	78.1	68.8	74.7	75.2	61.8	64.3	63.4
Kaoliang (or sorghum)	28.4	21.3	20.7	20.8	19.0	18.0	14.6
Millet	29.2	17.0	17.0	17.1	15.1	14.8	10.5
Corn	53.0	52.1	54.2	54.2	51.6	51.2	45.0
Soy beans	41.5	31.5	29.9	30.9	31.7	28.5	24.1
Sweet potatoes	66.0	75.2	74.6	67.1	69.2	74.8	65.5
Cotton (lint)		32.6	34.4	42.9	44.7	39.6	33.4
Peanuts	51.0	43.8	44.9	45.9	46.7	46.8	44.3
Sesame	54.3	39.2	26.1	47.0	48.3	43.2	28.4

TABLE 3.1 (*continued*)

FIFTEEN PROVINCES (*contd.*)				ACREAGE IN TWENTY-TWO PROVINCES			
1943	*1944*	*1945*	*1946*	*1946*	*1947*	*1948*	*1949*
46.6	48.5	49.0	51.1	107.0	106.5	106.1	105.7
54.8	55.1	54.1	53.7	96.6	95.0	93.1	92.0
100.7	103.2	100.4	108.3	136.7	140.1	147.2	144.1
15.3	15.1	14.7	14.1	92.4	91.0	90.2	90.7
67.1	67.8	66.5	65.4	92.4	91.0	90.2	90.7
19.7	19.5	18.7	19.0		126.1	125.6	128.0
14.2	13.8	13.8	14.0		62.5	61.3	62.5
52.3	51.3	50.6	50.5	107.2	105.6	105.4	106.1
28.1	27.2	27.0	27.0	89.6	90.0	87.4	90.9
87.8	90.1	93.3	96.8		131.0	131.9	134.5
48.2	52.7	55.9	57.6	75.4	86.7	85.1	71.3
44.5	46.9	47.7	48.8	104.8	103.9	103.0	105.2
46.1	48.5	49.7	50.7	102.5	102.6	102.1	102.1

TABLE 3.2 (*continued*)

FIFTEEN PROVINCES (*contd.*)				PRODUCTION IN TWENTY-TWO PROVINCES			
1943	*1944*	*1945*	*1946*	*1946*	*1947*	*1948*	*1949*
45.8	57.1	50.5	50.8	104.6	108.8	110.3	103.5
51.5	58.9	51.4	50.3	89.1	96.2	94.4	83.9
98.1	100.4	80.2	79.2	121.3	129.1	124.5	123.7
14.1	14.1	11.2	12.7	67.9	67.9	76.7	70.7
60.9	67.4	58.7	65.0	91.9	92.9	96.1	88.9
17.0	16.7	17.8	18.6		86.0	101.1	85.8
12.8	12.4	14.9	15.5		79.5	91.0	77.7
49.9	51.8	55.7	53.9	107.0	103.5	114.9	100.0
27.4	27.0	27.9	28.3	87.8	89.9	94.2	80.1
78.3	81.9	83.7	89.4		121.1	134.8	122.8
41.8	37.5	52.1	52.1	61.8	69.1	67.6	54.4
43.8	44.6	46.5	46.5	112.9	108.4	123.1	119.8
39.7	41.4	47.2	46.7	101.9	91.2	109.8	97.5

There are no data for spaces left blank in table.
Source: *The Statistical Yearbook of the Republic of China*, 1948 ed., pp. 74–77.

China. This was true despite the shrinkage in the total rice production in the area during the war.

The annual production of wheat in the fifteen provinces for 1937–43 was lower than the 1931–37 average for these provinces and that during 1944–46 was higher. The wheat production in the fifteen provinces, however, constituted only about 50 percent of what was produced in the twenty-two provinces. This percentage was much lower than either the corresponding percentage for the rice production or that for the population. The importance of wheat production to the economy of Free China must not, however, be overemphasized. In Free China, rice rather than wheat was the main foodstuff.

In 1937 the fifteen provinces produced approximately one third of the cotton normally produced in twenty-two provinces.[5] Despite the low ratio, this supply was amply in comparison with the demand for cotton in Free China, which had only a few modern textile mills in operation.

Free China: consumer goods produced by industry. In Free China, which was less industrialized than the coastal provinces and where imports were sharply curtailed by the war, the supply of manufactured and imported products was scarce. This was true of petroleum products, wheat flour, tobacco leaf, cotton yarn, and piece goods.

During the war attempts were made to improve the industrial production of consumer goods in Free China, partly from necessity and partly from the inducement of high profit. Consequently, there was a noticeable expansion in the production of such consumer goods as cotton yarn, paper, gasoline, alcohol, electric bulbs, printing inks and cigarettes.[6] While some of this expansion was impressive in terms of growth rate, the absolute magnitudes of production were mostly inconsequential for relieving much of the inflationary pressure on the consumption sector of the economy. For example, in 1944 (after allowing for the wartime expansion) Free China's production of cotton yarn, cotton piece goods, and wheat flour amounted to only 5.3 percent, 8.8 percent, and 5.3 percent of the corresponding prewar production of all China (excluding Manchuria).[7]

Free China: consumer goods from abroad. During the war, China relied heavily on imports to bridge the gap between supply of and demand for consumer goods in her domestic market. The role of imports was particularly important during 1938–41. Most of the imports of this period were for the foreign settlements in Shanghai and Tientsin. These settlements were then under the control of Western Powers, while the surrounding areas were under Japanese occupation. To maintain the supplies of food and raw materials needed for the residents and industries in the foreign settlements, the Nationalist government allocated a large amount of foreign exchange to finance the necessary imports. These consisted mainly of rice, wheat flour, raw cotton, petroleum products, tobacco, cigarettes, etc. In comparison with either the prewar or postwar imports, shipments in these few years were abnormally large. There was, however, no attempt on the part of the government either to regulate the end uses of these imports, or to maximize the utilization of its foreign-exchange resources by restricting nonessential consumer goods (e.g., cigarettes). To hold inflation by imports regardless of the cost seems to have been the policy of this period (see Chapter IV).

Prior to the Japanese occupation of Indo-China and Burma, Free China was a net importer of raw cotton, cotton piece goods, and a host of consumer goods, which were used to augment the supplies in domestic markets. The closing of the Burma Road and all other mainland transportation between Free China and the outside world reduced the inflow of these supplies to trickles; thus accentuating the inflationary pressure on the economy of Free China.

Conditions in the occupied areas. The supplies of foodstuffs and of manufactured consumer's goods in occupied China were severely curtailed during the war. In the metropolitan areas the usual food shortages were accentuated by the sharp curtailment of food imports during the war. Production of manufactured articles for consumption was hampered either by shortages in raw materials and fuel or by restrictions for diversification in favor of military needs. In fact, the flow of consumer goods into the open market was reduced not only in absolute magnitude but also in relation to the production of producer goods. In addition, it seems to have been an established wartime policy of Japan to export essential food supplies and raw materials from China to Japan and the territories under her control (i.e., Korea, Taiwan, and Manchuria) to feed the population and industries. Among such exports were iron, coal, raw cotton, salt, beans, wheat, and wheat flour.[8] In some cases, the expansion of export was attained by a corresponding expansion in Chinese production. In the case of wheat and raw cotton, the large exports from occupied China to Japan during 1938–40, were accompanied by Free China's substantial imports of the same commodities from Australia, Brazil, India, and the United States to feed the residents and to supply their textile mills in the foreign settlements of Shanghai and Tientsin, then under the control of the Western Powers.

Prewar supplies vs. postwar supplies of consumer goods

Agricultural products. The postwar production of virtually all the major food crops (rice, soybean, millet, kaoliang, etc.) declined. The annual production of raw cotton in 1946, 1947, and 1948 amounted to 62 percent, 69 percent, and 68 percent of the 1931–37 average respectively. Wheat, whose production in the three postwar years ranged from 4.6 to 10.3 percent higher than the 1931–37 average, and corn, whose postwar productions ranged 3.5 to 14.9 percent higher than the prewar average, were the only important exceptions[9] to the general downward trend (see Table 3.2).

The adverse effect of declining agricultural production was accentuated by the transportation difficulties which plagued postwar China. The ravages of war and the concomitant disruptions of China's main transportation arteries rendered the shipment of food and raw materials from their producers to their consumers in metropolitan areas increasingly difficult.

Manufactured products. Statistics concerning industrial production in postwar China are scarce and spotty; therefore, it is impossible to present a comprehensive survey of the supply of consumer goods produced by industries during the postwar years. It is clear, however, from the information available, that some generalizations can be made. First, there was a substantial reduction of virtually all the consumer goods, such as cotton yarn, matches, soap, and cigarettes, produced by domestic industries. Second, there was a substantial amount of unused capacity among the industries producing consumer goods as a result of the reduced production. The existence of excess capacity in the midst of inflation is contrary to the usual assertion that full employment is a necessary condition for inflation, and it also demonstrates the importance of studying conditions in each of the economic sectors. Third, the reductions in production were due either to high production costs or to raw material shortages, or to both. The high costs rendered it impossible for domestic products to compete with imported supplies. The raw material shortages prevented many factories from fully utilizing their production capacities. These shortages, caused by reductions of domestic raw material supplies and by sharp curtailments of imports after 1947, plagued the production of cotton textile products, cigarettes, soap, matches, rubber products, and other industrial consumer goods. For example, in 1946 seventy-three cigarette factories were operating; in 1947 only fifty-five factories remained, because of high production costs. During these two years, only 50 percent of the capacity of the forty-one match factories was in operation, owing to raw material shortages. Paper mills were operated at less than half of capacity because of insufficient supplies of pulp, waste paper, and other raw materials. Cement plants were operated at one-third of capacity.[10]

Imported supplies. After V-J Day, the Nationalist government tried to resume its policy (pursued during 1938–41) of using imports to supplement the deficient domestic supplies. However, the policy was substantially modified during the latter part of 1946 because of the dwindling foreign exchange reserves and unfavorable international payment conditions. After 1946 not only were the imports in general curtailed, but also the inflow of consumer goods was restricted to a few selected items essential to the Chinese economy (such as rice, wheat flour, raw cotton, petroleum, and petroleum products). Purchases of all the nonessential supplies (such as tobacco leaf and cigarettes) were reduced to a minimum or else completely suspended. These developments occurred despite the large amount of foreign aid made available to China after the war.

A study of the import statistics of the postwar years in conjunction with those of 1938–41 reveals the following characteristics of the trade policies pursued during the immediate postwar years:

1. In terms of physical quantity, the postwar period imported more raw cotton, gasoline, fuel oil, and cigarettes than from 1939 to 1941. On the other hand, the imports of wheat flour, cotton, rice, and tobacco leaf were higher during 1939–41 than in the postwar period.

2. A tendency in the postwar period was to emphasize the importation of raw materials (e.g., raw cotton and wheat) rather than

finished products (e.g., cotton yarn and wheat flour). The only exception to this generalization was the large importation of cigarettes into China during 1946 and 1947, amounting respectively to eighteen times and ten times the import of 1937. During 1939–41 this annual import of cigarettes amounted to only six or seven times that of 1937. The annual average of the tobacco leaf import for 1946–47 amounted to only 80 percent of its 1939–41 import.[11]

3. In both the 1938–41 period and 1946–48, raw cotton led all other imports both as the multiple of the 1937 import and as a percentage of the current total import. In these periods, the average values of cotton imports were approximately fifteen times the cotton imports of 1937. In terms of dollar values, the cotton imports constituted about 13.0 percent of the aggregate imports in 1939, 14.7 percent in 1947, and 12.6 percent in 1948. The value of raw cotton also represented 22.3 percent of the UNRRA imports to China during 1946 and 1947,[12] and about one-third of the ECA program as planned in 1948. In 1946 cotton imports amounted to more than 86 percent of domestic production. Because of the dwindling supply of domestic cotton during the postwar years, the textile mills depended more on imported supplies than on domestic crops. In fact, raw cotton was the commodity which caused the most trouble to the Chinese authorities during the postwar years. Despite the fact that cotton imports during these years were unrivaled by those for any other period in Chinese history, either in absolute magnitudes or in percentages of China's total annual imports, the expanded inflow of foreign supplies failed to compensate for the loss in domestic supplies.

4. While the domestic production of cotton piece goods during the postwar period was barely at the prewar level, an increasingly large portion of this product was exported to augment China's foreign-exchange earnings. This was done at the expense of domestic consumption.

5. Despite the established policy of relying on imports to supplement the deficiency of domestic supplies in metropolitan areas, the effective systems for controlling end-uses of the scarce imports were not established until the latter part of 1947. The absence of such control systems during 1938–41 and the months immediately after the war is a testimonial to the government's failure to maximize the

utilization of the imported supplies during the greater part of the Chinese inflation.

6. Despite the large inflow of imports during the postwar period, the total supply (represented by the sum of domestic production and import) of many consumer goods available during the postwar period fell short of the prewar level. This situation was due either to the fact that the expansion in domestic production fell short of the reduction in imports, or that the decrease in production exceeded the expansion in import, or that both imports and production declined.

INFLATIONARY PRESSURES FROM INVESTMENT EXPENDITURE

Inflationary effects of investment expenditures may be viewed from several angles. In the first place, they depend upon the nature of investment. Investment expenditures, for instance, may be classified as investments for use benefit or for ownership benefit.[13] Investments in bona fide industrial and commercial enterprises are examples of the former type of expenditures. Such investments, if properly utilized, are in a position to increase production in the economy. To that extent, they may have deflationary effects on the economy to compensate for whatever inflationary impact these expenditures may have caused. Investments for ownership benefit, on the other hand, are made solely for the benefit of the investors with little or no regard for their effect on the economy. In most such investments, the interests of investors are served at the expense of some other sectors of the economy. Holdings of inventories for speculative purposes or purchases of gold and foreign assets are outstanding examples of this type of investment.

A second angle from which the inflationary effects of investment may be studied is the rate at which investment is accumulated. Other things being equal, the faster the accumulation, the greater are the inflationary pressures. Thus a comparison between the rates of investment or capital accumulation during prewar years and those attained during the inflation, or a similar comparison between Free China and the areas under Japanese occupation, should shed light on possible inflationary effects of investment.

In the case of investment for use benefit, there is also the question of the extent to which additional productive capacities resulting from new investments are actually utilized. If the new productive capacities result in an expansion of production, the inflationary pressures may accordingly be reduced. If, on the other hand, new investments only result in increasing idle capacities rather than in production, the investment expenditures then have a doubly unfavorable effect on the economy. In addition to draining the scarce resources of the economy, such expenditures also render fruitless the production factors which could otherwise be fruitfully employed.

A third angle from which the inflationary effects of investments may be measured is the means by which these expenditures are financed. Normally, investments are financed either by domestic savings or by drawing on the international sector of the economy. Ex post investment and savings should always be equal. The criterion for measuring inflationary pressures of investment is therefore to be found not in the existence or lack of equilibrium between these two ex post factors, but in the process by which such an equilibrium is attained. Domestically, investment expenditures met by voluntary savings are generally considered noninflationary; whereas, those met by forced savings resulting from note issue, newly created bank credit, or deficit financing are inflationary. Investments involving the international sector, on the other hand, are met by exports, by grants, by loans, by investments from foreign countries, or by drains on the nation's own gold and foreign exchange reserves. An investment made possible by an expansion of current receipts has an implication quite different from one met by draining the gold and foreign exchange reserves. Similarly, the use of foreign grants or loans to finance investment for ownership benefit can mean a wasteful diversion of a country's limited financial resources from their use in employments valuable to the economy.

The discussion of the inflationary effects of investment will be divided into three sections: investments for use benefit; investments for ownership benefit; and financing of these investments. The first section deals with the patterns and rates of investments for use benefit; the second section is concerned with similar problems of investments for ownership benefit. The third section examines financing problems with a view to demonstrating processes by which the equilibrium between ex post investment and savings was attained during the Chinese inflation, and to studying the possible implications of these processes in terms of inflationary pressures on the economy.

Investment expenditures should normally include those for new constructions, new equipment, net changes in inventories, and net foreign investment. Since statistical data for these expenditures for the period of the Chinese inflation are not available, it is necessary to use substitute measurements for the purpose of this study. The inflationary pressures of investment expenditures will be studied on the basis of such heterogeneous indicators as changes in the production capacities of a few selected industries, the current supplies of capital goods either domestically produced or imported from abroad, the amount of gold sold by the Chinese government, or changes in a selected number of foreign asset holdings. In many cases, the choice of indicators is dictated mainly by considerations of expediency rather than by their efficiency as a criterion of measurement.

Investments for use benefit

Comparison between free China and occupied areas. First, during the war there was a substantial expansion in the capacities of producer-goods industries, such as cement, electric power, coal mining, and the iron and steel industries. Among these the pattern of growth was identical in occupied and Free China. Obviously, with both the Chinese and the Japanese authorities, expansion of such production and production capacities was considered an integral part of their war efforts. In virtually all these enterprises, the rates of growth were in excess of the corresponding rates for prewar years (see Table 3.3).

Second, there was a marked difference of investments in consumer goods industries in the two areas. In Free China, production of consumer goods industries and their capacities expanded along with the expansion of producer goods industries. Production and production capacities of such consumer goods as cotton textile products, wheat flour, soap, matches, and paper registered considerable expansion during the war. In the occupied areas, on the other hand, production of consumer goods, such as wheat flour and cotton yarn in north China (see Table 3.3), was drastically reduced during the war, while that of producer goods expanded. In fact, the unusually rapid expansion of the production of consumer goods in Free China may be construed as reflecting the remunerativeness of these enterprises as well as the lack of policy on the part of the Nationalist government in channeling the economy's limited resources to desired uses. Thus, despite her economic privation, Free China followed through the course of the war a haphazard path of attempting to expand production of both butter and guns. In the occupied areas, on the other hand, the policy was to expand the production of guns at the expense of butter.

TABLE 3.3. RATES OF PRODUCTION INCREASES (+) OR DECREASES (−) IN SELECTED INDUSTRIES

	FREE CHINA		NORTH CHINA		PREWAR CHINA	
Industry	*Period*	*Annual percent*	*Period*	*Annual percent*	*Period*	*Annual percent*
Pig iron	1938–42	+16	1937–44	+60	1925–32	+6
	1942–45	−25			1933–37	+8
Coal	1938–43	+7	1938–42	+24	1925–32	+2
	1943–45	−12	1942–45	−6	1932–36	+9
Electric power						
Generating capacity	1938–45	+11			1932–36	+7
Power generated	1938–45	+15	1938–44	+34	1932–36	+10
Cement	1938–45	+10	1937–44	+6	1925–31	+11
Alcohol	1938–45	+77	1938–44	+67		
Caustic soda	1938–44	+51	1938–42	+8		
			1942–44	−39		
Cotton yarn	1938–44	+35	1936–44	−13	1927–30	+4
					1930–36	
Wheat flour	1939–42	+34	1936–44	−10		
	1942–45	−33				
Paper (machine made)	1938–42	+67				
	1943–45	+4				
Soap	1938–41	+70				
	1941–44	−21				
Matches	1938–44	+18				

There are no data for spaces left blank in table.

Source: For Free China, *The Statistical Yearbook of the Republic of China*, 1948. ed., p. 144; *China Handbook 1937–1945* (New York, 1947), Chapter 11; and *China Handbook, 1950* (Taipeh, 1950), Chapter 9. For North China, Yen Chung-ping, ed., *Chung-kuo chin-tai ching-chi-shih tung-chi tzu-liao hsüan-chi* (Selected Statistical Data Relating to Modern Economic History of China) (Peking, 1957), pp. 146–50. For prewar China, Yen, *Selected Statistical Data Relating to Modern Economic History of China*, pp. 146–50; *Foreign Commerce Yearbook* (Washington, D.C.) 1935–37 and 1948–50 eds., and the *Statistical Yearbook of League of Nations* (Geneva, 1945), 1945 ed.

Third, there was in China's wartime investment policies a declining importance of enterprises associated with the export trade. In Free China, the most important exports were wood oil, bristles, tungsten, and tin. In occupied China, the exports consisted of soya beans and a few mineral products (coal, iron ore, etc.). During the war, virtually all these major exports of China, except those from occupied China to Japan and the territories under Japanese control, declined sharply in volume. Among the factors responsible for the reduction of exports were the transportation difficulties during the war and the loss of foreign markets under the control of enemy powers.

Comparisons between prewar and postwar conditions. First, there was a substantial expansion of capital investment in railways, shipping, highway transportation facilities, and electric power industries in postwar China. This expansion was made possible by Japanese-sponsored developments in occupied areas, by UNRRA imports, and by China's own government and private investments. Some of these investments were legacies of wartime expansion, but others were new investments after the war.

Second, there were definite indications that the production and the production capacities of consumer goods industries declined in postwar China in comparison with their respective prewar standards. This was particularly true of the cotton spinning industry, the most important of China's modern industries, as indicated by the decrease in spindleage and the trend of cotton yarn production.

Third, there was, in addition to the decline in capacities, a change in the extent to which the consumer goods industries were utilized after the war. For example, transportation, in which the postwar expansion of capital investment was most spectacular, declined in the ratios of output to capacity, indicating less than full utilization of their capacities. This trend was true of both railways and shipping, except for the ratio of the passenger transportation on railways. To a lesser extent, the output-capacity ratios of the electric power industry of the postwar years (particularly 1948) were also lower than those of the prewar period (see Table 3.4). Available fragmentary reports indicate that substantial unused capacities also existed during the postwar years among various mining and manufacturing industries. This phenomenon was clearly reflected by the unusually low production of steel and coal in the postwar years in comparison with the reduction of the corresponding production capacities. During 1946 and 1947 only 50 percent capacity of the match factories, 50 percent of the paper mills, and 33 percent of the cement plants were in operation.[14]

Many reasons account for the widespread existence of unused

TABLE 3.4. RATIO OF OUTPUT TO CAPACITY 1932–47

	RAILWAY		SHIPPING		ELECTRIC POWER
	Passenger kilometers per passenger car (in millions)	*tons-kilometers per freight car (in millions)*	*Passengers carried per ton of shipping capacity (in thousands)*	*Freight shipped per ton of shipping capacity (in thousand tons)*	*Power generated per kilowatt capacity (in thousand kv. hours)*
1932	1.82	.28			2.50
1933	2.05	.30			2.85
1934	2.04	.41			2.84
1935	2.13	.42			2.68
1936	2.13	.42			2.73
1937	1.04	.15	137.9	193.0	1.18
1938	.71	.10	99.6	87.1	2.07
1939	1.13	.06	23.8	18.5	2.26
1940	1.45	.01	34.7	16.2	2.75
1941	1.34	.08	71.1	17.2	2.87
1942	1.61	.10	78.9	9.9	2.75
1943	3.50	.13	236.2	41.7	2.28
1944	2.26	.10	137.5	29.5	2.21
1945	.67	.01	59.1	13.3	2.67
1946	4.85	.16	18.0	9.1	2.03
1947	3.14	.11	14.6	11.5	1.69

There are no data for spaces left blank in table.
Source: *The Statistical Yearbook of the Republic of China*, 1948 ed., pp. 280–84.

capacities. Disintegration of the transportation arteries because of the civil war was undoubtedly a main factor responsible for the low efficiency in utilizing the transportation facilities. Transportation difficulties rendered it impossible to employ fully the capacities of coal production. The unavailability or the high cost of raw materials and/or the competition of imported products curtailed the production of many of postwar China's manufacturing industries.

Fourth, there was a decline in the production of virtually all China's major exports during the postwar years. This situation was true of tungsten, antimony, tin, coal, manganese, iron ore, tung oil, soya bean, and possibly bristle[15] (see Table 3.5). As for mineral products, silk, tea, and soya bean, decreases in production were accompanied by contractions in exports. Thus the low productions in these cases could be a result as well as a cause of shrinking exports. Inflation, war, and the disruption of the transportation system in China contributed toward reducing postwar production. The curtailment of exports precluded any substantial investment in expanding production capacities.

In the case of cotton yarn and cotton piece goods, exports during the postwar years were much larger than the prewar trade, while their postwar production either declined (as in the case of yarn) or barely maintained their prewar level (as in the case of cotton piece goods). This development was a result of the desperate effort of the Nationalist government to augment the country's foreign exchange earnings after the war. The expansion of these textile exports, however, was attained at the expense of supplies for the domestic market, thus accentuating the inflationary pressure on the nation's economy.

Investments for ownership benefit

To estimate the investment for ownership benefit by the Chinese public during the inflation is a difficult undertaking because of the lack of comprehensive statistics. In the following discussion, four indices will be used to show the magnitude of such investment. They are the net gold purchases by the public from the government, holdings of the Hong Kong dollar in China, Chinese deposits in the United States, and Chinese investments in Hong Kong's textile industries during the immediate postwar years. While these four items may not constitute the entire investment for ownership benefit realized during the inflation, they cover the major part of such investment.

From 1941 through 1949, the Nationalist government purchased either from the United States or from the Chinese public about 8.72 million ounces of gold. Of this amount, from 300,000 to 400,000 ounces only were shipped to Taiwan in 1949; the balance (from 8.32 million to 8.42 million ounces) represented approximately the amount of the net gold sales[16] by the government to the public

TABLE 3.5. PRODUCTION AND EXPORT OF MAJOR EXPORT COMMODITIES

	Tung oil[a]	*Bristle*[b]	*Cotton yarn*[c]	*Soya beans*[a]	*Tungsten*[d]	*Antimony*[d]	*Tin*[d]	*Coal*[a]
Production								
Prewar[e]	6,000	65,110	882.8	11,011				
1937					13,991	12,742	13,424	36,913
1938					14,113	9,824	15,440	31,943
1946	4,500	48,619	607.3	8,400	2,638	426	1,960	14,860
1947	5,250		681.6	7,959	6,402	1,588	3,970	19,487
1948	5,750				9,327	3,251	1,632	15,000
Export								
Prewar[e]	70	4.9	7.35	2,301				
1937					16,522	12,524	13,080	1,800
1938					13,612	7,185	11,795	2,045
1946	35	4.8	.31	5.7	4,640	4,734	1,560	50
1947	80	4.4	8.34	60.4	6,113	8,258	4,116	16
1948	76	4.6	15.29	5.3	13,057	4,318	3,913	19

[a] 1,000 metric tons.
[b] Production figures represent number of hogs (1,000 units); export figures are in 1,000 metric tons
[c] million pounds. [d] metric tons.
[e] Tung oil figures are for 1931–37; cotton yarn, 1931–36; and soya beans, 1931. Bristle production figures are for 1936–37; export figures, 1935–36. All are annual averages.

All statistics except for soya beans do not include the data for Manchuria.

Source: Yen, *Selected Statistical Data Relating to Modern Economic History of China*, pp. 74–76 and 100–06; *Foreign Commerce Yearbook*, 1937–38 and 1948–49 eds.

during the inflation. At the United States official price of 35 dollars per ounce, the net sales amounted to about U.S. $300 million.

In early 1950 when the Communist regime gained control of the mainland, there were about 840 million Hong Kong dollar notes outstanding. Of this amount from 200 million to 300 million dollars were being circulated or held in China. At the rate of six Hong Kong dollars to one U.S. dollar, this holding had an equivalent of from 33 to 50 million dollars.[17]

The statistics published in the *U.S. Treasury Department Bulletin* and the *Federal Reserve Bulletin* in 1950 and 1951 indicate that just before the Communist victory in 1949, mainland China held about 50 million dollars of bank deposits and securities in the United States. Of these holdings, about two-thirds belonged to banks, while the remainder represented nonbank private holdings (see Appendix 5).

Up to 1948, modern cotton textile industries were virtually nonexistent in Hong Kong. Since then, they have grown rapidly and represent almost entirely the investments of former owners of textile mills in mainland China. From 1948 through 1950, about 200,000 spindles and about 4,000 power-bearing looms were installed in Hong Kong.[18] Including investments in working capital as well as those in plants and equipment, the capital funds used in developing this new industry in Hong Kong easily reached the order of U.S. $30 million. In addition, there was also a host of new factories producing enamel ware, rubber products, elastic supplies, wearing apparel, etc., representing capital exports from mainland China for which no estimates are available. From the viewpoint of mainland China, the investments in textiles and all other industries in Hong Kong, financed by capital from China, had the same status as holdings in gold, foreign currencies, foreign securities; they were all investments for ownership benefit. Of course, as far as Hong Kong was concerned, all undertakings for the development of industries in the Colony were considered as investments for use benefit.

Thus my estimates for various investments for ownership benefit: may be summarized as follows:

	U.S. $ million
Net gold purchases by the public from the government	300
Holdings in Hong Kong dollars	33–50
Deposits and securities holdings in the United States	50
Investments in textile industries in Hong Kong	30–40

Financing of investments during the inflation

Resources from the domestic sectors. During the administration of the Nationalist government, China's industries fell into two distinct groups. The first group consisted of private enterprises, and the second, the government enterprises. In the course of the inflation government industries became increasingly important vis-a-vis private enterprises. This trend was accentuated during the immediate postwar years when all heavy industries and textile mills in Manchuria and other occupied areas were taken over from the Japanese and were retained for government operation. The management of the heavy industries (including iron, steel, basic chemical industries, and virtually all the modern mining industries) was then considered a main function of the National Resources Commission of the Nationalist government; whereas, the China Textile Mills, another government agency, was specially created for operating textile mills formerly owned by the Japanese. Accordingly, our discussion of the investment financing will be based on this dichotomy of government and private enterprises.

The main sources of financing government enterprises were government appropriations and government bank loans. Long-term equity investment and the reinvestment of business profits (normally the main sources of business financing in a nonsocialistic economy) were relatively unimportant. This unbalanced situation was accentuated by the inflation.

The mining and manufacturing industries had a greater tendency to rely upon bank loans for financing than the communication industries did. The loans granted by government banks to the mining and manufacturing industries (see Table 3.6) ranged from 0.4 times the corresponding government appropriations during August–October, 1948, to 14.0 times in 1945. The loan-appropriation ratios for the communications industries, on the other hand, ranged only from .08 in 1946 and 1947 to 2.4 in August–October, 1948. While the magnitude of these appropriations and loans might not be comparable to that of military outlay, they had beyond doubt an important bearing on accentuating the inflation. In 1946 and 1947, for instance, the loans and appropriations to these economic enterprises amounted to more than 40 percent of the total military expenditures of the Nationalist government. Even in 1945

TABLE 3.6. RATIOS OF BANK LOANS TO GOVERNMENT APPROPRIATIONS FOR ECONOMIC USES AND RATIOS OF BANK LOANS PLUS GOVERNMENT APPROPRIATIONS FOR ECONOMIC USES TO GOVERNMENT APPROPRIATIONS FOR MILITARY EXPENDITURES

		1945	*1946*	*1947*	*1948 Jan.– May*	*1948 Aug.– Oct.*
1	Bank loans to communication industries / Government appropriations to Ministry of Communication	1.7	.08	.08	.15	2.4
2	Bank loans to mining and manufacturing industries / Government appropriations to Ministry of Economic Affairs and Natural Resources Commission	14.0	2.6	1.6	2.1	.4
3	Bank loans for food administration / Government appropriations to Ministry of Food	.07	.2	.14	.13	1.1[a]
4	Bank loans and government appropriations to communication enterprises / Government appropriations to Ministry of Defense	.06	.27	.24	.09	.07[a]
5	Bank loans and government appropriations to mining and manufacturing industries / Government appropriations to Ministry of Defense	.06	.14	.17	.08	.01
6	Bank loans and government appropriations for food administration / Government appropriations for military expenditures	.07	.09	.02	.1	.09
7	Total for 4, 5, and 6	.19	.50	.43	.27	.17

[a] Aug.– Sept.

Source: *The Statistical Yearbook of the Republic of China*, 1948 ed., pp. 235 and 262; *Chung-yang yin-hang yueh-pao* (The Central Bank Monthly), IV (1949), 122; and unpublished records of the Central Bank of China.

and the latter part of 1948, when the ratios of such loans and appropriations to military outlay were the lowest of the postwar years, they amounted to 19 and 17 percent respectively (see Table 3.6).

One marked feature of China's private industrial enterprises during the inflation was the mushrooming of small firms, a phenomenon that emerges from the statistics compiled by the Ministry of Economics of the Nationalist government (see Table 3.7). These statistics show that, despite the shrinkage of territory under the

TABLE 3.7. CORPORATION REGISTRATIONS, 1936-47

	Number of new corporations registered	*Average paid-in capital per newly registered firm (1937 yuan)*
1936	301	209,410
1937	198	370,942
1938	102	318,329
1939	142	50,745
1940	245	62,271
1941	397	44,131
1942	251	53,505
1943	422	20,995
1944	415	7,911
1945	347	5,102
1946	1,496	21,038
1947[a]	1,256	18,374

[a] Jan.–June

Source: *The Statistical Yearbook of the Republic of China*, 1948 ed., pp. 154–55.

control of the Nationalist government during the war, the number of new corporations registered with the government increased almost without interruption, from 102 in 1938 to 1,256 in the first six months of 1947. On the other hand, the real value of paid-in capital per corporation declined steadily from 370,942 yuan in 1937 to 5,102 yuan in 1945, and then rose to 21,038 yuan in 1946 (all the above amounts expressed in the yuan of 1937). Consequently, the total paid-in capital of the new corporations registered in 1946 amounted to less than 6 percent of the corresponding total of 1937, while the number of new firms registered in 1946 was twelve times as high as registered in 1938.

The decrease in real value of the paid-in capital of private firms may be construed as implying that private enterprises, like those controlled by the government, relied heavily on bank loans for financing. Unlike the government enterprises, however, access to loans from government banks was limited only to those private firms which were essential to national security and the livelihood of the people. Included in these two categories were the major firms producing and processing the major exports of China, and also those engaging in the production or distribution of supplies essential to daily living and military needs. It was the established policy of the government during the inflation that the facilities of government banks were limited only to these private undertakings and to government-controlled enterprises. Besides the government banks, private firms also borrowed from private banks or nonbank lenders. Because of the limited resources at their disposal, however, the private banks were not in a position to grant loans on a scale comparable to that of the loans from government banks. The term "nonbank lenders," when used in the Chinese context, does not refer to insurance companies, investment trusts, etc., as it usually does in the United States; in the Chinese context, the term refers to private money lenders and nonbank business firms with surplus funds at their disposal. While the role played by these lenders was not comparable to that of the government banks, these private lending facilities were as important to private firms during the Chinese inflation as were the private banks. Because of the unavailability of necessary data, however, it is difficult to make any meaningful comparison between the magnitude of such nonbank lendings and that of private bank lendings.

Government appropriations and bank credits were the chief resources for financing industrial investments in both postwar and Free China. The question to be examined is: From what sources did the government and the banks get the funds to provide for such appropriations and credits?

Obviously, during these years of heavy budgetary deficits, the appropriations were mainly provided for by note issues—a subject discussed at length in Chapter II.

The bank loans for financing industrial developments had a long maturity, and therefore should properly have been financed by funds derived from bond issues or time deposits. This rule of thumb, however, broke down entirely during the Chinese inflation. While bank loans for industrial developments during these years expanded the volume of savings and time deposits both in real terms and in relation to the bank loans outstanding with the banks shrank drastically. Bond issues (including government and corporate) became virtually impossible during the inflation. Instead, the bank often took recourse in such unconventional sources as rediscounts at the Central Bank, demand deposits, and even the funds accumulated from domestic remittances in transit (see Chapter VI) for financing industrial loans of long maturity. In the case of the Central Bank, the note issues and the credit on these notes were the financial sources for bridging the increasingly large gap between the Bank's cash receipts and outlays. In other words, as far as the domestic market was concerned, the investments exceeded what the economy could bear. The equilibrium between ex post investments and savings was attained by a host of roundabout processes, all of which led ultimately to the expansion of note issues and the bank credits pyramiding on these issues.

Resources from the foreign sector. In addition to domestic resources, factors in the international sector also contributed toward balancing ex post investments and savings. First, a substantial segment of the new investments for use benefit effected during the inflation were made possible by imports financed by foreign aid, loans, and investments. A large part of China's investments in railway and shipping facilities during the postwar years fell into this category. Second, some investments were financed by the government's own holdings in gold and foreign currencies. The imports of goods for investment for use benefit financed by the Central Bank's own foreign exchange holdings were an example of this type of investment.

The inflationary effects of investment should not be judged solely by the existence of an equilibrium, or the lack of it, between investment expenditures and available resources for meeting these expenditures. Consideration should also be given to the possible contributions of these investments toward slackening the tempo of the inflation, and the alternative uses of production factors which were absorbed by investment expenditures. For instance, instead of being used for purchasing ships and railway rolling stock (neither was fully utilized during the postwar years) the UNRRA funds and some postwar foreign credits could have been used to purchase scarce raw materials for the idle capacities of some industries. Instead of financing the import of such luxuries as high priced automobiles, refrigerators, powdered milk, woolen fabrics (none needed by the bulk of the Chinese populace) the foreign exchange holdings of the Central Bank could have been used to import staple food supplies. Instead of selling gold to the well-to-do at unusually low prices, the Nationalist government could have used its gold holdings to finance the import of commodities badly needed in China. A better utilization of foreign aid and foreign asset resources of the Central Bank would undoubtedly have improved its contribution toward stabilizing the economy.

SUMMARY

For the Chinese economy, consumption expenditures during the war were lower than in the prewar period. This situation was reflected by the reduction of manufactured products and imported supplies in Free China, and by the scarcity of consumer goods in occupied China. The curtailment of consumption (as the discussion of the redistributional effects of the inflation will show) was applicable mainly to government employees, teachers, and recipients of interest and rent, whose real income decreased sharply during the inflation. By comparison, the real incomes of farmers and factory workers were less vulnerable to the erosive effects of inflation. Business profits generally improved, since the Chinese inflation was basically of the demand-pull type. Accordingly, the consumption expenditures of farmers, wage earners, and recipients of entrepreneurial incomes were not so seriously affected as were those of other people.

During the inflation there were substantial investments for use benefit, despite the scarcity of producer-goods. A large part of such investments in producer-goods industries were undertaken by government or pseudo-government agencies and were financed mainly by government appropriations and government bank loans, rather than by equity investments. Investment for ownership benefit consisted almost invariably in converting Chinese resources into holdings in gold and/or foreign-asset holdings. These investments resulted in substantial drains on the foreign exchange resources of

China, and the effects on the economy was much more serious than that of investments for use benefit. On the whole, the investment expenditures resulted in a substantial amount of realized inflationary pressure on the economy, with government activities primarily responsible for the pressure arising from the investments for use benefit and private investments responsible for the pressure from the investments for ownership benefit.

CHAPTER IV

Foreign Exchange and Trade Policy: Inflationary Pressures in the International Sector

The development of China's trade and foreign exchange policies during 1935–49 will be divided into six stages. The first stage covered from November, 1935, to August, 1937, during which the Nationalist government attempted to peg the exchange rate of the yuan virtually without exchange or trade restrictions. The second stage covered from August, 1937, to August, 1941, during which a policy of "managed flexibility" (or managed peg)[1] was used without effective trade controls. The same policy was followed in 1946. The third stage covered the months from August to December, 1941, during which a comprehensive trade control was attempted for the first time to accompany the policy of managed flexibility. The fourth stage covered most of 1946, during which the policy of the second stage (managed flexibility without effective trade controls) was virtually reinstituted. The fifth stage covered 1947 and early 1948, during which the managed flexibility was accompanied by effective trade controls. The sixth and final stage covered almost entirely the year from May, 1948, to May, 1949 (with the exception of the months of August and September, 1948), during which time a policy of flexible exchange rate was followed, while the trade and exchange control remained in effect. Details of significant developments in each of these six stages will be discussed in the subsequent sections of this chapter.

It should be noted that the material covered in this chapter on China's experience with foreign exchange stretches over a period slightly longer than the duration of the Chinese inflation, which began in 1937, so that important developments during 1935–37, could be included.

STAGE ONE: A PEGGED RATE WITHOUT DIRECT CONTROLS (1935–37)

This period began with the introduction of the system of managed currency (commonly known as fapi) in November, 1935, when China abandoned the use of its traditional silver currency in favor of a system of managed currency;[2] and continued until August, 1937, when direct financial controls were instituted after the spread of the Second Sino-Japanese War from north China to Shanghai. The salient features of the currency system of this period were that:

1. The bank notes issued by the Central Bank of China, the Bank of China, and the Bank of Communications became the sole legal tender under the new currency system.
2. The use of silver for currency was prohibited. The public was required to surrender its silver holdings to the government in exchange for the legal tender notes commonly known as fapi.
3. The Central Bank of China bought and sold foreign exchange without limit at specified official rates.
4. The silver withdrawn from circulation was shipped and sold, mainly to the United States and the United Kingdom. The sales proceeds were used to create a foreign-exchange reserve which made possible the Bank's unlimited sales of foreign exchange in the market.

So far as the administration of foreign exchange was concerned, the monetary reform of 1935 brought about these results:

1. From November, 1935, to March, 1938, when the Chinese government drastically modified its foreign-exchange policy because of the Japanese interference, the external value of the Chinese currency was successfully maintained within the narrow range set by the official buying and selling rates for the pound sterling and the U.S. dollar. The rates first quoted were 1*s*. $2\frac{3}{8}$*d*. and 1*s*. $2\frac{5}{8}$*d*. per Chinese yuan for sterling, and $0.295 and $0.30 per yuan for the U.S. dollar. The sterling rates were changed in September, 1936, to 1*s*. $2\frac{1}{4}$*d*. and 1*s*. $2\frac{3}{4}$*d*. The dollar rates, on the other hand, were adjusted in February and in September, 1936. These adjustments were made primarily for technical reasons. They did not reflect any major change in the value of the Chinese currency.

2. The foreign-exchange policy pursued by the Central Bank permitted unrestricted arbitrage operations. For this reason, no appreciable discrepancy between the cross-rates derived from the official quotations for the U.S. dollar and sterling, on the one hand, and the relevant exchange quotation or cross-rate in markets abroad, on the other, existed. For instance, the Central Bank's sterling selling rate of 1*s.* 2⅜*d.*, and the dollar buying rate at U.S. $0.30 gave a cross-rate of U.S. $5.00869 to one pound sterling, while the dollar selling rate at U.S. $0.2950 and the sterling buying rate at 1*s.* 2⅝*d.* yielded a cross-rate of U.S. $4.84102 to a pound. So long as the dollar-sterling rate on the foreign market fluctuated within the spread set by these two cross-rates, no arbitrage transaction was possible; but when the dollar-sterling market rate went beyond either of these limits of the spread, it then became imperative for the Central Bank to adjust either its dollar rates or its sterling quotations.[3]

Until February, 1936, the Chinese policy aimed at keeping the sterling rates fixed (see Table 4.1); the Bank's dollar rates were adjusted when the dollar-sterling rate in foreign markets tended to deviate unduly from the cross-rates derived from the official quotations. After September, 1936, however, this policy was apparently changed. On September 9 the New York-London market rate rose to U.S. $5.0524 to one pound, and surpassed the limit set by cross-rate A, then prevailing ($5.05043). To cope with this situation, the Central Bank doubled the spread between the buying and selling rates for sterling from ¼*d.* to ½*d.*, and for the U.S. dollar from $0.005 to $0.01. Consequently, cross-rate A was raised to $5.13684 and cross-rate B, lowered to $4.80000, thereby providing a spread broad enough to contain the prevailing dollar-sterling market rate. In the meantime, the parities for both the dollar and sterling which, according to the interpretation of the Chinese authority, represented the averages of the relevant buying and selling quotations of the Central Bank, remained unaffected. Although this parity had no significance in actual operations, the Chinese government's intention was to keep both the yuan-dollar and the yuan-sterling parity rates stable, and to prevent the Chinese currency from being openly pegged to either the dollar or to sterling.

Evidently, the policy of keeping the value of the Chinese currency stable in terms of the sterling and the dollar was feasible only within a very restricted limit, for in actuality neither could the dollar-sterling market rate long remain stable, nor could the spread between the buying and selling rates be extended without limit. After 1941 the yuan-dollar rate became the only basis from which the relevant market cross-rates and the exchange rates, between yuan and other foreign currencies, were derived.

TABLE 4.1. OFFICIAL EXCHANGE RATES AND CROSS-RATES, 1935 AND 1936

	Nov. 4, 1935	*Feb. 4, 1936*	*Feb. 13, 1936*	*Sept. 9, 1936*
Yuan-Sterling rates				
(a) Bank selling	1*s*. $2\frac{3}{8}$*d*.	1*s*. $2\frac{3}{8}$*d*.	1*s*. $2\frac{3}{8}$*d*.	1*s*. $2\frac{1}{4}$*d*.
(b) Bank buying	1*s*. $2\frac{5}{8}$*d*.	1*s*. $2\frac{5}{8}$*d*.	1*s*. $2\frac{5}{8}$*d*.	1*s*. $2\frac{3}{4}$*d*.
Spread	$\frac{1}{4}$*d*.	$\frac{1}{4}$*d*.	$\frac{1}{4}$*d*.	$\frac{1}{2}$*d*.
Yuan–U.S. Dollar Rates				
(c) Bank selling	$29\frac{1}{2}$¢	30¢	$29\frac{3}{4}$¢	$29\frac{1}{2}$¢
(d) Bank buying	30¢	$30\frac{1}{2}$¢	$30\frac{1}{4}$¢	$30\frac{1}{2}$¢
Spread	$\frac{1}{2}$¢	$\frac{1}{2}$¢	$\frac{1}{2}$¢	1¢
Cross-Rate A $= \frac{(d) \times 240}{(a) \times 100}$	\$5.00869	\$5.09217	\$5.05043	\$5.13684
Cross-Rate B $= \frac{(c) \times 240}{(b) \times 100}$	\$4.84102	\$4.92307	\$4.88205	\$4.80000
Spread between Cross-Rates A and B	\$0.16767	\$0.16910	\$0.16738	\$0.33684

The yuan-sterling and yuan-dollar rates are in sterling and dollar equivalents per yuan respectively, and the cross-rates represent dollar equivalents per pound sterling. Cross-rate A is obtained by dividing the bank selling rate for sterling into the buying rate for the dollar; cross-rate B, by dividing the buying rate for sterling into the selling rate for the dollar. In both cases, the quotients obtained are multiplied by a constant $\frac{240}{100}$, so that the cross-rate will be in U.S. dollar equivalents per pound sterling.

STAGE TWO: MANAGED FLEXIBILITY WITH SOME FINANCIAL CONTROLS (1937–41)

The major developments during this period were the restriction of withdrawals from bank accounts; the abandonment of the policy of a pegged exchange rate; and the loan arrangements with foreign banks for supplementing the government's diminishing monetary reserves and the dwindling receipts from exports. Although some trade controls were contemplated by the government, they were never successfully enforced.

Restrictions on deposit withdrawals

In August, 1937, when Sino-Japanese hostilities spread from north China to Shanghai, there were large withdrawals of deposits from Chinese banks and unusually heavy pressure on the foreign-exchange market. To cope with the situation, the Chinese government proclaimed on August 13 a two-day bank holiday. In the following week, it promulgated a set of emergency bank regulations. These regulations limited cash withdrawals from the currency deposit accounts in the banks to 5 percent of the outstanding credit balance, or a maximum of 150 yuan a week; and prohibited the withdrawal of time deposits before their maturity, and required that these be converted on maturity into current deposits subject to the restrictions on withdrawals. Because of the practical difficulties involved, these restrictions were applicable only to deposits made before August 13, not to those made thereafter. To relieve the stringency in the money market caused by these restrictions a *Wei-wah* check system was introduced to enable payments in excess of the cash available, including interbank settlements. New deposits made after the announcement of the restriction were accordingly divided into cash accounts and *Wei-wah* accounts. The former could be freely transferred, withdrawn, or converted into foreign currencies. The balances in the latter accounts, on the other hand, were used only for interbank transfers and were not convertible into cash or foreign currencies. Because of these restrictions, the value of the *Wei-wah* check was discounted in terms of cash payment. The discount rate was about 4 per mill in November, 1937. Despite their inadequacy as long-term solutions, these restrictive measures did succeed in temporarily relieving the pressures on the foreign-exchange market and contributed appreciably to the economic stability maintained during the first eight months of the war.

Another important change was in the regulation requiring the sale of the foreign exchange proceeds from major exports to the Central Bank at the official rate.[4] This regulation was never effectively enforced. The failure was because most of the maritime customs, whose service was essential for checking exports, were then under the control of Japanese, and because the increasing discrepancy between the official rate and the market rate of exchange made it impossible for exporters to surrender their exchange proceeds at the official rate without incurring heavy losses.

The abandonment of fixed exchange rate

On March 10, 1938, the Federal Reserve Bank of China was instituted in Peiping by the puppet government of north China, and a new bank note was issued for circulation in the northern provinces to displace the Chinese fapi. At the time the fapi was still a freely convertible currency. It would have been possible, therefore, for the Japanese to utilize the fapi notes withdrawn from circulation in north China to drain the reserve of the Central Bank of China, which would then have been obligated to redeem the fapi with foreign currency without restriction. In order to guard against such drains, the Chinese government imposed a new set of restrictive measures. The most important change was the withdrawal of an unlimited supply of foreign exchange at the official rate fixed by the Central Bank. This old policy of supplying foreign exchange without limit was substituted by an allotment system, under which the Central Bank supplied foreign exchange at the old official rate to meet the over-sold positions of commercial banks, but only to an amount to be decided by the Bank. The amount of exchange thus allotted usually fell far short of the demand. The allotment, amounting to about 30 to 50 percent of the amount requested by commercial banks during the initial weeks of the operation of the system, dwindled steadily both in absolute magnitude and in percentage. Toward the end of 1938, the allotment was reduced practically to nothing.[5]

When the amount of the allotment dwindled, the external value of the Chinese currency in the free market accordingly depreciated. Gradually, the official quotations, which had been almost identical with the market rates, became nominal.

Loans from banks: the Sino-British Stabilization Fund (1939–41)

In an attempt to maintain the value of the fapi currency, an agreement was reached in March, 1939, among four banks to establish a Stabilization Fund of £10,000,000. Two of these banks were the Chinese government banks (the Bank of China and the Bank of Communications), and two were the British banks (the Hong Kong Shanghai Banking Corporation and the Chartered Bank of India, Australia and China). The amounts required were advanced by those banks in the following proportions:

The two Chinese banks in such proportion as agreed on:	£5,000,000
The Hong Kong and Shanghai Banking Corporation	3,000,000
The Chartered Bank	2,000,000
Total	£10,000,000

The main function of the Fund was in the Chinese currency by operating in the exchange market in Hong Kong and Shanghai.

The management of the Fund was vested in a five-man committee, which met in Hong Kong and was known as the Hong Kong Committee. Two members were jointly appointed by the Chinese banks, one was appointed by each of the two British banks, and one, who had to be a British subject, was appointed by the Chinese government with the concurrence of the British Treasury and the participating British banks. A member of the committee might appoint an alternate, who in the member's absence was entitled to attend committee meetings and to exercise the power of that member. The duties of the committee were to determine the operational policy best suited to achieve the objectives of the Fund, and to give instructions to the Hong Kong Bank and the Chartered Bank, which were the Fund's agents for operations in the Shanghai market.

Until all the subscriptions of the British banks were repaid, interest payable in sterling at the rate of 2.75 percent per annum on the outstanding balances of these subscriptions was to be paid in London to the two British banks.

The establishment of the Sino-British Stabilization Fund marked an important change in the financial policy of the Chinese government. Instead of allotting foreign exchange at the unrealistically pegged official rate, the Chinese authority attempted to slacken the depreciation of fapi by open-market operations, mainly through the two British banks. While every effort was made to prevent the

Chinese currency from further depreciation, the rate at which the Fund sold exchange (usually represented by the selling rate of these British banks) was in the neighborhood of the market rate.

The active operation of the Stabilization Fund, however, lasted for only three months, from March to June, 1939. On March 10, 1939, when the Stabilization Fund began its operation, the market rate of exchange for the Chinese currency was $7\frac{13}{16}$*d.* to one yuan, and it rose to $7\frac{14}{16}$*d.* toward the end of the month. The rate was maintained at $7\frac{13}{16}$*d.* in the first part of April, and rose to $8\frac{1}{4}$*d.* during the latter part of the month. This stable situation continued until the beginning of June, 1939, when the depletion of its sterling resources forced the Fund to withdraw its support in the market. The market rate then dropped to a new low level of $6\frac{1}{2}$*d.*

From June, 1939, until the outbreak of the war in Europe, the Chinese government, in view of the withdrawal of the Fund's support, introduced several new regulative measures in the hope of tightening the money market in Shanghai and of bolstering foreign-exchange receipts from exports. None of these palliatives, however, was fruitful. The depreciation of the Chinese currency continued. At the beginning of August, 1939, the sterling rate of fapi was reduced to $3\frac{1}{4}$*d.* This downward trend was interrupted by the outbreak of World War II in Europe. This resulted in a heavy repatriation of funds abroad, and consequently brought about a temporary appreciation of the Chinese currency in the foreign-exchange market. During October and November, the sterling rate of fapi rose well above 5*d.*, and then remained stable in the neighborhood of $4\frac{1}{2}$*d.* In the course of the repatriation of funds, the Stabilization Fund was actually in an over-bought position.

In short, after August, 1937, the inflationary pressures began to bear fruit in the form of rising prices and the depreciating external value of yuan. While the rise of prices was unchecked, the Nationalist government tried desperately to slow down the depreciation of the foreign-exchange rate by drawing heavily on its meager monetary reserves and on loans from foreign banks. Because of the absence of effective exchange and trade controls, not even the resources available were fully utilized. In retrospect, it is thus not difficult to see the pitfalls in these trade and exchange policies and the reasons for their failure.

STAGE THREE: MANAGED FLEXIBILITY WITH EXCHANGE AND TRADE CONTROLS (1941–44)

This period covered August to December, 1941, during which a policy of a managed flexibility was accompanied by both exchanges and trade controls.

In Stages One and Two, the foreign-exchange operations of the Chinese government were carried out with no effective support from trade restrictions. Whatever trade regulations existed, they were not effectively enforced. The Sino-American-British Stabilization Board, which came into full operation in August, 1941, as the successor of the Sino-British Stabilization Fund, was responsible for instituting China's first system of import quotas. In general, however, even the trade restrictions introduced by this Stabilization Board were too liberal to ensure the full utilization of China's limited resources. Not until 1947, did the role played by trade restrictions become really significant.

Organization and functions of the Stabilization Board

Foreign-exchange policies of the period were built on the loans from the American and British governments and the Chinese banks, amounting to U.S. $50 million, £5 million, and U.S. $20 million respectively. These resources, in total the equivalent of U.S. $90 million, were for purchasing excess Chinese currency in the market with a view to maintaining its external values. It was understood that the Chinese currency, purchased with the American and British funds, would be repurchased by the Chinese government at the original purchase rate.

The Sino-American-British Stabilization Board, consisting of members—three Chinese, one British, and one American[6]—appointed by the Chinese government, administered these funds. Each member was authorized to appoint one alternate.

Although this new board was an organization of the Chinese government from a legal point of view, its authority was derived from the cooperation of the American, British, and other foreign governments. After the outbreak of the Sino-Japanese War in 1937, the Chinese government lost control over the maritime customs administration functioning in the coastal areas; without the assistance of the customs, the government was in no position to check imports and exports, or to enforce the trade and foreign-exchange controls in the country.

The establishment of the Stabilization Board of China, however, entirely changed the situation. To facilitate the foreign control of the Stabilization Board, the Chinese government agreed with the government of the United States, members of the British Commonwealth, and the government of the Netherlands (East) Indies to the following arrangements:[7]

1. Imports into China from the United States were not permitted, unless the Stabilization Board or its designated agent provided the dollar exchange required for such an import. Exports from China to the United States were not permitted, unless the sales to the Board of the foreign-exchange receipts from such an export had been arranged.

2. All remittances from the United States and other American territories to China had to be paid to agents designated by the Chinese authority.

3. The British government instructed all the British banks dealing with Chinese yuan to open accounts with the London office of the Bank of China with a view to centralizing all yuan-sterling transactions there.

4. The government of Hong Kong prohibited, except by special permit, the holding or shipment of fapi notes or any transaction (including that of bills of exchange, promissory notes, deposit receipts or entries in bank accounts) involving Chinese currency, and required all banks in the colony to quote only official rates for the fapi.

5. The American, British, and Dutch banks in China, following the instructions of their respective governments, pledged their full cooperation with the Stabilization Board in confining their foreign-exchange dealings only to the transactions permitted by the Board at its specified rates.

The Board and the Foreign-Exchange Control Commission

Besides the Stabilization Board, the Nationalist government also set up in September, 1941, an Exchange Control Commission presided over by the Minister of Finance, Dr. H. H. Kung, and composed of representatives of the Ministry of Finance, the Joint Administration of Four Government Banks, and the Central Bank of China. The functions of the Commission as announced were to study the policy of exchange control; to screen applications for the purchase of foreign exchange; to control the sales of foreign-exchange proceeds derived from exports; to supervise remittances from Chinese residing abroad; to study the disposition of foreign-exchange assets frozen in foreign countries; to study the utilization of foreign loans and credits; and to plan and to supervise gold and silver operations in the domestic market.

Apparently there was a certain amount of overlapping in the functions of the Commission and the Stabilization Board. The former, however, exercised authority only over the Nationalist government's foreign-exchange transactions and the operations of Chinese banks in or with Free China; while the latter was in a position to enforce foreign-exchange restrictions over Chinese banks in the foreign concessions in Shanghai and over the transactions of foreign banks with both Free China and the occupied areas. The division of power between the Board and the Commission, nevertheless, was often controversial. At that time many in China believed that foreign-exchange control should have been ministered by the Chinese government rather than by a committee of foreign representatives who in their opinion often overemphasized the interests of their own countries. Moreover, they argued, the operation of the Board should have been limited to its own resources, and the foreign-exchange proceeds derived from exports and inward remittances should have been kept by the Chinese government to meet its own needs. Later, however, all such foreign-exchange receipts were transferred to the Board, which in turn reimbursed the Central Bank of China with foreign-exchange payments for government requirements; the Board undertook the examination of commercial applications, and the Commission screened the government applications, including those of government enterprises.

The Shanghai Policy

More than 90 percent of the foreign exchange paid out by the Stabilization Board during the months prior to the Japanese attack on Pearl Harbor was to meet applications originating in Shanghai and Hong Kong. Most of these applications were for financing imports to the foreign concessions in Shanghai.

The main objectives of the so-called Shanghai Policy of the Board were to provide raw materials for industries in the foreign concessions of Shanghai and food for the residents. By so doing, the Board hoped to ensure employment and livelihood of millions of residents and refugees who crowded the Shanghai concessions.

Many Chinese economists believed that the failure of the Sino-British Stabilization Fund had been mainly due to its attempts to supply the exchange market in Shanghai and Tientsin. Since the foreign concessions in Shanghai and Tientsin were under foreign administration, they felt that the Chinese government no longer needed to provide the foreign-exchange requirements of these cities. To operate in the Shanghai market, the economists argued, only facilitated the flight of capital from these areas and helped provide the enemy with essential supplies. The Chinese and foreign authorities, however, believed that foreign-exchange operations in Shanghai were essential to maintaining the prestige of the fapi currency, and that the withdrawal of such operations would likely mean a total collapse of the Chinese currency in free market. The maintenance of the foreign-exchange market in Shanghai ensured the supply of raw materials essential to Shanghai industries, and thereby saved millions from being unemployed. Moreover, since the Board was mainly supported by foreign loans, the American and British interests in the foreign concessions naturally played an important part in the Board's decisions.

The operation of the Board

The headquarter of the Board was in Hong Kong, which was a convenient center for supervising the Board's operations in Shanghai and Free China. In addition, the Board had a branch office in Kunming, which at that time was the most important entrepot for imports into Free China via the Burma Road. After the occupation of Hong Kong by the Japanese in December, 1941, the Board moved to Chungking.

When the Board was instituted, three sets of foreign-exchange rates were in the Chinese market: (1) the Central Bank's rate of U.S. $29.5 (equivalent to 100 Chinese yuan) for the dollar and 14¼*d.* (equivalent to one yuan) for the sterling, both rates were nominal; (2) the Bank of China's and the Bank of Communications' rate (also known as "trading rates") of U.S. $7.5 and $4\frac{1}{2}$*d*., at which rates the Sino-British Stabilization Fund had provided foreign exchange to importers; and (3) the black-market rates, of which the April averages were U.S. $5.9375 and $4\frac{1}{8}$*d*. In order to maintain a realistic level, the Board fixed its exchange rates at U.S. $5.3438 to 100 yuan and $3\frac{3}{16}$*d*. to one yuan for the dollar and sterling when its operation began in August, 1941. The markets of that month averaged U.S. $5.3438 and $3\frac{19}{32}$*d*. These rates were used until January, 1942, when the Board, in compliance with the request of the Ministry of Finance of the Chinese government, announced the new rates of U.S. $5.0625 per 100 yuan and $3\frac{1}{64}$*d*. per yuan. Under the operation of the Board, all foreign-exchange purchases and sales were handled by appointed banks and only at the rates which were stipulated by the Board.

Unlike its predecessor, the Sino-British Stabilization Fund which had confined activities only to open-market operation, the new Board allocated the foreign exchange on the basis of an import quota system determined after careful deliberation and discussion with qualified representatives of the industrial and commercial interests in Shanghai. Under the system, the Board established quotas for all major imports, and provided foreign exchange only for imports within the limits set by these quotas. The quotas were designed primarily for meeting the immediate needs of the foreign settlements in Shanghai. Imports for stockpiling purposes were not permitted. Thus, instead of covering all importers, the Board would allocate the quotas only to established importers in the lines of business concerned so that the imports would ultimately be sold to bona fide end-users. The imports were classified with a schedule determining the order of priority of foreign-exchange allotments. When the Board's operation in Shanghai was suspended after the Pearl Harbor attack, the Board had already completed a quota system covering most of the major imports. The import quota system was the first of its kind ever used in China. Despite the imperfections it provided an important bases for postwar trade controls.

Although a detailed record of the Board's operation is not available, it is not too difficult to obtain an approximation of the foreign-exchange resources used by the Board during its operation.

Allotments from Aug. 19, 1941, to Nov. 22, 1941[8]	U.S.$ 12,430,548.54	£ 1,739,960
Allotments from Jan. 1942, to March, 1944[9]	7,865,835.45	2,110,463
Total	$ 20,296,383.99	£ 3,850,423
Deduct: Amount of Hong Kong dollars and Burmese rupees purchased by the Board		1,758,708
Total net allotments	$ 20,296,383.99	£ 2,001,715

Out of a total sum (equivalent to U.S. $90 million, including both U.S. dollars and pounds sterling) appropriated to the Board, only U.S. $20 million and £2 million were used. At the dollar-sterling rate then prevailing, these totals amounted to about U.S. $8.5 million more than the original advances made by the Chinese government bank, which amounted to U.S. $20 million.[10] In other words, the Board relied very little upon the American and British funds during its operation, although their presence contributed appreciably to strengthening its position. Thus when the Board was abolished in 1944, it had no difficulty in liquidating what it had borrowed from foreign creditors.

The abolition of the Board

The Japanese occupation of the foreign concession in Shanghai and in Hong Kong after Pearl Harbor deprived the Board of a major part of its original work of providing foreign exchange for the import requirements of Shanghai. As transportation reduced to a trickle the trade between Free China and the outside world, the activities of the Board in Free China were reduced. In April, 1943, the Chinese Ministry of Finance, to compensate for the adverse effects of the unrealistic foreign-exchange rate, announced a special subsidy, equivalent to 50 percent of the official rate for the remittances of foreign governments and missionaries in China. Since the Central Bank of China advanced all such subsidies, the proceeds from such remittances were also kept by the Bank rather than transferred to the account of the Board, as previously arranged. Consequently, the function of the Board as the collector of inward remittances was also lost.

It is also important to understand the attitudes of the American, the British, and the Chinese governments toward the Board. The Chinese financial authorities, particularly the Ministry of Finance and the Central Bank, considered the existence of the Board, over which they had no control, an usurpation of authority which belonged to them. The basic agreement which brought the Board into existence was one of the many unfair treaties imposed upon China by foreign powers, which should naturally be abolished when all such treaties were being abandoned. This view, however, was not shared by some of the Chinese members of the Board, who felt on the basis of their practical experience that because of chaotic economic conditions in China, foreign (particularly American) participation would certainly assist economic stabilization. But the views of the Ministry and the Bank finally prevailed.

The American government was eager to promote goodwill in China and was willing to abandon any treaty considered unfair by the Chinese. In the meantime, the amount of the American remittances was rapidly increasing with the expansion of United States military activities in China. Abolition of the financial agreement gave the United States authority a free hand in pressing for an adjustment in the exchange rate, thereby reducing the cost of American operations in China.

On the other hand, the British, who knew that the continued existence of the Board would permit them to participate in the administration of China's foreign-exchange and trade controls and that this would be beneficial to their postwar trade with China, were rather eager to have the Board retained; but they were unable to convince the Americans and the Chinese. The Board was abolished in 1944.

In comparison with the Sino-British Stabilization Fund, the operation of the Board was definitely a great improvement for several reasons. First, while the Fund mainly confined its operations to the purchase and sale of the Chinese national currency with the resources at its disposal, the Board controlled not only the exchange but also the trade. By introducing the system of import quotas, the Board provided an important foundation for the import-quota system used in postwar China. Second, through the system of U.S. General Licenses and special arrangements with other countries, the Board obtained the cooperation of not only the American, the British, and the Hong Kong governments, but also the influential foreign banks in Shanghai. This international cooperation greatly facilitated the control of China's exports and imports, and thereby made clandestine financial transactions difficult. Third, the *modus operandi* of the Stabilization Board represented a pattern under which foreign and Chinese experts might have possibly cooperated to solve the economic problems of China. Some economists contended that many of the blunders committed during the postwar years might have been avoided had the work of the Stabilization Board not been terminated in 1944.

The above commendations, however, do not imply that there existed in the operating mechanism of the Board a perfect trade-control system. In comparison with China's elaborate import-quota systems that developed after 1946, and the trade controls in Europe, the controls then instituted by the Board were rudimentary.

STAGE FOUR: MANAGED FLEXIBILITY WITHOUT EFFECTIVE TRADE CONTROL (1946)

Like all historical developments, the foreign-exchange policy of postwar China was a result of theories and facts developed during the years immediately preceding. A knowledge of such theories and facts is therefore essential to a thorough understanding of the postwar policy.

The leaders in Free China generally believed that one of the main factors responsible for the hyperinflation in China was the shortage of commodities during the war. Supplies were inadequate to meet demand, and prices rose rapidly. If therefore imports of commodities could be facilitated following the reopening of the sea ports at the conclusion of the war, the rise in commodity prices would be checked. They thought that despite the expansion of the note issue and the continued depreciation of the value of the currency in terms of commodity prices, changes in the official quotations of gold and foreign exchange should be avoided, because in the eyes of the public those quotations were often the most sensitive barometers for the future trend of the inflation.[11] Adjustments in those quotations would only lead to a further reduction of public confidence in the fapi notes, and would thereby accentuate the tempo of the inflation. And finally with the surrender of the Japanese in 1945, the Nationalist government gained an undue self-confidence which resulted in underestimating the strength of the Chinese Communists. Virtually all the Nationalist military leaders believed that the Communists would be defeated, either by negotiation or by war, within a few months. The financial authorities, who based their calculations on the advice of the military leaders, were accordingly misled, and they concluded that the heavy drains on the exchange reserve during the months immediately following V-J Day was only a passing phenomenon of the transitional period, one which would soon end with peace and prosperity.

The first of China's foreign-exchange systems instituted after World War II was based on the regulations promulgated in February, 1946. It contained the following important provisions:

1. Only the banks especially authorized by the Central Bank of China (the appointed banks) were allowed to buy or sell foreign exchange under the conditions stipulated by the Central Bank of China.

2. All foreign-exchange proceeds derived from exports were sold to the Central Bank through the appointed banks at the rate fixed by the Bank.

3. The Central Bank sold foreign exchange through the appointed banks only for approved imports, personal requirements, and other authorized payments.

4. A new Central Bank rate of 2020 yuan to one U.S. dollar was established; in fact, it became the basic rate on which all bank transactions in foreign exchange were conducted. The old official rate of twenty yuan to one dollar, which was established in 1941, and which no longer realistically reflected the external value of yuan, was not abolished, but remained applicable to only a few specially approved outlays of the government.

Despite the provision for the adjustment of the exchange rate from time to time, the initial rate of 2020 yuan to one U.S. dollar remained unchanged for five months. On the other hand, the restrictions on imports turned out to be so lenient that even the importers of many nonessential commodities were provided with the cheap foreign exchange by the Central Bank. In the meantime, the overvaluation of the yuan in terms of foreign currency, together with the chaotic conditions resulting from the war, greatly hampered the exports from China. There was thus an unusually heavy drain on the official reserve.

During those months the economic conditions in the country remained relatively stable, but this stability was attained at an enormous expense to the nation's specie and foreign-currency reserves. The drains on these reserves might have been greatly reduced had there been better coordination between the financial and fiscal policies of the Chinese government. In many respects there was a close resemblance between the policy of this period and that of the Stabilization Fund of 1939–41.[12] In both cases there was a tendency to rely too much on foreign-exchange operations as the means for stabilizing the economy. In both cases cheap foreign exchanges were liberally provided to meet import requirements, without effective trade control.

STAGE FIVE: MANAGED FLEXIBILITY WITH EXCHANGE AND TRADE CONTROLS (1946–48)

The high lights of this period were the adoption of the systematic trade controls at the end of 1946, and the organization of the Foreign Exchange Stabilization Fund Committee of 1947–48. The operation of this committee will be discussed first, and the trade controls will be studied in the next section.

The Foreign Exchange Stabilization Fund Committee of 1947–48

Organization and functions of the Committee. At the beginning of March, 1947, just before Mr. Pei Tsu-yee had resigned from the governorship of the Central Bank, the old exchange rate of 3320 yuan to one U.S. dollar became so unrealistic than an adjustment was made to a new rate of 12,000 yuan to one U.S. dollar, a few points above the prevailing market rate. Immediately after the readjustment there was a heavy repatriation of foreign currency, mainly through the redemption of foreign-currency notes in China presented to the Central Bank; and the foreign-exchange receipts from exports and inward remittances were also increased. Consequently, in the month of March the foreign holdings of the Central Bank had a net gain of about U.S. $30 million. Two months later, however, the market rate began to rise, and the new official rate became unrealistic. Virtually all exports from China and remittances to the country came to a standstill, and the drain on the

Bank's reserve again gained momentum. In order to cope with this situation, the Central Bank in August, 1947, adopted a new foreign exchange policy with the following salient points:

1. A specially appointed Stabilization Fund Committee, consisting of representatives of foreign-exchange banks in Shanghai, announced on each business day, on the basis of the market conditions, the Fund's rate of exchange which displaced the Central Bank rate as the basis for transactions.

2. All foreign-exchange requirements were met on the basis of the Fund's rate except the foreign exchange for the importation of such essential raw materials as cotton, cereals, coal, and coke, and a part of the government's requirements, which the Central Bank continued to sell at the old official rate of 12,000 to one U.S. dollar.

3. A Foreign Exchange Stabilization Fund Committee decided the Fund's rate with a view to maintaining an equilibrium between supply and demand in the foreign-exchange market. The Fund Committee consisted at first of three members but was later increased to five. To plan and supervise day-to-day operations, the Fund Committee had a technical committee consisting of representatives of the Fund and four leading foreign-exchange banks, the Bank of China, the Bank of Communications, the National City Bank of New York, and the Hong Kong Shanghai Banking Corporation.[13]

4. The Stabilization Fund Committee was not actually backed by any foreign loan or any earmarked reserve, but was allowed to draw its necessary working fund either in foreign exchange or in local currency from the Central Bank. In fact, the Bank not only kept all the accounts for the Fund but also handled its routine work.

5. The import and export control system remained unaffected.

Theoretical bases for rate adjustment. Unpublished records of the Central Bank summarized the basic principles on which the Fund's operation was based as follows:

1. In adjusting its exchange rate, particular attention was usually paid to the possible effects upon the local market. The market conditions in the Shanghai Stock Exchange, good indicators of the nation's financial condition in general, were usually studied with special care.

2. Whenever the exchange rate was adjusted, the Central Bank,

the Food Supply Commission of Shanghai, the Textile Control Commission and other relevant government agents were requested to coordinate their market operations and to tighten the money market in Shanghai so that the bullish effect of such an adjustment on commodity prices might be minimized.

3. Rate adjustment was avoided when an important political meeting or conference was in session.

4. No adjustment was to be made whenever rumors anticipating such a change were rampant in the market.

5. Usually the Fund's rate was adjusted when the drain on the official reserve was heavy or when such a drain was anticipated.

6. An adjustment was usually made when the Fund's rate lagged so much behind the market quotation as to hamper the export trade of China.

7. Adjustment in the Fund's rate was avoided when there was a large government outlay pumping into the market.

8. When the dollar-sterling cross-rate derived from the Fund's rates became unduly out of line as compared with the cross-rate prevailing in Hong Kong, an adjustment in the relevant Fund rate usually followed.

9. While an objective of the Fund was to make the official exchange rate as realistic as possible, it had no intention of competing with the black-market for inward remittances, for it was feared that a diversion of such remittances from the market might tend to accentuate the rise of the black-market rate.

To what extent these tests were actually applied in determining the Fund's rate is not clear. It is apparent that not all were compatible with one another, and that not all could be applied simultaneously. Nevertheless, they did reflect to some extent the basic policy of the Fund.

In order to maintain the objectivity of its work, the Stabilization Fund Committee used to help its rate adjustment the following criteria:

THE GENERAL PRICE INDICES. As a primary guide for rate adjustment, the average of the wholesale price indices of Shanghai, Canton, and Chungking, as compiled by the Central Bank of China, and the prices of China's chief exports as compiled by the Fund itself were used.

THE HONG KONG MARKET QUOTATIONS. The telegraphic transfer rate for Shanghai yuan quoted in Hong Kong was then probably the most reliable indication of the market value of the Chinese yuan. A comparison of this rate with the Fund's rate for Hong Kong dollars was always a good indication as to how realistic the latter was. Similarly, the cross-rate derived from the Hong Kong T/T rates on New York and on Shanghai was considered as the market valuation of Chinese yuan in terms of U.S. dollars. The exchange rates of Hong Kong and the corresponding rates in the Shanghai black market were usually closely related, although not identical.

AVERAGE EXPORT RATE AND INDICATED RATE. The export rate was defined as:

$$\text{export rate} = \frac{\text{Shanghai price of an export in yuan}}{\text{corresponding f.o.b. U.S. dollar price in Shanghai}},$$

where the f.o.b. dollar price was derived by deducting the shipping costs from the corresponding c.i.f. price quoted in the world market. An individual export rate was obtained for each of the main export commodities of China, including tung oil, bristles, black and green tea, feathers, hog casings, cotton piece goods, hides, goat skins, weasels, and wool. The average export rate was then derived from these individual rates, duly weighted by the value of each commodity actually exported in the year 1947. The indicated rate was derived by adding 15 percent for profit and interest charges to the average export rate. However, the indices and the formulae were not necessarily used with mathematical precision, particularly when the policy on rate adjustment was strongly influenced by public opinion.

Effects of the Fund's operation. Before it was straitjacketed by political pressure, the flexible rate policy of the Stabilization Fund Committee was quite successful, although the achievement in general was not so impressive as that of its successor, the foreign-exchange certificate systems. Because of the Fund's operations, the drain on the Central Bank's reserve reduced appreciably. Except October, 1947, when the ratio of the Fund's rate to the market-exchange rate dropped to 60 percent from 70–90 percent for the earlier months,and except the months after February, 1948, when the Fund was reduced to a state of inactivity, exports from China maintained a high level of more than U.S. $10 million a month. Inward remittances also increased during the first three months of the Fund's operation. These improvements, together with a tightening of control over imports, resulted in a great reduction in the nation's trade deficit. This reduction played an important role in slowing down drains on the foreign-exchange reserve of the Central Bank, although curtailment of government requirements also contributed to such an improvement.

Not very long after the institution of the Stabilization Fund Committee, its flexible rate policy aroused a great deal of public criticism and was often blamed as a "prime mover" in the inflation. The intensity of such criticisms increased when the inflation turned from bad to worse toward the end of 1947; and the operation of the Fund was greatly hampered. During the last few months of its existence, when mounting criticism made further rate adjustment politically unfeasible, the Fund's activities were virtually paralyzed. After March, 1948, the ratios of the Fund's rate to the black-market rate were reduced to about 25–50 percent as against the 80–90 percent in the early months of the Fund's operation, so that the disadvantages of the rigid rate policy again became prevalent.

Did the flexible rate policy really accelerate China's inflation? This question aroused many fruitless arguments during the last phase of the Fund's operation. The argument against the Fund's policy centered around two points: The continued upward adjustment of the Fund's rate tended to undermine public confidence in the Chinese currency and thereby to accentuate the tempo of the nation's inflation. And although rice, wheat, flour, cotton, coal, and coke, were still imported at the fixed official rate (twelve thousand yuan to one U.S. dollar) under the Fund's system, many other essential commodities (petroleum and petroleum products, etc.) were purchased at the Fund's rate. For instance, in Shanghai the public utilities were operated under foreign management with imported fuel and supplies which were purchased or paid for with foreign exchange obtained at the Fund's rate. When the Fund's rate was raised, the cost and therefore the rates of such utilities were raised, and a corresponding adjustment followed in the cost-of-living indices. The rise in prices gave an impetus to a further rise in the black-market exchange rate and called for a new adjustment in the Fund's rate. The vicious circle continued.

On the other hand, the Fund's experts argued: the fiscal deficit and the expansion of note issues, and not the changes of the Fund's rates, formed the real "prime mover" of the inflation. The rise of the Fund's rate usually lagged behind that of prices and the black-market rate. The upward adjustment of the Fund's rate was therefore an effect rather than a cause of the rising prices. In its statement issued on May 18, 1948, the Fund pointed out that from August 19, 1947 (the day on which the Fund first came into operation), to the middle of May, 1948, the wholesale price index of Shanghai rose by about ten times, and the black-market rate for U.S. dollars by about fifteen times; whereas during the same period the Fund's rate rose only sevenfold. This clearly showed, the statement continued, that the Fund's rate had actually been following rather than leading the prices and the market rate (see Table 4.2). Since China was a country with deficit payment and since the Central Bank normally sold more foreign exchange to the market than it purchased, a high Fund rate was more effective for withdrawing money from the market than a low, unrealistic rate; it was therefore a useful asset in combating the inflation.

The controversy concerning the Fund's flexible rate policy involved one of the basic principles on which the nation's anti-deflationary operations were based. From the outbreak of the war in 1937 until the institution of the Stabilization Fund Committee in 1947, the Chinese government pursued a pegged foreign-exchange rate policy. It believed that an upward adjustment of the official exchange rate caused a further rise in the market rate and thereby accentuated the inflation. After March, 1947, a definite shift in government policy favored a flexible rate. Although the significance of this new policy was not fully realized at the time, it is not too difficult to evaluate it in retrospect, particularly in the light of the experience with the exchange certificate systems later adopted. The following is probably a fair verdict on the flexible rate policy.

First, when an inflation is mainly psychological and speculative, and monetary factors (such as the expansion of currency in circulation) are well under control, a rigid price and exchange-rate policy is preferable. On the other hand, when the monetary factor is predominant and unwieldy, a policy of keeping price and exchange-rate flexible and realistic undoubtedly is better than one of rigid

TABLE 4.2. FOREIGN-EXCHANGE FUND RATES, 1947 AND 1948

Date of adjustment	$\frac{\text{Fund rate index}}{\text{market rate index}} \times 100$	$\frac{\text{Fund rate}}{\text{purchasing price parity}} \times 100$	*U.S. dollars*	*Pounds sterling*	*Hong Kong dollars*
			(yuan per foreign currency unit)		
1947					
Aug. 19	63	90	39,000	124,800	7,800
21	59	91	38,500	123,200	7,700
23				120,000	7,500
29				117,000	7,312.5
30				115,000	7,187.5
Sept. 3	53	82	38,000	113,000	7,062.5
6	54	87	40,000	118,000	7,375
9				120,000	7,500
11	51	87	40,500		
12				122,000	7,625
18	49	89	42,500	125,000	7,779.95
26	52	72	46,000	135,000	8,402.34
29	54	70	49,500	146,000	9,086.98
Oct. 9	53	64	55,300	163,000	10,145.05
24	46	61	55,000	165,000	10,269.53
Nov. 1				172,000	10,705.21
4	50	72	59,500	187,000	11,638.8
7				182,000	11,327.6
18				188,000	11,701.04
20	51	45	64,500	197,000	12,261.2
25	57	50	73,000	225,000	14,003.91
Dec. 19	52	50	83,000	259,000	16,120.05
23				270,000	16,804.69
30	52	58	89,000	290,000	18,049.48
1948					
Jan. 12	46	58	113,500	375,000	23,339.84
27	44	68	119,500		
Feb. 3	46	77	131,500	413,000	25,704.95
9	45	73	135,000		
20	37	71	149,000	447,000	27,900
Mar. 9	33	51	195,000	585,000	36,900.16
17	43	52	255,000	765,000	47,000
Apr. 6	48	57	324,000	972,000	60,496.88
May 17	49	41	474,000	1,422,000	88,504.69

The dollar-yuan purchasing power parities are computed on the basis of the wholesale price indices of Shanghai and of the United States compiled by the Central Bank of China and the United States Bureau of Labor Statistics.

The spaces left blank in table indicate no change in the exchange rate between yuan and the foreign currency concerned.

Source: Unpublished records of the Central Bank of China.

price and exchange rates. For the former policy, under the circumstances, can be more anti-inflationary and prevent unjustifiable windfalls in favor of a privileged few.

Second, no matter which policy is pursued, proper coordination and overall planning are always essential. Without them, a squeeze on one sector of the economy and a windfall on another may result with no justification whatsoever. Under these circumstances, the merit of a right policy is lost and its objective often misunderstood. The Fund's policy represented a step in the right direction but there was no bold, over-all program, which was needed to bring out the full effect of the policy.

Third, the economists who have studied China's economic conditions during the inflation have generally agreed that regardless of which policy was pursued, the prices of subsistence commodities (particularly foodstuffs) should have been kept stable so that the cost of living for the populace would not have been disturbed. To prevent undue windfalls, a ration system for distributing such commodities should have been instituted, together with the price control or subsidy required to attain such a stabilization.

The abolition of the Stabilization Fund Committee. In order to solve the difficulties confronting the Fund, experts of the Fund and of the Central Bank reviewed the whole exchange policy and recommended improvements and substitutes for the Fund's rate system. In May, 1948, just before Chang Kia-ngau resigned from the Central Bank, three alternative policies were formulated and brought to Nanking for consideration by the premier. These alternatives were as follows:

THE FOREIGN-EXCHANGE CERTIFICATE SYSTEM. This system had been under serious consideration by the Central Bank and the Stabilization Fund Committee since the beginning of 1948. In March, 1948, all the details of the plan (including texts of the regulation and circular letters) were completed. It was actually adopted at the end of May. This system will be dealt with in a subsequent discussion.

THE EXPORT-IMPORT LINK SYSTEM. Under this system the import licenses would be issued only to exporters, who could either use the privilege themselves or sell it to others. Under this arrangement no question of fixing the foreign exchange rate would be involved; the rate would be determined by the price of the import license. This system is different from the exchange-certificate system because the former covered only the export and import transactions and not the noncommodity transactions (such as remittances, payments of service, etc.); whereas, the latter covered all transactions. A draft proposal for this system was also worked out and was discussed at great length. One possible advantage of this system would have been the avoidance of all the difficult problems arising from rate fixation. The system would have been relatively cumbersome in its operation, however, and could not have offered any satisfactory solution to the problems concerning noncommodity transactions.

THE USE OF AN APPROVED FORMULA FOR RATE ADJUSTMENT. Some of the Fund's experts suggested that the basic formula for rate adjustments should be first approved by the Executive Yuan (or the cabinet), and the Fund would be responsible only for semi-automatic adjustments based thereon. The primary objective of this proposal was to shift the responsibility of the rate adjustment from the Fund and the Central Bank to the cabinet. This, of course, would not have solved the technical or even the political difficulties confronting the Fund.

Before the Executive Yuan had time to execute these proposals, the cabinet under the premiership of Chang Chun resigned. Chang Kia-ngau, the governor of the Central Bank, was succeeded by O. K. Yui. On May 31, 1948, the new cabinet, upon the recommendation of O. K. Yui, adopted the foreign-exchange certificate system in place of the Fund system.

While possible substitutes for the Fund system were studied, and before the foreign-exchange certificate system was adopted, the Central Bank and the Fund also introduced a makeshift arrangement which provided that an importer deposit in local currency an amount equivalent to 50 percent of the value of the approved import with the Central Bank. This amount was computed at the Fund's rate prevailing on the day of deposit when the import license was issued. The foreign exchange required for the import was settled upon the arrival of the cargo in China.[14] The main purpose of this ruling was to offset possible windfalls which might have resulted from an unduly large discrepancy between the Fund's and the market rate. Instead of attaining the expected result, this regulation provoked a great deal of complaint in business circles[15] and finally was abolished when the basic policy was changed to foreign-exchange certificate system.

The trade controls of 1946–49

The only period during the inflation in which China had a comprehensive system of trade controls in operation was 1946–49. This system had the following points:

1. There were two basic rates at which foreign exchanges were sold at the Central Bank: the official rate and the Bank rate. The official rate was a nominal rate applicable only to government purchases of foreign exchange. The Bank rate, which referred to the rate quoted by various stabilization boards and funds in the early years of the inflation and to the foreign-exchange certificate rate in 1948 and 1949, was usually applicable to authorized purchases for nongovernment uses. For most years of the Chinese inflation, the official rate was much lower than the Bank rate, which in turn was lower than the open market rate.

2. Imports (excluding those for military uses) were classified into three major groups: imports by government; nongovernment imports restricted by a quota on individual commodities (commonly known as the quota imports); and nongovernment imports restricted by a group quota (commonly known as nonquota imports).

3. The government imports consisted of such basic civilian supplies as rice, coal, wheat, and wheat flour, as well as items for the government's use. They were imported directly by the government and were financed by foreign exchange made available at the official rate. All nongovernment imports required prior permission of the government. An import license carried with it automatically an authorization to purchase foreign exchange from the Central Bank at the Bank rate.

4. All exporters were required to sell their earnings in foreign exchange to the Central Bank at the Bank rate.

5. Because of the overvaluation of Chinese yuan to foreign currencies, China's export trade was greatly hampered during the postwar years. To ameliorate this situation, the Nationalist government adopted a number of measures for promoting exports. Among these measures were the provisions for low-interest loans to exporters, including packing credits, which assisted exporters in the preparation

for the shipments; and the so-called "change-over" under which arrangement the Central Bank provided low-interest loans in Chinese currency against letters of credit received by Chinese exporters. For commodities which the domestic cost exceeded the foreign market price—a situation often resulting from the unrealistic exchange rate of the Chinese currency—the government undertook to export, absorbing whatever losses were involved. The export regulation also permitted a manufacturer to use up to 5 percent of the value of his export receipt to import packing materials required for his export. The import of raw materials was permissible, providing that the products derived from such materials were for export and that the foreign exchange earned was surrendered to the Central Bank.[16]

The export-import control system was a new experience in the Chinese economy and contributed appreciably to improving the efficiency of the foreign-exchange control during the years after 1947. Even in its final form, however, the system was far from being perfect.

The most important defect was that while it was relatively easy to determine the aggregate quota for each import, the allocation of the aggregate among individual importers often involved difficult administrative problems. The quotas for the quota imports were allocated among importers on the basis of the volume of trade during the prewar years and/or during the early months of 1946. Consequently, a large number of small importers were included among the participants and rendered the system administratively cumbersome and wasteful. For example, about 90 percent of the total petroleum quota was allocated to five major oil companies, and 10 percent was divided among some sixty small firms. The administration of nonquota imports, for which only an aggregate quota in U.S. dollars was announced without any detailed breakdown for individual commodities, was particularly unsatisfactory. Unlike the quotas for individual commodities the approval or rejection of an application for the nonquota imports was mainly decided by the officials in charge. Theoretically, the import priority of these commodities was determined by the need in the domestic market. In fact, however, the amount of foreign exchange available for the nonquota imports was usually so small in comparison with the amount requested by the importers that it was impossible to establish a rational order of priority. Consequently, the administration of the nonquota imports caused more criticism than any other phase of the trade-control system.

Another important defect of the import-control system was the lack of control over the price of imports, thereby facilitating unauthorized remittances from the country by inflating the c.i.f. cost of imports to cover more than the actual import needs. In the case of gasoline, for instance, the c.i.f. costs at which importers applied for the purchase of foreign exchange from the Central Bank were sometimes from 20 to 30 percent higher than the actual cost. The difference, as some oil companies claimed, represented the remittances covering the companies' profit, overhead charges, and other foreign exchange expenses which otherwise were not permitted under China's exchange regulations.

When a quota was allocated to an importer, it became his established privilege. The incentive to make any reduction in the cost of imports to compete with other importers vanished, although such competition was essential to the full utilization of the foreign exchange allocated to importers by the Central Bank. To attain this, however, the trade controls needed one of two provisions: the import quota of any commodity or any group of commodities, instead of being distributed on the basis of an established percentage, should have been awarded only to an importer who could offer the most favorable terms of trade, including a minimum c.i.f. cost, prompt delivery, etc. Periodic adjustment of an announced quota should have been made on the basis of prices, delivery, and other performances of an importer in comparison with those of an average importer. Quotas of the importers whose performances excelled the average should have been increased, and those whose holders failed to attain the average standard should have been reduced.

Lack of control over the extension of letters of credit through the appointed banks was another important defect of the trade-control system. According to the practice established at the time of the institution of the trade controls in December, 1947, an appointed bank of the Central Bank gave a letter of credit to an importer upon the latter's presentation of an import license issued by the Export-Import Board. After a letter of credit was established, the issuing bank then claimed a 100 percent foreign-exchange coverage from the

Central Bank for financing that import. If the importer failed to consummate his shipment before the license expired, he applied for an extension of the license. If such an extension was granted, the validity of the letter of credit automatically and accordingly extended often without the prior knowledge of the Central Bank. The abuse was particularly serious in the case of capital goods for which the validity of a letter of credit fully covered by the Central Bank lasted as long as several years. Because of these arrangements and the inadequacy of the checking system in the Central Bank, it was not difficult for an importer or an appointed bank, if they so wished, to keep for a long period of time the foreign exchange of the Central Bank without making any actual import. Consequently, a large amount of the Bank's foreign-exchange resources was frozen for long-term commitments of great uncertainty, while the country was badly in need of funds for financing the imports designed for immediate needs.

STAGE SIX: THE FLEXIBLE EXCHANGE RATE WITH DIRECT CONTROLS (*1948–49*)

During May, 1948, to April, 1949, a policy of a flexible exchange rate was followed while the trade and exchange controls remained in effect. This period was characterized by the use of two systems of foreign-exchange certificates. The basic principles of these two systems were almost identical except that the certificates were known as "the Foreign-Exchange Surrender Certificate" in the one case, and as "the Foreign-Exchange Clearing Certificate" in the other. In addition, the survey of this period includes also the trade and exchange policies pursued by the Nationalist government after its move from Nanking to Canton.

The systems of Foreign-Exchange Certificate

The Foreign-Exchange Surrender Certificate System as announced by the Central Bank in May, 1948, had these chief characteristics:

1. For the inward purchase of foreign-exchange proceeds derived from exports and remittances, the Central Bank issued through its appointed banks a Foreign-Exchange Surrender Certificate upon the receipt of the exchange proceeds in an amount equivalent to the exchange surrendered.

2. Any holder of an import license or of an authorization to purchase foreign exchange for nonimport requirements was permitted to use the exchange certificate to buy foreign exchange from the appointed banks at the prevailing certificate rate. The certificate alone, however, could not be used for purchasing foreign exchange from the Central Bank.

3. Originally the expiration date of the certificate was not more than seven days from the date of issue, and the expiration date under no circumstances was extended. This validity period, however, was later extended to thirty days.[17]

4. The owner of a certificate was permitted to transfer it to a qualified importer, or to any other person authorized to purchase foreign exchange from the Central Bank, but transfer for any other purposes was prohibited.

5. If the supply of exchange certificates in the market exceeded (or fell short of) the demand for them, the Central Bank intervened by buying (or selling) certificates in the market to avoid violent fluctuations in the price of the certificate.

6. A foreign-exchange certificate issued in one port permitted use of the certificates for meeting authorized foreign-exchange requirements in other ports.

7. The exchange certificate was divisible into any number of certificates of any denomination, provided the total amount remained unchanged.

8. Unlike the official rates under the previous foreign-exchange systems, the certificate rate was determined by the market rather than by the Central Bank. The latter, however, influenced the market through the purchase or sale of the certificates in the market.

The Foreign-Exchange Surrender Certificate System, which functioned quite successfully until its abolition on August 19, 1948, following the monetary reform, represented a major step on the part of the Chinese government toward a realistic foreign-exchange policy. During almost the entire period from May to August, 1948, the certificate rates were successfully maintained above 70 percent of the black market rate. Throughout the months of its operation, the Surrender Certificate System enabled the Central Bank to maintain an overbought foreign-exchange position ranging from U.S. $4.8 million to U.S. $10.4 million per month.

After the monetary reform in August, 1948, the new exchange was pegged at four gold yuan to one U.S. dollar. The Foreign Exchange Certificate System, which was built upon the principle of a flexible exchange rate, was suspended.

The pegged-rate policy however was short-lived. In the middle of November, 1948, the official rate became again unrealistic and the usual shortcomings came to the fore. The Clearance Certificate System was then introduced. The *modus operandi* of the system of Foreign-Exchange Clearance Certificate was practically the same as that of the Surrender Certificate System. There were two important differences, however, between the certificate systems. The clearance certificates were valid for sixty days from the date of issue and restrictions on the purchase of the clearance certificates were much less severe. Limitations for preventing undue pressure on the market, which had been stressed in the regulations of the earlier system, were obviously absent. In fact, when the government decided to resume open-market operations in gold, in commodities, and in the foreign-exchange certificate of March, 1949, for withdrawing surplus cash from the money market, purchases of the certificates for maintaining the value of the currency holdings were implicitly encouraged.

Like its predecessor, the Clearance Certificate System[18] enabled the Central Bank to maintain an overbought position in its foreign-exchange dealings in the market throughout its operation from November, 1948, through the following May. This situation was accentuated by the fact that since the turn of the year the military victories of the Communist army in north and central China made the Shanghai merchants extremely hesitant in making further imports into China.

The decrease in imports, which in turn curtailed the demand for the clearance certificates, brought forth two difficult problems for the Central Bank. The reduction in demand resulted in widening the discrepancy between the certificate rate and the foreign-exchange rate in the black-market, and thereby deprived the certificate system of its chief merit. The shrinkage in the certificate market also hampered the Bank's open-market operations, for the Clearance Certificate was then considered as one of the major weapons used by the Bank to control the market.

To offset this bearish tendency, the Central Bank and the China Mission of Economic Coordination Administration (or ECA) of the United States Government made an arrangement which required the importers of petroleum products and the buyers of chemical fertilizers to pay their imports or purchases in the clearance certificates. Under the ECA program, petroleum products were imported by a limited number of established importers who were required to pay the Central Bank an amount in the foreign Exchange Certificates equivalent to the U.S. dollars provided by ECA for such imports. Chemical fertilizers, on the other hand, were directly imported into China by ECA and then were sold in the domestic market.[19] It is estimated that under this arrangement about U.S. $25 million of the certificates were absorbed from the market. The bearish market condition was also responsible for the long validity of the clearance certificate and the implicit encouragement on the part of the Central Bank in certificate purchases for purposes other than financing authorized imports or nonimport requirements.[20]

The trade balance of the south China ports (Canton, Swatow, and Amoy) was usually favorable, and the resulting excess certificate supplies were mainly absorbed by the Central Bank, which maintained the certificate rate in these cities on a basis of the Shanghai price and the relevant remittance charges among Shanghai and the southern ports. After the occupation of Shanghai by the Communists, the main market for the exchange certificates was lost. To cope with this situation, the Central Bank announced in June, 1949, that it would first redeem all the certificates issued in south China. Because of the breakdown of the gold yuan, the redemption was made in foreign currencies. The certificates issued in Shanghai were registered, but redemption was not effected because of the evacuation of the Bank from Canton in October, 1949.

As a whole, China's experience with the foreign-exchange certificate system was encouraging. The suspension of the Surrender Certificate System in August, 1948, was necessitated by the monetary reform, which abandoned the policy of a flexible exchange rate in favor of a fixed-rate policy. The Clearance Certificate System was abandoned in May, 1949, in order to adapt the foreign-exchange policy to the new situation resulting from the Communist occupation of Shanghai. In neither case was suspension of the system caused by the failure of the system itself. The foreign-exchange certificate systems had several merits.

The certificate system enabled the Central Bank to follow a policy of flexible exchange rates without entailing irrational public criticism which often made the Bank hesitate to adjust its foreign-exchange rate. The flexible-rate mechanism provided by the certificate systems ultimately narrowed the gap between the official and the market rates, thereby enabling the Bank to buy more foreign exchange from the market than it sold. The certificate mechanism also enabled the Central Bank to borrow foreign exchange from the market without undue losses to exporters, even under conditions of hyperinflations; for the certificates issued by the Bank were sold in the market at a realistic price. The establishment of the exchange-certificates system gave the Central Bank another "big stick" to control the money market. Under these certificate systems, the Central Bank relied upon sales (or purchases) of the certificates to tighten (or loosen) the money market. Unlike gold, which often disappeared because of hoarding or because of being smuggled out of the country, exchange certificates had to be used within a specified period to cover authorized imports of nonimport requirements. In selling exchange certificates to the market, the Central Bank, of course, had to be extremely cautious in not unduly depressing the certificate rate in the market and in not rendering the effective foreign-exchange rate unrealistic.

During the period from October, 1947, to June, 1951, Greece also had a foreign-exchange certificate system, but there were important differences between the Chinese and the Greek systems. Under the Greek system, the price of the exchange certificate represented a flexible premium which was added to a fixed official rate to yield a composite effective rate usually known as an "official rate with certificate." Under the Chinese system the certificate rate represented an effective official rate. The Chinese certificate rate daily fluctuated. Under the Greek system, the official rate (without certificate) and the price of the certificate, for most of the time, were fixed and only occasionally adjusted; although, in both cases, the certificate rates were subject to the influence of the respective central banks through their operations in the certificate market.

The Greek certificate was issued in U.S. dollars and pounds sterling; whereas, the Chinese certificate was issued in U.S. dollars only. The Greek certificate was valid for 120 days from the date of its issue. The longest validity period for the Chinese certificate was only 60 days.

Besides China and Greece, Peru also used a certificate system. The principles of that system were very similar to those of the Greek and Chinese certificate systems, although there were important differences in details. The Peruvian system was established in September, 1948.[21]

It is rather difficult to say to what extent these certificate systems are interrelated. The Chinese system was developed primarily by Albert Shao, an assistant general manager of the Central Bank during 1947–49. So far as this writer can recall[22] we had no knowledge of the operating details of the Greek system when the Chinese regulations of the certificate system were prepared.

The foreign-exchange administration after the Communist occupation of Shanghai (May–October, 1949)

Background. Because of the proximity of the south China ports to Hong Kong and of the continued depreciation of the Chinese currency, Hong Kong dollars were used in Kuangtung, Kwangsi, and many other southern provinces, not only as a store of value but also as a medium of exchange. Many futile attempts were made by the Chinese authorities to forbid the use of Hong Kong currency in South China. In August, 1948, when the gold yuan was first issued, about H.K. $80 million of the Colony currency circulating in China was redeemed at the Central Bank as a result of the government decree which prohibited the use of all foreign currencies in the country. Despite these efforts, the Colony dollars continued to dominate the south China markets. It was estimated that out of more than H.K. $800 million of notes outstanding, there were then $200 million to $300 million circulating or hoarded in China.[23] Even at best, the Chinese currency only supplemented and never superseded the role of Hong Kong dollars as *de facto* standard money in south China.

In the months immediately before the Communist occupation of Shanghai in May, 1949, the gold yuan notes began to show signs of collapse under a double-barreled pressure of mounting commodity prices and an acute shortage of note supply resulting from lagging adjustment in the denominations of the bank notes. After the Communists took Shanghai, the public first in Kwangtung and then gradually in all the other provinces held by the Nationalist government rejected the gold yuan notes. Until the issuance of the silver yuan notes in July, 1949, Hong Kong dollar notes and the silver and nickel coins held over from prewar days became the chief media of circulation in the non-Communist area.

The prevalence of smuggling was a dominant feature of trade in south China. The geographical proximity of the south China ports to Hong Kong and Macao, where foreign goods were imported without duty,[24] and the multiplicity of communication lines between China and those two foreign colonies made it extremely difficult to check smuggling. It is estimated that at least 70 or 80 percent of the trade between south China and those colonies was done through smuggling. After a series of conferences which dragged on for more than a year, a customs agreement was finally signed in October, 1948, between the Chinese and the Hong Kong governments. That agreement provided that no major Chinese exports were allowed unless duly certified by the Central Bank of China, and that the Chinese Maritime Customs was permitted to install stations in Hong Kong territory to make the necessary inspections. Smuggling, however, continued to flourish under Hong Kong's traditional policy of free trade. In fact, anything short of a full-fledged cooperation between the Chinese and Hong Kong authorities (as in the case of the operations under the Stabilization Board in 1941) would never have been able to impose an effective check on smuggling. To effect such cooperation, however, would have required a drastic modification of Hong Kong's free-trade policy, on which her postwar prosperity was based, and might therefore have run counter to the interests of the Hong Kong government. But so long as smuggling existed, it had an important bearing upon any trade or exchange-control system instituted in south China.

Another important factor which hamstrung such financial controls in the southern provinces was that a large part of the exports was made on consignment rather than by letter of credit. This arrangement was necessary because these exports usually required transshipment in Hong Kong, long the chief entrepôt for international trade in that area. Letters of credit from foreign importers as a rule covered only shipments from Hong Kong and not those from south China ports; nor was it the custom of the small shipping companies which provided transportation between Hong Kong and those Chinese ports to issue the shipping documents needed for letter-of-credit transactions.

Many years before World War II and also those following it, China was invariably a deficit country. The unusually large demand for industrial and other supplies in Shanghai and in its neighboring areas mainly contributed to the trade deficit. After the Communists took over Shanghai, the drain on the Nationalists' foreign-exchange resources for supplying imports to that area accordingly disappeared. The international payments for south China were as usual favorable to China. Moreover, because of the wide circulation of Hong Kong dollar notes in south China, importers easily covered the cost of their imports by selling them for Hong Kong currency in the Chinese market. The purchase of foreign exchange from the Central Bank therefore became unnecessary.

These peculiarities of south China made obsolete the old import-quota system designed primarily for the situation in Shanghai with a view to prevent undue drains on the foreign-exchange resources of the Central Bank. To meet these changing conditions, a revised foreign-exchange and trade-control system was instituted in the summer of 1949, after the transfer of the Nationalist government to Canton.

The foreign-exchange deposit certificate system. This certificate system, promulgated in June, 1949, represented the first major change in foreign-exchange administration after the occupation of Shanghai by the Communists. The system contained the following salient features:

1. The foreign exchange received for an export covered by a letter of credit or by authorization to purchase was surrendered to the Central Bank in exchange for an exchange-deposit certificate (in duplicate) with a value equivalent to 80 percent of the exchange proceeds surrendered.

2. The original of the certificate could be used for withdrawing foreign exchange from the Central Bank either for financing imports or for any other purpose at the discretion of the holder. The duplicate of the certificate, which represented an import license, could be

sold to any importer in the market if the holder himself did not wish to import.

3. For an export on a consignment basis, the exporter was required to make a margin deposit equivalent to 20 percent of the prospective foreign-exchange receipt with the Central Bank or its appointed agent in order to obtain the export certificate authorizing the release of the export by the Chinese Maritime Customs. If the exporter failed within a specified period (i.e., thirty days for exports to Hong Kong and Macao, sixty days for export to southeast Asia and the Philippines, and ninety days for export to all other countries) to surrender the full amount of exchange proceeds on the consignment, the 20 percent margin deposit was unconditionally forfeited.

4. The old import-quota system was abolished. With the exception of commodities included in the list of prohibited imports, all others were imported without restriction so long as the importer held an import license (i.e., the duplicate of the exchange-deposit certificate) with a value equivalent to that of the import.

The new system provided an indirect link by which the aggregate import into China was limited to only 80 percent of the value of the exports; thereby a margin of 20 percent of the foreign-exchange proceeds derived from exports was left to meet government or other noncommercial requirements. To utilize his exports proceeds, an exporter had two alternatives: He could surrender a margin deposit of 20 percent to the Central Bank and keep the other 80 percent for his own disposition; or he could surrender all his export proceeds, and then recover 80 percent of those proceeds by immediately cashing the original of the exchange-deposit certificate. In addition, he also received a license authorizing imports equivalent to 80 percent of the value of the proceeds originally surrendered as a compensation for his 20 percent contribution to the Central Bank, for which he received no other *quid pro quo*. If the license was sold for, say, 10 percent of the value of its authorized imports, the net cost of the exports reduced from 20 to 10 percent.

The margin deposit of 20 percent was in fact a tax on exports from China. It was different, however, from ordinary export duty in that it was payable in foreign currency to the Central Bank rather than in Chinese currency collectible by Chinese customs, as would be the case of a customs duty.

The four-month experience in operation revealed that exporters generally preferred to surrender the margin deposit in exchange for the privilege of holding the balance of the exchange receipts derived from their trade. Hundred percent deposits were occasionally made in order to obtain the license needed for importing into China. In such cases, withdrawals up to 80 percent of the original deposit were usually made as soon as the certificate was issued. There was therefore no possibility for the Central Bank to borrow foreign currencies from the market, as it had originally expected, under the certificate mechanism.

Since the new foreign-exchange system required merely an outright surrender to the Central Bank of 20 percent of the exchange proceeds, the problem of providing the necessary local currency by the Bank for the purchase of exchange proceeds was thereby solved. After the breakdown of gold yuan, the lack of local-currency funds for purchasing foreign exchanges became a major problem of the Central Bank. In south China smuggling was rampant. Smuggling rings were openly organized, and usually enabled traders to evade both the duties on imports and the 20 percent levy on the foreign-exchange receipts derived from export. Since the usual charges by smuggling agencies amounted to only about 10 percent, the 20 percent levy put the new foreign-exchange system in an impossible position to compete with the smuggling trade.

At the beginning of September, 1949, revisions in the foreign-exchange regulations were made. The percentage of the margin deposit was reduced from 20 to 10 percent. Commodities other than those included in the prohibited list could be imported even without an importer's license. An import license up to 90 percent of the value of the export could be issued without the surrender of an equivalent amount of foreign exchange and the issuance would be made only upon the request of merchant.[25]

Except for two weeks in June, there was an apparent tendency for the exchange yield from margin deposits to remain constant, whether the levy was 10 percent or 20 percent (see Table 4.3). For most of the weeks listed in the table, the collection amounted to about H.K. $200,000. Thus, although the reduction in the percentage of levy resulted in doubling the amount of export routed through the official channel, the change failed to increase the

TABLE 4.3. STATISTICS OF MARGIN DEPOSITS COLLECTED BY THE CENTRAL BANK IN CANTON, 1949

	20 PERCENT SYSTEM			10 PERCENT SYSTEM		
Week ending	*U.S. dollars*	*Hong Kong dollars*	*Total*[a]	*U.S. dollars*	*Hong Kong dollars*	*Total*[a]
June 18	8,535.64	448,725.50	499,939.34			
25	138.00	981,324.12	982,152.12			
July 2	1,029.85	276,215.27	282,394.37			
9		205,913.25	205,139.25			
16		219,274.80	219,274.80			
23	172.81	192,545.51	193,582.37			
30	432.01	201,589.76	204,181.82			
Aug. 6		474,526.48	474,526.48			
13		267,570.12	267,570.12			
20	22,171.60	119,035.48	252,065.08			
27		120,448.44	120,448.44			
Sept. 2		45,033.86	48,033.86			
10				579.78 (2,334.43)[b]	336,065.41	350,072.01
17				1,984.23 (10,654.14)[b]	72,329.84	134,454.67
24				623.23 (19,671.81)[b]	55,827.20	173,858.05
Oct. 1				7,992.43 (10,888.42)[b]	198,350.51	263,681.01
Total	32,479.91	3,555,202.59	3,750,082.05	11,179.67 (43,548.80)[b]	662,572.96	992,065.74

[a] In Hong Kong Dollars.
[b] Figures include collections received by the Chungking office of the Central Bank of China.
There are no data for spaces left blank in table.
Source: Unpublished records of the Central Bank of China.

collection in foreign exchange by the Central Bank. This system was automatically abandoned when Canton was taken over by the Communist government.

SUMMARY

It is obvious, however, from the discussions in this chapter that China's exchange and trade policies during the inflation represented a gradual evolution from a policy of pegged exchange rate to one of flexible exchange and from no direct control to a full-fledged system of trade and exchange controls. But even in 1949, controls over capital transactions were almost nonexistent, while other trade and exchange controls were by no means perfect.

Despite the convincing evidences supporting the use of the flexible rate under the unstable conditions of inflation, the progress of the Chinese policy toward that direction was slow and sometimes halting. On several occasions (such as 1946 and August, 1948), the Chinese government even reverted to the policies which were apparently less rational than those they replaced. On other occasions, the administration of a rational policy was hamstrung by political considerations. The Nationalist government put too much emphasis on the foreign-exchange operations as an antidote against inflation and ignored the importance of fiscal and other reforms.

The experience seems to indicate that, unless the basic problems of inflation are solved, any attempt to peg external value of a depreciating currency at a specified level is doomed to fail. Before the inflation is under control, the best policy to follow (particularly in the case of an underdeveloped country) is to regulate imports and nontrade payments but leave the exchange rate unpegged. In other words, I advocate a system of controlled trade and payments with the exchange rate left free. This arrangement, I believe, minimizes the drain on a nation's foreign-exchange resources. It may at the same time avoid many of the complications arising from the disequilibrium between the external and internal values of a depreciating currency. This conclusion shows clearly the absurdity of the attempt on the part of the Chinese government in early years of inflation to peg the exchange rate without effectively controlling the trade and payments.

CHAPTER V

Trade, Payment, and Foreign Aid: Inflationary Pressures in the International Sector

The discussion in this chapter falls into three parts. The first examines how the financial policies of the Nationalist government affected the trade and payments which were normally the components of China's international account. The second part considers the contribution of American aid programs in relieving the inflationary pressures on the foreign sector of the Chinese economy. The third consists of observations from the discussions in this chapter.

CONSEQUENCES OF THE TRADE AND FOREIGN-EXCHANGE POLICIES

The overvaluation of the Chinese currency

During most of the years under inflation the Chinese currency was overvalued in terms of price parity (see Charts 5.1a–5.1c). This overvaluation was particularly obvious in the official rate of exchange as quoted by the Central Bank. This trend was true of the postwar years (1946–49) when the official rate was subject to frequent adjustment, as well as the war years (1942–45) when the rate was pegged at twenty yuan to one dollar. Moreover, the availability of cheap foreign exchange at the Central Bank resulted in holding the market rate below the parity derived from the changes in Chinese prices in relation to those of the United States. From September, 1940, to March, 1948, as charts show, the market rate was mostly lower than the price parity. The opposite, however, was generally true in the months prior to September, 1940, and months after March, 1948.

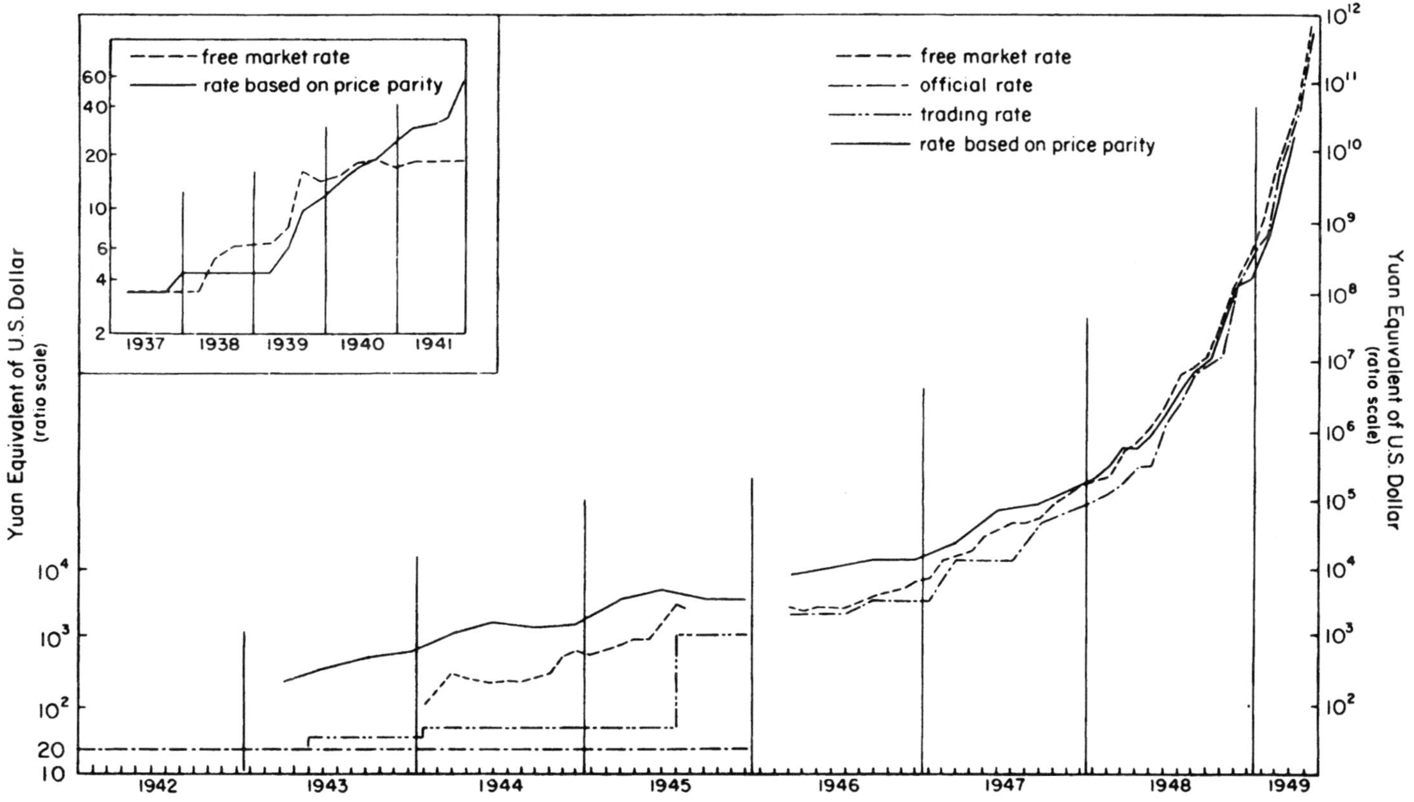

CHART 5.1. FOREIGN EXCHANGE RATES OF YUAN, 1937–49

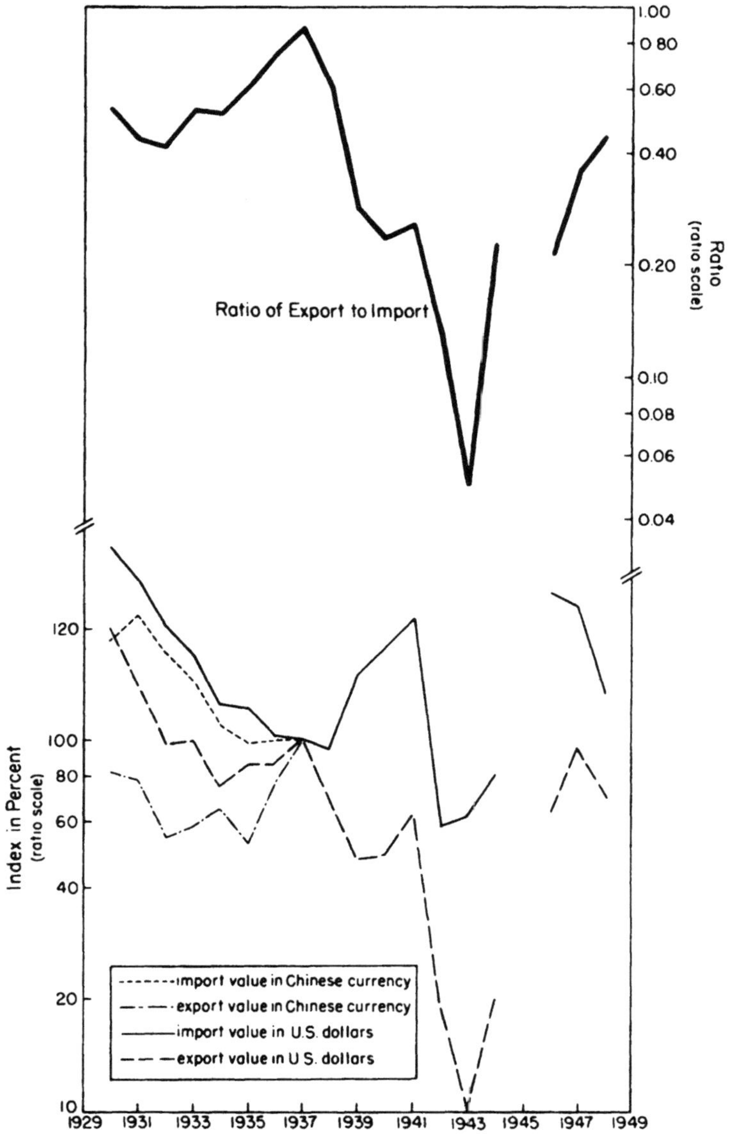

CHART 5.2. INDEX AND RATIO OF CHINA'S EXPORT AND IMPORT, 1930–49

The indices use 1937 as the base year. They are compiled on the basis of the amounts in both Chinese currency and U.S. dollars for the prewar years. For the postwar years, the instability in value seriously limits the value of the statistics expressed in Chinese currency, and therefore only the indices based on the trade values of U.S. dollars are used.

Adverse effects on the trade balance

The ratio of the export index to the import index, given in Chart 5.2, shows that the trade deficit (a standing feature before 1937) increased substantially during the inflation. The deficit came from the discrepancy between expanding imports and dwindling exports. For most of the years under inflation, the volume of imports, shown in the lower portion of Chart 5.2, was unusually large as compared with the 1937 volume. This was particularly true in 1939–41 and 1946–47. On the other hand, the volume of exports lagged far behind the 1937 level, and declined almost uninterruptedly during 1937–41. Even the spurt after the war failed to regain all the ground lost.

To explain these adverse developments in China's trade account, it will be necessary to examine briefly the elasticities of the nation's imports and exports and the behavior of the terms of trade under inflation.

Elasticities of imports and exports. Imports to China consisted mainly of supplies essential to the maintenance of the populace and the industries in her metropolitan areas. Cereals, raw cotton, petroleum, and petroleum products usually led the import list. While China's total demand for these products was inelastic, her demand for imports varied substantially in accordance with (among other factors) the availability of indigenous supplies and the cost of imports compared with that of domestic purchases.[1] On the other hand, because China's demands in the world market were relatively insignificant, the elasticities of supply were generally high.

The bulk of China's exports consisted of a few agricultural products and mineral ores, of which the production was not readily adjustable. Most of these products went for export with little or none for the domestic market. In terms of the world market, however, Chinese supplies were mostly insignificant. An inevitable consequence of these conditions was a highly elastic foreign demand for Chinese exports and a highly inelastic supply of these products in China. Thus a slight change in the quality or price of China's exports resulted in a substantial change in the foreign demand for these products, but not necessarily in their supply.

These features of China's exports and imports, which had at least in part been responsible for her chronic trade deficit, assumed new dimensions during the inflation. The shortage in domestic supplies and the overvaluation of the Chinese currency made it both necessary and economical to import rather than to purchase in the domestic market many of the supplies essential to the maintenance of the nation's metropolitan economy. The sudden spurt of imports during 1939–41 and 1946–47 particularly exemplified this situation. On the other hand, the inflation and the exaggeration of the external value of the Chinese currency contributed to a substantial reduction in the flow of export products from their producing areas in interior China to her metropolitan areas for shipment to foreign countries.

Terms of trade. In the statistical studies that follow, three terms of trade are considered. They are the net barter terms, the gross barter terms, and the income terms. The net terms of trade are the ratio of the price index of exports to the corresponding price index of imports. They measure primarily the gain or loss in international trade resulting from relative changes in the prices of imports and exports. A fall (or rise) in the value of the net terms shows that imports become higher (or cheaper) in relation to exports, and that the terms of trade therefore become unfavorable (or favorable) for the country. The net terms of trade, however, indicate nothing of the changes in the balance of payments. To make up in part for this deficiency, the gross barter terms are used. Represented by the ratio of the quantum index of exports to the quantum index of imports, the gross terms compare the *total money value* of exports with the *total money value* of imports after allowing for the changes in both factors caused by changes in the price index. A rise (or fall) in the value of the gross terms shows that more (or less) exports are being exchanged for a given value of imports, and indicates a development unfavorable (or favorable) to the nation's trade. The income terms of trade are obtained by dividing the import price index into the export value index. The function of the income terms is to measure the changes in a nation's capacity to import, or the quantity of imports obtainable from her export income. An improvement in the net terms, if accompanied by a large decline in the physical volume of exports, may leave a country worse off rather than better off in her command over imports. The income terms are designed to overcome the deficiency of the net barter terms of trade. A rise (or fall) in the income terms indicates increase (or decrease) in the nation's ability to purchase from abroad.[3]

The behavior of the three terms of trade for the periods 1937–41 and 1946–48 are shown in Chart 5.3, from which the following facts appear:

First, during 1937–41, the gross terms invariably showed an upward trend, indicating a trade situation unfavorable to China.

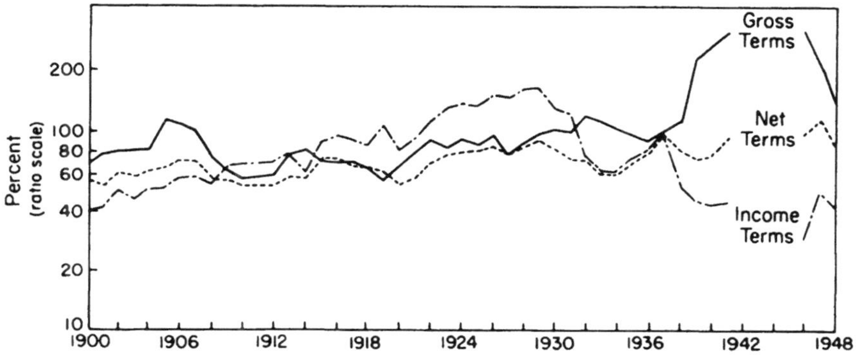

CHART 5.3. CHINA'S GROSS, NET AND INCOME TERMS OF TRADE, 1900–48 (in percentage)

The so-called "ideal formula" was used in compiling the price and quantum indices for the years prior to 1930, and 1913 was the base year. The price indices for the post-1936 years were obtained by dividing the relevant quantum indices into the value indices—a method which has been commonly used in compiling the price index. For the convenience of comparing the data of various periods obtained from different sources (see below), adjustments were made by equating the last index of the series for 1900–30, with the first index of the relevant series for 1930–36, the last index number of the second series with first index number of the relevant series for 1936–41, and so forth.

Source: The price and quantum indices for the years prior to 1930, Franklin L. Ho, *Index Number of the Quantities and Prices of Imports and Exports of the Barter Terms of Trade in China, 1867–1928* (Tientsin, 1930); for 1930–36, United Nations, *Statistical Yearbook, 1950* (New York, 1951). The value indices for 1930-48 and the quantum indices for 1936–41 and 1946–48 were compiled by myself.

The income terms, reflecting China's capacity to purchase from abroad, declined. During 1938–40, one factor which accounted for these unfavorable developments was the deterioration of the net barter terms of trade, which indicates a rise of import prices in relation to those of exports. This downward trend of the net terms reversed in 1940–41, when export prices rose in relation to import prices as a result of the war in Europe. The resulting improvement in the net terms, however, was not sufficient to reverse the downward trend of the income terms, although it did slow down the rate of decline of the latter.

Second, during the postwar years, the situation substantially changed. Instead of showing a rising trend, the gross terms continuously declined, indicating trade conditions favorable to China. As for the net and income terms of trade, favorable conditions reflected by a rising trend are observable only in the comparison between 1946 and 1947, but not in 1948, when that trend declined. This discrepancy among the movements of the gross, net, and income terms can probably be accounted for by those imports financed by foreign-aid programs, for these programs induced the expansion of the physical volume of imports to China even though the net and income terms turned against her.

Third, on the whole, the income terms were invariably much lower during both the periods of 1937–41 and 1946–48 than before 1937. This is a clear indication of China's dwindling capacity to import during the inflation, resulting from either an increase in the gross terms or a decrease in the net terms, or from both.

Decrease in overseas remittances

According to the latest estimate, there are about twelve million Chinese residing in various parts of the world outside mainland China and Taiwan, most of them in southeast Asia and many in North America.[3] It was traditional practice among those emigrants to remit part of their incomes to China to support their relatives and charitable institutions or to purchase land and houses. Real estate in their native city or village, where many such emigrants intended to spend their old age, was usually considered the most desirable investment for savings.

Until the Communist dominance of mainland China in 1950, there were two main channels through which these remittances were normally routed: the modern banks and the open market. The business derived from such remittances was shared by those two channels in accordance with the terms and services each was able to offer. The most important of these, of course, were the exchange rate and the promptness of transmission. Since many such remittances were destined for the interior villages of the Kwangtung and Fukien provinces, where most of China's emigrants came from, it was necessary for banks providing such remittance services (such as the Bank of China and the Overseas Chinese Banking Corporation of Singapore) to cooperate with the post offices in China to deliver remittance to interior villages where the volume of business did not warrant the establishment of a separate branch bank.

The nucleus of the open market consisted of money shops, which, though incomparably smaller than modern banks in their operation, usually had the advantage of their specialization in remittances between designated points, as well as intimate personal relations with both remitters and remittees. Consequently, they often offered a speedier and more reliable service than the modern banks. Moreover, because of personal relations with the customer and because of loose administrative procedures, the money shops were often in a position to advance payments in China before the remittances were received from abroad—a concession usually not permissible in normal banking operations. The modern banks, on the other hand, usually excelled in serving remittances destined for cities where they had a branch office or a direct paying agent. Since their reliability was not predicated upon personal relationship, their commission charges were invariably lower than those of the money shops.

With the establishment of exchange controls in China after World War II, the choice between the services of the money shops and of the banks often was either to follow legal procedure, or to use illicit facilities to evade the restriction imposed by exchange regulations. Because of the exchange regulations, modern banks often were permitted to redeem remittances only at rates that unrealistically overvalued the Chinese currency. Under these circumstances, the use of illicit channels provided by money shops became a necessity if a desired remittance was to be effectively transmitted to China without incurring undue losses. This situation was particularly common in southeast Asia during the postwar years. It is estimated that during those years only 10 to 15 percent of the remittances from the Chinese emigrants went through official banking channels.

For remittances via the open market, Hong Kong played an important role in serving as an intermediary for redirecting such remittances, since many went first to Hong Kong and from there to China. This unusual position of Hong Kong stemmed from the following factors: first, the stability of the Hong Kong currency made it widely acceptable for circulation in the southern provinces of China to which most of the remittances were destined. Thus remittances to China were often in the Hong Kong dollar rather than in the depreciating Chinese currency. Second, the value of the Hong Kong dollar was widely known even in remote villages in the Kwantung and Fukien provinces, where the quotations of other foreign currencies were not as readily available. Consequently, it

TABLE 5.1. INWARD REMITTANCES THROUGH OFFICIAL CHANNELS TO CHINA (U.S. $ thousand)

	1940		*1941*		*1946*	
Country of origin	*Value*	*Percent*	*Value*	*Percent*	*Value*	*Percent*
United Kingdom	4,447.6	16.41	3,387.8	20.11	5,192.7	34.00
Hong Kong	304.0	1.12	608.6	3.61		
Malaya	12,528.2	46.23	5,512.6	32.72	4,694.3	30.74
Burma	198.0	.73	417.2	2.48	753.9	4.94
Philippines	1,607.0	5.93	1,990.5	11.81		
Indonesia	3,511.4	12.96	597.1	3.54		
Thailand	619.1	2.28	1,179.9	7.00		
United States	3,886.0	14.34	3,154.0	18.72	4,631.5	30.33
Total	27,101.3	100.00	16,847.7	100.00	15,272.4	100.00

The original figures were given in different foreign currencies. They were converted into U.S. dollars on the basis of the relevant foreign-exchange rates given in *International Financial Statistics* and *Federal Reserve Bulletin.*

The percentage figures may not add up to totals because of rounding.

There are no data for spaces left blank in table.

Source: *Chung-hua min-kuo t'ung-chi nien-chien* (The Statistical Year Book of the Republic of China) (Nanking, 1948), p. 434.

would have been administratively difficult to redeem remittances in foreign currencies other than the Hong Kong dollar. For this reason, even remittances from southeast Asian countries through official banking channels were often in the Hong Kong dollar. Third, during most of the Chinese inflation, the remittances from Hong Kong to China were not restricted in Hong Kong and could be effected with great convenience and promptness. It was common, therefore, as a hedge against the inflation in China, for residents in south China to keep their proceeds from remittances in Hong Kong until the money was needed.

Before 1937 emigrants' remittances to China amounted to the approximate equivalent of 100–130 million U.S. dollars, most of which was from southeast Asia.[4] Although the Chinese population living abroad and their wealth have expanded appreciably since the war there were many factors which restricted remittances to China during the postwar years. First, there was an increasing tendency among the overseas Chinese (especially in southeast Asia) to settle permanently in foreign countries instead of returning to China for retirement, as they had done before the war. This inclination naturally discouraged them from remitting savings to China towards their old age. Second, exchange regulations restricted the outflow of funds to foreign lands after World War II and became increasingly common in southeast Asia. Before the war, for instance, remittances from Malaya to China had no limitations. Since the war family remittances to China from that country have been limited to forty-five Malayan dollars (equivalent to about fifteen U.S. dollars) a month for each person.

Excessive drains on the official reserves

Discussions in this section are based on the statistics compiled by the writer during his association with the Central Bank of China after World War II (see Table 5.2). In order to avoid the unfavorable repercussions on the market which information on the losses of monetary reserves might cause, publication of the statistics relating to the amount, the composition, and the changes of the official exchange and specie reserves was suspended after 1937. From then on such information was considered top secret, available only to a few persons in the Chinese government and occasionally to the U.S. government for planning foreign-aid programs. The official reserves referred to in the present discussion are confined only to the foreign exchange and specie holdings of the Central Bank. They do not include the holdings of other government banks and government agencies (such as the National Resources Commission, etc.), which also held foreign exchange for their business operations; for these holdings were not considered a part of the currency reserve, as were the holdings of the Central Bank.

On the basis of the financial and political history of China, and for the purpose of studying the vagaries of the official reserves, the period under consideration is divided into the following stages: 1935–39, 1939–41, 1942–45, and 1946–49.

Although little information concerning conditions before 1937 is available, the following points may be noted.

1. Before November, 1935, neither trade restrictions nor foreign-exchange control existed in China. The Central Bank of China, then relatively uninfluential, was more important as a government treasurer than as a controller of the money market. The foreign exchange rate fluctuated according to market conditions. Private banks and other nonbanking interests imported and exported silver and gold whenever the need arose. Under these circumstances, the official foreign-exchange reserve was not likely to be a substantial one.

2. After the adoption of the managed currency system, silver coins were withdrawn from circulation and gold and silver nationalized. In order to peg the external value of the new paper currency at a stipulated level, the Central Bank of China purchased and sold foreign exchange without limitation at fixed buying and selling rates. The operation was financed primarily by a foreign-exchange reserve created by selling in London and New York the silver withdrawn from the Chinese circulation. According to the statistics published by the Chinese customs, China exported during 1936–39 about U.S. $243.3 million worth of silver and gold, virtually all going to London and New York.[5] Since specie exports from China became a government monopoly after November, 1935, the above export may therefore be considered a rough approximation of the total government shipment.

3. There are no records of how heavy the drain was on official reserve during the period 1935–37, when the external value of the Chinese currency was successfully pegged within the narrow limits stipulated by the buying and selling rates of the Central Bank. The stability attained during those years might partly be attributed to improvements in China's trade balance. But it is also a fact that during this period there were heavy government expenditures in foreign currencies on the military supplies and equipment necessary to defend the nation against a possible Japanese invasion. A large portion of such purchases are not shown in the Chinese customs returns on which the trade statistics are based. Moreover, the trade balance, despite improvement, was still in deficit. For these reasons

the drain on the government's foreign-exchange reserve during these years could have been substantial.

4. After the withdrawal of its policy of unlimited sales of foreign exchange in March, 1938, and before the institution of the Sino-British Stabilization Fund in the following March, the Central Bank allotted about £4.6 million (or U.S. $18.4 million) of foreign exchange. Most of this amount was allotted during March, April, and May, 1938. Toward the end of the year, the official allotments were reduced to virtually nil. In the light of the foreign-exchange policy of the Chinese government during those years, it is reasonably certain that the reserve of the Central Bank could not have been high during the months before the Sino-British Stabilization Fund came into operation for otherwise the government would never have let its currency depreciate as it did.

During 1935–39 at least U.S. $243 million of the official holdings must have been lost. This estimate includes both the losses due to maintenance of the market and those due to the government's purchases of military supplies from abroad.

The history of China's official exchange reserve in the second stage (1939–41) may be very well represented by the operations of the Sino-British Stabilization Fund and the Sino-American-British Board established in March, 1939, and April, 1941. The first stabilization fund, as has been pointed out in Chapter IV had an initial resource of £10 million, or about U.S. $49 million at the dollar-sterling cross-rate then prevailing. Most of those funds dissipated during the first three months of the Fund's operation. The total resources of the Sino-American-British Board were about U.S. $90 million. The Board suspended active operations in December, 1941, as a result of the Pearl Harbor attack. An unpublished official report of the Board showed that until then an equivalent of about U.S. $28.5 million of the Board's total resources had been used. The combined two sums had a total of about U.S. $77.5 million in losses in official reserves during the stage from 1939–41. These losses, like that of the previous period, fell far short of trade requirements. During these three years, the trade deficit amounted to about U.S. $1,000 million, and was particularly sizable because of the large imports needed for the maintenance of production and economic order in the foreign concessions in Shanghai and Tientsin.

Despite the liberal amount of foreign exchange supplied by these stabilization funds, it was the market, not the official reserves, which primarily financed the expanding imports. The government policy did contribute, however, to maintaining the external value of the Chinese currency and thereby encouraged the influx of imports.

The stage 1942–45 was the most encouraging one during the whole span under consideration. The Japanese occupation of the foreign concessions in Shanghai caused the painful drains on the exchange reserve to disappear; and the large expenditures by United States military and civilian personnel in China made possible a rapid accumulation of a dollar balance. According to the report of the U.S. Treasury Department, China's net short-term assets in the United States, which amounted to U.S. $133.3 million at the end of 1941, rose to U.S. $349.8 million at the end of 1942, U.S. $572.5 million at the end of 1943, and U.S. $582 million at the end of 1945.[6] During this stage, therefore, China's official dollar holdings increased by about U.S. $449 million. Prior to the American participation in the Stabilization Board in 1941, the Chinese currency was more closely linked to the pound sterling than to the U.S. dollar. Accordingly, a large part of China's foreign-exchange reserve in the prewar years was in British currency. After 1941 the dollar superseded the sterling as the leading currency in the Chinese reserve, and constituted virtually the entire reserve of the Chinese government.

In 1946 there was a net loss of U.S. $443.6 million in total reserves, including a loss of U.S. $338 million in the dollar reserve, U.S. $89 million in gold, and U.S. $16.7 million in sterling currencies (see Table 5.2). In 1947 the total loss was reduced to U.S. $227.2 million which included a loss of U.S. $160.8 million in the dollar reserve, U.S. $24.2 million in gold, U.S. $28.8 million in sterling currencies, and U.S. $13.5 million in silver. This reduction of the official reserve in 1947 was made possible by the following factors: the pursuit of a more stringent foreign exchange and foreign trade policy than that of 1946 after the installation of the import quota system; and the suspension of gold sales by the Central Bank at the beginning of the year. In fact, as a result of the drastic depreciation of the external value of the Chinese currency and the proclamation of the "emergency laws" in February of that year, there was a repatriation of gold and foreign-currency notes from the market to the Central Bank for a brief period.

The year 1948 was by far the most eventful of the postwar years for the history of China's official exchange reserve. During the first four months of that year, the sterling liabilities of the Central Bank exceeded its sterling assets. By the end of April, even the dollar balance, which had been the mainstay of China's exchange reserve, became negative. Except for the specie holdings, which had been kept stable in the neighborhood of U.S. $126 million during the early months of the year and which had been intended primarily for deflationary operations in the domestic market, the reserves of the Central Bank were entirely exhausted. During May to August, due to the successful operation of the foreign-exchange certificate system, the exchange market for commercial transactions became virtually self-sustaining, although a large part of the government requirements was left uncovered. Then came the monetary reform in August, which forced the sale of private holdings in foreign assets to the Central Bank and resulted in a large inflow of gold and foreign currency into the coffers of the Bank. The Bank's balance at the end of October, 1948, was U.S. $197.6 million, which registered an increase of U.S. $160 million over the balance for August. This change resulted from an increase of U.S. $106 million in the Bank's dollar holding, of U.S. $41 million in the amount of its gold holding, of U.S. $12.3 million in the reserve of sterling currencies, and of U.S. $0.7 million in silver.

From the beginning of November, 1948, through March, 1949, when the Nationalists withdrew from the Shanghai area, the reinstitution of the exchange certificate system and the bearishness of the market caused by the uncertainty of the political situation reduced imports into China. There was no drain on the official reserves during these months as far as the nongovernment transactions were concerned. Government spendings in foreign currencies and the gold operations of the Central Bank however reduced the reserve of the Bank by U.S. $96.6 million.

Although detailed statistics for the Bank's reserve are not available, certain general developments in the months after March, 1949, are known.

TABLE 5.2. SPECIE AND FOREIGN-EXCHANGE HOLDINGS OF THE CENTRAL BANK OF CHINA, 1945–48 (FIGURES IN MILLION)

End of month	*U.S. dollar equivalent of gold*[a] 1	*U.S. dollar equivalent of silver*[b] 2	*U.S. dollars* 3
1945			
Dec.	198.9	43.5	571.4
1946			
Jan.	198.9	43.5	559.0
Feb.	198.9	43.5	546.5
March	197.5	43.5	547.5
April	196.2	43.5	508.0
May	191.7	43.5	490.3
June	184.9	43.5	445.5
July	180.4	43.5	407.1
Aug.	169.1	43.5	356.9
Sept.	162.7	43.5	324.2
Oct.	155.6	43.5	272.6
Nov.	136.0	43.5	244.8
Dec.	110.0	43.5	233.4
1947			
Jan.	88.0	33.8	213.0
Feb.	83.0	33.8	198.7
March	83.1	33.2	216.5
April	84.3	33.4	225.4
May	85.6	31.6	190.6
June	85.7	29.4	177.3
July	85.9	27.1	154.1
Aug.	85.8	27.1	132.5
Sept.	85.8	31.2	122.2
Oct.	85.8	30.0	100.7
Nov.	85.8	30.0	92.5
Dec.	85.8	30.0	72.7
1948			
Jan.	85.8	30.0	50.5
Feb.	96.5	30.0	19.0
March	96.5	30.0	11.7
April	96.6	29.3	−5.9
May[d]	96.6	29.3	−10.0
Aug.	103.6	29.0	−87.7
Sept.	141.2	29.6	−52.8
Oct.	144.6	29.7	18.3
Nov.	142.8	29.0	12.2
Dec.	120.7	29.0	1.3
1949			
Jan.	126.0	29.0	−11.3
Feb.	139.7	29.0	−29.6
March	134.8	24.3	−50.9

The amounts listed represent the net balance after allowing for liabilities due. Negative values indicate an excess of liabilities over assets.

[a] Conversion of gold into dollars is made on the basis of $35 per ounce.

[b] Conversion of silver into dollars is made on the following exchange rates:

Date	*U.S. cents per ounce*	*Date*	*U.S. cents per ounce*
Dec. 1945–Dec. 1946	90	June 1947	65
Jan. 1947–March 1947	70	July 1947–Aug. 1947	60
April 1947	74	After Aug. 1947	70
May 1947	70		

TABLE 5.2 (continued)

Pounds sterling[c] 4	Hong Kong dollars[c] 5	Indian rupees[c] 6	U.S. dollar equivalent of the holdings in sterling currencies (4, 5, and 6) 7	U.S. dollar equivalent of total holdings (1, 2, 3, and 7) 8
9.6	21.3	2.0	44.3	858.1
9.4	21.0	1.8	43.2	844.6
9.8	20.7	1.2	44.6	833.6
10.2	16.4	2.1	45.4	821.5
10.9	16.1	1.8	48.2	795.8
9.6	15.5	1.9	43.0	768.4
10.8	15.3	.9	47.4	721.3
9.2	14.8	.03	40.4	671.4
8.9	14.7	.02	39.3	608.7
8.7	14.8	1.0	38.7	568.4
6.5	19.3	−.4	31.0	502.5
5.2	18.4	3.9	26.7	451.0
5.2	26.2	1.4	27.5	414.4
5.4	20.1	2.0	27.0	361.9
6.1	16.8	1.7	29.2	344.7
10.1	47.5	1.7	52.7	385.5
10.2	17.8	1.6	45.6	388.8
10.1	40.0	1.4	50.8	358.6
5.5	48.0	1.2	34.3	326.6
5.5	31.7	3.3	31.2	298.2
2.3	29.5	3.2	17.8	263.1
1.8	21.0	1.1	12.7	251.9
1.8	29.4	1.2	15.0	231.6
1.3	2.8	5.8	7.4	215.7
−1.1	16.2	−2.5	−1.3	187.2
−2.7	6.0	−2.2	−9.9	156.3
−3.2	−2.8	−1.9	−14.0	131.5
−4.0	−1.1	−2.3	−15.4	122.4
−4.0	−6.2	1.2	−17.2	103.6
−3.7	−10.9	.6	−17.4	98.4
−5.7	−2.7	.1	−8.3	36.6
−6.4	3.4	1.5	−1.5	116.4
−5.2	6.5	2.7	4.0	197.6
−13.1	−.3	4.5	−8.9	175.0
−12.0		3.6	−8.4	142.5
−8.0	−.1	2.7	−8.1	138.2
−7.3	2.4	4.1	−.8	138.2
−7.6	3.9	−3.4	−7.1	101.1

[c]Conversion of sterling currencies into dollars is made on the basis of the following exchange rates:

U.S. $4 = £1 (Dec. 1945 – Dec. 1948) 1s. 3d. = 1 Hong Kong dollar
U.S. $3 = £1 (After Jan. 1949) 1s. 6d. = 1 Indian rupee

[d] Based on data for May 15.

Source: Unpublished records of the Central Bank of China.

An unpublished record of the Central Bank shows the geographical distribution of the Bank's gold holdings as of February 4, 1949.

Locale	*Thousands of fine ounces*
Shanghai	242.7
Canton	211.4
Amoy	572.9
Taiwan	2,555.9
New York	343.7
Others	28.6
Total	3,955.2

Most of the holdings in Shanghai and New York were used up during March, April, and May, 1949, for gold operations in the Shanghai market. Virtually all the holdings in Canton and Amoy were used for meeting urgent government expenditures after the Nationalist's evacuation to Canton. During that period, specie and Hong Kong dollar notes were used even for domestic paymets of the government because of the total rejection of the gold yuan notes by the public. The balance of the gold reserves left in mainland China was later seized by the Communist regime when it gained the control over the country. A large part of the holding in Taiwan was transferred from Shanghai in early 1949 under the instruction of President Chiang. In fact, when the Nationalist government retreated from the mainland to Taiwan, the gold holdings stored in the island were the only asset left in the government reserve.

The silver holdings amounting to U.S. $24.3 million at the end of March, were later used for coining silver dollars, which were used for circulation in China after July, 1949. The silver coins were then used primarily for military payments when the paper money issued by the Central Bank was no longer accepted in market.

Despite the negative balances shown in Table 5.2, the U.S. dollar notes and the sterling currencies left in vaults of the Central Bank at the end of March, 1949, were spent to meet government expenditures, both in China and abroad, incurred during the interim months between the collapse of the gold yuan in May, 1949, and the issuance of the silver yuan in July of the same year. During these months, gold and Hong Kong dollar notes, which constituted the bulk of China's holdings in sterling currencies, became the most important means for meeting government's domestic expenditures.

AMERICAN AID AND THE CHINESE INFLATION

During these years of inflation, China received from the United States a total of $2,422.4 million in grants and $1,101.0 in credits, which gave a total of more than $3.5 billion.[7] The total note circulation in China was estimated at about $400 million in the middle of 1937, and at $2.6 million at the end of April, 1948.[8] Since government deficits and excess note issues were the primary causes of the Chinese inflation, why did not American aid, which amounted to much more than the total note circulation in China, halt the inflation? To answer this question, it is necessary to separate these credits and grants into the following categories:

Loans raised and repaid from 1937 to 1949. The Chinese government received and repaid these loans during the inflation. Their contribution toward halting the inflation, therefore, was at best only limited.

Military aid. Its direct contribution as an anti-inflationary measure was rather limited, despite its importance to China's national defense. Had there been no such military aid, the drain on the resources of the Chinese government and the concomitant increased inflationary pressure on the economy would have been much worse. On the other hand, many military procurements financed by this aid would probably never have been obtained had that aid not been available.

Foreign aid in financing capital investments. While capital investments might have contributed to China's economic stabilization in the long run, these usually had little or no anti-inflationary effect.

Credits financing the purchase of United States surplus properties in the Pacific and the Far East. This aid was different from outright grants or credits because most of the surplus properties thus purchased by the Chinese government were either appropriated for military use or sold in the open market at unduly low prices. Besides, a large portion of those properties were actually resold in bulk at a loss or merely wasted because of improper or inefficient management. To this extent the foreign aid used to finance the purchase of surplus properties failed to produce anti-inflationary effects as an outright aid might have done.

The UNRRA and BOTRA programs.[9] The primary objectives of these programs were relief and rehabilitation. As carried out in China, these programs had little effect in combating inflation.

Foreign aid designed primarily for economic stabilization. To this category belong the United States Treasury Credit of 1942, the China Relief Program of 1947, and ECA (Economic Cooperation Administration) Program of 1948. While none of these aids represented an all-out effort to halt the monetary inflation, economic stabilization was their chief concern.

The present discussion is primarily directed to the aid programs grouped under the last two categories.

United States Treasury Credit of 1942

Among all the forms of foreign aid, the Treasury Credit of 1942, amounting to U.S. $500 million, had the most immediate bearing on the anti-inflationary policies of the Chinese Government.[10] The credit was used as follows:

Distribution	*U.S. $ million*
Gold purchase	220
Redemption of dollar bonds and certificates issued by the Chinese government	200
Printing of Chinese bank notes in the U.S.A.	55
Purchase of cotton and textile products	25
Total	500

The gold purchased was mainly for sales in China during 1946, after a small part of the shipment was paid out to the public in Free China to fulfill the forward contracts sold by the Chinese government banks in earlier years.[11] The textile purchase consisted mainly of raw cotton to supplement the cotton supply in the Shanghai area in 1946.

The UNRRA program

The following table shows in categories the assigned value of the over-all UNRRA supply program for China.[12]

Commodity	*Equivalent U.S. $ million*	*Percent*
Food	131.8	25.4
Clothing, textiles, and footwear	112.5	21.7
Medical and sanitation supplies	32.7	6.3
Agricultural rehabilitation	71.7	13.8
Industrial rehabilitation	169.1	32.8
Total	517.8	100.0

The United States contributed $474.0 million of this total.

According to the reports of the Chinese customs, the UNRRA supplies, arriving during 1946 and 1947, had the following breakdown:[13]

Commodity	*Percent in total UNRRA imports*
Raw cotton	22.3
Cereal (mostly rice, wheat, and wheat flour)	12.7
Fertilizers	11.3
Machinery and tools (including 3.8 percent for manufacturing cigars and cigarettes)	9.6
Explosives for industrial use	5.1
Chemicals and chemical compounds	1.3
Medicines, drugs, etc.	2.3
Timber	2.2
Vehicles and vessels	3.5
Ships and boats	*.6*
Motor tractors, trailers, trucks	*1.6*
Locomotives, railway carriages, etc.	*.2*
Others	*1.1*
Animal products, canned goods, and groceries	3.1
Metals and ores	4.9

The statistics in the customs reports, classified differently from the UNRRA report, are useful for providing details not given in the latter.

Cereal imports (particularly that of rice) constituted the major part of the food program. Virtually all the allotments listed under clothing, textiles, and footwear were used to purchase raw cotton from the United States. A large part of the fund for agricultural rehabilitation went for financing fertilizer imports. The program for industrial rehabilitation was designed as shown on next page.[14]

Beyond doubt, the UNRRA program was extremely important in rehabilitating postwar China. It supplied more than U.S. $100 million worth of supplies and services for railways, telecommunications, public utilities, and other industries. It also provided a host of welfare programs, which contributed substantially to relieving the hardships of the Chinese people during the postwar years. Plagued by inflation and by dwindling foreign-exchange reserves, China was hardly in a position to purchase the needed industrial supplies without the assistance of UNRRA. The rehabilitation of the communications system and the industries would have been delayed, and the economic conditions in the country would have been far worse.

Industry	*Percent*
Transportation and communications	45
Roads	*9*
Railways	*17*
Waterways	*17*
Telecommunications	*2*
Public utilities	6
Building industry	14
Coal mining	4
Machine tools	6
Petroleum, oil lubricants	3
Materials (chemical)	7
Industrial rehabilitation services	1
Others	14
Physical rehabilitation	*.1*
Surplus property commitments	*8.9*
China Air Transport	*1.0*
China Waterways Transport	*.5*
Hong Kong Operations (transhipment costs)	*3.5*
European Regional Office charges	*.1*

Since the UNRRA was the first of its kind, the program also had many important defects.

Originally the Chinese government was to make appropriations for local currency needs. When the local currency expenditures rose with the expansion of the UNRRA activities, the problem of obtaining funds became increasingly difficult to the mission in China. The estimated expenditures for implementing the UNRRA program were in the equivalent of about U.S. $190 million, of which $113 million were appropriations on the part of the Chinese government.[15] Apparently these sums were substantial in comparison with the total expenditures of the Chinese government, which amounted to U.S. $1,717.4 million in 1946 and U.S. $1,258.4 million in 1947 (see Table 2.4). Therefore, despite the generous appropriations of UNRRA, the program still resulted in a substantial drain on the already hard-pressed finances of the Chinese government. To assure effective operation, the program (as it was in the later phases of its operation) had to be self-sustaining both in dollars and in yuan.

In planning its program in China, the UNRRA failed to give consideration to its relations with the over-all economic conditions prevailing in the country. Postwar China was undoubtedly in need of large-scale relief and rehabilitation. Whether the nation was in a position to bear the cost of such an undertaking at the tempo planned by UNRRA without unduly straining its economy should also have been considered. In the opinion of this writer, many of the welfare and long-range development projects should have been slowed down and postponed if the inflationary effects of such expenditures on the economy were duly considered.

The UNRRA operations in China could have been substantially simplified had the established channels been used for distributing its supplies. Instead, for an operation scheduled to last about two years, UNRRA chose to set up a host of new enterprises as its own affiliates or subsidiaries, such as the National Highway Transport, the China Air Transport and the China Waterway Transport.[16] Later on there was even a tendency to make some of these enterprises (such as the China Aviation Transport and the China Waterway Transport) permanent organizations in China—an undertaking which should properly belong to a long-range development program rather than to one for relief and rehabilitation.

Compared with the experience of later United States aid programs, the system under which many of the UNRRA supplies were distributed in China was unsatisfactory. Most of the UNRRA foodstuffs (e.g., rice, wheat, and flour) were distributed through philanthropic agencies or among the employees of private and public offices. There was no organized distribution system with the coverage that a program of UNRRA's magnitude should have had. Because of this haphazard approach, pilferage and misuse of aid supplies resulted.[17] The UNRRA cotton program permitted the owners of textile mills to receive more than 800 pounds in return for a bale of yarn weighing 400 pounds. Later experience with ECA operations showed that an exchange ratio of about 600 pounds to one bale of yarn would have adequately provided both for the production costs and also for profit to the mills. Besides the favorable exchange ratio, the UNRRA operation also relieved the textile mills from such burdens as carrying their usual cotton stocks and marketing their products. Before these aid programs came into operation, it had been necessary for the mills to carry a cotton stock equivalent to from 2½ to 3 months' consumption at their own expense in order to ensure their continuous operation. Whether or not their products sold at a profit depended on market conditions and the mill's sales effort. Under the UNRRA and the ECA operations, both these problems were taken care of at no expense to the mills. This favorable treatment of the textile mills, together with the absence of an effective progressive taxation in China, made it possible for mill owners to accumulate large profits during the postwar years. The rapid expansion of the textile industries in Hong Kong during the late 1940s represented to a substantial extent the flight of the industrial earnings from China to the British colony because of the chaotic conditions on the mainland.

It is highly questionable if some UNRRA imports could have been utilized to benefit the Chinese populace. One example of this type of import was machinery for manufacturing cigars and cigarettes, which amounted to 3.8 percent of the value of the total UNRRA supplies received by China in 1946 and 1947. Another was the import of woolen products. They mainly included woolen clothing, blankets, and rugs. I believe that the UNRRA funds should have been much more efficiently employed to purchase cotton bedding and clothing in place of the woolen articles. Nor do I believe that the qualifications of some UNRRA experts sent to China were commensurate with what UNRRA paid for their services. Whenever substitutions could have been made with local recruits, it would have been more economical to use such personnel; but it seems to me that this was not the policy UNRRA followed.

The China Relief Program of 1947–48

This was a part of the Foreign Relief Program approved by the United States Congress in 1947. The main objective of this program was to provide China with some essential imports during the interim period between the end of the UNRRA program and the beginning in 1948 of the comprehensive United States program later known as the ECA Aid Program. Deliveries under this program during the first half of 1948 were as follows:[18]

Cereals	$35,412,900
Seeds	88,400
Insecticides	609,900
Medical supplies	5,185,300
Estimated shipping costs	5,084,500
Total	$46,381,000

The cereals shipped under the program were distributed under a specially established rationing system in five major cities (Shanghai,

Peiping, Tientsin, Canton, and Nanking) to ensure the populace in these metropolitan areas with an adequate supply of staple food (e.g., rice or wheat) at minimum cost. These relief supplies, however, covered only 40 percent of the food needed for rationing; the other 60 percent, according to the original plan, was to have been provided by the Chinese government, either by import or by procurement from domestic production.[19]

Most of the medical supplies and insecticides provided for under the China Relief Program did not arrive in China until the end of 1948, when the program was already integrated with that of the ECA of 1948. A large portion of the medical supplies was distributed without charge through hospitals and philanthropic institutions. Part of the pesticides was distributed free, and part sold through commercial channels.[20]

All local-currency proceeds from sales of relief supplies, beside meeting the administrative expenses of the program in China, were used for financing welfare, relief, conservation, and other projects in China. During its brief operation of less than a year, the United States mission in charge of the relief program undertook commitments for over 260 projects: about 55 percent were for public works, 43 percent for medical purposes, and 2 percent for miscellaneous projects.[21]

The China Relief Program made important contributions to the Chinese economy in helping institute the food rationing program in the major Chinese cities, and in providing relief and employment through its local-currency projects. As with many other aid programs, however, the primary objective was not to combat inflation.

Despite the nature of the relief program, I do not believe it justifiable for the relief mission during the brief months of its operation to have sponsored so many projects, of which many were traditional measures for combating deflation[22] rather than inflation. The multitude of project commitments, together with the fact that local-currency proceeds were often committed or spent before received, indicates clearly that the Relief Mission gave little or no consideration to the inflationary pressure of local-currency expenditures on the Chinese economy. It is therefore not difficult to understand why many projects were weeded out when the ECA Mission took over the program late in 1948.[23]

It should be noted that many of the American officials in charge of the China Relief Mission were former members of the UNRRA Mission in China. This was undoubtedly a main reason accounting for the similarity between the policies of these missions.

The ECA Program of 1948

As originally planned, this program was to have a total appropriation of $275 million with the following general breakdown:

	U.S. $ million
Commodity program	203.8
Program for rural reconstruction	2.5
Program of industrial replacement and reconstruction	67.5
Administrative expenses in Washington, D.C. and in China	1.2

As of March 11, 1949, about a month before Shanghai was occupied by the Chinese Communists, commodity procurements amounted to over $190 million which was distributed as follows:

	U.S. $ thousand
Rice	44,560
Wheat & wheat flour	20,617
Petroleum	46,000
Cotton	69,790
Fertilizer	9,202
Coal	286

Because of the uncertain military conditions in China, the industrial program was suspended in 1948 and its appropriation was made available for other ECA operations. The rural-reconstruction program was also hamstrung. In fact, it was not fully developed until the Nationalist government moved from the mainland to Taiwan late in 1949.

During its brief operation on the Chinese mainland from mid-1948 to mid-1949, ECA developed a host of commodity and local-currency programs. Among them the following deserve special attention: the food-rationing program, the cotton program, the petroleum program, and the counterpart fund projects.

The food rationing program. Virtually all the rice, wheat, and wheat flour imported under the ECA program were directly distributed to the residents of seven major cities, Shanghai, Nanking, Peiping, Tientsin, Canton, Tsingtao, and Swatow. The purpose of this rationing program was to ensure each resident of those cities a minimum amount of food staples at a minimum cost. This was merely a continuance of the policy which the China Relief Mission had adopted early in 1948. The only important modification was that the rationing program under ECA covered seven instead of five cities, including Swatow and Tsingtao in addition to those originally covered.

The cotton program. Cotton was directly purchased from United States suppliers by ECA for distribution to textile mills in China. For the cotton received, the mills were required to repay ECA in yarn at a predetermined exchange ratio. A part of the cotton yarn thus produced was then further distributed among weaving mills in exchange for cloth at a specified ratio and for delivery within a specified period of time. The cotton-yarn and the yarn-cloth exchange ratios were so determined that they usually allowed not only for the costs of raw material, labor, and overhead but also for a profit margin of about 10 percent. The principle of that program was similar to that of the UNRRA cotton program, except that there were significant adjustments in the various exchange ratios to reduce excess profits of the mill owners.

The petroleum program. The appropriation for petroleum and petroleum products was used to finance imports through regular commercial channels. Before the ECA program came into operation, petroleum products were imported by four leading oil companies[24] and by a score of small importers under a quota system. Within the limits of the quotas allocated, these companies and importers were allowed to purchase the necessary dollar exchange from the Central Bank of China. Under the ECA program, the old system for importing petroleum products remained unchanged, except that the dollar exchange paid by the Central Bank for petroleum imports was refunded by ECA. To obtain the dollar exchange, the importers were required to pay to the Central Bank the equivalent in Chinese yuan on the basis of the prevailing certificate rate for American dollars. The Bank in turn was responsible to ECA for the credits in the counterpart fund account.

As originally planned, the petroleum program was to have had a double-barreled effect on China's financial position. It was not only to relieve the Central Bank from providing dollar exchange of its own for petroleum imports, but also to yield yuan proceeds for the Bank to meet its counterpart fund obligations to ECA. During the early part of 1949, the purchase of foreign-exchange certificates for the ECA petroleum imports (virtually the only major imports remaining) became the main source of the demand for the certificates in Shanghai market. In fact, the petroleum program made it possible for the price of the certificates to stay at a realistic level despite the shrinkage of imports to China. Without this support, the operation of the foreign-exchange certificate system would never have been so successful as it was (see Stage Six, Chapter IV).

The counterpart fund programs. As with United States aid programs in other countries, the Chinese government was required to deposit in the designated ECA account in the Central Bank the equivalent in Chinese currency for the value of aid supplies received. The funds thus deposited were used to meet local-currency requirements for ECA administrative expenses, the expenses of the rural reconstruction program, and those of various public works and welfare projects sponsored under the program. Because of the continued depreciation of the Chinese currency, the Chinese government was required under the agreement to maintain the purchasing power of the credits to the counterpart fund until their withdrawal from the Central Bank. The value of counterpart funds was maintained on the basis of the wholesale price index. The maintenance-of-value provision for the counterpart fund and the fact that no substantial local-currency proceeds were realized from various commodity programs often made withdrawals from the counterpart fund accounts far in excess of the sale proceeds from the aid supplies.[25]

Comments on the aid programs

The best form of foreign aid for stabilizing an economy like that of postwar China should include these features.

1. The dollar funds made available by foreign aid should be used to finance the importation of a few commodities essential to the local economy, such as rice, raw cotton, and petroleum products.

2. Imported commodities should be sold for local currency at prices which either maximize sales receipts or minimize inflationary pressures on the subsistence cost of the people. For instance, the rationing of rice at a cost slightly below market price should satisfy

the latter condition, and sales of gasolines at realistic market prices should attain the former condition.

3. In programming the utilization of local currency proceeds from sales of the commodities under the aid programs, the monetary impact as well as the welfare and production aspects of such spending should be considered. A portion of the proceeds should be sterilized so as to contract the volume of currency circulation in the aid-receiving country, if inflation is plaguing that country. In fact, if such sterilization did result in improving the economic stabilization of the country, its contribution to the public welfare can be as important, if not more so, as any local-currency project. The publicity value of such a stabilization program, if considered at all, would probably be unsurpassed.

4. Domestic reforms coordinated with the foreign aid program should be imperative, if the benefit of aid to the receiving country is to be maximized. The planning of such reforms should be a joint undertaking of the aid-giving government and the aid-receiving government. Concrete proposals from the giver would always be preferable to a vague demand for reform on the part of the receiver.

5. The planning of commodity programs should include the distribution of commodities in the receiving country and the control of their uses.

6. If the proposed programs exceed the provided funds, a screening committee should be formed to decide the allocation of funds. The committee should consist of the senior officials of both governments who are in a position to make over-all decisions rather than represent sectional interests.

Earlier discussion points to the fact that as anti-inflationary measures, the foreign aid received by China during and after the war failed to have a full effect on the economy. The following are probably among the main causes responsible for such a result.

First, there was a lack of proper coordination between the aid programs and the stabilization plans of the Chinese government. The Chinese government, on the one hand, failed miserably in effecting the domestic reforms expected by the aid-giving countries, particularly by the United States. On the other hand, foreign officials directing aid programs often tended to be overenthusiastic in promoting welfare and public-works projects financed by local currency, and also failed in considering the inflationary impact of such projects on the Chinese economy.

Second, not all aid programs had an effective system for distributing aid commodities and/or controlling their end-uses. This was particularly true of the United States Treasury Credit of 1942 and the UNRRA program after V-J Day. Consequently, a part of the aid supplies was not fully utilized for stabilizing the economy.

Third, the Chinese government tended to overemphasize the importance of the unfavorable psychological effects on the market that an upward adjustment of the selling prices of aid commodities might bring. This illusion resulted in its keeping the selling prices for such commodities at an unduly low level and prevented the sales proceeds from reaching maximal figures.

Despite such defects, foreign-aid programs, financed major imports essential to China, did make important contributions toward reducing the country's trade and payment deficits. But because of the difficulties involved in these various aid programs, their contribution toward stabilizing the Chinese economy was not entirely commensurate with the amount of the appropriations involved.

SUMMARY

During the prewar years, the trade balance was invariably unfavorable to China. The deficits were met by remittances from Chinese emigrants abroad, foreign expenditures in China, and exports of gold and silver. The contributions of foreign credit and of investments were usually small during those years. In 1931–33 specie shipments consisted mainly of gold. But in 1934–35 silver exports became a dominant feature because of U.S. silver-purchasing policy and the attendant high silver prices in the world market.

In 1936–37, China's trade balance registered a rather unexpected recovery, which may be attributed to the following factors: the volume of several of the major imports (including cotton, rice, tobacco, liquid fuel, etc.) was drastically curtailed; not only was the flight of capital (a major disturbing factor during the early years) stopped, but also were indications of capital repatriation because of the stabilization of the Chinese currency; and the net terms of trade (i.e., changes in the prices of exports in relation to those of imports) were improved.

In 1938 while the downward trend in the physical volume of imports continued, China's exports also began to dwindle, and this reduction was more severe than that of imports. The war began to show its effects on the nation's trade.

During 1939–41, because of the actual need for maintaining the people and the industries in the foreign concessions in Shanghai, and because of the cheap foreign-exchange rate in relation to domestic prices, there was a great expansion of imports. To a certain extent that expansion was made possible by the policies of the Sino-British Stabilization Fund in 1939–41 and those of the Sino-American-British Stabilization Board in 1941. A comparison of the import statistics with the drain on the resources of these stabilization funds seems to indicate that a major portion of the imports during those years was met by the foreign-exchange supplies in the market, which were relatively abundant as a result of capital repatriation following the outbreak of World War II in Europe.

After the spread of the war to the Pacific at the end of 1941, the volume of the exports and imports of China was drastically reduced. On the other hand, United States expenditures in China were greatly increased because of the expansion of American military activities in China, and American aid to China was also increased. Consequently, China had at the end of the war an unprecedentedly large reserve of foreign exchange.

During the years immediately following V-J Day, China's trade deficits were usually large. They were met by the foreign-aid programs (particularly those of the UNRRA and ECA) and by the liquidation of the foreign-exchange holdings of the Chinese government accumulated during the war. The monetary reform of 1948 helped to replenish the government's reserve just as it was on the verge of exhaustion. This replenishment, however, was attained at a great expense to government prestige, and precipitated the economic chaos which plagued the country after the monetary reform.

Because of the expansion of trade deficit, the shrinkage of emigrant remittances, and the flight from the fapi currency, the chronic payment deficit of China was substantially widened during the inflation.

In an attempt to maintain the external value of the yuan, the Chinese government supplied the market with foreign exchange at an unduly low cost. When this policy became unfeasible because of limited resources, an elaborate system of exchange and trade controls emerged. During the months just before its evacuation from the mainland, the policy of the Nationalist government clearly drifted toward a policy which would maintain the rigid trade and exchange controls but not the external value of the yuan. These changes in policy, however, were usually too slow and ineffectual to influence the tide of inflation.

In short, the initial "shock" from the Chinese inflation originated in the budgetary deficit in the government sector. Inflationary pressures later spread to the household and business sectors. When these three sectors failed to absorb the pressures, attempts were made to pass the burden on to the international sector. Because of the constant inflow of foreign loans and because of the large accumulation of reserves of gold and foreign exchange in the early stage of the inflation, the international sector did absorb a part of these pressures. However, when the monetary reserve had dissipated and when the payment deficit expanded with the intensification of inflation, it soon became increasingly difficult for the international sector to accommodate these outside pressures. The gravity of the problem was accentuated by the faulty trade and foreign-exchange policies pursued by the Nationalist government, which substantially reduced China's exports and the receipts from emigrant remittances. While United States aids did contribute to the narrowing of the gap in China's international account, many of the aid programs (particularly the postwar programs) were too inadequate and restrictive to provide any comprehensive solution to China's payment problems. Thus during most of the postwar years (particularly 1947–49), the ex post equilibrium in the international account was attained by drastically curtailing nongovernment imports. This curtailment resulted in a substantial amount of an unrealized inflation potential haphazardly distributed among various economic sectors without due consideration of either equity or the welfare of the economy.

CHAPTER VI

Bank Credit, Velocity, and Inflation

This chapter examines the roles played by monetary and banking factors in the Chinese inflation. The discussion falls into three parts: the first examines the effects of inflation on China's banking system; the second, the possible contributions of monetary factors (particularly the velocities of money circulation) toward accentuating the tempo of inflation; the third, the gold sales and the credit policy, both of which the Central Bank used to control the money market during the inflation.

EFFECTS OF INFLATION ON THE BANKING SYSTEM

Background[1]

In prewar China the banks were usually classified in four major groups: the government banks, the modern banks, the native banks, and the foreign banks. Those in the last three categories were also known as private banks. At first the government banks consisted of the Central Bank of China, the Bank of China, and the Bank of Communications. The Central Bank was organized in 1928 by the Nationalist government, and was designed as a government treasury. Before 1935, the Bank of China and the Bank of Communications were predominantly privately owned corporations. The former was organized in 1907 primarily to serve as a central bank for China; the latter was organized in 1906 to handle, among other functions, the funds of the government-owned postal and communication systems. In 1935 both banks were reorganized to allow active governmental participation in their management. This was done with a view to strengthening governmental control over the banking system of the country. Because of their long history, the Bank of

China and the Bank of Communications were in 1935 more influential than the Central Bank. Therefore, the direct control of these banks by the government indirectly strengthened the position of the Central Bank in the financial market.

To these three banks, were later added the Farmers Bank of China, the Central Trust, the Postal Remittances and Savings Bank, and the Central Cooperative Bank. The Farmers Bank was first established in 1933 as the Agriculture Bank of Hunan, Hupeh, Anhwei, and Kiangsi Provinces and was reorganized in 1935, as the Farmers Bank. Its primary function was to provide farm credits. The Postal Remittances and Savings Bank was first established as the banking department of the Chinese Post Office. It was reorganized in 1930 into an independent agency under the Ministry of Communications to facilitate the payment of remittances from Chinese emigrants abroad to their recipients in rural areas. These remittances, as will be recalled from the discussions in Chapter V, played an important role in the balance of international payments of China. The Postal Bank, using post offices in rural areas as its agents, was in a unique position to supplement the inadequacy of the ordinary banks whose activities were usually confined to urban areas. The Central Trust was established to handle military purchases from abroad on behalf of the Nationalist government and was later developed into a special agency, mainly for the management of government-controlled trade. The Central Cooperative Bank, the youngest of the government banks, was established after World War II also for administering rural credit. But in actuality both the Farmers Bank and the Cooperative Bank were operated more as financial organizations for the Nationalist party than as agricultural banks for the country.

The government banking system in China was a result of an evolutionary process, often influenced by political considerations, which had no relevance to a rational banking system.

In September, 1939, a Joint Administration of the Government Banks[2] was established to coordinate the policies of the government banks. It operated under the direction of a board consisting of the premier of the Nationalist government, several cabinet ministers, and representatives of all the government banks. The Administration, as originally intended, was to coordinate all phases of the banks' operations; but later developments seem to show that a major part of its work consisted in examining various loans granted by the government banks and in occasionally reviewing the banks' credit policies in general. During the postwar years, the existence of the Administration often hindered rather than helped the development and enforcement of a rational credit policy. The Joint Administration was finally abolished in 1948 to give the Central Bank a free hand in formulating its own credit policy.

Private banks in prewar China comprised three groups: foreign banks, modern banks, and native banks. In early years, the foreign banks dominated the foreign-exchange market in China because of their connections abroad. Before the institution of the managed currency system in 1935, the foreign-exchange quotations of the British-owned Hong Kong and Shanghai Banking Corporation were *de facto* official quotations in the Shanghai market. Gold prices and the yuan rates for most foreign currencies were derived from the sterling rate quoted by that Bank and the relevant cross-rates prevailing in the London market. During the operation of the Sino-British Stabilization Fund and the Sino-British Stabilization Board in the period 1939–41, the leading British and American banks in Shanghai directly participated in China's foreign-exchange administration. In the domestic market, some of the foreign banks also benefitted from their being depositories for revenues from customs duties and salt taxes, which were pledged by the Chinese government for servicing its foreign debts. In addition, they were all protected by extraterritoriality. After World War II most of these privileges of the foreign banks were dissipated and their status became almost comparable to that of a Chinese private bank.

The native banks were financial institutions of indigenous origin. Unlike modern banks, they were mostly unincorporated enterprises with little or no paid-up capital. The bulk of their business was conducted on the basis of personal relations. Because of their loose organization and limited resources, these financial institutions were by nature incompatible with a modern economy. So, as the Chinese economy grew and became modernized in the course of several decades, the importance of the native banks declined.

The system of modern banks was entirely a product of Western influence and was first introduced into China in the latter part of the nineteenth century. It owed much of its later development to the leadership of the Bank of China.

After the World War II, the old trichotomy of modern, native, and foreign banks became obsolete. Instead the Chinese banking system became divided into the following generally accepted classification: Government-owned banks included the Central Bank and other government banks. Private banks included the provincial, municipal, *hsien* banks, privately-owned modern banks, foreign banks, and native banks.

Hereafter the term "government banks" will be used to denote the government banks other than the Central Bank; "private banks," to denote nongovernment banks, including modern, native, and foreign banks; and "member banks," to denote all banks other than the Central Bank, including the government banks and private banks.

Development of central banking under inflation

The war and the ensuing inflation brought about many important developments in the central banking system of China. This may be seen by reviewing the evolution of the various functions of the Central Bank from the time of its institution in 1928.

Note issue. Before 1935 note issuance was not solely a privilege of the Central Bank, but one shared by several government and well-established private banks, including foreign banks. In fact, it was considered one of the important operations of any established bank. The reserves of note issues were administered by the issuing bank themselves, although there were basic government regulations which had to be observed. These basic regulations included among others the formal procedures for obtaining such an issuing privilege, the reserve requirements for note issues, and the rules concerning the convertibility of the notes. Within this legal framework the banks had virtually a free hand in managing their note circulation. Since good management and free convertibility were necessary conditions for a wide acceptance of bank notes, the private note-issuing system, functioning under the principle of free competition, was fairly satisfactory. After the monetary reform in November, 1935, all private issues were withdrawn, leaving only the notes issued by the government-owned banks as the nation's legal tender. In 1942 the issuing privileges of the government banks (excluding the Central

Bank) were suspended, and the Central Bank became the sole bank of issue.

Bank clearings. Before the war, Chinese modern banks, native banks, and the foreign banks in Shanghai formed three independent groups. Each had its own clearing system with the Bank of China which, being a member of all three groups, served as an agent for intergroup clearings. The centralized clearing system was then virtually nonexistent in other Chinese cities. During the war the modern clearing system administered by the Central Bank was instituted first in Chungking and later in all the major cities in Free China. After V-J Day, similar systems were installed in Shanghai, Tientsin, Canton, and all other important centers in the country. In Shanghai, the new clearing system, replacing the old decentralized arrangement, drastically changed the structure of financial market. Under the new system, the banks in Shanghai, as has been indicated, were divided into the following major groups: the government-owned banks (including the Central Bank and government banks) and private banks. A clearing settlement in favor of the former group was usually considered as an indication of a tight money market; one against it was indicative of an easy money market.

Not until 1946, therefore, did the clearing functions of the Central Bank actually come into operation on a nationwide scale. Even then the clearing was confined to the settlement of local transactions. A system of interregional clearing at par had never been developed. Oftentimes, money transferred from one region to another region was either subject to a discount or at a premium, depending upon market conditions.

Foreign exchange. The evolution of China's foreign-exchange policy has been dealt with at length in Chapter IV and requires no amplification here. Suffice to say that up to November, 1935, neither China's foreign-exchange market nor her trade was subject to effective government control. There was no positive foreign-exchange policy to be enforced. The function of the Central Bank as its administrator was accordingly limited. After the adoption of the managed currency system in 1935, the Central Bank, being responsible for maintaining China's foreign-exchange rates at pegged levels, became the sole administrator of the nation's foreign-exchange policy and in effect the supervisor of its market. This situation lasted until the institution of the Sino-British Stabilization Fund in 1939. Under the Stabilization Fund and the Sino-American-British Stabilization Board that followed, the foreign-exchange administration became a joint undertaking of these international organizations, in which the Central Bank had a limited voice. Not until 1944, when the Stabilization Board was abolished, was the function of foreign-exchange administrator returned to the Bank; and not until the early months of 1946 was the importance of this function fully demonstrated.

Rediscount policy. The rediscount system was first developed in the early 1930s in Shanghai by the Joint Reserve Board of the Bankers' Association and the Native Bankers Guild. The rediscount facilities of the Central Bank were not developed, however, until the institution of the Joint Head Office of Government Banks in 1939.

Under the British system, the interest rate of the Bank of England is usually higher than the market rate, so that no recourse will be made to rediscount at the Bank until all other borrowing possibilities are exhausted. Under the American system, the rediscount rate of the Federal Reserve Banks is usually lower than the market rate of interest, but it has not been a practice for member banks to borrow unnecessarily from the Reserve Banks. In China, the interest rate of the Central Bank as a rule was lower, in fact much lower, than the corresponding rates charged by member banks. Nor was it an established practice among either the private banks or the government banks to refrain from borrowing from the Central Bank. On the contrary, because of the attractively low rediscount cost, the lending facilities of the Central Bank were often exploited as important sources of profit. Consequently, the market remained constantly in the Bank, so to speak, instead of being kept away from it, as has been the case in American and British practice.

Although the Central Bank provided the rediscount facilities, it did not have a free hand in administering its credit policy. The rediscount rate, as well as the extent to which the rediscount facilities were available to government banks, was decided at the committee meetings of the Joint Head Office of the Government Banks (or JHOGB), which consisted of representatives of the Central Bank, the government banks, the Ministry of Finance, and the ministries of the Nationalist government (the Ministries of Economic

Affairs, Communications, and Food) whose subsidiaries often borrowed from government banks. The borrowing ministries and the government banks who handled such loans with the funds provided by the Central Bank were both for credit expansion and cheap money policy. Oftentimes, a rediscount by the Central Bank was made a condition for a government bank's lending to a government enterprise, when the loan was approved by the JHOGB. Since neither the Central Bank nor the Ministry of Finance had a veto power at the meetings of the JHOGB, attempts on the part of the Central Bank to modify its cheap money policy were usually rejected by the JHOGB. The existence of the JHOGB, whose original purpose was to control the bank credit of government banks, actually became a deterrent to the development of a rational rediscount policy of the Central Bank.

Open market operations. Because of the declining importance of the market for government bonds during the Chinese inflation, the usual open market operations based on such securities became unfeasible. Instead, the Central Bank relied mainly upon sales of gold, foreign exchange, foreign-exchange certificates, and commodities for its open market operations. According to estimates of the proceeds derived from such sales in relation to the amount of note expansion for the corresponding period, the importance of these operations to the Central Bank's control over the money market was beyond doubt (see the discussion of gold operations in section 3 of this chapter). Because of the resultant drain on the Bank's limited reserve, these sales operations were often too expensive to be used as a standing weapon for market control. This was particularly true when the official selling prices of gold or foreign exchange were maintained at an unrealistically low level.

Sales of commodities provided another important alternative in the Bank's market operations. To be effective, however, such operations were confined to staple commodities which had a ready and organized market in China. One of the commodities was cotton textile products. During the postwar years, a substantial amount of textile products was sold by the Central Bank for open market operations. But the products were virtually all in the possession of some other organization (such as UNRRA, ECA, and the China Textile Industries Corporation, a government agent which controlled most of the textile mills taken over from the Japanese after the war). Thus the proceeds derived from the sales of the textile products were mostly needed for future expenditures of these organizations rather than withdrawn from circulation. In the case of the UNRRA and ECA supplies, the Central Bank was obliged to provide a counterpart fund in favor of these agencies. Sometimes these counterpart deposits were redeemable on the basis of a specially devised unit of account so that the real value of the deposit remained unaffected by the inflation (see Chapter V). The continued rising prices usually made the sales proceeds, received by the Bank, fall far short of the amount it later paid out. For these reasons, any effect of the commodity sales on the money market was at best only temporary. These effects were not so unequivocal as those obtained through the sales of gold and foreign exchange directly owned by the Nationalist government.

These facts point to the conclusion that the Bank might have effectively supplemented its other market operations by using a portion of its foreign-exchange holdings to import such staple commodities as cotton, cotton yarn, etc., for sale in the domestic market, alongside the gold and foreign exchange. Such a commodity program would have helped not only to drain excess purchasing power from the market but also to provide necessary raw materials for the nation's industries and to supplement essential commodity supplies in the market. These operations, however, required long-range planning on the part of the Central Bank—a condition which the Bank's administration, subject to frequent changes and to the influence of domestic politics, was not always in a position to fulfill.

Deposit reserve. According to the Central Bank Act promulgated in 1935, one of the functions of the Central Bank was to serve as the custodian of the deposit reserves of private banks. This provision, however, was not put into effect until the Regulation for Controlling Private Banks was promulgated in August, 1940. The regulation required all private banks to maintain a reserve at the Central Bank in an amount not less than 7 to 15 percent of its deposit liability in the case of time deposits and 15 to 20 percent in the case of demand deposits. The effective ratio for such a reserve was to be determined from time to time within the above-mentioned ranges by the Central Bank, after consultation with the Ministry of Finance. At first, these reserve deposits were made with any of the government-owned banks. It was not until June, 1941, that the Central Bank became the sole depository of these reserves.

The importance of the reserve-deposit ratio as a regulator of the money market in China, however, must not be overemphasized. First, the reserve requirements were applicable only to the deposits in private banks, not to those in government banks. The discussion in the latter part of this chapter will show that despite the importance of the deposits in private banks before the war, their share or participation in the total deposits declined sharply after the war in the course of the inflation. In 1932 about 56 percent of the total deposits of the entire banking system (including the Central Bank) was in the hands of private banks, 37 percent in government banks, and less than 8 percent in the Central Bank. In 1945 the deposits with the Central Bank rose to more than 71 percent, and those with government banks to about 27 percent, while those in private banks dropped to less than 2 percent (see Table 6.3). Under the circumstances, the most important item for control in regulating the total volume of bank credit was the deposits in the Central Bank and then the deposits in government banks. It is therefore ridiculous to expect that the manipulation of the deposit-reserve ratios applicable only to private banks had any significant effect on China's financial market.

It may be argued, of course, that since the government banks were government institutions, they would naturally adhere closely to the policy of the government and would not need any additional control over their deposit liabilities. But most of the government banks owed their existence to political considerations or to historical development. Operating on a self-sustaining basis and being actively engaged in commercial banking, they sometimes put their interests above the general welfare of the national economy. Their existence represented an anomaly in the Chinese banking system. To subject them to controls similar to those governing private banks would therefore have been a necessary makeshift arrangement before the entire banking system could be reorganized and rationalized.

This study indicates that, under an inflation caused primarily by the government's printing press, the expansion of note issues usually exceeded that of bank deposits, and the efficiency of the reserve-deposit ratio as a controller of the money market tends to decline as the process spirals. Because of the unusually low ratio of private bank deposits to note issues during the postwar years, the effect on the money market of an adjustment of such a ratio was necessarily insignificant.

Control of government banks. One function of the JHOGB was to screen loans granted by the government banks, to which the usual banking regulations did not always apply. According to the agreed

TABLE 6.1. LOANS GRANTED BY GOVERNMENT BANKS EXCLUDING THE CENTRAL BANK, 1937–46 (*billion yuan*)

	Loans outstanding[a]	*Loans approved by JHOGB*[b]	*Cumulative total of loans approved*
1937	.661		
1938	.962		
1939	1.282	.532[c]	.532[c]
1940	1.476	.696	1.228
1941	2.229	1.545	2.773
1942	9.564	2.662	5.435
1943	13.885	11.096	16.531
1944	54.871	33.025	49.556
1945	342.583	75.804	125.360
1946	4,277.046	738.872	864.232

[a] Figures represent the outstanding balance at the end of the designated year.
[b] Figures represent the amounts approved during the year.
[c] Total amount for 1937–39.

Source: *Chung-yang yin-hang yueh-pao* (The Central Bank Monthly), IV (1949), 120–21.

procedures, all loans which exceeded a specified amount required the prior approval of the JHOGB, and those under that amount were left to the discretion of the individual banks. The purpose of this arrangement was apparently to cover a substantial portion of the banks' loans without at the same time imposing an undue administrative burden upon the JHOGB.

The statistics, however, reveal that the actual results did not conform with this expectation. The amount of loans approved by the JHOGB (see Table 6.1) was inordinately small in comparison with the corresponding amount of the loans outstanding. This is particularly true for 1945 and 1946. It is possible that the loans approved during a given year are not necessarily included in their balance outstanding at the end of the year. Some of these loans might have been granted and repaid during the same year. Some, though approved, might not actually have been used until the following year. In neither case would the amount be included in the year-end balances. Despite these possible distortions, the cumulative total of the loans granted and the corresponding outstanding balances should not be entirely unrelated. The substantial discrepancy between the figures in the two columns is indicative of the inadequacy of the JHOGB's control over the lending operations of the government banks. Because of the lack of necessary information, it is difficult to project this loan-and-balance relation into the years after 1946, but the circumstantial evidence seems to indicate that the control of the JHOGB over the loan assets of government banks was loosened rather than tightened.

Control of government funds. One of the main functions of a central bank is sole custodian of government funds. While this principle is almost axiomatic in countries where a central banking system is fully developed, it was never successfully enforced in China. Up to the early 1930s, a large part of China's customs revenues and salt-tax receipts was designated as security for foreign credits by international treaties and loan contracts, and was deposited with designated foreign banks in China.

After the transfer of China's customs administration from foreign control to the Chinese government in the early 1930s, deposits from the customs revenues were transferred from the foreign banks to the Central Bank. However, not until the inflation reached an acute stage during the 1940s was the importance of government-fund administration to market control fully realized. Thereafter many attempts were made to enforce the so-called National Treasury Act promulgated in 1939 with a view to concentrating public deposits in the Central Bank.[3] In July, 1946, the Nationalist government issued a new order outlining in detail the procedures for handling deposits and remittances of government funds and prohibiting explicitly the handling of such remittances and deposits by banks other than the Central Bank.[4]

The enforcement of this regulation with respect to the private banks encountered little difficulty because the amount of government deposits in those banks became insignificant during the postwar years and because the banks were not in a position to offer any effective opposition. The situation was somewhat different for government banks. To them, a strict enforcement of the regulation was a substantial curtailment of their business activities. Moreover, they had the influence and the voice in the JHOGB to prevent, or at least to minimize, possible adverse effects of the regulation on their business. After protracted negotiations between the Central Bank and government banks, an agreement was reached in 1948. The government banks would refrain from accepting deposits and remittances of government offices, and all such deposits in their custody would be transferred to the Central Bank. Government banks would be allowed to continue the handling of funds belonging to government enterprises, which were not considered as the "government offices." The Central Bank would provide the necessary advances or other forms of financial assistance to the government banks if the deposit transfer resulted in undue difficulties to the banks.

This agreement evidently constituted an important step toward the concentration of government funds in the Central Bank, although the solution was far from satisfactory. For instance, the ambiguity in the definition of public-enterprise funds offered an important loophold for abuses. There was not enough time between the enforcement of the agreement, reached in late 1948, and the occupation of Shanghai by the Communists in early 1949 to see the full effect of such a transfer on the banking system.[5]

Effects of inflation on other banking operations

The principal assets of a nonissuing bank normally consist of cash assets, loans, discounts, and investments; the principal liabilities are deposits and net worth accounts. The cash assets include primarily cash in vault and deposits with central and other banks. The loans, discounts, and investments, representing the earning assets of the bank, cover all the long-term and short-term advances, discounts of bills, and investments in securities. The deposit liabilities include all those in time deposits, demand deposits, and savings deposits. The net-worth accounts consist of all capital and surplus accounts (including paid-up capital), proprietary reserve accounts, and undistributed profit. While the earning assets provide a bank with income, its deposit liabilities are met by the primary and secondary reserves of the bank, which consist respectively of cash assets and investments. The net-worth assets, representing the excess of a bank's total assets over its total liabilities, is a cushion to protect the depositors and other creditors of the bank—a protection additional to what its non-net-worth assets can provide. It follows, therefore, that the larger the cash assets in relation to the deposits, the more liquid is the position of the bank. Similarly, the larger the net-worth assets in relation to its deposit liabilities, the greater is the protection to its depositors. In this section, the effects of inflation upon various assets, liabilities, and net-worth accounts of the Chinese banks will be examined.

Effects on net-worth accounts. As a result of the protracted inflation, the value of the capital assets of the Chinese banks, both private and government, became ridiculously low in comparison with their deposit liabilities or total assets (see Table 6.2). During 1932–36 when conditions in China were normal, the ratio of net worth to deposit liability ranged from 4.4 to 5.6 percent for government banks and from 15.4 to 17.9 percent for private banks. These percentages were not too far from the corresponding ratios for the banks in the United States.[6] In 1946 the ratio dropped sharply to 0.02 percent for government banks, and 3.0 percent for private banks; that is to say, while the money value of deposit liabilities expanded in the course of inflation, the adjustment in the banks' capital accounts lagged. In upsetting the prewar capital-deposit relationship, the inflation seriously impaired the stability of the Chinese banking system.

Effects on cash assets. When inflation is rampant, when interest rates are high, and when a rise in commodity prices is expected, the liquidity preference of banks, it is generally believed, should normally be low. This, however, was not true of the Chinese banks. The statistics in Table 6.2 show that neither government banks nor private banks lowered the ratio of cash assets to deposits during the inflation. On the contrary, the cash-deposit ratio at 20.9 percent for private banks in 1946, was actually higher than any of the prewar ratios. This seemingly abnormal phenomenon may be attributed to several factors. First, all banks in China, except government banks, were required to maintain a deposit reserve with the Central Bank amounting to not less than from 5 to 10 percent in the case of time deposits and from 10 to 15 percent in the case of demand deposits. This legally required reserve was in addition to the cash in the bank's vault and the clearing balance, which a bank usually maintained at the Central Bank to facilitate settlements of bank clearings. Neither the cash in vault nor the clearing balance was counted toward the legal deposit reserve. Second, even though the clearing reserves were not a legal requirement, there existed, like the British system, a minimum level below which the reserve-deposit ratio could not fall without unduly impairing the prestige and the smooth operation of a bank.[7] One therefore should not be surprised to find a prewar cash-deposit ratio lower than the postwar ratio, as during the earlier years the reserve requirement was nonexistent and the banks' cash reserves might be more effectively utilized than they were after the war.

Effects on investment portfolio. The investment portfolios of Chinese banks (see Table 6.2) were ridiculously small in comparison with those of the American and British banks. Even during the prewar years when conditions in China were normal and when government securities were still an attractive investment yielding more than 10 percent per annum, the ratio of investments to deposits of the government and private banks never exceeded 20 percent. In 1946 the ratio for private banks dropped to 1.0 percent, but the government banks maintained the high level of 19.5 percent. This was due probably to the latter's special obligation to hold government securities. During the years from 1932 to 1952 the investment-deposit ratio of the American banks ranged approximately from 40 to 67 percent, and the British banks ranged from 37 to 67 percent.[8]

The small investment portfolio of the Chinese banks was caused mainly by the absence of a fully developed security market in China. Even the small market developed around government bonds and corporation securities during the 1930s was destroyed by inflation. The small investment portfolio meant a low secondary reserve for deposits in Chinese banks. The low secondary reserve, if not adequately compensated for by large cash assets, in turn meant the low liquidity of these banks. This was another of the unfavorable changes in the Chinese banking system brought about by the protracted inflation. Another important difference between the investments of

Chinese banks and of the American and British banks was the effect of war financing upon the relation between investment and loans. In both the United States and the United Kingdom, the percentage of bank investment increased in relation to loans, indicating the expansion of bank holdings in government securities. The reverse was true of the Chinese banks because the deficits in Chinese budgets were met mostly by direct advances from the Central Bank which were not transferable to other banks.

Effects on the deposit-loan ratio.[9] The deposit-loan ratio of the Central Bank was unusually low in 1934 and 1935, reflecting improvement in the fiscal conditions of the Nationalist government during these years (see Table 6.3). After 1936, however, the ratio rose almost without interruption until it reached a peak of 622.1 percent in 1943, reflecting the continual deterioration of government finance during the period. Similarly, the decline of the loan-deposit ratio of the Central Bank during 1944–46, at least in part, can be attributed to the improvement in government finance following the institution of the collection-in-kind system for land and of some commodity taxes.

In the case of government banks, the series of the loan-deposit ratio may be divided into two sections: one for 1932–41, when government banks shared with the Central Bank the privilege of note issues, and another for 1942–46, when the Central Bank became the sole bank of issue. Within each of these periods the loan-deposit ratio showed an upward trend. This upward trend was abruptly interrupted in 1942, when the ratio dropped to 45.6 percent from the 151.0 percent in 1941. The break in 1942 was caused mainly by the suspension of note issue by government banks, as the note issue was presumably a main factor which enabled the banks to expand their loan in amounts substantially above that of the deposit received.

Similarly, the series of the loan-deposit ratio of private banks may be divided into two sections: one for 1932–40 and another for 1940–46. The general trend for the first period was apparently downward; for the second period, upward. The downward trend may be explained by the rising importance of the Central Bank and government banks in both note-issue and loan facilities in relation to the similar functions of the private banks. The sudden drop of

TABLE 6.2. PRINCIPAL ASSETS AND LIABILITIES OF THE CHINESE BANKS, 1932–36 AND 1946
(*million* yuan *for 1932–36 and billion* yuan *for 1945–46*)

ASSETS

End of year	*Cash*		*Loans and discounts*		*Investments*		*Others*	
	(*yuan*)	(*percent*)	(*yuan*)	(*percent*)	(*yuan*)	(*percent*)	(*yuan*)	(*percent*)
The Central Bank								
1932	39.0	33.1	163.1	96.7	.3	.2	1.9	1.1
1933	64.6	26.4	220.8	90.2	.2	.1	1.4	.6
1934	52.6	19.3	166.6	61.1	155.4	57.0	4.0	1.5
1935	87.4	13.8	383.2	60.4	252.9	39.9	12.9	2.0
1936	275.2	36.4	539.3	71.2	37.6	5.0	21.4	2.8
1945	37.3	6.3	1369.8	232.2	.9	.2	275.2	46.7
1946	1116.7	23.6	7321.9	155.0	366.8	7.8	1170.9	24.8
Government Banks								
1932	93.7	12.1	627.9	81.4	90.3	11.7	26.1	3.4
1933	68.4	7.6	821.0	91.0	61.9	6.9	40.2	4.5
1934	38.2	3.8	955.2	96.0	55.5	5.6	45.8	4.6
1935	79.7	5.4	1400.0	95.1	99.1	6.7	42.4	2.9
1936	531.7	27.7	1374.6	71.6	112.9	5.9	72.8	3.8
1946	169.2	10.0	1855.2	106.0	340.9	19.5	173.9	9.9
Private Banks								
1932	146.9	12.5	1170.7	99.6	135.5	11.5	18.7	1.6
1933	178.8	12.4	1274.5	88.1	194.7	13.5	41.6	2.9
1934	194.0	11.2	1502.1	86.8	258.9	15.0	28.4	1.6
1935	247.5	14.7	1412.4	83.9	241.8	14.4	21.5	1.3
1936	265.0	14.1	1552.2	82.8	350.6	18.7	54.8	2.9
1946	62.9	20.9	312.3	104.0	3.3	1.0	22.5	1.5
Total: All Banks								
1932	279.6	13.2	1961.7	92.7	226.4	10.7	46.7	2.2
1933	311.8	12.0	2316.3	89.3	256.8	9.9	83.2	3.2
1934	284.8	9.5	2623.9	87.5	469.8	15.7	78.2	2.6
1935	414.6	10.9	3195.6	84.3	593.8	15.7	76.8	2.0
1936	1071.9	23.6	3466.1	76.2	501.1	11.0	149.0	3.3
1946	1348.8	19.9	9489.4	140.1	711.1	10.5	1367.4	20.2

The compilation is based on several unpublished consolidated balance sheets compiled by the Auditing Department of the Central Bank of China and formal reports submitted to the Bank by three government banks, eight provincial banks, fifty-four commercial banks, fifty-two banking corporations, and seventy-two native banks. The *Yearbook* covers only the statistics of the "modern banks" which, according to the usual definition, includes only those of government and private banks operated as incorporated enterprises but not the native banks. It is hoped that by expressing the absolute amounts as percentages of deposit liability, the distorting effects stemming from these discrepancies can be substantially reduced.

Source: *Chung-kuo yin-hang nien-chien* (The Chinese Bank Yearbook) (Shanghai, 1931–35), 1931–35 eds.; and unpublished records of the Central Bank of China.

TABLE 6.2 (*continued*)

LIABILITIES

Deposits		Remittances payable		Others		Capital and surplus accounts	
(*yuan*)	(*percent*)	(*yuan*)	(*percent*)	(*yuan*)	(*percent*)	(*yuan*)	(*percent*)
168.5	100			1.4	.8	27.4	16.3
244.7	100			1.2	.5	35.8	14.6
272.6	100			1.1	.4	103.7	38.0
634.0	100			4.7	.7	103.5	16.3
757.0	100			7.5	1.0	104.9	13.9
589.8	100			1080.9	183.2	5.9	1.0
4724.8	100			5143.9	108.9	44.3	.9
771.5	100	9.2	1.2	26.1	3.4	43.2	5.6
902.2	100	9.8	1.1	40.2	4.5	43.4	4.8
994.9	100	12.3	1.2	45.8	4.6	47.4	4.8
1472.3	100	33.5	2.3	42.4	2.9	79.6	5.4
1919.4	100	35.6	1.9	75.0	3.9	85.2	4.4
1750.0	100	179.4	10.3	588.0	33.6	.4	.02
1175.5	100	17.7	1.5	17.3	1.5	205.2	17.5
1447.3	100	15.0	1.0	20.4	1.4	248.8	17.2
1730.2	100	31.8	1.8	27.8	1.6	267.3	15.4
1683.2	100	32.6	1.9	19.8	1.2	265.8	15.8
1874.9	100	38.3	2.0	45.5	2.4	336.1	17.9
300.3	100	50.5	16.8	47.9	16.0	9.0	3.0
2115.5	100	26.9	1.3	44.8	2.2	275.8	13.0
2594.2	100	24.8	1.0	61.8	2.4	328.0	12.6
2997.7	100	44.1	1.5	74.7	2.5	418.4	14.0
3789.5	100	66.1	1.7	66.9	1.8	448.9	11.8
4551.3	100	73.9	1.6	128.0	2.8	526.2	11.6
6775.1	100	229.9	3.4	5779.8	85.3	53.7	.8

the ratio from the 187.3 percent of 1935 to the 82.8 percent of 1936 was because of the suspension of the note-issue privilege of private banks after the monetary reform in November, 1935. During the second period, the ratio rose almost without interruption from 60.2 percent in 1940 to 175.7 percent in 1946.

Because of the absence of relevant balance-sheet data, it is difficult to determine definitely what resources other than deposit liability were used by the Chinese banks to finance their loans when the latter exceeded the deposits received. The fragmentary

TABLE 6.3. LOANS AND DEPOSIT LIABILITIES OF CHINESE BANKS, 1932–48

End of year or month	*Central Bank*			*Government banks*			*Central and government banks*		*Private banks*		
	1	*2*	*3*	*1*	*2*	*3*	*1*	*2*	*1*	*2*	*3*
1932	8.0	8.3	96.7	36.5	32.0	21.4	44.4	40.3	55.6	59.7	99.6
1933	9.4	9.5	90.2	34.8	35.5	91.0	44.2	45.0	55.8	55.0	88.1
1934	9.1	6.4	61.1	33.1	36.0	94.2	42.2	42.4	57.8	57.6	86.5
1935	16.7	7.9	60.4	38.9	27.4	90.6	55.6	35.3	44.4	64.7	187.3
1936	16.6	25.3	127.2	42.2	33.9	67.3	58.8	59.2	41.2	40.8	82.8
1937	21.2	23.7	105.6	43.0	47.5	104.4	54.2	71.2	35.8	28.8	76.1
1938	24.7	33.2	161.0	45.5	48.5	127.3	70.1	81.7	29.9	18.3	73.0
1939	22.3	33.3	202.3	52.8	55.1	146.0	75.1	87.4	24.9	12.6	70.8
1940	20.2	41.5	345.1	54.7	50.0	152.4	74.9	91.0	25.1	9.0	60.2
1941	17.5	39.5	413.5	59.8	51.8	151.0	77.3	91.3	22.7	8.7	70.4
1942	34.1	76.7	346.5	54.6	16.2	45.6	88.7	92.8	11.3	7.2	98.3
1943	48.0	85.6	622.1	34.6	9.3	96.0	83.6	94.9	16.4	5.1	110.4
1944	61.0	90.7	428.1	28.1	6.4	63.3	89.1	97.1	10.9	2.9	77.5
1945	71.1	91.9	397.6	26.7	7.0	80.1	97.8	98.9	2.2	1.1	154.8

1946										
March						89.4		10.6		
June						92.9		7.1		
Sept.						91.6		8.4		
Dec.	88.9	170.3		9.3	100.5	91.2	98.1	8.8	1.9	175.7
1947										
March						82.5		17.5		
June						89.3		10.7		
Sept.						85.9		14.1		
Dec.						83.8		16.2		
1948										
March						85.9		14.1		
June						86.8		13.2		

1 The percentage participation in deposits held by banks.
2 The percentage participation in loans granted.
3 The ratio of loan assets to deposit liabilities.
There are no data for spaces left blank in table.
Source: *The Chinese Bank Yearbook*, 1932–48 eds.; *The Central Bank Monthly*, Vols, I–IV (1946–49); and *Chung-hua nin-kuo tung-ch'i t'so yao* (The Statistical Abstract of the Republic of China) (Nanking, 1947), pp. 70–72.

information derived from the combined balance sheets compiled by the Bank of China and the Central Bank, however, does indicate that the expansion of the note issues played an important role in filling the gap. If this is correct, then it is not difficult to explain the high ratio (i.e., more than 100 percent) of the government banks during 1937–41 and of the Central Bank during 1936–46. The high ratio for the Central Bank is understandable. Its loans consisted predominantly of advances to meet government deficits, which were in turn used for government purchases in open market and other public outlays. It is unlikely that all such loans were redeposited with the bank, and that the deposits received from nongovernment sources were adequate to meet the ever expanding needs of the government without supplementation by a new note issue. The high loan-deposit ratio of government banks during 1937–41 may be similarly explained. Before these banks surrendered their privilege of note issue, they participated actively in financing government deficits, mainly through the purchase of government securities. After the suspension of note issue, which curtailed severely the resources at their disposal, this responsibility of government banks was accordingly reduced.

The unusually high loan-deposit ratio of private banks in 1943, 1945, and 1946, which reached 110.4, 154.8, and 175.7 percent respectively, is rather difficult to explain. One possible explanation is that the ratio of capital assets to deposits in these banks was high in comparison with that of government banks. In 1946, this ratio was 3.0 percent for private banks against 0.02 percent for government banks (see Table 6.2). The difference in the capital-deposit ratio alone, however, is not adequate to account for the excess of loans over deposits. An examination of the combined balance sheet reveals that the possible resources, which, besides those mentioned previously, might be used to meet the expansion loans, were those derived from Remittance Payable and Other Liabilities. In fact, the existence of these two liability accounts enabled private banks to expand their earning assets to a level substantially higher than their deposit liability. While the nature of the accounts included under Other Liabilities is not clear, the use of proceeds derived from a bank's remittance liability to finance its excessive loan expansion is clearly not a commendable banking policy.

Effects of inflation on the relation among the banks

The change in the relative positions among the various groups of banks, as reflected by changes in their percentage shares in deposit liabilities and loan assets, is shown in Table 6.3. During the early 1930s, the shares of private banks in both deposits and loans were slightly higher than the corresponding shares of the Central Bank and the government banks put together. The first reversal of this relationship occurred in 1935, when the deposit holdings of the Central Bank rose to 16.7 percent and the government banks to 38.9 percent of the entire banking system of China, as against their shares of 9.1 and 33.1 percent respectively in the preceding year. These changes raised the total share of all the government-owned banks to about 55.6 percent. In 1936, because of the monetary reform in the preceding year, the percentage of total loans outstanding accounted for by the Central Bank rose abruptly to 25.3 percent from 7.9 percent in the previous year, cutting the private banks' share in the loan market to 40.8 percent. Afterward, the shares of private banks in both deposits and loans dwindled, while those of the Central Bank and government banks expanded steadily. This trend continued, and the private banks' share in 1945 was only 2.2 percent for deposits and 1.1 percent for loans.

In the meantime, the division between the Central Bank and government banks did not remain constant. While the percentage shares of all the government-owned banks (including the Central Bank and government banks) in deposits and loans rose in relation to the corresponding proportions of private banks, the Central Bank's shares vis-a-vis those of government banks also increased. This situation was particularly obvious in 1935–36 and in 1942–45. The shift after 1942, being far more decisive than the early change, was apparently a result of the suspension of note issue by government banks and of the establishment of the Central Bank as the sole note issuer.

The fact that after 1936 the Central Bank had a larger share of total loans than of total deposits reflects the rise of the Bank's loan-deposit ratio above the unity level. It was the high loan-deposit ratio of the Central Bank that was primarily responsible for keeping the corresponding ratio for all government-owned banks above the unity level. Moreover, the Table 6.3 also shows that for most of the years between 1932 and 1945 private banks' share in deposits was greater than their share in loans.

For the postwar years, detailed data for bank loans are not available, and the available information does not permit the separation of deposits in the Central Bank and government banks. For these reasons, only the percentage shares in deposit holdings of all the government-owned banks vis-a-vis those of private banks are shown in Table 6.3. These statistics show that during the thirty-month period ending June, 1948, the percentage share in deposits of private banks rose from a range of 7.1 to 10.6 percent of the deposits for all banks during the first six months of 1946, to a range of 10.7 to 17.5 percent during 1947 and the first half of 1948, as against a participation of 2.2 percent in 1945. In other words, the importance of private banks not only increased immediately after the war but continued to do so during the postwar years.

This improvement in the position of private banks was mainly, if not entirely, due to the reopening of the major seaports where private industrial and commercial activities played a much more important role than they did in interior China. Despite this betterment, the postwar position of private banks still fell far short of that attained in the early 1930s, when these banks controlled more than half the deposits and loans in the entire banking system. Their postwar percentage share remained inordinately low in comparison with the Central Bank and government banks. This decrease in private banks' participation is particularly significant when considered in the light of the increased number of private banks established in China during and after the war. To divide a dwindling pool of deposits among an increasing number of private banks meant an increased instability in China's banking system.

Besides the deposit assets and the loan liabilities, the changes in the number of institutions in various groups of banks is also indicative of the impact of inflation upon China's banking system. The statistics in Table 6.4 show a cross-section of the system as it appeared before and after the war. The government, provincial, and modern private banks all used the system of branch banking. Most of the native banks, the municipal banks, and the *hsien* banks, on the other hand, operated as independent units without branches of their own. A comparison of the prewar and postwar statistics indicates that there

TABLE 6.4. NUMBER OF FINANCIAL INSTITUTIONS IN CHINA[a]

	1936		*1937*		*June, 1946*		*June, 1947*	
	Head Office	*Branch*	*Head office*	*Branch*	*Head office*	*Branch*	*Head office*	*Branch*
Central Bank and government banks	4	390	4	491	6	964	7	776
Provincial, municipal, and *hsien* banks	25	331	26	464	20	972	26	970
Modern private banks	135	611	134	672	206	837	200	794
Native banks and money shops	995		782		348	75	995	53
Trust companies					17	5	21	7
Insurance companies					112	114	139	391
Cooperative banks					463	1	331	4

[a] The number of offices is given for the end of the year or month.

Source: For prewar data, *The Chinese Bank Yearbook*, 1936 and 1937 eds.; and for the postwar data, unpublished records of the Central Bank of China.

was a great increase in the number of new banks and their branches in almost all groups. The increase was particularly spectacular in the case of the branch offices of provincial, municipal, and *hsien* banks. The expansion of modern private banks was also substantial. The number of native banks and money shops for 1947 almost trebled that of 1946. But compared with their prewar numbers and with the changes that occurred in the modern and local government banks during the decade from 1936–37 to 1946–47, the increase in the number of native banks and money shops in 1947 was rather small. The expansion of the Central Bank and government banks during the decade was also impressive. This was particularly true of the multiplication of their branch offices.

The spectacular expansion in banking activities during these years was because of the lucrative financial enterprise under inflation and of the policy of the Ministry of Finance of the Nationalist government. During the protracted inflation, the deposit liabilities of banks were of course always fixed in terms of the money unit. On the other hand, the depository banks were free to use their funds either for lending at exorbitant rates of interest or for investing in gold, commodities, etc., to profit from inflation. The disproportion between the deposit liabilities of a bank and equity investment during the inflation, as previously noted, also added to the attraction of the enterprise.

During the war there was little evidence of any positive and effective policy on the part of the Chinese government to cope with the problems of banking regulations arising from inflation. In August, 1940, a "Temporary Banking Regulation for the Emergency Period" was promulgated. Among other regulations, the policy required the prior approval of the Ministry of Finance for the establishing of a new bank or a branch office of an old bank in China. Experience has since proved that the intent of this regulation was merely to restrict, not to stop, the opening of new banks or branches. In fact, all those who could fulfill the none too strict formal requirement and knew the way to get around government "red tape" usually had no difficulty in obtaining the required approval for entry into or expansion of their banking business. After the conclusion of the war, the Ministry of Finance adopted a policy which permitted the reopening of all the private financial institutions closed by the Japanese and which allowed the merged banks to regain their separate entities. In the meantime, the provincial, municipal, and *hsien* banks, which had been the favorites of local warlords, were allowed to multiply on a hodge-podge basis rather than as an integral part of a well-planned banking system. Not until February, 1947, did the Chinese Government explicitly prohibit further additions of private and local-government banks. But this prohibition was applicable only to a few designated metropolitan areas (Shanghai, Tientsien, Canton, etc.).

The expansionist banking policy was one of the most obvious blunders the Nationalist government committed during the inflation.[10] The blunder can be attributed partly to a lack of understanding on the part of officials in both the Ministry of Finance and local governments as to the undesirability of the mushroom growth of atomistic banking institutions in an unstable economy. But it was apparently not entirely unrelated to self-interest on the part of those officials.

EFFECTS OF BANK CREDIT AND VELOCITIES ON INFLATION

This section will examine the effects, if any, of monetary factors in accentuating the inflation in China with particular emphasis on the following situations: the possible effects of bank credit on the tempo of Chinese inflation; the role of the velocity of money circulation as a determining factor in the course of the inflation; and the interest rates and the credit policies of the government-owned banks.

Volume of bank credit and inflation

The role played by bank credit during the Chinese inflation is examined first by comparing changes in the volume of bank deposits with corresponding changes in note issues, and second by comparing the changes in credit again with the rate of price changes. The factors which led in the surging spiral were obviously the leading motivating forces of the inflationary process. If changes in the volume of bank credit significantly accentuated the tempo of Chinese inflation, then the rate at which the credit multiplied undoubtedly exceeded either the rate of price changes or of note issue expansion, but if the reverse was the case, then the role played by the volume of bank credit was not a major motivating force in the inflation.

The comparison between note issues and bank credit will be made for two periods: the first covers from 1932 through 1935, and the second, from 1935 through June, 1948. The absence of statistical data makes it impossible to extend our comparison beyond the middle of 1948. During the first period, as indicated in our previous discussion, private banks as well as the Central Bank and government banks were authorized to issue notes. After the monetary reform of 1935, all the notes issued by private banks were withdrawn from circulation, and the Central and government banks became the only note-issuing banks. This situation lasted until 1942, when the Central Bank became the sole bank of issuance.

Because of the multiplicity of notes issued in the first period, the ratios of note issues to bank deposits, used as a basis of comparison, are computed for the various banking groups, as well as for all banks. Because of the withdrawal of the notes of private banks and the unavailability of separate deposit statistics for the Central Bank and government banks, only one set of the ratios of note issues to deposits is computed for the second period.

The currency-deposit ratios for 1932–35 remained fairly stable. The ratio for the Central Bank and government banks fluctuated around 0.30, and ratio for all banks around 0.40 (see Table 6.5*a*). After 1936, however, the ratio fluctuated widely (see Table 6.5*b*).

TABLE 6.5a. RATIO OF NOTE ISSUES TO DEPOSITS, 1932–36

Date	*Central Bank*	*Other government banks*	*Central Bank and government banks*	*Private banks*	*All banks*
1932	.24	.35	.33	.47	.40
1933	.30	.29	.30	.45	.37
1934	.32	.33	.33	.47	.40
1935	.29	.34	.32	.65	.45
1936	.42	.32	.38		.38

TABLE 6.5b. RATIO OF NOTE ISSUES TO DEPOSITS, 1936–48

Date	*Ratio for all banks*	*Date*	*Ratio for all banks*
		1946	
1936	.38	Nov.	.65
1937	.54	Dec.	.66
		1947	
1938	.59	Jan.	.78
1939	.75	Feb.	.83
1940	1.08	March	.89
1941	1.28	April	1.05
1942	1.72	May	.73
1943	2.63	June	.74
1944	2.13	July	.81
1945	2.13	Aug.	.85
1946			
Jan.	1.33	Sept.	.84
Feb.	1.32	Oct.	.96
March	1.28	Nov.	1.10
April	.93	Dec.	1.14
		1948	
May	1.03	Jan.	1.11
June	.65	Feb.	1.09
July	.51	March	1.03
Aug.	.58	April	.97
Sept.	.58	May	.92
Oct.	.81	June	.94

Source: *The Chinese Bank Yearbook*, 1932–47 eds.; and *Chung-hua min-kuo t'ung-chi nien-chien* (The Statistical Yearbook of the Republic of China) (Nanking, 1948), 1948 ed.

The series for the ratio are divided into three sub-sections. The first subsection covered 1936–43. During those years there was a steady expansion of note issues in relation to deposits, that is, during the initial stage of the inflation, deposits became submerged in the flood of note issues as a result of the latter's rapid expansion. The second subsection covered 1943 to July, 1946, during which the movement of the note-deposit ratio showed a downward trend. The decrease of the currency-deposit ratio during 1943–45 was due mainly to the expansion of official deposits in the government-owned banks. This downward trend continued in the first half of 1946 because of the inclusion of the deposits of private banks in the areas formerly under Japanese occupation, because of the rapid expansion of deposits in government-owned banks, because of the large-scale gold and foreign-exchange operations of the Central Bank, which slowed down the expansion of the note issues. The third subsection covered all the months from August, 1946, to June, 1948. During these months the note-deposit ratio had an upward trend rising from its low level of 0.51 attained in July, 1946, to values exceeding unity in late 1947 and early 1948. Despite this upward trend the note-deposit ratios of this period remained mostly below the unity level because of the low points reached in 1946. In other words, because of the rapid expansion of note issues in relation to the volume of bank deposits, the expansion of the latter during the first subsection could not have intensified the inflationary spiral. The motivating force of the inflationary process came primarily from the expansion of note issues. During the second subsection, however, the expansion of bank deposits outpaced that of note issues. Hence the expansion in bank deposits did have an amplifying effect. In the third subsection, the note issues again expanded faster than deposits, and the latter thus did not intensify the inflation.[11]

Changes in the money value of bank deposits, however, do not reflect all the possible effects that bank deposits may have had on the Chinese inflation. On the contrary, under conditions such as those in China where production was not readily expansible, the distribution of the monetary purchasing power among the various sectors of the economy usually determined the allocation of the nation's available resources for different uses. A reduction either in the absolute volume of bank deposits in nongovernment accounts or in their rate of expansion in relation to that of government deposits or note issues could mean a diversion of resources from the private to the public sector, and vice versa. One of the most effective means of reducing deposits in private accounts is to curtail bank loans to nongovernment borrowers since bank loans usually constitute an important source of private deposits. Moreover, the expansion of note issues in relation to bank deposits, unless it is duly offset by counterbalancing adjustments, would necessarily mean an increase in the banks' ability to lend. To stop inflation then requires not only the suspension of note expansion but also the elimination or reduction of the banks' excess capacity for creating credit through the adjustment of the legal deposit-reserve ratio.[12]

For comparison with the price changes, the statistical series for the deposits in various groups of Chinese banks are deflated by the corresponding price indices. In order to do this, each of these series is divided into two sections: one for 1932–45, and another for January, 1946, to June, 1948, or the early months of 1949, depending upon the availability of data.

For the first period, the wholesale price index of Chungking is used as the deflator. While the price index of Chungking for 1937–41, was not identical with the corresponding indices of Shanghai, which were of prime importance to the development of the Chinese inflation during the early years, the discrepancy is not so substantial to cause undue distortions in the results. The price index of Shanghai for 1941–45 primarily represents the value of the notes of the Japanese-controlled puppet government rather than that of the fapi notes issued by the Nationalist government. Hence, the Chungking index is used for the period 1937–45. For the second period, from 1946 to 1948 or 1949, the deflation is made on the basis of the Shanghai monthly price index.

With the exception of 1938, in the case of the deposits in private banks, and 1938 and 1939, in the case of the deposits in the Central Bank and government banks, the real values of the deposits were drastically reduced during the inflation (see Chart 6.1a). The sharpest and steadiest reduction occurred in private bank deposits. The reduction in real value of the deposits in the Central Bank extended only to 1941 and in government banks to 1943. After these points their curves reverted to an upward trend, although none ever returned to the level of 1937.

For the second period (i.e., the postwar years), separate statistics for the deposits of the Central Bank and government banks are not available. For this reason the study of the period must be confined to comparisons between the deposits in all the government-owned banks (including the Central Bank and government banks) and those in private banks. During these years the real values of note issues and deposits were mostly below the unity level (see Chart 6.1b). The loss of real value was largest in the deflated index for the note issues and smallest in the index for the deposits in private banks. The deflated index for deposits in the government bank for most of the time was located between these two indices. This order of

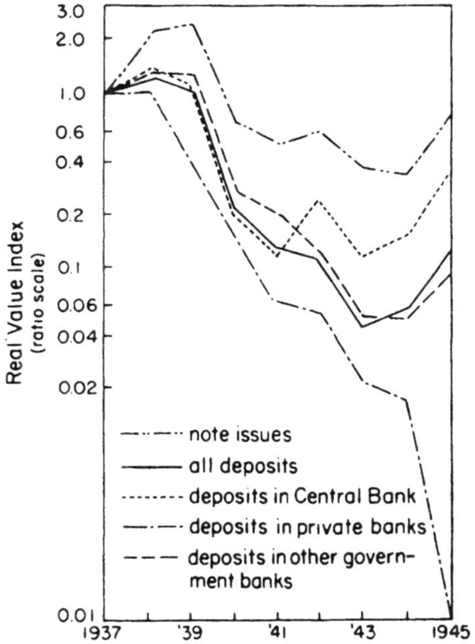

CHART 6.1a. REAL VALUES OF NOTE ISSUES AND BANK DEPOSITS, 1937–45 (CHUNGKING WHOLESALE PRICE INDEX = 1)

magnitude was directly opposed to that of 1937–45 (see Chart 6.1a). The relative importance of deposit money as a circulating medium in the metropolitan areas, which dominated the economic activities of China during the postwar years, was one of the possible factors causing the relative expansion of bank deposits.

Our earlier discussions have shown that during the Chinese inflation increases in prices usually exceeded the expansion of note issues. This situation is clear from the fact that all the mean year-to-year link relatives of the price indices are higher than the corresponding mean relatives of note issues for all the periods under consideration (see Table 1.1). Similarly, the expansion of bank credit lagged behind not only the price changes but also the rate of note expansion for most of the inflation period. The former phenomenon was evidenced by the shrinkage of the real value of bank credit, and the latter by the dominance of the downward trend of the note-deposit ratio. It is thus clear that with the possible exception of a brief period of time (such as the note-issue expansion in 1937 and early 1938), neither the volume of the note issues nor

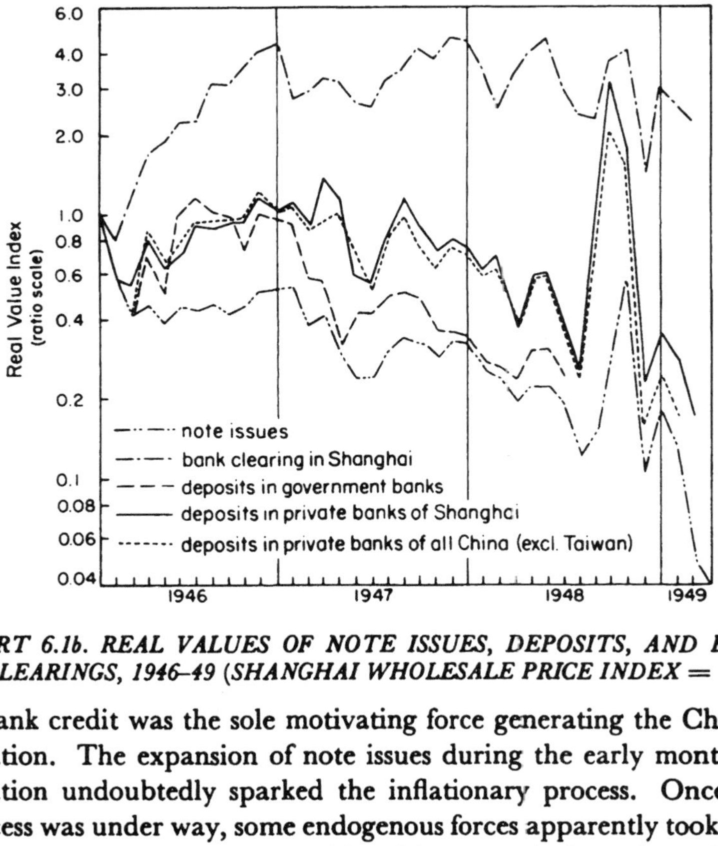

CHART 6.1b. REAL VALUES OF NOTE ISSUES, DEPOSITS, AND BANK CLEARINGS, 1946–49 (SHANGHAI WHOLESALE PRICE INDEX = 1)

of bank credit was the sole motivating force generating the Chinese inflation. The expansion of note issues during the early months of inflation undoubtedly sparked the inflationary process. Once the process was under way, some endogenous forces apparently took over and propelled the spiral toward its ultimate explosion. One of such endogenous forces was the velocity of money circulation.

Velocity of money circulation and inflation

For the purpose of this study, two versions of velocities are used. The first version is represented by the ratio of the price link relative to note issues, and the second concerns the velocity of bank deposit.

The ratio of price changes to the corresponding note issue changes (i.e., the price-currency ratio) is one of the basic measurements used in this discussion of the general pattern of the Chinese inflation (see Chapter I). It has been frequently employed as an approximation of the velocity of money circulation in studies of underdeveloped countries when no better alternative was available.[13] Reflection, however, reveals that the price-currency ratio is a hybrid, which is meaningful only under certain conditions. If the production in physical units is assumed to be constant, then the change in national income is in proportion to the change in price; and the price-currency ratio is a good approximation for the income velocity of money. If in the volume of production the relationship between the magnitudes of note issues and bank credit, and that between their velocities of circulation remain constant, the changes in the price-currency ratio should adequately reflect changes in the transaction velocity of money.[14] In view of the instability in the relationship between the volume of note issues and the volume of bank deposits and the uncertainty of the relationship between the two velocities, the usefulness of the price-currency ratio for measuring the transaction velocity also becomes questionable. On the other hand, the earlier studies of consumption and production gave no evidence of drastic changes in physical production during the Chinese inflation. Therefore, it seems more justifiable to use the price-currency ratio for measuring the income velocity than for representing the transaction velocity. It is on this basis that our discussion of the velocity of money circulation will be developed.

As shown in Chapter I, the ratio of price changes to that of note issues tended to rise with the intensity of inflation. This trend was obvious not only in the comparisons among periods, but also in the changes within a period (see Tables 1.1 and 1.2). This was true in the fapi area and in all other monetary areas representing the subprocesses of the Chinese inflation, as well as in the inflations of other countries.

From Charts 6.2, 6.3 and 6.4, where the ratios of price changes to those of note issues for various areas are shown, the following observations may be derived:

1. There was an obvious tendency for the price-currency ratio to

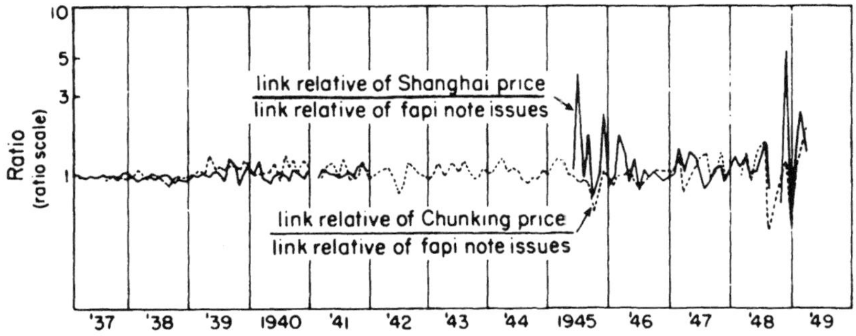

CHART 6.2. RATIO OF MONTHLY LINK RELATIVE OF WHOLESALE PRICE TO LINK RELATIVE OF FAPI NOTE ISSUES, 1937–49

increase (or decrease) with intensification (or slackening) of inflation, and this upward (or downward) trend usually developed along a zigzag course, indicating that leads or lags were generally involved in the course of such changes (see Chart 6.2).

2. In the case of Chungking, the spiraling process generated by the price-currency ratio had almost a continuous trend of divergency, reflecting the increasing tempo of inflation (see Chart 6.2).

3. The situation of Shanghai was slightly different. Here the spiraling process was divided into four phases. The first phase

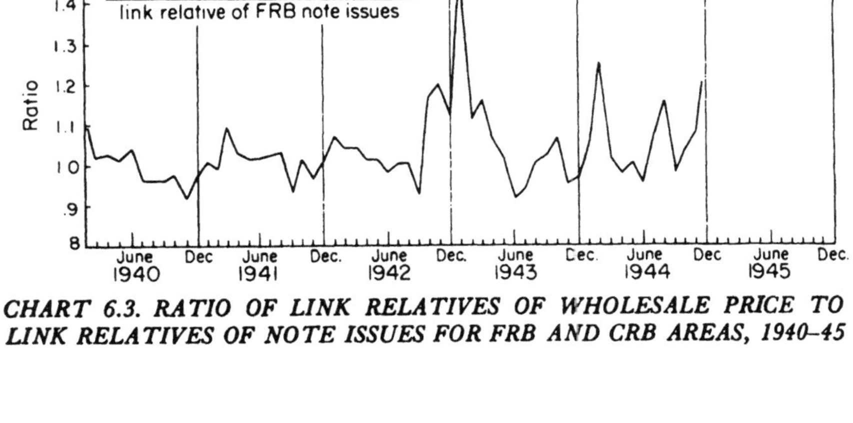

CHART 6.3. RATIO OF LINK RELATIVES OF WHOLESALE PRICE TO LINK RELATIVES OF NOTE ISSUES FOR FRB AND CRB AREAS, 1940–45

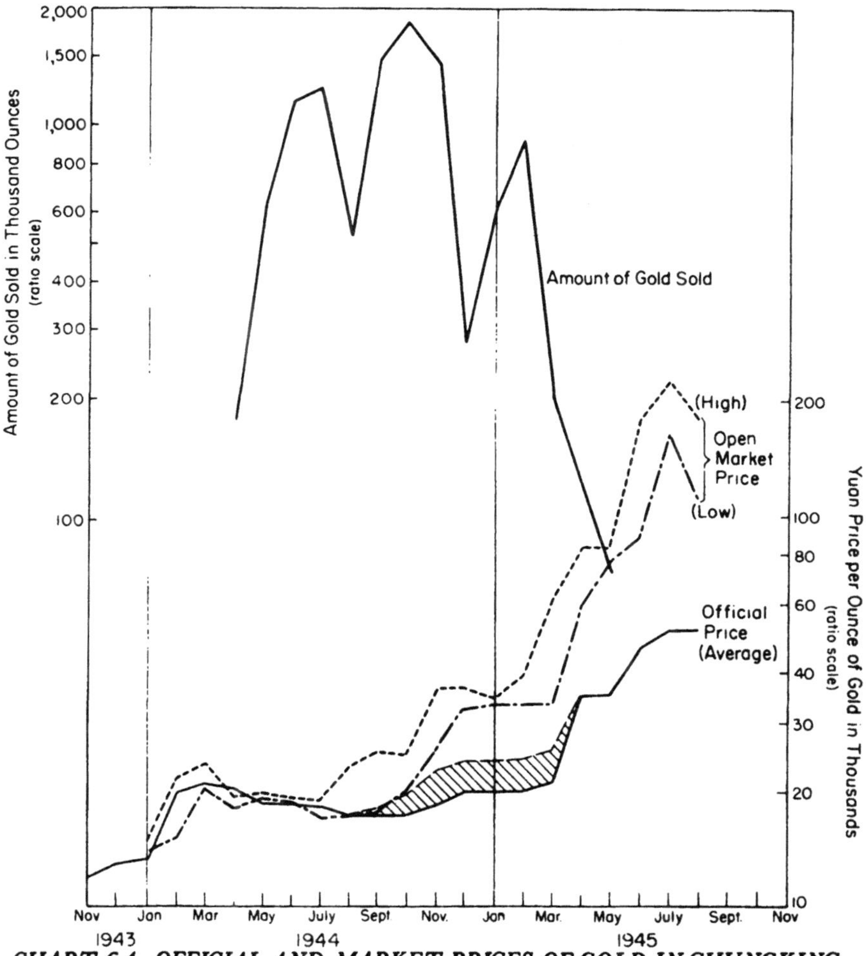

CHART 6.4. OFFICIAL AND MARKET PRICES OF GOLD IN CHUNGKING, 1943–45

The shaded area represents the adjustment in the official prices resulting from the required bond purchase.

Source: Chu Ssu-huang, *Min-kuo ching-chi-shi* (The Economic History of the Republic) (Shanghai, 1947), pp. 428–29; and unpublished records of the Central Bank of China.

covered 1937–41. The second phase, extending from January, 1942, through May, 1945, covered developments in the CRB area (see Chart 6.3). In both these phases, the price-currency ratio generated a divergent spiraling process. In the third phase, covering the period from June, 1945, to the end of 1946, the spiraling process became convergent. The convergency indicated the slackening of inflation during the months immediately before and after V-J Day. This temporary relief reflected, in part at least, the public belief then prevailing that economic stabilization would be forthcoming with the end of World War II. In the fourth phase, covering approximately 1947–48, the spiraling process reverted to its trend of divergency, and reached its climax toward the end of 1948, when the system of gold yuan plunged the nation's economy into unprecedented chaos. The fifth phase, consisting of the early months of 1949, the spiraling process became convergent again. This change to convergency may be construed as a temporary respite after the financial convulsion occurred in the concluding months of 1948. In fact, it is reasonably certain that the spiral would have reverted to a state of divergency, if there had been sufficient data to extend the course of the spiral for a few more months.

4. The relation of the prices to the note issues in the CRB and the FRB currency areas was similar to the corresponding relation of the fapi area. In the case of the FRB note area (see Chart 6.3b), most of the price-currency ratios for the years under consideration were above the unity level, with a general tendency for the ratio to rise with intensification of inflation. In the case of the CRB currency area (see Chart 6.3a) the situation was slightly different, although the basic principle that the ratio rose with the intensity of inflation remained unchanged. As was shown previously (see Table 1.3), the annual averages of the price-currency ratio in the CRB case stayed below the unity level during 1941–43 and then rose suddenly to 1.07 in 1944, when the inflation in that currency area turned from bad to worse.

The relationship between the period-to-period changes of note issues and of prices shown in previous discussions exemplifies clearly the spiraling process which was discussed in Chapter I and Appendix 1. This lead-and-lag relationship between note issues and prices explains, in part at least, such a paradoxical phenomenon as the shortage of the medium of circulation in the midst of the plethora of note issues.

The usual procedure for determining the velocity of bank deposits is to divide the volume of deposits into the corresponding debits to bank account. Wherever the statistics for debits are not available, the volume of bank clearings is often used instead to compute the velocity.[15]

In this study of the velocity of deposit money during the Chinese inflation, several problems occur. First, although the velocity has been studied on the basis of both the debits and the clearings, none of these studies has gone beyond the postwar years. Second, the difficulty arises from the statistics of deposits. The facilities of bank clearings were available in a few major cities and Shanghai, which was by far the most important in the country. In order to utilize these statistics for prewar bank clearings, the regional data for bank deposits are needed; but these are not available. After 1945 only the statistics for deposits in the Shanghai private banks were published. The statistics for the clearings among the Shanghai banks covered transactions involving both the private- and government-owned banks. For other cities with clearing facilities, the regional statistics for bank deposits are nonexistent. Thus, if the velocity is to be measured by the ratio of the Shanghai clearings to the deposit liabilities of the private banks in Shanghai, the velocity will be exaggerated. On the other hand, if it is computed on the basis of the Shanghai clearings and the total deposit liabilities of all banks (including all the private- and government-owned banks in China), the velocity will be unduly low. In view of the complications involved in computing the velocity on the basis of the clearing-deposit ratio, the procedure using the deposit liabilities of Shanghai private banks and the related debits is obviously preferable. This preference holds not only because of theoretical considerations but also because of the complications involved in matching statistics of bank clearings and deposits. Unfortunately, the debit-deposit ratios are available only for 1947 and 1948, whereas the data for the clearings and deposits cover all the postwar years. For the purpose of comparison, I have computed all three versions of velocity based on (i) the Shanghai clearing for all banks and the deposit liabilities of the private banks in Shanghai, (ii) the Shanghai clearings and the deposit liabilities of all banks in China, and (iii) the deposit liabilities of the Shanghai private banks and their related debits. The results are shown in Table 6.6.

The velocity of money circulation tended to increase with the intensity of inflation. This trend was true regardless of whether the

TABLE 6.6. VELOCITIES OF BANK DEPOSITS, 1946–49

	Ratio of Shanghai clearings to demand deposits		*Ratio of debits to deposits*
	Shanghai private banks[a]	*All banks*[b]	
1946			
Jan.	8.53	.36	
Feb.	11.95	.48	
March	15.50	.81	
April	17.45	.86	
May	25.66	1.33	
June	27.72	.85	
July	23.93	.83	
Aug.	30.38	1.10	
Sept.	28.77	1.14	
Oct.	32.56	1.71	
Nov.	30.91	1.39	
Dec.	36.76	1.43	
1947			
Jan.	21.33	1.05	19.77
Feb.	28.32	1.72	24.63
March	20.93	1.84	21.32
April	24.10	2.81	22.57
May	40.57	2.18	36.60
June	42.02	2.10	38.05
July	33.89	2.29	37.99
Aug.	28.51	2.33	32.63
Sept.	43.78	2.92	39.58
Oct.	49.65	3.46	46.67
Nov.	52.43	4.03	46.26
Dec.	56.78	4.16	61.49

1948			
Jan.	53.85	3.88	54.70
Feb.	30.88	2.87	36.43
March	81.75	4.74	23.42
April	72.91	4.38	79.18
May	80.10	4.90	86.80
June	81.51	4.06	65.44
July	89.88		108.56
Aug.	27.71		50.64
Sept.	10.88		15.76
Oct.	22.34		21.31
Nov.	52.81		74.69
Dec.	76.80		100.82
1949			
Jan.	79.81		
Feb.	118.50		
March			

[a] Ratios are those of Shanghai bank clearings to the outstanding balance of demand deposits in Shanghai private banks.

[b] Ratios are obtained by dividing the balance of demand deposits in all banks (including the private banks in Shanghai and all government owned banks) into the bank clearings of Shanghai for the corresponding period.

There is no data for the spaces left blank in table.

Sources: *The Central Bank Monthly* Vols. I–IV (1946–49) and unpublished records of the Central Bank of China.

velocity referred to that of bank deposits, or to the ratio of price changes to note issues, or whether the velocity of deposits was measured on the basis of bank debits or bank clearings. This behavior of the velocity, which was found not only in the Chinese inflation but also in other inflations (see Chapter VIII), is of great importance. In fact, the high velocity of money circulation converted the Chinese inflation from a fruitful means for augmenting government receipts into a process which in a few years' time melted away virtually all the income of the government in real terms. Recent studies indicate that the role of the velocity can be important under a mild type of inflation as well as under hyperinflation.[16] Some economists believe that unless both the volume and the velocity of money are controlled, no central bank would be in a position to make its monetary policy fully effective.[17]

Conclusion

The expansion of money supply, whether represented by note issues or by the sum of note issues and bank deposits, lagged behind the rise of the price index. The only exception to this generalization was found in the early stage of the inflation, when the money supply occasionally took a significant lead over the price increases.

During the Chinese inflation, both price indices and note issues usually expanded much faster than bank deposits. This indicated that the volume of deposits was definitely not a major force in generating the inflationary process.

The velocity of money circulation increased with the intensification of the Chinese inflation regardless of whether the velocity was measured on the basis of the ratio of price changes to currency changes, or whether it referred to the velocity of bank deposits. This characteristic of the velocity had undoubtedly been a major factor in making the Chinese inflation, like other great inflations, self-propagating after it gained momentum.

GOLD OPERATIONS AND INTEREST POLICIES

The gold operations[18]

History of the gold policy. Before September, 1939, the purchase and sale of gold in China were unrestricted. Then the Nationalist government promulgated the law which for the first time not only nationalized gold but also prohibited private gold transactions in the country. This decree remained effective, at least on paper, until June, 1943. The primary objective of the gold nationalization in 1939, like that of silver, was to convert the nation's specie holdings into foreign exchange for replenishing its monetary reserve.

After 1941 the trade between Free China and the outside world was reduced to a trickle. In the meantime, the inflation in China turned from bad to worse. Because of these changes, the prohibition on gold transactions was lifted in June, 1943. In September, 1943, the Chinese government formally reversed its early gold policy. Instead of buying it from the public, the Central Bank began to sell gold with a view to reducing the volume of money in circulation. While the initial sales were met with the gold then in the Bank's vault, the operation was financed primarily by the U.S. Treasury Credit of $500 million granted in 1942. Of this total, $220 million were used for the purchase of gold from the United States to make possible the subsequent sales operations in China.[19]

At first the gold sales were made on a cash basis. But, before long, the lag in gold shipments from the United States made it necessary to seek recourse in sales for future delivery. In addition to direct gold sales, the Central Bank, through its designated agents, also accepted gold savings deposits in fapi on the basis of the official gold price prevailing at the time of deposit. These deposits had maturities of one, two, and three years, bearing an annual interest of 2, 3, and 4 percent respectively. Both the principal and the interest were payable in gold upon the maturity of deposits.

The official prices of gold were 12,000, 13,000, and 14,300 yuan per ounce at the end of November and December, 1943, and January, 1944, respectively. Within the first nine days of February, 1944, five upward adjustments were made to raise the price to 21,500 yuan per ounce. The official price remained virtually stable, with the exception of some minor adjustments in both directions until September, 1944.

Up to July, 1944, the official and the market prices of gold were very close to each other, and no major difficulties were therefore encountered in administering the gold sales (see Chart 6.4). After that, the official price was subjected only to occasional adjustments and became increasingly unrealistic in terms of the market quotation, which soared with the inflation. To curtail unjustifiable windfalls and the public's rush for gold, the Chinese government in September, 1944, revised its gold regulation to require gold buyers to purchase, in addition to paying the official price, government bonds equivalent to 10 percent of the value of the gold purchased. At the end of October the percentage of the required bond-purchase was raised from 10 to 20 percent. The bond thus purchased yielded an interest of 10 percent per annum and were repayable after three years. Because of the rapid depreciation of the Chinese currency and the exorbitant interest rates prevailing in the market, the purchase of such low-interest bonds was almost tantamount to an outright contribution to the government. It might therefore be considered as a disguised upward adjustment of the official gold price. The official prices with the bond purchase were even then too low. On November 23, 1944, the official gold price was set at 20,000 yuan per ounce, giving a total cost of 24,000 yuan per ounce when the cost of the required bond purchase is included. In March, 1945, the official price was changed to 35,000 yuan per ounce, and the required bond purchase was abolished. In June the price rose further to 50,000 yuan.

Despite these upward adjustments the discrepancy between the official and the market quotations of gold became increasingly large. In order to avoid an undue drain upon its gold reserve, the government finally suspended its gold sales in May, 1945, and the purchase-gold-by-deposit arrangement in the following month.

After the suspension of these sales operations, the market price of gold zoomed in the early part of July, 1945, to an unprecedented height of 225,000 yuan an ounce. In the following month, however, it slumped to 170,000 yuan, when the Central Bank delivered gold it had sold during previous months on the forward basis. In the latter part of September, 1945, the Japanese surrender led to a large-scale dishoarding of gold, and its market price dropped to a low level of about 70,000 yuan per ounce.

When the financial market was reopened in Shanghai in March, 1946, the Central Bank used the open market operation in gold as a major antidote for combating inflation. During this period the old rigid-price policy, under which the selling price of gold changed only on rare occasions, was abandoned. In addition to the public allotments to goldsmiths, the Bank also made undisclosed sales through its agents in the open market. In both cases, the Bank's quotations were determined daily, and sometimes several times a day, on the basis of the actual market conditions. The accentuation of inflation, however, made it necessary for the Bank to suspend its gold sales in February, 1947, because of the drain on the government's diminishing gold reserve.

The emergency regulations announced by the government in February, 1947, not only suspended the Bank's gold sales, but also prohibited gold transactions in the open market. The prohibition, however, was enforced effectively for only a few months. After that, clandestine transactions in gold again became rampant.

The Monetary Reform Act of August, 1948, reiterated the prohibition of gold dealings and required the surrender of all private specie holdings. Under the threat of severe penalty and because of the realistic buying rate of the Central Bank, 1,677,163.6 ounces[20] of gold, as well as a large amount of silver and foreign currencies, were sold to the Central Bank for gold yuan during the first six weeks following the proclamation of the monetary reform. The purchase of gold, silver, and foreign exchange, though greatly strengthening the specie and foreign currency reserves of the Central Bank, caused a large increase in the note issue of the Bank and increased the inflationary pressure on the economy.

In November, 1948, the gold sales operation was reinstituted. Instead of selling at the market rate, however, the financial authority erroneously reverted to the old outdated policy of selling gold at pegged prices. The selling rate was first fixed at 1,000 gold yuan to one ounce of fine gold. When the gold price in the market began to rise and the gap between the official and the market quotations became increasingly large, a deposit of 1,000 yuan in addition to the official price of 1,000 yuan was later required for each ounce of gold purchased. In addition, the gold purchases for each individual were limited to ten ounces. After December 15 the quota was further reduced to one ounce per person for every three months, and the gold was sold only against a residence registration card. These restrictions, designed primarily to reduce the drain on the gold reserve of the Bank, accentuated the rise of gold prices in the market and thereby intensified the rush for gold purchases at the Central Bank. Sales against residence certificates were suspended on December 24, 1948. On January 5 of the following year the gold sales were resumed. The Bank's selling price was then raised from 1,000 to 2,000 yuan per ounce. In addition, gold buyers were also required to pay an equilization charge representing the approximate difference between the official gold price of 2,000 yuan an ounce and the yuan equivalent of gold derived from the Bank's exchange certificate rate. The latter equivalent was computed on the basis of the official gold-dollar cross-rate of fifty to one ounce of fine gold. Since the exchange-certificate rate under the system then in force was flexible and close to the market quotation, the equalization charge mentioned above became an increasingly important part of the gold price, and the original quotation of 2,000 yuan was soon reduced to a negligible fraction. On January 17 the gold sales were once more suspended. On February 1 a new gold bond (i.e., a bond purchasable with domestic currency and redeemable in gold) was issued in place of the gold sales. Although the bond was regularly quoted in the Shanghai Security Exchange, the daily transactions never reached a significant magnitude. Their effect on the money market could therefore have been only nominal.

Toward the end of February, 1949, the gold operation was again resumed. The emphasis at this time, however, was shifted from stabilizing the gold price to maximizing the amount of paper money to be withdrawn from circulation. There was no official price announced by the Central Bank. Gold sales were made at rates which might produce a maximum deflationary effect on the money market with a minimum amount of gold. In most cases, the Bank's sales were made at the prevailing market price; that is, the sales were started at a high price which was reduced gradually when the market supply of gold was increased by the sales. The operational policy was determined in daily morning meetings by a specially organized committee consisting of experts of the government banks.[21] The meetings usually began with an estimate of the possible local currency receipts, the disbursements of the Central Bank and other government institutions for the day, and the potential supply of funds in the market (e.g., the clearing balances of private banks at the Central Bank, expected payments by the Bank, etc.). In case of excess disbursements over receipts and a market with high potential liquidity, deflationary operations were adopted to drain the surplus money from the market. The gold sales were in fact only one of many weapons used for attaining this objective. In addition, sales of commodities, foreign currencies, foreign-exchange certificates, gold bonds, delays in Bank payment, and the temporary suspension or restriction of loans by the government banks, were also used for deflationary operations. The simultaneous use of these multifarious measures with proper coordination, instead of an isolated application of gold or some other operation as the measure for controlling the money market, was the chief characteristic and the advantage of the system of open-market operations inaugurated during this period.

Evaluation of the gold operation The gold operation of the Chinese government may roughly be divided into six major phases. The first extended from the beginning of the gold operation in 1943 to February, 1946. During this period, the gold operation consisted mainly of over-the-counter sales by government-owned banks to individual purchasers. Transactions were mainly on a "retail" basis. The second phase lasted from March, 1946, to February, 1947. The gold sales during this period were primarily in the form of open market operations through brokers or agents in the Shanghai market. The sales therefore were conducted at the "wholesale" rather than the "retail" level. The third phase started in March, 1947, and ended with the monetary reform in August, 1948. During this period no major gold policy was in active operation. For most of these months the Central Bank, in an effort to replenish its gold reserve, bought more gold from the market than it sold, but the amount of transactions was negligibly small. The fourth phase extended from August through October, 1948, during which the Central Bank purchased a large amount of gold and foreign currency from the public, instead of selling to them. The fifth phase started in November, 1948, when the Nationalist government, in an attempt to redress the mishaps resulting from the ill-fated monetary reform, reverted to gold sales over the bank counter at a rigidly fixed price. The sixth phase covered March and April, 1949. During this period, the policy of selling gold in Shanghai's organized market at the wholesale level once more replaced over-the-counter sales.

In terms of both the scale and the duration of operations, the first and the second phases were by far the most important. The first phase was significant because it represented the formative stage of subsequent gold policies. It was also the phase during which the controversial negotiations between the U.S. Treasury and the Chinese officials concerning the shipment of U.S. gold to China were completed. The Chinese requested that $220 million of the $500 million credit granted by the American government in 1942 be paid in the form of gold for the domestic operation in China. This request at first met strong opposition by the U.S. Treasury on the ground that the gold operation had been wasteful and ineffective as an antidote against inflation. But the Americans finally yielded to the Chinese request because of the latter's insistence.[22]

Despite the publicity it received in the United States, the operation during this initial phase was less significant both in terms of magnitude and of actual effect than that of the second phase. About 3.36 million ounces of fine gold were sold by the Central Bank during the second phase against a sale of 3.34 million (including both the outright sales and the deposits redeemable in gold) in the first phase. Moreover, the ratio of monthly receipts from gold sales to the monthly increment in note issue of the second phase had an average of 27.12 percent and a range of 3.12–58.61 percent, against an average of 4.38 percent and a range of 0.01–35.86 percent for the first phase (see Table 6.7).

In the fifth phase the Chinese government reverted to the crude policy of selling gold over the counters of government banks at a rigid official price. As expected, the efficiency of the operation was low in comparison with the experience of the second and last phase. This was demonstrated by the low average ratio of the sales receipts to the monthly increment in note issue—10.34 percent for this period as against 27.12 percent and 85.61 percent for the second and the sixth phases respectively (see Table 6.7).

The gold operations of the sixth phase are worthy of special note because of the changes in operational technique. During the seven weeks ending April 22, 1949, for which the comprehensive operational statistics have been available, the weekly ratio of the gold sales receipts to the increment in note issues averaged 85.61 percent with a range of 29.42–147.56 percent, and the gold sales were made at an average rate of 79,100 ounces a month. It is clear therefore

TABLE 6.7. STATISTICAL SUMMARY OF GOLD OPERATIONS IN CHINA, 1943–49

Phase	RATIO OF GOLD SALES RECEIPTS TO NEW NOTE ISSUE: *Average (percent)*	RATIO OF GOLD SALES RECEIPTS TO NEW NOTE ISSUE: *Range (percent)*	GOLD SOLD: *Average monthly rate (ounces)*	GOLD SOLD: *Total for period (ounces)*
1 1943–Feb. 1946	4.38	.01– 35.86	66,980	3,343,590
2 March 1946–Feb. 1947	27.12	3.12– 58.61	280,360	3,364,300
3–4 March 1947–Oct. 1948[a]				
5 Nov.–Dec. 1948	10.34	3.17– 12.63	340,200	680,300
6 March–April 1949	85.61[b]	29.42–147.56[b]	79,100	237,110
			Total	7,625,300

[a] No gold sales policy in operation. [b] Weekly rate for figures.

Source: For phase 1, *The Statistical Yearbook for the Republic of China*, p. 258; for phases 2 to 6, unpublished records of the Central Bank of China.

that the high efficiency of this phase of gold operation was attained at a relatively low cost. This high efficiency resulted from the depreciation of the gold and foreign-currency value of the notes in circulation. The policy of selling gold at a realistic market level, rather than at an unduly low quotation undoubtedly also contributed to the improvement.

The use of gold sales as an anti-inflationary measure was not exclusive to China. Similar policies were adopted during and after the World War II in Greece, India, Egypt, and several other Middle Eastern countries.[23] The following are some general observations on gold operations:

First, the large-scale sales of gold, particularly in the countries where the international movement of the specie was restricted, tended to depreciate the gold price in the local market in relation to the prices of other commodities. Sometimes, even the relation between the gold price and the foreign-exchange rate was distorted when the local gold market had been successfully segregated from the world market.

Second, although the principle underlying China's gold policy was not entirely groundless, the efficiency with which the policy was put into effect certainly left much to be desired. Had the gold, together with the foreign-exchange holdings, of the Central Bank been sold at a constantly realistic price, the cost involved in attaining the deflationary effect would certainly have been substantially reduced. Moreover, according to the experiences of some of the countries in the Middle East, a combination of gold sales with an issuance of lottery-bearing bonds by the government would have offered a preferable alternative to outright gold sales, that is to say, instead of selling gold directly to the public, it might have been used as a prize for government lottery bonds. The bait of the prize, according to experiences in these countries, would have enabled the government to float bonds at a cost much lower than would otherwise have been possible.

Third, gold sales at best can only temporarily relieve inflationary pressure on the money market; they do not provide any fundamental solution to the problem of inflation. Such a solution can be found only by eliminating the basic factors (e.g., fiscal deficit, credit expansion, etc.) that generate the inflationary process.

Interest rate and credit policy

The interest structure of the Chinese money market during the years under consideration consisted of four groups of rates. At the bottom of the ladder were the Central Bank rates, the rates charged by the Bank on advances or rediscounts to other banks, and on its loans to government agencies. These rates were decided by the monetary authority (specifically the Joint Head Office of Government Banks) rather than the market conditions. During most of the inflation, the rates were kept at an unusually low level in relation to the changes in prices and the market rates of interest. Following closely the rates of the Central Bank were the rates of the government banks. The rates of the government banks were also subject to control of the Joint Head Office of Government Banks. To keep interest rates of these banks at a low level, the Central Bank was usually obligated to make available its lending facilities to the government banks. In fact, when the normal sources of bank deposit dwindled, lending from the Central Bank became a main source of loanable funds for the government banks.

Next were rates of private banks (including both the modern and native banks). These rates were too subject to the control of the monetary authority. Any change in the interest rates of these banks in a given region required the prior approval of the branch of the Central Bank operating in the region, since these rates were subject to a much greater regional variation than either the rates of the Central Bank or government banks. As a whole, the lending facilities of the Central Bank were not so readily available to the private banks as they were to government banks. Accordingly, the government control over the rates of private banks was usually much looser, and these rates were more sensitive to the changes in market conditions than the rates of government banks.

On the top of the ladder were the interest rates prevailing in the free market. These were rates applicable to loans by nonbank lenders. Since the lending facilities of the Central and government banks were not accessible to these lenders, the monetary authority only influenced the market rates through the effects of the credit policy of the Central Bank on the supply of and demand for loanable funds in the market.

The behavior of various interest rates are shown in Charts 6.5–6.7.

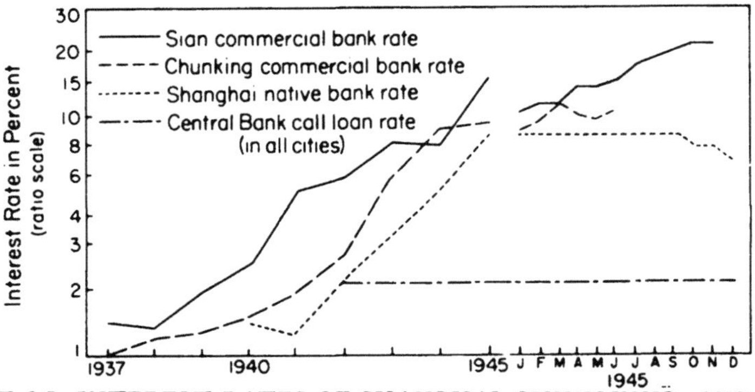

CHART 6.5. INTEREST RATES OF SHANGHAI, CHUNGKING, AND SIAN, 1937–45 (in percent per month)

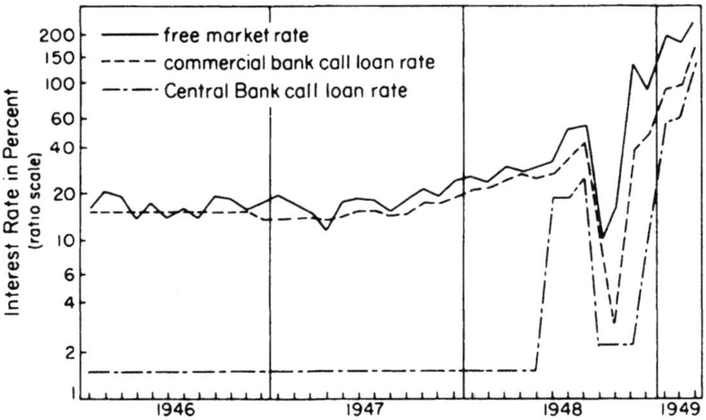

CHART 6.6. SHANGHAI INTEREST RATES, 1946–49 (in percent per month)

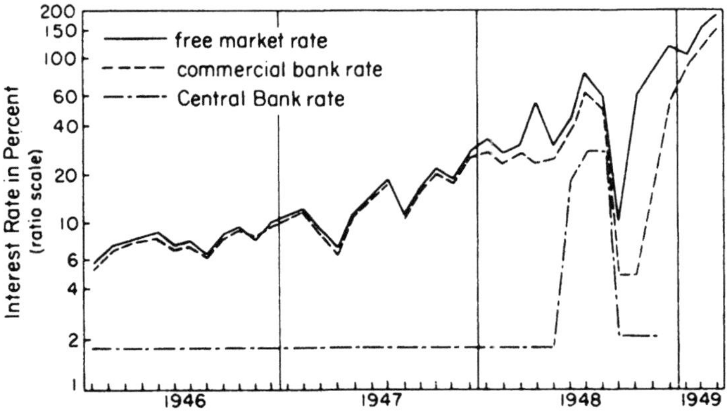

CHART 6.7. CHUNGKING INTEREST RATES, 1946–49 (in percent per month)

With the exception of the period from May to August, 1948, and the months after November, 1948, the interest rates of the Central Bank and the government banks were incredibly low. Even during these months when a realistic rate policy was attempted, the differences between the rates of these banks and the market quotation were still appreciable. The association between the private bank rate and the market rate of interest was close, despite the control of the former by the Central Bank. There was, however, a tendency for the lead of the market rate to increase during the later stages of the inflation. The experience in August, 1948, showed that the Central Bank, by manipulating its rates and by providing cheap loans, did influence the market rate of interest. But such an influence was only temporary when the fundamental problems of the inflation were not yet solved. Because of the cheap money policy of the government, even the market rate of interest was not always high enough to reflect the full impact of the inflation. This is shown by a comparison of the increases in the market rate and the changes of the price indices during the period under consideration—a subject discussed at length in the next chapter.

CHAPTER VII

The Redistributional Effects of the Chinese Inflation

The redistributional effects of an inflation may be examined from two angles: one is the lead-lag hypothesis; the other is based on the debtor-creditor relation.[1]

The lead-lag hypothesis implies that inflation works in favor of the factors of production which lead in an upward adjustment during inflation and against the factors which lag in such an adjustment. In this connection, the comparison between changes in wage and profit is particularly significant. Since interest and rent are tied to contractual arrangements and are invariably lagging in adjustment, wage and profit are the only two factors which are in a likely position to compete with one another for the lead in adjustment in the course of inflation. Since profit is closely related to the difference between price and wage, the profit-wage relation is often studied on the basis of the relation between price and wage for the reason of expediency.

The debtor-creditor hypothesis implies that, so long as debt is specified in fixed monetary units, inflation invariably works in favor of the debtor and against the creditor. Because of the erosive effects of inflation on the purchasing power of money, the real value of a given amount of money that the creditor receives at the time of repayment is usually less than the sum commands at the time of his lending. Moreover, during the period of acute inflation, the rate of interest usually falls short of the rate of price increase, thereby precluding the interest payment from adequately compensating the loss due to currency depreciation. Studies of the lead-lag hypothesis are usually based on the changes in the distribution of aggregate income and product (e.g., the national income, personal income) among various income groups.[2] The unavailability of the data for income and product precludes the use of such an approach to the present study. The best alternative is to compare changes in prices, wages, material costs, to changes in the values of foreign currencies, gold, and stocks. In some cases, the wage and price data of China are so inadequate that some makeshift substitutions are necessary.

For studying the debtor-credit relation, the usual approach is to segregate business firms into debtors and creditors depending on whether a firm's monetary liabilities exceed or fall short of its monetary assets.[3] This approach is likewise not feasible because financial statistics of business firms are not available. Instead, the examination is based on the relation between the rate of interest and change in commodity prices.

PRICE VERSUS COST IN INDUSTRIES

This study of the relative changes in product prices and labor costs is divided into two parts: the first refers to the prices and costs of Chungking for 1937–47; the second, to those of Shanghai for 1946–48. The former represents mainly the conditions prevailing during the war; the latter, those of the postwar years.

The Chungking study is based on the money-wage index compiled by the Directorate General of Budgets, Accounts and Statistics of the Nationalist government and the price indices for raw materials, semimanufactured goods and manufactured goods compiled by the Central Bank of China. The price series cover the years 1937–49, but wage data are available only for 1937–47. For this reason, the Chungking study cannot be extended beyond 1947. To facilitate comparison, the wage index and the price index for raw materials are expressed in percentages of the price index for semimanufactured goods for the period under consideration. The ratio of the wage index, or that of the index of raw-material cost, to the index of semimanufactured goods should be above (or below) the unity level (or 100 percent), if the wages or raw-material costs rose (or fell) faster than the price of semimanufactured goods. If so, then producers of semimanufactured goods would have been in a relatively unfavorable (or favorable) position compared with that of labor or suppliers of raw materials. This means that the inflation resulted in a redistribution of income in favor of (or against) laborers and suppliers of raw materials at the expense (or in favor) of the entrepreneurs of the manufacturing industry.

Similarly, the percentages of the wage index and the price index for semimanufactured goods in the corresponding index of manufactured goods were computed for studying the redistribution effects

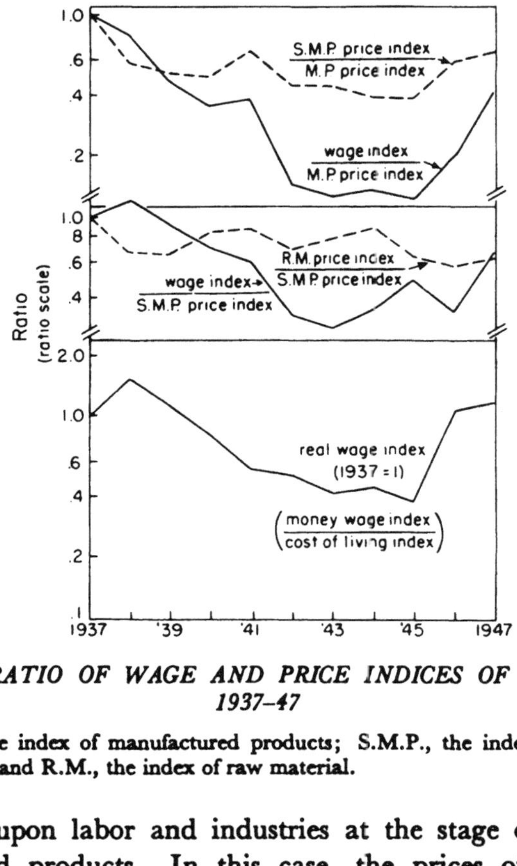

CHART 7.1. RATIO OF WAGE AND PRICE INDICES OF CHUNGKING, 1937–47

M.P. denotes the index of manufactured products; S.M.P., the index of semimanufactured goods; and R.M., the index of raw material.

of inflation upon labor and industries at the stage of producing manufactured products. In this case, the prices of semimanufactured products represent the material cost.

No attempt has been made to compile any composite index for wage and material costs. Because of the wide variations in proportion at which these factors were used in various Chinese industries, no one combination can represent the actual conditions. Regardless of what these proportions were, all such combinations, being weighted averages of the labor and material costs, would have to lie somewhere between these two costs. Therefore, the indices representing wage and material costs in Chart 7.1 should indicate the range within which all the weighted averages of such costs would be located.

These are the conclusions derived from the study of relative changes of various cost and price indices:

1. The position of the industrial entrepreneurs during the inflation was favorable. The prices of both the semimanufactured and the manufactured goods rose during inflation, not only relative to the 1937 level but also to their respective raw material and wage costs.

2. During the initial years of the war (1937–39), there was a tendency for the rise in prices of manufactured products to surpass the rise of semimanufactured products, and the rise in prices of semimanufactured goods to surpass that for raw materials. Since more industrial products than raw materials were normally imported into China before the war, this phenomenon may be attributed to the curtailment of imports into China, because of a change in the government's trade policy or because of the Japanese blockade.

3. Both the advantages to producers of manufactured products over semimanufactured products, and the advantages of semimanufactured products over raw materials decreased during the postwar years (1946–48). These phenomena may be accounted for by the curtailed flow of indigenous raw materials from their producing areas to the industrial centers because of civil strife and the inflation. The import of manufactured products was not as seriously impeded.

4. During the period under consideration, the real wage in Chungking was higher than that of the base period (January–June, 1937) only in 1938, 1946, and 1947 (see Chart 7.1). The high real wage in 1938 was the result of the rise in Chungking's money wage in relation to its cost of living. This was made possible by the large-scale wartime migration of government offices and industries into interior China from the coastal areas. The cost-of-living index of Chungking, like China's commodity price in general, slumped during 1945 and the early months of 1946. The money wage, on the other hand, continued to climb in these periods with virtually no interruption, which reflected the bullish atmosphere prevailing in the country. Consequently, the average real wage for 1946, rose above the prewar level. The high real wage for 1947 was accounted

for mainly by the stable cost-of-living index during the months following the financial crisis in February. After that crisis, the tempo of the inflation did temporarily slacken for several months before conditions became worse.

5. Aside from the three years mentioned above, the real wage was invariably lower than the base period. This continuous downward trend started in 1939, and reached its lowest trough in 1945. During the war years, the rise in wage lagged in relation to the prices of both semimanufactured and manufactured products.

All these indications point to the fact that the Chinese inflation was of the demand-pull type rather than the cost-push type.

Because of the interruptions resulting from the Japanese occupation in Shanghai, there are no appropriate statistics which can be used to show the relative changes in the prices of raw materials, semi-manufactured goods, and manufactured goods. Nor are the wage statistics as complete as those of Chungking. The indices required for the study of the changes in money and real wages for the period 1940–45 are unobtainable.

Because of the deficiency in price indices, a special set of indices based on the prices of raw cotton, cotton yarn and undyed cloth (grey sheeting) has been compiled to represent raw materials, semi-manufactured, and manufactured products respectively. Since the cotton textile industries were the most important industries in Shanghai and its neighboring cities,[4] these indices should be somewhat representative of the conditions of the manufacturing industries in that entire area.

The best available substitute for the wage-rate index is the cost-of-living index compiled by the municipal government of Shanghai. This substitute is suggested because, particularly during the later stage of the inflation, wage payments based on the cost-of-living index became a common feature in the labor contracts of industries in Shanghai. Although nominally the index was compiled by the municipal government, the process of the compilation was subject to the strong influence on the part of both labor and management, a process resembling in many respects that of collective bargaining. With this substitution the quotient of the wholesale-price index to the cost-of-living index is used to represent price-wage ratio, and its excess over the unity level may be used to gauge the degree of profit inflation in favor of the entrepreneurs and at the expense of the wage-earners. Also, the reciprocal of the price-wage ratio is used to measure the real wage received by the laborers at various stages of the inflation.[5]

As in the case of the Chungking study, the ratios of labor and materials costs to the prices of semimanufactured or manufactured products were computed for Shanghai on the basis of the series just mentioned. Since our study is now confined only to the cotton-textile industry, it is feasible to combine the wage and material costs. According to the experience of the textile mills in postwar Shanghai, labor and overhead charges constituted 15–20 percent, and raw materials 80–85 percent of product price. In the average, the wage and material costs were weighted by the ratios 20 percent and 80 percent respectively. Because of the unavailability of data, the overhead charges were not included in the average. But in view of the small percentage of the overhead cost in product price, the changes in the weighted average of wage and material costs should be adequate to reflect approximate changes in the entire cost structure. The results are shown in Chart 7.2.

Throughout the months under consideration, the index of wage-material cost was lower than the corresponding index for product price, regardless of whether the product was yarn or cloth. This excess of product price over costs reflects clearly the existence of a profit inflation in favor of industrial entrepreneurs. As a whole, the discrepancy was larger during the early postwar months than in the later ones. The reduction in the lag of wage adjustment was partly responsible for reducing the profit margin in the latter part of the inflation. The discrepancy between the index of wage-cotton cost and of the yarn was on the whole larger than the discrepancy between the index of wage-yarn cost and of the cloth. The profit margin based on the cost of imported cotton was usually greater than the profit on the cost of domestic cotton; that is, the profit was generally greater in the spinning industry than in the weaving, and greater for the yarn productions using imported cotton than those using domestic cotton.

The high profit in the spinning industry can probably be explained by the fact that many textile producers in China operated both spinning and weaving mills. Under such vertical combinations, the price-cost relation for weaving products was entirely different from the similar relation between cotton and yarn, which were produced by two independent groups of producers. Even when spinning and weaving were done by independent mills, these industries usually consisted of well-organized, modern enterprises with good market information and adequate financial backing by modern banks. The prices of spinning products and those of weaving products are closely

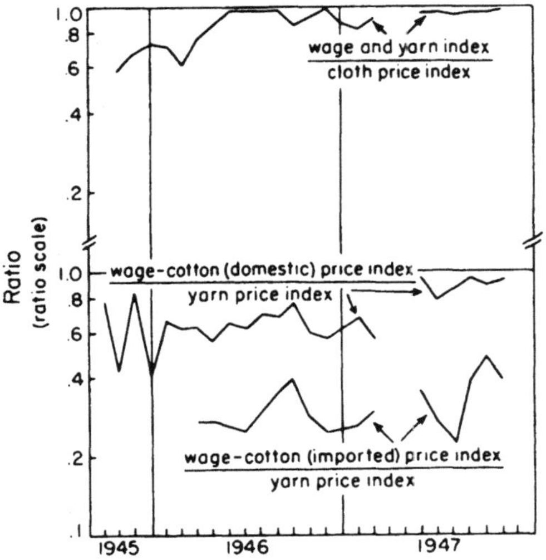

CHART 7.2. RATIO OF SHANGHAI INDICES OF WAGE, COTTON, COTTON YARN AND CLOTH, 1945–47

The wage-yarn, wage-cotton (domestic), and wage-cotton (imported) indices are respectively the weighted averages of wage and yarn-price indices, wage and cotton (domestic) price indices, and wage and cotton (imported) price indices. In each case, the wage index carries a weight of 20 percent, and the materials-price index a weight of 80 percent.

Sources: Chu Ssu-huang, *Min-kuo ching-chi-shih* (Economic History of the Republic of China) (Shanghai, 1947), pp. 545–46.

associated with each other. Neither the spinning mill nor the weaving mill were in a position to take advantage of one another. Cotton (i.e., domestic supply) and yarn, on the other hand, were produced by two entirely different groups of producers, one at the agricultural level and the other at the manufacturing level. In China, agriculture was usually associated with small rural producers without access to either market information or modern banking facilities. For this reason they were often in a relatively unfavorable position in dealing with industrialists from urban areas. The low cost of imported cotton resulted from the overvaluation of Chinese currency in terms of foreign money. The availability of a large supply of low-cost imported cotton was in fact another important factor which caused a profit in the spinning industry. Since the raw materials used in Chinese mills usually consisted partly of imported cotton and partly of domestic cotton, the actual cost curves, which varied from mill to mill according to the type of cotton used, should lie somewhere between the two curves showing the ratios of the composite price index of wage and cotton to the price index of yarn, as shown in Chart 7.2.

THE FARM INCOME

During 1938–40, the real income of farmers dropped below the 1937 level (see Table 7.1). The income index began to rise in 1940, and reached the peak of 115 (1937 = 100) in 1941. After 1941, however, the index reverted to a downward trend. During 1944–46, the farmers' real income again dropped below the 1937 level. All these changes in real income reflected changes in the prices received by farmers in relation to the changes in the prices paid by them. Although during the inflation the farmers were not so well situated as the business men, they were on the whole more fortunate than the *rentiers* and most of those living on wages salaries.

TABLE 7.1. INDICES OF FARM PRICE AND INCOME, 1933–46
(*1937* = 100)

	Prices received by farmers	*Prices paid by farmers*	*Farmers' real income*
1933	90	80	113
1934	87	81	107
1935	87	83	105
1936	96	88	109
1937	100	100	100
1938	108	124	87
1939	157	184	85
1940	381	396	96
1941	1,052	915	115
1942	2,931	2,774	106
1943	10,738	10,722	100
1944	27,132	33,354	81
1945	108,119	123,917	87
1946	229,359	265,816	86

Source: *Chung-hua-min-kuo tung-ch'i nien-chien* (The Statistical Yearbook of the Republic of China) (Nanking, 1948), p. 96.

INCOME OF TEACHERS AND GOVERNMENT EMPLOYEES

Teachers, professors, military, and civilian employees of the government bore the major burden of the inflation. Their salaries were calculated on the basis of an adjusted basic salary and the cost-of-living index. The adjusted basic salary was determined by discounting their prewar salaries according to a schedule which progressed by brackets. For example, if the rate of discount was 50 percent for the first hundred dollars of their prewar salaries, then it became 60 percent for the second hundred dollars, 70 percent for the third hundred, and so on. The cost-of-living indices were compiled on a fairly realistic basis, and were usually quite similar to those of wage earners. Instead of being adjusted monthly on the current cost-of-living index as wages did, however, these salaries during the most part of the inflation were adjusted only occasionally, in most of the cases not more than once every three or four months. If these salaries were adjusted according to the cost-of-living index once every three months, then the loss of 10, 20, and 30 percent per month in the purchasing power of yuan resulted in a reduction of 18.7, 34.9, and 48.9 percent respectively in the real income over that three-months period.[6]

The government employees stationed in isolated localities suffered another important loss resulting from the lag in salary payments. This lag particularly penalized the army personnel stationed in areas remote from the financial centers supplying the cash for their salaries. To an extent the lag in payment was inevitable because of administrative and transportation difficulties, but there were also cases in which salary payments were purposely delayed by administrative or commanding officers in order to facilitate their personal benefit.

This highly progressive discount schedule and the lags in salary adjustments and payments, often reduced the remuneration of a government employee during the war and postwar years to something between 6 to 12 percent of his prewar salary. During those years a monthly salary equivalent to thirty U.S. dollars would have been considered high. A private in the army often received less than one U.S. dollar a month. Such incredibly low remuneration accounted in large measure for the low morale and the corruption among government employees and military personnel, and for the ultimate collapse of the government on the Chinese mainland.

PRICES OF GOLD, SECURITIES, AND FOREIGN CURRENCIES

This section examines the changes in the gold prices, the dollar-yuan exchange rate, and the prices of securities in relation to the changes in the wholesale price index during the Chinese inflation. Because of the unavailability of some of these prices for other areas, the quotations of the Shanghai market are used as the basis for the study. Because of the Japanese occupation of Shanghai during the war and because of frequent changes in the financial policies of the Nationalist government, it is impossible to obtain some of the quotations for the entire period under consideration. Gold prices, for instance, are not available during the months when gold transactions were prohibited. This situation is also true for the prices of securities. In fact, there are only a few stocks whose price data are available for the entire span of 1937–49. To cope with these deficiencies, many adjustments became necessary.

During 1937–49 two types of stocks were traded in the stock exchange of Shanghai: those whose stated values were in Chinese currency, and those whose stated values were in a foreign currency (usually the Hong Kong dollar). Most of the stocks in the first category were issued by corporations in China and controlled by the Chinese. The stocks in the second category belonged mostly to corporations controlled by foreign interests, and the securities were traded in the Hong Kong and the Shanghai market. The common stocks of Wing-on Textiles, Mayar Silk, and Standard Shirts exemplify the first type, and the common stocks of the Wheelock Company, the Ewo Cotton Mill, the Ewo Breweries, and the Shanghai Dock Yard represent the second.

The study of the prices of government bonds is confined only to those based on the local currency. The prices of the Consolidated Bonds, whose data are available during most of the inflation period, are used as indicators of the bond market. There is no attempt to cover the prices of those bonds whose values are in units other than the local currency (see Chapter II).

The results of these price studies are shown in Tables 7.2, 7.3, and 7.4, from which the following observations are derived:

1. The price of gold has a comparable, but not as high, multiple as the price index.

TABLE 7.2. PERCENT OF INCREASE (+) AND DECREASE (−) IN REAL VALUES OF GOLD PRICES AND DOLLAR EXCHANGE RATES, 1938–49

	Bond quotations	SHANGHAI		CHUNGKING	
		Gold price	*Dollar exchange rate*	*Gold price*	*Dollar exchange rate*
1938	+ 1.1	+ 6.9	+ 7.0[d]		
1939	+ 4.7	− 1.0	− .5		
1940	− 7.3	− 1.9	− 1.8		
1941	− 3.1	− 2.1	− 3.8		
1942	− 6.6	− 1.4	− 1.8	−17.3	
1943	− 7.4	+ 2.7[b]		− 1.0	− 3.8
1944	−19.8	− 0.1	−26.9[e]	+ .6	+13.4
1945		+21.5[c]	+29.7	+ 5.3	+ 7.3
1946	+12.9	− 1.9	− .5	+ 7.4	+ 7.6
1947	+ 9.0	+ 6.8	+ 6.5	+ 6.8	+ .8
1948	+10.6	+14.9	+16.9	+ 8.9	− 3.6[f]
1949[a]	+12.7	+51.2	+50.2	+15.2	
Average	+ 0.6	+ 8.3	+ 6.8	+ 3.2	+ 3.6

[a] Jan.–April. [b] Jan.–Oct. [c] Jan.–May, Oct.–Dec. [d] May–Oct. [e] Aug.–Dec. [f] Jan.–June.

The percentage increase or decrease in the real value of gold prices is derived from the ratios of the link relatives of gold prices to the corresponding link relatives of wholesale prices. The ratio for each year is obtained by averaging the monthly ratios available for the year. The percentage changes are obtained by subtracting each of these yearly averages by one. The percentage changes for the dollar rates and the bond prices are computed by similar procedure. Because of frequent changes in government policies concerning gold, foreign exchange, and bonds, their quotations are not available for all the years of inflation.

There are no data for spaces left blank in the table.

Source: Wu Kang, *Chiu-chung-kuo t'ung-ho peng-chang shih-liao* (Historical Materials Relating to the Inflation in Old China) (Shanghai, 1958), pp. 140–52; and *Chung-yang yin-hang yuch-pao* (The Central Bank Monthly) (Shanghai, 1946–49), Vols. I–IV.

2. The gold policies of the Nationalist government apparently had an important bearing on the gold price in the free market, as well as the official quotations. In Chungking, for instance, the real value for gold registered a decrease of 17.3 percent and 1.0 percent

in 1942 and 1943 respectively. In both years, the government sold a large amount of gold in Chungking. In 1946 when the Nationalist government conducted its large-scale gold operations in Shanghai, there was a drop of 1.9 percent in the real value of gold in that market. The effects of these operations, however, seem to be more

TABLE 7.3. PERCENT OF INCREASE (+) AND DECREASE (−) IN REAL VALUES OF SHANGHAI STOCKS, 1938–49

	Chinese currency stocks		*Foreign currency stocks*	
	1	*2*	*1*	*2*
1945				
Nov.	− .15	−.45	+3.37	−.26
Dec.	+ .16	+.38	+ .26	+.33
1947				
Oct.	− .10	−.25	+ .13	−.06
Nov.	+ .01	−.17	+ .73	+.43
Dec.	+ .20	+.10	+ .16	+.06
1948				
April	− .06	−.26	+ .27	
May	+ .05	−.15	+ .19	−.04
June	− .25	−.32	+ .09	−.02
July	− .35	−.32		
Aug.	− .22	+.05		
1949				
Jan.	− .23	−.47		
Feb.	+1.16	−.65		
March	− .14	−.79	− .03	+.04

1 The month-to-month percentage change of stock prices after deflation by the corresponding changes in the wholesale prices of Shanghai.

2 The similar changes in stock prices after deflation by the corresponding changes in the dollar-yuan rates of free market.

There are no data for spaces left blank in the table.

The method used for computing these deviations is similar to that used for Table 7.1.

Source: *The Central Bank Monthly*, Vols. I–IV; and *Min-kuo ching-chi-shih* (The Economic History of the Republic) (Shanghai, 1948), p. 533.

significant to the regional than to the national market. This was true during the postwar period when both Shanghai and Chungking were under the control of the Nationalist government, and during the war period when these cities were governed by different authorities. From 1945 to 1949, while the gold prices of Chungking showed a steady increase in real terms, the corresponding prices of Shanghai fluctuated widely in both directions. In 1946 when the gold price

TABLE 7.4. PRICE INDICES OF GOLD, DOLLAR, AND SECURITIES AT BENCHMARK DATES OF THE CHINESE INFLATION

	Base period (=1)	*December 1941*	*August 1945*	*October 1945*	*June 1948*	*August 1948*	*March 1949*	*May 1949*[a]
					(thousand)		*(trillion or 10^{12})*	
Wholesale price index								
Shanghai	1937[b]	15.98	86,400	75,726	176,960	985,400	2.43	1,261
Chungking		28.48	1,795	1,184	455	1,551	.30	1,368
Gold price								
Shanghai	1937	11.36	10,527	98,600	192,058	925,637	2.27	1,252
Chungking								
Dollar-yuan rate								
Shanghai	1937	6.78	36,395	186,462	135,175	665,280	1.60	870
Chungking								
Foreign-currency stock								
Wheelock Co.	1937	5.72[a]		56,446	311,498		2.61	
Ewo Cotton Mill	1937	2.52[a]		20,654	119,738		.69	
Chinese-currency stock								
Wing-on Textile Mill	1940	2.81		1,013	797	38,000	.006	
	1941	1.00		360	3,707	13,521	.002	
Government bond Consolidated C	1937	1.29	1,080	1,073	94,100	6,806		

[a] First week. [b] Jan.–June.

There are no data for spaces left blank in table.

Source: *The Central Bank Monthly*, Vols. I–IV; *The Economic History of the Republic*, pp. 521–34; and Wu Kang, *The Historical Materials Relating to The Inflation in Old China*, pp. 141–52.

of Shanghai dropped 1.9 percent in real values, the gold prices of Chungking climbed without interruption.

3. From 1937 to May, 1949, the dollar-yuan rate multiplied by only $870(10^{12})$ times as compared with $1{,}252(10^{12})$ times and $1{,}261(10^{12})$ times for the gold price and the wholesale-price index of Shanghai, respectively. There was a close association between the movement of gold prices and that of the dollar-yuan rate. In the Shanghai market the only important difference between the movements of these two sets of quotations occurred in 1941, when the dollar value of gold appreciated in the world market as a result of the war in Europe. The high dollar value of gold during and after World War II was undoubtedly a leading factor in the discrepancy between the multiples of the gold prices and the dollar rates shown in Table 7.4.

4. The prices of the foreign-currency stocks followed closely the prices of gold and foreign currencies. In some instances the prices of these stocks rose more than both the dollar-yuan exchange rate and the wholesale prices,[7] reflecting the joint effect of the depreciation of yuan and the high business profits during the Chinese inflation. The behavior of the local-currency stocks, on the other hand, was entirely different from that of the foreign-currency stocks. The valuation of these stocks has to rely mainly on the business prospect of the firm concerned, not on the depreciation of the Chinese-currency. During the Chinese inflation, the prices of the Chinese-currency stocks lagged in relation to the prices of commodities, gold, and foreign currencies, but rose faster than the prices of government bonds. In August, 1948, the quotation for the stock on the Wing-on Textile Mill, one of the most favored Chinese currency stocks, was 13.5 million times as high as the average quotation of that stock for 1941. During the same period (from 1941 to August, 1948), the price of the Consolidated "C" Bond, the most favored among government bonds, registered an increase of about 5.3 million times.

5. From 1937 to August, 1948, the period from which the relevant quotations are available, the price of government bonds multiplied by 6.8 million times, as against a multiplication of 985.4 million times of the wholesale price index of Shanghai over the same period. While this comparison shows the staggering loss incurred by the bond holders during the inflation, the fact that the government

bonds, with no assurance of repayment in excess of their face value, appreciated so much in its market prices is indeed surprising.

PRICES VERSUS INTEREST RATES

To facilitate the study of the price-interest relations, the real rates of interest have been computed for both Chungking and Shanghai. The results obtained are shown in Table 7.5. It should be noticed that the detailed comparisons based on the monthly data in the table are confined only to 1945–49. Because of the unavailability of monthly data, the study for 1937–44 is made on the basis of the annual averages. In selecting the interest data, preference is always given to the series which most realistically reflect the conditions then prevailing in the market. For this reason, the market rate of interest is used during the postwar years, when monthly data were available, but for the years before and during the war, when the data were incomplete, the commercial bank rates were used for Chungking and those of the native banks for Shanghai.[8]

In the eight years from 1937 to 1944, the real interest rates of Shanghai and Chungking were positive only in 1937 and 1938 (see Table 7.5).[9] The presence of the positive rates in Shanghai in 1937 and 1938 is understandable, for during those initial years of the war the rise in commodity prices was slight in comparison with the usual high interest then prevailing in the Chinese money market. After 1938 the rise in prices was accelerated with the accentuation of the inflation, but the money rate of interest had a constant tendency to lag behind in the upward climb. Consequently, the rate of interest in Shanghai became negative and remained so until the end of the war in 1945. A similar situation existed in Chungking. The real rate of interest was invariably negative from 1939 to 1944, although the negative rate for 1944 was rather low because of the relative economic stability in Free China during the second part of the year.

In 1945, the real interest rate of Shanghai was positive in September and December, when wholesale prices registered a fall of 21 percent and 11 percent respectively. The fall in September came at the conclusion of the war, and that in December represented a brief respite following an abrupt rise in the preceding month. The year 1945 was the first since 1938 in which Chungking's real rate

TABLE 7.5. REAL RATE OF INTEREST IN CHUNGKING AND SHANGHAI, 1937–49

	Chungking	*Shanghai*		*Chungking*	*Shanghai*
1937	+ .8	+ .12	1941	−6.9	− 5.6
1938	+ .6	+1.57	1942	−3.0	− 7.0
1939	− 2.4	−5.9	1943	−4.2	− 7.8
1940	−12.3	−4.8	1944	− .6	−16.3

	1945		1946		1947		1948		1949	
	Chungking	*Shanghai*	*Chungking*	*Shanghai*	*Chungking*	*Shanghai*	*Chungking*	*Shanghai*	*Chungking*	*Shanghai*
Jan.	− 9.0	−12.1	+ .9		−15.6	− .8	−15.5	−18.1	−24.9	+11.5
Feb.	−19.6	−19.3	+ 1.2	−36.1	−19.0	−24.5	− 1.0	−14.6	−56.2	−72.0
March	−14.1	−20.4	+ 3.6	−17.5	−41.9	+ 9.5	−22.3	+20.1	−52.7	−45.9
April	+ 1.8	− .9	−10.5	+14.0	− 6.1	−32.3	+29.3	+10.0		
May	− 3.1	−12.1	+ 3.4	−20.4	−11.9	−23.5	− 1.5	−10.9		
June	+ 6.9	−77.1	−16.9	+17.5	−20.5	+ 0.9	−32.1	−27.4		
July			−19.7	+ 6.0	−18.9	+26.9	−37.5	−48.8		
Aug.		−47.1	+ 5.7	+ 8.4	+ 3.3	+ 9.1	+57.9	−16.0		
Sept.		+24.8	− 8.1	− .2	− 6.8	−10.3	−55.4	+ 1.6		
Oct.		− 1.3	− 2.2	+11.6	−15.1	−12.7	+ 2.2	− 7.9		
Nov.		−58.0	− 3.3	+16.6	+ 3.8	+ 6.9	+13.7	−82.7		
Dec.		+20.2	− 2.3	+ 9.3	− .7	− 1.6	+42.1	− .9		
Average	−.2	−16.9	− 5.7	− .8	−12.5	− 4.4	− 1.7	−16.3	−44.7	−35.5

There are no monthly data for spaces left blank in table.

of interest became positive. During the first six months of the year for which the monthly interest data of Chungking were available, positive real interest occurred in April and June, and the semiannual average rate was −6.2 percent. The positive average rate for the entire year, which was +0.20 percent, was therefore primarily the result of developments during the second part of the year, when the prices slumped in Free China after V-J Day.

In 1946, economic conditions in Chungking and in Shanghai were again at variance. Because of the repatriation refugees from Free China to the coastal provinces, commodity prices in Chungking remained fairly stable during the first half of the year except for April, and actually registered slight decreases in January, June, and July. In Shanghai, on the other hand, the tempo of the inflation was in general accentuated during the first part of 1946, but slackened appreciably after June when the open-market operations of the Central Bank in gold and foreign exchange were in full swing. Although both these cities had a positive real interest in a number of months during the year, Chungking's positive rates occurred mainly in the early part of the year (January, February, March, May, and August) and those of Shanghai concentrated in the later months (April, June, July, August, October, November, and December).

In 1947 Shanghai had positive rates during five months (March, June, July, August, and November), but Chungking only in two (August and November), because of the economic instability in the latter city during the year. In 1948 Chungking had five positive-rate months (April, August, October, November, and December) against three in Shanghai (March, April, and September). The frequency of the positive rates in Chungking was the result of its relatively high market rate of interest, which was in general subject to less effective controls and less influence from the Central Bank rates than that of Shanghai. This situation was particularly true during the last quarter of 1948 following the monetary reform in August. In the early months of 1949, however, the unprecedentedly rapid increases virtually drove the positive real rates out of the picture—the positive rate in Shanghai in January, 1949, was the only exception.

A study of these statistics shows that the negative real interest rate usually occurred when the rate of price rise was abruptly accentuated.

However, it does not follow that a large percentage increase in price was necessarily accompanied by a negative real rate of interest. During the last four months of 1948, for instance, the monthly increases in the price index of Chungking were all well above 50 percent, and some exceeded 150 percent, yet the real rates of interest during those periods were all positive. Similarly, in January, 1949, Shanghai had a rather high positive real interest rate, although the price for that month was 2.6 times higher than for the preceding one. It seems, therefore, that the negative real interest is a possible, but not a necessary or sufficient, condition of hyperinflation. In fact, a comparison of interest rate with the rate of increases in prices may not provide an adequate definition for hyperinflation.[10]

The prevalence of the negative real rate of interest during the inflation means that in general borrowers in that period gained at the expense of lenders and holders of paper money. The cheap loans of the Central Bank and other government banks were in fact a disguised form of subsidizing borrowers. However, it should not be inferred that these blessings were unequivocal.[11] In the first place, the real rate of interest was not invariably negative. Even during the later stages of the inflation, as shown in Table 7.5, there still was occasionally a positive real interest; sometimes at a very high level. Therefore, only those in a position to maneuver successfully among such vagaries really benefited. In the second place, when the money rate of interest was low in comparison with the expected rises of commodity prices, the temptation to "overtrade" was usually irresistible. During the Chinese inflation, therefore, it was not unusual to find business firms relying mainly on borrowed money for their operations while their equity investment was kept at a minimum proportion. Business firms also tended to borrow on terms much shorter than those required for financing, as it was usually difficult under inflation to obtain long-term credit. Under these circumstances, to arrange credit renewals and to obtain new loans for the payment of the old became a routine function of management. Many of these loans were raised from sources outside the organized money market. All these operations, of course, involved unusually high risks and required exceptional shrewdness on the part of management to keep a business in equilibrium. Finally, there were the uncertainties arising from the payment of wages on a cost-of-living basis, as well as other factors leading to varying cost of production. Because of such complications, it was not uncommon during the inflation in China for borrowers to run into financial difficulties or even to go bankrupt.

When the war ended in 1945 and when the expected restoration of foreign and metropolitan supplies caused an abrupt slump in the prices of the markets of interior China, all the firms following dubious financial policies became panicky, and many went bankrupt. In the Chungking area alone 201 manufacturers out of 723 closed down. In Kweichow Province, about 60 percent of the 1500 manufacturing units were suspended. In Sian, 14 mining companies ceased operations. The panic was not confined to mining and manufacturing undertakings, but also affected commercial firms, particularly those that hoarded commodities with money borrowed at a high money rate of interest. The sudden drop in prices made even cheap loans bear a high real interest, and the low marketability of commodity holdings because of the slump made it impossible to liquidate short-term liabilities without incurring heavy losses when they came due. Consequently, in interior China a large number of commercial firms which had flourished during the war were swept out of business. Banks which had overextended their resources also ran into difficulties when they found their debtors unable to meet overdue liabilities. Seven modern and native banks in Chungking were suspended during the crisis.[12]

In the effort to cope with the situation, the government through its banks granted about 10 billion yuan in low-interest loans during the few months immediately following V-J Day. The panic soon disappeared when the inflation spiral reverted to its upward swing. The situation would have worsened, of course, had the inflation not resumed. Meantime, because of the resumption of the inflationary process and the cheap money policy, many of the concomitant irrational developments accordingly continued.

The cheap money policy brought many irrational results which would never have occurred in a normal economy. Among other things, the cheap money policy of the government banks resulted in windfalls to their debtors at the expense of other income shares and the stabilization of the entire economy.

It was often argued that the cheap money policy during the

inflation was justifiable and necessary because it was essential to encourage production. Industrial productions in Free China did multiply during 1939–45. But in terms of absolute magnitude, the actual expansion was rather negligible because of the low production in 1939, and there was no convincing evidence in agricultural production to substantiate such an argument.

BANKS VERSUS DEPOSITORS

Another angle from which the debtor-creditor relationship may be examined is the redemption of pre-inflation deposits with and loans from banks. Although these deposits and loans would normally be repaid at par, the continued depreciation of the Chinese currency made this usual arrangement inequitable. Under the circumstances, to redeem the depositors or bank loans at par without allowing for the depreciation in yuan would mean an outright confiscation of the creditors' claims. To protect the interest of such depositors and banks, the Nationalist government promulgated in December, 1947, a regulation providing that all the deposits with and loans from banks prior to December 9, 1941, should be redeemed at a multiple of the original amount. The multiples used for such a purpose started from 700.67 yuan for each yuan of deposit or bank loan made prior to December 9, 1941, and rose gradually to a maximum ratio of 1703.46 to one yuan for claims established prior to August, 13 1937. No adjustment, however, was provided for claims established after December 1941.[13]

The wholesale price index of Shanghai in December, 1947, was 15,662,800 times the price in August, 1937, and 1,048,748 times the price in December, 1941. In Chungking, the corresponding multiples in the price index were 42,218 and 1,443 respectively. Thus, even in terms of Chungking prices the redemption schedule as provided in the regulation was grossly unfair to the creditors, regardless of whether they were banks or depositors.

The banks, being intermediaries between their depositors and borrowers, were in a neutral position with little to gain or lose under the new regulation, so long as the deposits were all lent out to the borrowers. This, however, was not in actuality the case. During the inflation many Chinese banks, including those of high standing, did invest the funds received from their depositors in gold or foreign assets (such as foreign currencies and securities in foreign currencies). In doing so, these banks reaped handsome profits and accumulated large assets abroad, particularly in the United States, Hong Kong, and Switzerland. Early in the inflation (1937–39) these banking operations were facilitated by the government policy of making foreign currencies available to the public at an unduly low cost. The bankers were in a favorable position in effecting these operations because of their knowledge of the financial market, while the bulk of the Chinese public was still unaware of the significance of inflation. During and after World War II, the fortunes of these bankers were further multiplied by their investments in booming stock markets in the United States. This favorable position of the Chinese bankers remained untouched until January 20, 1953, when the Communist government required all the banks in mainland China to redeem their deposit liabilities on the basis of a new schedule much stiffer than the one used in the 1947 regulation. The new regulation required, *inter alia*, the transfer of these deposit liabilities, after being bolstered by the stipulated multiples, to the government, if these deposits remained unclaimed after a specified date.[14]

SUMMARY

It now appears evident that the Chinese inflation was primarily a profit inflation which worked in favor of the recipients of profits at the expense of those receiving other income shares. A profit inflation may be desirable on at least one ground: the recipients of profits (or entrepreneurs) usually belong to upper-income brackets and have a higher propensity to save than do the recipients of low incomes. Since savings are helpful in arresting an inflation, a profit inflation (to the extent that it is conductive to an increase in savings) has a built-in stabilizing effect. An inflation of this type should facilitate the diversion of a nation's resources to military use during war time and to the reconversion of industry from military to non-military production after war. On the other hand, a proper government policy should not permit a profit inflation to pour the "booty" arising from the inflation without restriction into the laps of the entrepreneurs. As an adjunct to profit inflation, a high taxation of profits and of incomes above the exemption limit must be imposed so that the "booty" is ultimately transferred from the entrepreneurs to the government. "It is expedient to use entrepreneurs as collecting agents. But let them be agents and not principals." This, according to Keynes, is the right procedure for "virtuous" war finance.[15]

In the Chinese situation, the absence of effective tax measures made it impossible for the government to collect the "booty" which profit inflation poured into the laps of the entrepreneurs. Consequently, these entrepreneurs became, not collecting agents of the government, but the rightful owners of such "booty"; and worse still, the profiteers, despite their huge windfall, had no such propensity to save as is normally expected. Because of their expectation of a further depreciation in Chinese currency, they usually invested whatever liquid resources they had in commodities, precious metals, and foreign currencies for hedging against inflation. This hedging process precipitated a further rise in price of these articles and a further fall in the value of the local currency. The larger the "booty," the greater the inflationary pressure on the economy—particularly in the form of swelling investments for ownership benefit. The spiraling process, thus, became as automatic as wage payment based on the cost-of-living.[16]

During the Chinese inflation, money wages did lag in adjustment relative to the rise of commodity prices, but the lag confined mostly to the remunerations of government employees and school teachers. The real incomes of farmers and industrial workers were not so seriously affected as the incomes of those working for the government. During the later stages of the inflation, the money wages of industrial workers were mostly paid on the cost-of-living basis.

In the debtor-creditor relationship, the Chinese inflation worked definitely in favor of the debtors. This was proved by the prevalence of negative real interest during the inflation and by the favorable position of banks vis-a-vis their depositors.

In short, in the course of the Chinese inflation, excess profits arising from war or inflation were not duly taxed. Instead, a large part of the war cost was imposed through spiraling processes upon a limited number of government employees, military personnel, school teachers, and recipients of rental and interest incomes, with virtually no regard for their ability to pay. This haphazard process of distributing the burden of war not only incited the inflation, but also demoralized the underpaid teachers and employees in public offices. This inequitable distribution of the burden produced widespread graft and corruption among the civil servants, and it undoubtedly was an important factor in the downfall of the Nationalist government.

CHAPTER VIII

A Comparison of the Chinese and Other Inflations

Comparisons of the Chinese inflation with other inflations will be made with reference to the behavior of prices and note issues, the relationship between the internal and external values of the currencies, the effects of inflation on the incomes and expenditures of government in real terms, and the relationship between interest rates and the rate of price changes. The choice of the countries studied is primarily based on the availability of data and the relevance of such experience to what happened in China. Because of these considerations of experience and relevance, there is no attempt to make the coverage in all the sections of this chapter consistent and no pretense in this study at a comprehensive survey of all the great inflations.

THE BEHAVIOR OF PRICES AND NOTE ISSUES UNDER INFLATION

For comparing the behavior of prices and note issues with the Chinese experience, three cases of open inflation have been chosen: Germany during 1914–23, Greece during 1939–45, and Hungary during 1945–46. The use of the note issues to represent money supply should not be interpreted as a minimization of the importance of bank credit to a modern economy. Because of the lack of proper data for bank credit in most of the countries under consideration, its inclusion in money supply would have resulted more in confusion than in clarification. Moreover, in the course of both the Chinese and the German inflations, the relative importance of bank credit declined substantially as the inflationary process intensified (see Chapter VI). In such cases, the inclusion of bank credit in the study would not necessarily bring in much information otherwise unobtainable.

The discussion in this section will focus on: (1) the ratios of price and note issue indices at the beginning of an inflation to the corresponding indices at the end of the inflation; (2) the distribution of the month-to-month link relatives of prices and note issues; and (3) the ratios of the month-to-month link relatives of prices to the corre: ponding link relatives of note issues. The purpose of the first is to measure the cumulative effects of inflation on prices and note issues. The function of the second is to study of the rate of price increases and currency expansions. The intention of the third is to show the behavior of the velocity of money circulation during the inflation.

The cumulative effects of inflation on prices and note issues

Based on the index compiled by the Central Bank for the twelve-year span from the middle of 1937 to the end of April, 1949, the commodity prices in Shanghai multiplied by $151.73(10^{12})$ times, and the volume of the note issues expanded by $2.20(10^{12})$ times. From 1914 to 1923, the price index of Germany multiplied by $1.26(10^{12})$ times, and the note issue expanded by $1.57(10^{11})$ times. Thus the increases in the prices and the note issues during the Chinese inflation were both greater than the corresponding increases during the German inflation (see Table 8.1).

The Chinese multiples were also higher than the corresponding statistics of Greece for 1939–44. If, however, the Greek series were prolonged to include all the months up to June, 1953, when the economic order in the country was well under control, then the increase of the Greek note issues would be higher than that of the Chinese currency, although the increase in the Greek prices would have been smaller than that of the Chinese prices. The Chinese note issues would probably have regained its lead in expansion over the Greek currency, if the statistics of the Chinese note issues were extended to cover the months from May to December, 1949, the last and the darkest stage of the Nationalist's control over the Chinese mainland.

It is quite evident in Table 8.1 that none of the countries under consideration ever experienced such a phenomenal inflation as

TABLE 8.1. RATIOS OF INDEX AT THE END OF INFLATION TO INDEX AT THE BEGINNING OF INFLATION

	INFLATION PERIOD	RATIOS[a] Price index	Note-issue index
China	July 1937–April 1949	151.73(10^{12})	2.20(10^{12})[b]
Germany	1914–1923	1.26(10^{12})	1.57(10^{11})
Greece	1939–November 1944	.21(10^{12})	.77(10^{9})
	1939–June 1953	21.55(10^{12})	18.21(10^{12})
Hungary	July 1945–July 1946	399.62(10^{27})	22.60(10^{15})

[a] Ratios are obtained by dividing the initial index for the prices and note issues into the corresponding final index of an inflation.

[b] Ratio allows for the conversion of the CRB notes to fapi in 1945, at the rate of two hundred to one fapi yuan.

Source: For Germany: C. Bresciani-Turroni, *The Economics of Inflation* (London, 1937), pp. 162 and 442. For France: J. H. Rogers, *The Process of Inflation in France, 1914–1927* (New York, 1929), p. 143. For Greece: D. Delivanis and W. C. Cleveland, *Greek Monetary Development* (Bloomington, Indiana, 1949), Appendix tables; and section on Greece in International Monetary Fund, *International Financial Statistics* (Washington, D.C., 1948–50, 1953, and 1954), Vols. I–III, VI, and VII. For Hungary: B. Nogaro, "Hungary's Monetary Crisis," *The American Economic Review*, XXXVIII (1948), 526–42; N. Kaldor, "Inflation in Hungary," *Manchester Guardian*, December 7 and 13, 1946; and W. A. L. Coulborn, *A Discussion of Money* (London, 1950), p. 204. For China: Wu Kang, *Chiu-Chung-kuo t'ung-ho peng-chang shih-liao* (Historical Materials Relating to the Inflation in Old China) (Shanghai, 1958), pp. 92–97 and 122; and unpublished records of Central Bank of China.

Hungary did immediately after World War II. Within a brief span of thirteen months, the Hungarian prices increased by 399.62(10^{27}) times and the note issues by 22.6(10^{15}) times. On the other hand, none of the four inflations under consideration lasted so long as the Chinese, which had a life span of about twelve years. If the inflations in the Chinese mainland and Taiwan after 1949 were considered as continuations of the pre-1949 inflation, then the Chinese inflation had a continuous life history of fifteen (1937–52) years. This was longer than the duration of the Greek inflation which, even including the years from 1945 to 1953, had a duration of only about fourteen years (1939–53).

The rates of price increases and currency expansions

In order to compare the intensity of various inflations, the five highest month-to-month link relatives, representing the worst conditions in the course of each inflation, were taken from the price

TABLE 8.2. HIGHEST MONTHLY LINK RELATIVES OF THE FOUR INFLATIONS[a]

Rank of link relative[b]	PRICES *Date*		PRICES *Link relative*	NOTE ISSUES *Date*		NOTE ISSUES *Link relative*
China						
1	April	1949	82.01	April	1949	26.32
2	Nov.	1948	12.95	March	1949	3.28
3	Feb.	1949	9.72	Sept.	1948	3.22
4	March	1949	6.10	Feb.	1948	2.86
5	June	1945	4.76	Dec.	1948	2.55
Germany						
1	Oct.	1923	296.86	Nov.	1923	160.12
2	Sept.	1923	253.17	Oct.	1923	88.56
3	Nov.	1923	102.33	Sept.	1923	42.48
4	July	1923	38.58	Aug.	1923	14.54
5	Aug.	1923	12.62	July	1923	2.64
Greece[c]						
1	Nov.	1944	94.90	Oct.	1944	95.07
2	Oct.	1944	89.95	Sept.	1944	13.21
3	Sept.	1944	20.09	Nov.	1944	9.04
4	Dec.	1945	4.62	March	1945	2.73
5	Aug.	1944	4.49	June	1945	2.37
Hungary						
1	July	1946	$4.18(10^6)$[d]	June	1946	95,702.02
2	June	1946	8,467.21[e]	July	1946	2,756.09
3	May	1946	314.81	May	1946	151.02
4	April	1946	19.11	April	1946	12.77
5	Feb.	1946	6.03	March	1946	6.49

[a] Each link relative above is computed on the basis that data for preceding month equals 1.

[b] From worst to least inflation.

[c] Statistics for Greece cover 1944–45. The inclusion of 1945 is necessary because of the high link relatives for some of the months in 1945. Because of the unavailability of the wholesale prices for the early part of the inflation, the cost-of-living index of Greece is used instead.

[d] Index for the fourth week of July, 1946, with the data for second two weeks of June, 1946, equals 1.

[e] Index for the second two weeks of June, 1946, with the data for May, 1946, equals 1.

Source: See Table 8.1.

and the note-issue indices of the four countries. These link relatives are shown in Table 8.2. The inflation of Hungary, with prices multiplying $4.18(10^6)$ times in July, 1946, and note issues expanding 95,702 times in the month preceding, was by far the most intensive among the four inflations. The German inflation, whose highest month-to-month link relative (with the preceding month = 1) for its price index was 296.86 and that for its note issue was 160.12 would be ranked next. The inflation of Greece, whose highest link relatives were 94.90 for its price index and 95.07 for the note issue, was third. The Chinese inflation, who highest link relatives were 82.01 for the price index and 26.32 for note issue, was the mildest of

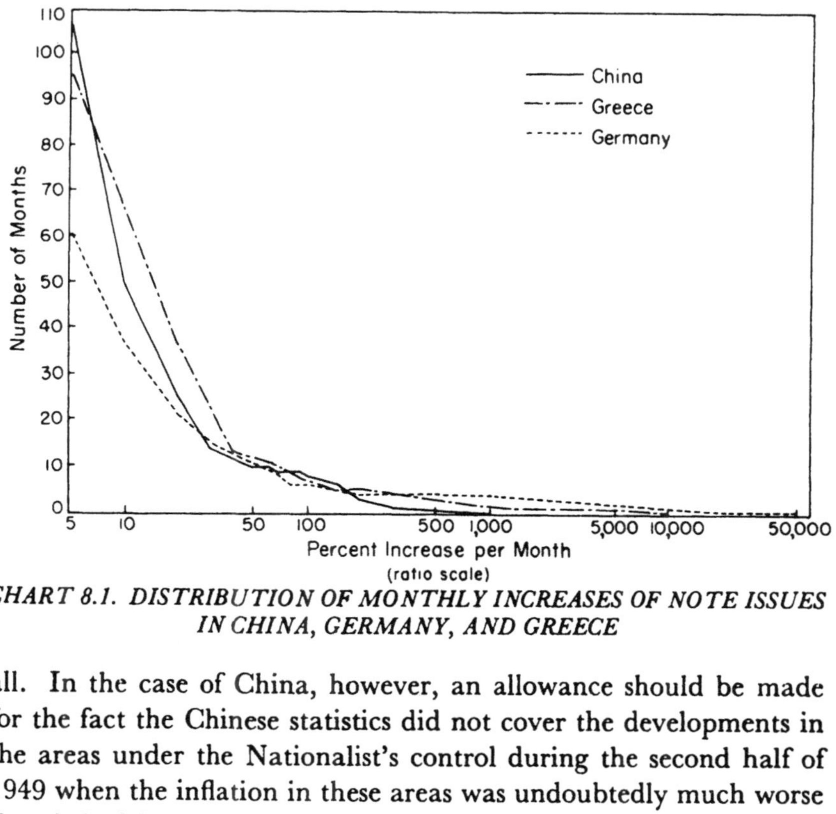

CHART 8.1. DISTRIBUTION OF MONTHLY INCREASES OF NOTE ISSUES IN CHINA, GERMANY, AND GREECE

all. In the case of China, however, an allowance should be made for the fact the Chinese statistics did not cover the developments in the areas under the Nationalist's control during the second half of 1949 when the inflation in these areas was undoubtedly much worse than it had been in the early part of the year.

Another criterion to measure the intensity of inflation is to compare the frequency distribution of various link relatives reflecting the month-to-month changes in prices and note issues. To facilitate this study, frequency distributions covering the link relatives with value of 1.05 or more, representing a monthly increase of 5 percent or more, was prepared (see Charts 8.1 and 8.2). Even excluding the months immediately after April, 1949, China had 85 months with an increase of 5 percent or more in the case of price indices and a similar increase in 106 months in the case of note issues. Both of these frequency figures are higher than the corresponding figures for Germany and Greece; that is to say, if a monthly increase of 5 percent or more in prices or note issues is used as a criterion for inflation, then the Chinese inflation lasted longer than either the

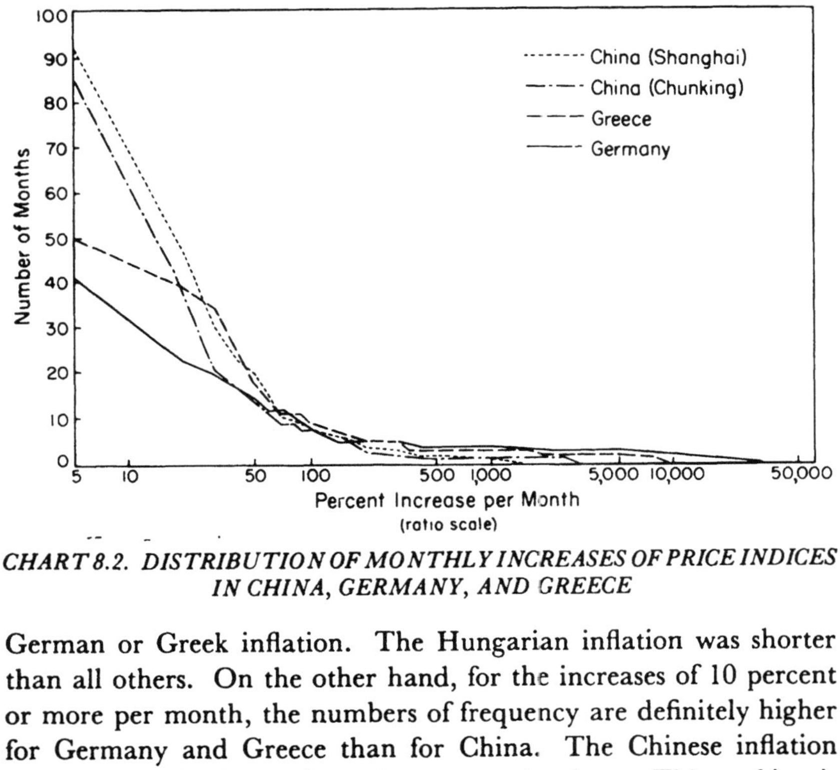

CHART 8.2. DISTRIBUTION OF MONTHLY INCREASES OF PRICE INDICES IN CHINA, GERMANY, AND GREECE

German or Greek inflation. The Hungarian inflation was shorter than all others. On the other hand, for the increases of 10 percent or more per month, the numbers of frequency are definitely higher for Germany and Greece than for China. The Chinese inflation actually had the lowest intensity among the three. This ranking is true regardless of whether the comparison is made on the basis of the link relatives of the note issues or that of commodity prices.

The ratio of prices to note issues

To study changes in commodity prices in relation to the changes in the volume of note circulation, the ratio of the link relative of price indices to that of note issues of the corresponding period is used. The statistical results are presented in Table 8.3. The following are the conclusions derived from the analysis of the price-currency ratios.

First, in the case of Germany, all the annual averages for the link relatives from 1914 through 1918 were below unity. From 1919 to 1923, when the inflation reached an acute stage, the ratios were invariably above the unity level and had a steady upward trend. In 1923 the ratio reached its record high of 1.21.

TABLE 8.3. AVERAGES OF THE RATIO OF MONTHLY LINK RELATIVE OF PRICES TO NOTE ISSUES

Greece				*Germany*	
1939	1.02	1947	0.99	1914	.96
1940	.98	1948	1.01	1915	.98
1941	1.15	1949	.96	1916	.99
1942	1.01	1950	1.00	1917	1.00
1943	1.02	1951	.99	1918	.98
1944	2.13	1952	.98	1919	1.07
1945	.97	1953	.99	1920	1.01
1946	.93			1921	1.04
				1922	1.12
				1923	1.21

Each link relative is computed with the data for the preceding year equals 1.
Source: See Table 8.1.

Second, during 1939 and 1940, the rate of increase of the Greek price indices and note issues was almost at par. In 1941, however, the increase in the currency circulation was outpaced by that of prices. Consequently, the annual average for the price-currency ratio rose to its first peak of 1.15. From October, 1942, to April, 1943, the inflationary process temporarily slackened mainly for psychological reasons. The Western Allies' military successes in North Africa gave rise to the belief among the public that liberation from German occupation and therefore the end of inflation were in sight. Accordingly, the values of the price-currency ratios dropped. But when it was found that the liberation resulted only in intensifying the inflation, the ratio rose again from a level below unity to its record peak of 2.13 for the average of 1944.

Third, in both Germany and Greece, the price-note ratios increased when the tempo of inflation accentuated, and decreased when economic conditions improved. This phenomenon was very similar to what occurred during the Chinese inflation, (see Chapter I) and may therefore be considered a common feature of inflation.

EXTERNAL VALUE OF THE CURRENCIES UNDER INFLATION[1]

The difficulties encountered in adjusting the foreign-exchange rate in the course of inflation were by no means an experience unique to China. Similar developments were found during recent inflations in France, Greece, and Japan, and during the inflations of France, Germany, and Poland after World War I.

In March, 1947, Japan fixed her foreign-exchange rate at fifty yen to one U.S. dollar. The official rate was about 30 percent above the price parity. But the latter soon outpaced the official rate, and readjustment of the official rate became necessary. When the new official rate of 270 yen per U.S. dollar was established in July, 1948, it was again well above the price parity. But by March, 1949, the official rate was once more in danger of being outpaced by the price parity, and the adoption of a new rate of 360 yen to one U.S. dollar became necessary. After January, 1951, the new rate, which had been higher than the price parity at the time of its adoption, again lagged behind the rising price parity.

The lack of necessary data has prevented a studying of the behavior of the Greek foreign-exchange rate and price parity during World War II, when hyperinflation was rampant in that country. But a study of developments since 1945 adequately demonstrates the nature of the foreign-exchange rate policy pursued by the Greek government and the difficulties encountered during these years. Until the institution of the certificate system (see Chapter IV) in October, 1947, the Greek government adopted a fixed-rate policy, under which the official quotation was adjusted only occasionally. Even after the adoption of the certificate system, the flexible-rate system was actually in force only from October, 1947, to June, 1948. Thereafter, the improvement of economic conditions in Greece made it possible for the Greek authorities to revert to a *de facto* fixed-rate policy, although the certificate rate was not formally abolished until June, 1951. During the first part of 1945, the official rate was equal to less than one-third of the price parity. From

February, 1946, to September, 1947, the official rate rose to about 50 percent of the price parity. During the latter part of 1948 and almost all of 1949, the official rate was maintained within a spread that ranged from 60 to 70 percent of parity. After October, 1949, this discrepancy between the official rate and parity was further reduced as a result of improvements in Greece's domestic economy.

In France the Allied authorities in 1942 set the official rate of the franc at 400 francs per pound and 100 francs per dollar. At France's insistence the official rate was reduced to 200 francs per pound and 50 francs per dollar in February, 1943. The rate was retained after the liberation of metropolitan France. At this rate, the franc was greatly overvalued in terms of the parity calculated from the price indices of the United States and France. The situation was temporarily improved by the adjustment of the official dollar rate from 50 to 119.10669 francs.[2] But the discrepancy increased steadily in the course of 1947, when the price parity rose with the rise of commodity prices in France, while the official foreign-exchange remained unchanged. During 1948 and the greater part of 1949, the basic quotation was raised to 214.71 francs for one U.S. dollar and a multiple-rate system was formally instituted to provide several official quotations (including the official rate, the official free-market rate, and the average rate derived from these two rates). These changes contributed appreciably to narrowing down the gap between the official quotations and the price parity, although the existence of the multiple-rate system made a clear-cut comparison between these quotations and the parity rather difficult. In September, 1949, the single official-rate system was reinstituted in place of the multiple-rate one. The official rate was quite realistic in terms of the price parity in 1950, but the discrepancy between the two was again widened after 1951 as a result of the rise of commodity prices in France. In cases where the "parallel" market quotations (represented by either the free-market rate in Switzerland or that in the domestic market) were available, official rates were usually low in relation to those parallel rates.[3]

In general, the foreign-exchange experiences encountered during the Chinese inflation after World War II were quite similar to that of the French inflation during 1919–26, and of the Polish inflation during 1921–24. In both cases, there was a general tendency for the depreciation of a currency in terms of domestic prices to outpace its depreciation in terms of foreign currency, and for the discrepancies between the price parity and the exchange rate to increase when the tempo of inflation was accentuated.[4] On the other hand, during the German inflation after World War I (as shown by authoritative studies on the subject[5]) the depreciation of the external value of the mark for most of the time led the internal depreciation of the currency. This relation between the external and internal values of a depreciating currency, however, applied only to the German mark; it was not true in most of the belligerent and neutral European countries.[6]

In the light of this discussion, it seems that the foreign-exchange experience of Germany during 1919–23, was rather an unusual one, probably precipitated by the heavy reparation payments. The lead of internal depreciation over the external depreciation has been a more common phenomenon of inflation by far. This situation was particularly true during and after World War II, when the dollar and sterling exchange rates maintained by the neutral countries and re-established in the liberated and conquered areas in Europe were often purposely overvalued in terms of the price parity. There were many factors responsible for the overvaluation of the currencies. During the immediate postwar years, there was a tendency for many nations to overvalue their currencies with a view to raising their prestige for countering inflation.[7] Moreover, to set and to maintain temporarily the external value of a currency at a given level can usually be done before the basic problems of inflation are solved, so long as the necessary foreign-exchange reserves are available. Since foreign exchange is trade in an organized market, its rates are much more amenable to government manipulation than domestic prices, behaviors of which are subject to the influence of numerous unrelated markets. The availability of foreign aid after World War II has made the task of manipulating foreign-exchange market even easier than the prewar years. As was pointed out earlier, these are exactly the factors which might explain the overvaluation of the Chinese currency during the postwar years. This policy of overvaluation has been one of the major factors from which the economic problems in many countries have stemmed.

The previous review also shows that any attempt to peg the exchange rate at a fixed level before the stability of domestic economy was assured would likely be confronted with serious difficulties. For, to fix the foreign-exchange rate prematurely while the rise in domestic prices continued would usually result in overvaluing the home currency in relation to foreign money, and might thus bring about disequilibrating rather than equilibrating effects on the economy.

LOSS IN REAL GOVERNMENT INCOMES AND EXPENDITURES DURING INFLATION

One feature common to the experiences of China and Germany was the shrinkage of government incomes and expenditures in the course of inflation. In Germany, the real values of government expenditures and incomes in October, 1923, were reduced to the rate of 1.49 and 0.02 of the 1913 mark per year respectively. In April, 1919, the income and expenditure expressed in the 1913 mark were at the rate of 1286.0 million marks and 6039.48 million marks per annum respectively. Thus, in real terms, the ratio of the expenditure of April, 1919, to the expenditure of October, 1923, was 4,053 million to one. The similar ratio of the 1919 income to that of 1923 was 64,300 million to one. The ratio of income to expenditure for October, 1923, was 1.6 percent, as against 21.3 percent in April, 1919 (see Table 8.4). In December, 1948, the annual

TABLE 8.4. CHANGES IN GOVERNMENT REVENUES AND EXPENDITURES DURING THE GERMAN AND CHINESE INFLATIONS

	Government expenditures	*Government revenues*	*Revenues as percent of expenditures*
Germany (1913 marks)			
a. April 1919	6039.48 million	1286.0 million	21.3
b. Oct. 1923	1.49	.02	1.6
Ratio of *b* to *a*	1:4053 million	1:64300 million	
China (1937 yuan)			
c. 1936–37	1884.0 million	1307.7 million	69.4
d. Dec. 1948	1.48	.25	16.9
Ratio of *d* to *c*	1:1274.2 million	1:5245.5 million	

Source: For Germany: Breciani-Turroni, *The Economics of Inflation*, pp. 422, 437–38; for China: chapter III.

expenditures and incomes of the Chinese government amounted to 1.48 and 0.25 units of the 1937 yuan respectively. At these amounts, the expenditures were only one-1274.2 millionth that of 1936–37; and the incomes, one-5245.5 millionth that of 1936–37. Compared with the German experience, the Chinese losses in incomes and expenditures were far less staggering in magnitude, although the Chinese figures refer to a period of more than eleven years as against a period of four years for Germany.

While the prime motive of inflation is to raise the government income, both the Chinese and German governments lost virtually all their real incomes in the process of inflation. In both cases, the loss was more serious in government incomes than in government expenditures. A major factor leading to such losses was the rise in the velocity of money circulation in the course of inflation.

INTEREST RATES AND THE RATE OF PRICE INCREASES

Some experts contend that one of the characteristic symptoms of inflation is that "the rate of interest tends to approach the rate of increase in prices, because lenders always consider the hoarding of goods as an alternative to lending."[8] This contention, however, has no equivocable support from either the Chinese or the German experiences. In Germany, the Reichbank rate from 1914 through 1918 was invariably higher than the average annual percentage increase in commodity prices (see Table 8.5); but from 1919 to November, 1923, the rate of price increases mostly exceeded the corresponding rate of interest. From June, 1922, to November, 1923, the Reichbank rate was negligibly small in comparison with the rate of price increases despite the repeated adjustments in the bank's interest rate. In China, the prevalence of the negative real interest in the free market during the inflation, and the increasing lag in interest rates behind price increases with the intensification of the inflation (see Table 8.4) are all strong evidence against this contention.

A possible explanation for the lag in interest rates may be found in the failure on the part of the public to anticipate the rate at which the tempo of inflation accentuates. It is possible at an advanced stage of inflation to have interest rates so fixed in loan contracts that

TABLE 8.5. INTEREST RATES AND PRICE CHANGES DURING THE GERMAN INFLATION, 1914–23 (in percent)

	The Reichbank rate	Price increases[a]		The Reichbank rate	Price increases[a]
1914	.4167	2.5	1923 Jan.	1.00	88.8
1915		1.5	Feb.		100.5
1916		.2	March		−12.6
1917		2.6	April	1.50	6.7
1918		1.7	May		56.8
1919		10.6	June		137.3
1920		6.3	July		185.8
1921		8.5	Aug.	2.50	1,162.3
1922 June		8.8	Sept.	7.50	2,431.7
July	.50	43.1	Oct.	75.00	29,586.2
Aug.	.58	90.9	Nov.		10,132.6
Sept.	.67	49.5	Dec.		73.8
Oct.		97.2			
Nov.	.83	103.9			
Dec.		27.8			

[a] The yearly price increases for 1914–21 are computed on the basis of the annual averages of the link relatives.

There was no change in interest unless indicated.

Source: Bresciani-Turroni, *The Economics of Inflation*, p. 44; and F. D. Graham, *Exchange, Prices and Production in Hyperinflation, 1920–23* (Princeton, 1930), p. 65.

an anticipated change in prices may be allowed for. However, such allowances will not likely be adequate, so long as prices are rising at a rapidly increasing rate, while the anticipation of the public, as is usually the case, relies mainly upon past experience.

Epilogue

If I had to live again the ordeal of the Chinese inflation I would suggest the following monetary and fiscal programs for coping with the problems:

The government's outlay in domestic currency should be budgeted on a monthly basis rather than on an annual basis.

The purchasing power required for the budgeted expenditures should be obtained through these channels: tax collections, issue of banknotes, sales of government gold, sales of foreign exchange held by the government, sales of government properties, borrowing from the domestic market, and any other appropriate measure in attaining that objective.

The principle of minimum cost should be strictly observed in considering all these alternatives. If, for instance, the sale of imports in the domestic market could yield more local-currency revenue than the sale of foreign currency, the government should use its foreign-currency reserve to purchase such imports for domestic sales rather than selling foreign currency in the domestic market. If the cross-rate between gold and U.S. dollars is favorable to gold in comparison with the similar cross-rate abroad, gold then should be imported for domestic sales. Similarly, if a tight local money market permits issuance of some new paper currency without unduly depreciating its purchasing power or increasing the money value of government outlay, the new currency should then be issued to meet the government's need. To follow such a policy would naturally require the government to hold in ready reserve an adequate supply of new bank notes, gold, foreign currency, securities, and a host of commodities for sale. The operation, like that of a department store, would appear to be difficult, but the types of operation actually in use, as the experience in China testified, would not be too numerous.

Ten or fifteen such usable alternatives should be quite adequate for an economy like postwar China. Moreover, even this limited number of alternatives has to be developed gradually in the course of operation, permitting the administrators of these operations to learn by experience.

The following is an illustration of this proposal.

Suppose the total government expenditures (including both foreign and local currency outlays) were U.S. $600 million a year. Assume that 25 percent of this outlay was met by nonborrowing revenue of the government, 25 percent by note issues, and the remaining 50 percent by gold or foreign currency reserves of the government. The gold or foreign currency could be used either for direct sale in the domestic market or for the purchase of commodity imports for domestic sales. Assume also that the nation's balance of payment would be in equilibrium after excluding the government expenditures in foreign currencies. Under this assumption, the gold and foreign-currency reserve of the government amounting to more than U.S. $845 million (roughly an approximation of the conditions in postwar China at the beginning of 1946), would have been sufficient to meet the nation's need for about three years.

In actual operation, as was shown in Chapter V, about U.S. $500 million of the entire Chinese reserve was dissipated during the twelve-month period ending February, 1947. By August, 1948, the entire reserve of U.S. $845 million virtually disappeared. My proposed plan, if successfully executed, would have substantially slowed down the drain on the official monetary reserve.

More important, however, is that under the proposed program of planned inflation, the expansion of the note issues would have meant an annual increase of about 25 percent in the volume of currency circulation. This estimate is based on the assumption that the total Chinese currency in circulation in 1937 had a value equivalent to about U.S. $500 million. Compounded at a rate of 25 percent per annum, the note issues at the end of 1948 would have been approximately thirty-four times the issues at the beginning of 1937. In actuality, China's note circulation expanded from 1.3 billion yuan in January, 1937, to 24,558,999 billion yuan at the end of 1948, representing an expansion of 19 million. That this proposed program could have reduced the intensity of inflation is too obvious to require further elucidation. Moreover, as the Chinese experience testifies, if the intensity of inflation had been reduced, so would have been many of its undesirable secondary effects. This in turn would have meant a further reduction in fiscal deficit and inflation.

While the proposed program might have contributed to reducing the intensity of inflation in a short run, it would not have offered any fundamental solution to the problem of inflation. The solution to the problem has to be predicated upon a drastic expansion in the nation's production, the development of an effective means of augmenting revenue and/or the curtailment of government activities. With the military and political situations in China as they were during the postwar years, the Nationalist government had neither the strength nor the necessary environment effectively to pursue these objectives. Only peace within the country and an effective large-scale foreign-aid program could have changed the situation. Up to 1949, neither was in existence.

Appendix 1 Mechanics of Inflationary Spiral

Many attempts have been made by the use of mathematical models to depict the inflationary process arising from struggles for income shares among various production factors.[1] The general hypothesis is that, even in the absence of an inflationary gap and in the disturbances originating from monetary factors, the struggle among various income groups, either to expand or to maintain their income share, provides a condition sufficient to generate an inflationary spiral.

I think the inflationary spiral is a dynamic process similar to the one used by Samuelson to demonstrate the cobweb theorem.[2] The purpose of this appendix is to develop, with the assistance of the mechanics of the cobweb theorem, a set of rigorous models, which depict various types of inflation and cover many of its essential characteristics as developed in early studies of inflation.

This discussion is based on the following premises:

1. Both price and wage are cost-determined, or substantially so; that is to say, price is a function of the wage cost, and wage is a function of the cost-of-living, which is in turn determined by prices.

2. In a closed economy, in which foreign trade is either nonexistent or unimportant, price or money income may ultimately be decomposed into wage and profit. In countries like the United Kingdom or Japan, where imports for raw materials are essential, the decomposed elements may include the cost of imports as well as wage and profit.[3] The amount of rental income either is assumed to be constant in the course of inflation, or is considered to be a derivative which may ultimately be resolved into profit and wage.

3. There is a constant struggle among the factors of production (i.e., labor and capital, under our assumptions) to maintain or increase their real incomes or their income shares in comparison with the preinflation condition. The entrepreneurs' attempts to protect their profit share are often characterized by their adherence to the target pricing policy, which may be in the form of either a fixed percentage mark-up over cost, or a target percentage return on sales or investment.

4. Full employment is not a necessary condition for bringing the cost-price spiraling mechanism into operation. It is essential, however, that

labor be in a position to effectuate a substantial portion, if not the entire amount, of its desired wage adjustment without unduly increasing unemployment. First, this condition implies that there must be a profit margin and also monetary resources at the disposal of entrepreneurs, either ex post or ex ante, sufficient to absorb the wage increase; second, that labor must be in a position to bargain effectively with its employers, either because of the strength of its union organization, or because of the scarcity of labor supply in relation to demand.

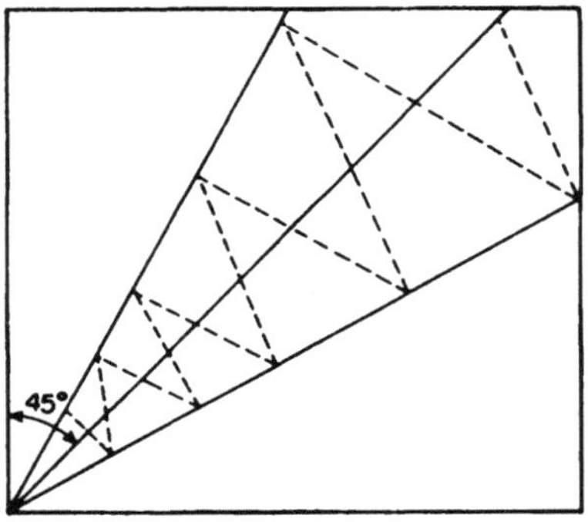

CHART 1a

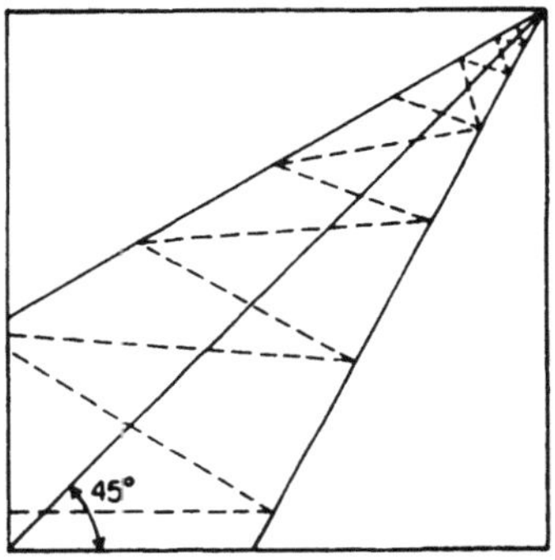

CHART 2a

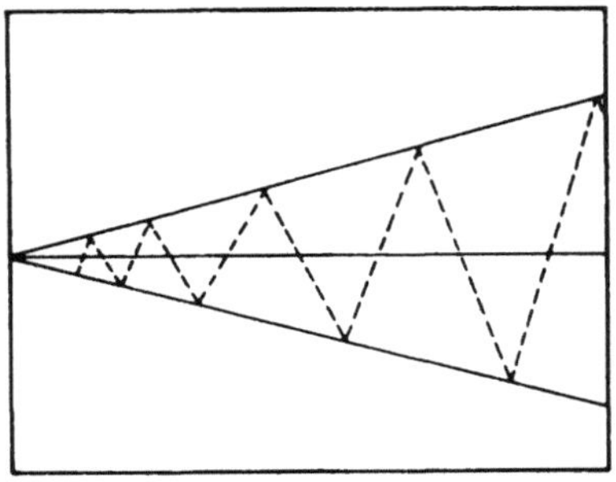

CHART 1b

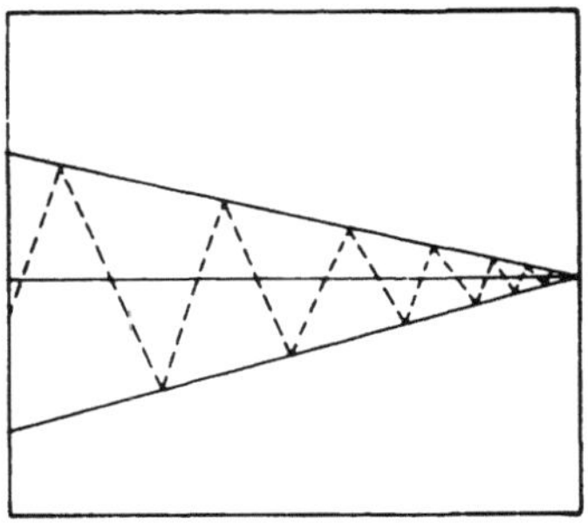

CHART 2b

The mathematical models in this study are constructed on the basis of the period-to-period link relatives which show percentage changes of the variables concerned from one period to another. The struggle for income shares between any two factors of production (for example, between wage and profit) are conceived diagrammatically in either of two forms.

In the double-entry diagram, the vertical axis represents the rate of profit (or its link relative, or index), and the horizontal axis, the wage rate (or its link relative or index). A change in one of these two rates, which would bring about an immediate and equal adjustment in the other, is shown by a straight line passing through the origin and forming a 45° angle with either of the axes. Any deviation of actual observation from this line reflects the struggle between these two factors for absolute or relative income shares. An entry above the 45° line indicates a change in favor of the factor represented by the vertical axis, and an entry below the line indicates a change in favor of the factor on the horizontal axis. Under inflation, the entries of successive periods tend to move farther away from either or both these axes when the number of periods increases. If the spiral is a divergent one, the entries move farther and farther away from the 45° line; and the reverse is true if the spiral is convergent. These spiraling processes are shown in Charts 1a and 2a. Chart 1a illustrates the divergent spiral; Chart 2a represents the convergent one.

Alternatively changes in the income shares between two factors may also be shown by first computing the ratio of their link relatives for each period, and then by plotting these ratios in a diagram, where the vertical axis represents the ratio, and the horizontal axis, the time. Diagrams of this type, as shown in Charts 1b and 2b, would usually give a much clearer picture of the relative changes than does the double-entry diagram. But this clarity is attainable only at the expense of the details concerning the absolute changes in these factor incomes, which are also accounted for in the double-entry diagram.

Since our prime interest is the basic principle underlying the spiral, the discussion is confined only to the bare bone of the principle.

The basic model

Let Q_t and W_t be the link relatives showing period-to-period changes in profit and wage respectively. Q denotes the profit relative at the initial equilibrium, and W, the corresponding wage relative. For this discussion, I make the following assumptions:

1. The price or money income may ultimately be resolved into two factor incomes: wage and profit. Thus:

$$P = \eta Q + (1 - \eta) W, \text{ or} \tag{2.1}$$

$$P_t = \eta Q_t + (1 - \eta) W_t, \tag{2.2}$$

where η and $(1 - \eta)$ denote respectively the percentages of the profit share and the wage share in the total money income. It is assumed that the percentage of each of these income shares remains constant for all periods.

2. In addition to the distortions arising from the interclass struggle, the inflationary process is being multiplied at a constant rate of α percent per period. That is

$$P_t = \alpha P_{t-1}, \text{ or}$$

$$P_t = \alpha^t P. \tag{2.3}$$

In (2.1)–(2.3), P represents the price index at the initial equilibrium, the P's with subscripts denote the price index of any subsequent period, and the subscripts $(t - 1)$ and t denote the period.

3. The wage rate for a given period t is determined jointly by the general trend of inflation mentioned in (2.3); and the concomitant changes in the income distribution between wage and profit. As a manifestation of the wage-earners' effort to maintain their income share, wage-earners will press for a corresponding adjustment in wages, if and when profit increases. And this adjustment is assumed on the basis of the following equation:[4]

$$W_t = \alpha^t W - (-\beta)^t (Q_1 - Q), \tag{2.4}$$

where β is a coefficient denoting the relationship between the deviation of the current link relative from the corresponding value of the trend (i.e., $W_t = \alpha^t W$), on the one hand, and the amount of the initial "shock" (i.e., $Q_1 - Q$) on the other. The higher the value of β is, the stronger is the resiliency of wage in response to a change in profit, and vice versa.[5]

From equations (2.1) to (2.4), I solve for Q_t as follows:[6]

$$Q_t = \alpha^t Q + (-\beta)^t \frac{(1 - \eta)}{\eta} (Q_1 - Q). \tag{2.5}$$

The next to be examined is what is the value of β in relation to η, α, and $(Q_1 - Q)$, if the spiraling process is to continue, while the amplitude of the period-to-period fluctuations remains within specified limits. The term "limits" means that in no period under consideration would any of the wage or profit link relatives fall below the corresponding index at the initial equilibrium; that is to say, the discussion is predicated upon the following conditions: $W_t > W$, and $Q_t > Q$ for all values of t, when $t \geqq 1$. The substitution of equations (2.4) and (2.5) in these conditions yields the following result:

$$W_t = \{\alpha^t W - (-\beta)^t (Q_1 - Q)\} > W \tag{2.6}$$

$$Q_t = \{\alpha^t Q + (-\beta)^t \frac{(1 - \eta)}{\eta} (Q_1 - Q)\} > Q. \tag{2.7}$$

The relation shown in (2.6) is true for all values of t, if and only if[7]

$$|W(\alpha^t - 1)| > |\beta^t (Q_1 - Q)|, \tag{2.8}$$

or

$$|R_w^{1/t}| > |\beta|,$$

where

$$R_w = \frac{\alpha^t - 1}{\dfrac{(Q_1 - Q)}{W}}.$$

Similarly, relation (2.7) holds, if and only if

$$|Q(\alpha^t - 1)| > \left|\beta^t\left(\frac{1-\eta}{\eta}\right)(Q_1 - Q)\right|, \qquad (2.9)$$

or

$$\left|\left\{\frac{R_q\eta}{(1-\eta)}\right\}^{1/t}\right| > |\beta|,$$

where

$$R_q^{1/t} = \frac{\alpha^t - 1}{\frac{(Q_1 - Q)}{Q}}.$$

If $W = Q$, then $R_q = R_w = R$. The conditions expressed in (2.8) and (2.9) may thus be rewritten, as follows:

$$|R^{1/t}| > |\beta|, \qquad (2.10)$$

and

$$\left\{\frac{R\eta}{(1-\eta)}\right\}^{1/t} > |\beta|. \qquad (2.11)$$

The limitation imposed on the value of β in relation to $\sqrt[t]{R}$ and $\{R\eta/(1-\eta)\}^{1/t}$ implies that, in computing its income share, labor can claim not more than what the entrepreneurs are in a position to pay. Excess claims may result in an undue reduction in profit, and may in turn reduce employment and the income share of labor. On the other hand, if the wage-price spiral is to be in effective operation, β must have a value significantly different from zero. This implies that labor must be in an effective bargaining position, either because of the strength of the labor union, or because of the scarcity of the labor supply in relation to demand.

In short the inflationary spirals as represented by equations (2.4) and (2.5) resolve into two parts: the trend effect (represented by the factor $\alpha^t Q$ in the case of profit or by $\alpha^t W$ in the case of wage); and the oscillating effect (represented by $(-\beta)^t(Q_1 - Q)$ for wage and by $(-\beta^t)\frac{(1-\eta)}{\eta}(Q_1 - Q)$ for profit). While the trend effect determines the general slope of a spiral, the oscillating effect determines the amplitude of the fluctuations around the trend.

It is assumed that during inflation the value of α is invariably greater than unity (a necessary condition for an upward trend). It follows, therefore, that the greater is the value of α, the steeper is the slope of the trend.

The amplitude of the fluctuations of both the wage and profit spirals varies directly with the value of β. In the case of profit, the behavior of the spiral is also affected by the value of η: the greater is the percentage of the wage share ($= 1 - \eta$) in total income in relation to the corresponding percentage share of profit ($= \eta$), the greater is the amplitude of fluctuation around the trend; and vice versa.

The spiral is divergent or convergent according to whether β is greater or less than unity. If β has a value exceeding unity, the value of $(-\beta)^t$ and therefore the deviation of the actual spiral from the basic trend ($\alpha^t W$ or $\alpha^t Q$) increases as t increases. The spiral has the appearance of the one shown in Charts 1a and 1b. Conversely, if the value of β is less than 1, the factor $(-\beta)^t$ converges to zero as t approaches infinity. The deviation of the actual spiral from the trend decreases as t increases, with the spiral ultimately converging to the trend (see Charts 2a and 2b).

It should also be noted that if the value of β exceeds unity and becomes unduly large in terms of the criteria given in relations (2.8) and (2.9), there is the possibility that either Q_t or W_t, representing the period-to-period link relatives of profit and wage may drop during some period below the preinflation level (i.e., W or Q). This, of course, is a deviation from the basic inflationary trend. Thus any model which does not satisfy in general the condition $W_t > W$ or $Q_t > Q$ is to be excluded from our consideration of the inflationary spiral. This point will be further explored in the next section.

Types of spiraling processes

Based on previous discussions and on the relations between $\sqrt[t]{R}$ and β, at least eight types of spiraling processes for wages and a corresponding

TABLE 1. TYPES OF INFLATIONARY SPIRALS[a]

	$\beta < \sqrt[t]{R}$		$\beta > \sqrt[t]{R}$	
	$R < 1$	$R > 1$	$R < 1$	$R > 1$
$\beta < 1$	*a*: $W_t > W$, convergent	*b*: same as *a*	*c*: possibility of $W_t < W$ and/or convergent	*d*: same as *c*
$\beta > 1$	*e*: impossible	*f*: $W_t > W$, divergent	*g*: possibility of $W_t < W$ and/or divergent	*h*: same as *g*

[a] $R = \dfrac{(\alpha^t - 1)}{\dfrac{(Q_1 - Q)}{W \text{ (or } Q)}}$. The relations $\beta < \sqrt[t]{R}$ and $\beta > \sqrt[t]{R}$ should be true for all values of t when $t = 1, 2, 3 \ldots .$

series of the profit spirals are derived. The different types of wage spirals are shown in Table 1. Of the eight processes only three types *a*, *b*, and *f* satisfy the conditions of $W_t > W$, for all values of t, when $t = 1$. Of these three, types *a* and *b* have convergent spirals, and type *f* is divergent.

For the purpose of illustration, let us consider the types *a*, *b*, *f*, and *h*, by assigning a numerical value to each of the relevant coefficients shown in equations (2.4) and (2.5). For the sake of simplicity, let us assume that

$Q_1 = 102$, $Q = W = 100$, $\eta = \frac{1}{3}$, and $\dfrac{(1-\eta)}{\eta} = 2$ for all the four types considered. The values of α and β, varying from type to type, will be assigned when each type is discussed.

Type a. Assume that $\alpha = 1.01$ and $\beta = .25$. Thus, $t = 1$, $\sqrt[t]{R} = \left\{\dfrac{(1.01)^t - 1}{.02}\right\}^{1/t} = .50$; and $\left\{\dfrac{R\eta}{(1-\eta)}\right\}^{1/t} = \left\{\dfrac{R}{2}\right\}^{1/t} = .25$. Therefore both $\sqrt[t]{R}$ and $\left\{\dfrac{R\eta}{(1-\eta)}\right\}^{1/t}$ have a value equal to or greater than β, which is assumed to have a value of .25. Applying the relevant numerical values to equations (2.4) and (2.5), the result shown under type *a* of Table 2 is obtained. This is a type in which the spiral converges to a common trend of $Q = W$ as t becomes infinitely large. The values of the trend for various periods are shown in the next to last column of Table 2.

Type b. Assume that $\alpha = 1.04$ and $\beta = .5$. Thus,

$$\sqrt[t]{R} = \left\{\frac{(1.04)^t - 1}{.02}\right\}^{1/t} > 1, \text{ and } \left\{\frac{R\eta}{(1-\eta)}\right\}^{1/t} > 1, \text{ when } t \geqq 1.$$

The substitution of the assumed numerical values in equations (2.4) and (2.5) gives the result shown under type *b* of Table 2. Like type *a*, the spiral of this case also converges to the trend (see last column) as the value of t becomes infinitely large. Unlike type *a*, the values of both $\sqrt[t]{R}$ and $\left\{\dfrac{R\eta}{(1-\eta)}\right\}^{1/t}$ exceed one, instead of having values of less than unity.

Type f. Assume that $\alpha = 1.04$ and $\beta = 1.05$. Thus $\sqrt[t]{R} = \left\{\dfrac{1.04^t - 1}{.02}\right\}^{1/t}$, which has a value exceeding both unity and β, when $t = 1, 2, 3 \ldots.$ Substituting the numerical values in equations (2.4) and (2.5), the result is shown under type *f* of Table 2. The trend values applicable to this case are shown in the last column. Unlike the convergency of types *a* and *b*, this case has a divergent spiral, indicating that the inflationary process, if not promptly stopped, ultimately results in "explosion."

Type h. This type shows the property of the model in the case of $|\beta| \geqq |R^{1/t}|$ or $\left\{\dfrac{R\eta}{(1-\eta)}\right\}^{1/t}$, a situation which contradicts the conditions specified in (2.10)–(2.11). Assume, for this purpose, that $\alpha = 1.04$ and $\beta = 2.5$. Since $\eta = \frac{1}{3}$, as has previously been given, then $R = \left\{\dfrac{(1.04^t - 1)}{.02}\right\}^{1/t} \leqq 2$. Substituting numerical values in equations (2.4) and (2.5), I obtain the results under type *h* in the table. The trend values in this case are the same as those of type *f* (see final column Table 2). Since $\beta > 1$, the spiral of this case is a divergent one. But because of the assumed relation between β and $R^{1/t}$, the link relative Q_t falls below the

TABLE 2. INFLATIONARY SPIRALS RESULTING FROM ASSIGNING VALUES TO CASES a, b, f, AND h IN TABLE 1

	Type a[a]			*Type b*[a]			*Type f*[a]			*Type h*[a]			*Trend* (α^t)	
	$\alpha = 1.01, \beta = .25$			$\alpha = 1.04, \beta = .5$			$\alpha = 1.04, \beta = 1.05$			$\alpha = 1.04, \beta = 2.5$				
	Q or Q_t	W or W_t	$\frac{W_t}{Q_t}$	Q or Q_t	W or W_t	$\frac{W_t}{Q_t}$	Q or Q_t	W or W_t	$\frac{W_t}{Q_t}$	Q or Q_t	W or W_t	$\frac{W_t}{Q_t}$	$\alpha =$ 1.01	$\alpha =$ 1.04
Initial equilibrium	100.0	100.0	1.000	100.0	100.0	1.000	100.0	100.0	1.000	100.0	100.0	1.000	1.00	1.00
1	100.0	101.5	1.015	102.0	105.0	1.029	102.9	106.1	1.031	94.0	109.0	1.160	1.01	1.04
2	102.3	102.1	.998	109.0	107.5	.986	109.2	105.8	.969	133.0	95.5	.718	1.02	1.08
3	102.9	103.0	1.001	111.5	112.3	1.007	110.8	114.3	1.032	49.5	143.3	2.895	1.03	1.12
4	104.2	104.0	.998	116.9	116.5	.997	118.2	114.2	.969	273.3	38.9	.142	1.04	1.17
5	105.0	105.0	1.000	121.1	121.3	1.002	119.7	123.8	1.034	−269.6	316.3	−1.173	1.05	1.21
6	106.0	106.0	1.000	126.1	126.0	.999	127.4	123.2	.967	1,102.6	−362.3	− .329	1.06	1.26

[a] It is assumed that $Q_1 = 102$, $Q = W = 100$, $\eta = \frac{1}{3}$, and $(1 - \eta)/\eta = 2$.

pre-inflation level ($Q = 100$) in all the odd-number periods. On the other hand, W_t is smaller than $W(= 100)$ in all the even-number periods.

The convergency or divergency can be viewed in terms of the ratio of W_t/Q_t as well as W_t or Q_t, as implied in our early discussions. The values for the ratio W_t/Q_t are shown in Table 2. If the ratio is to be used as the basis of this study, the basic equation, which can be readily derived from equations (2.4) and (2.5), should be as follows:

$$\frac{W_t}{Q_t} = \frac{\alpha^t W - (-\beta)^t(Q_1 - Q)}{\alpha^t Q + (-\beta)^t\left(\frac{1-\eta}{\eta}\right)(Q_1 - Q)}$$

$$= 1 + \frac{1}{\left\{\frac{\eta\alpha^t Q}{(-\beta)^t(Q_1 - Q)} + (1 - \eta)\right\}} \qquad (2.12)$$

Thus far, there has been no allowance for change in the value of η in the course of inflation. How would the conclusions be altered by a change in the value of η? From the relation (2.11), which is

$$|\beta^t| < \left|\left\{\frac{\alpha^t - 1}{(Q_1 - Q)/Q}\right\}\left(\frac{\eta}{1 - \eta}\right)\right|,$$

it is obvious that the smaller the value of η the narrower are the limits within which the value of β^t fluctuates without deviating from the basic trend of inflation. The implication is that the smaller the income share for profit, the smaller is the capacity of entrepreneurs to absorb wage increases.

These models have the following implications:

1. If the trend of inflation is maintained, then the increase in any of the income shares (wages or profit) in a given period, arising from the oscillating effects, cannot go beyond the limits set by the increases accumulated from the trend effect up to that period. This conclusion is implied in the relation (2.10) and (2.11).
2. An adjustment involving an increase in wage or profit during a given period in excess of the original "shock" (i.e., $\beta > 1$) invariably results in an explosive type of inflationary spiral. Wage adjustment in anticipation of future price increases, or price increases in excess of cost increases are examples of this type of adjustment.
3. The smaller the income share for profit (i.e., the lower the value of η), the smaller the capacity of entrepreneurs to absorb wage increases.
4. The models developed in the preceding discussions have been compared with the actual experience of China, Germany, and the United States. The result of these comparisons (shown in part in Charts 3–5) shows that the underlying principle of the cobweb process of adjustment may be applied not only to the relations between wage and profit (or

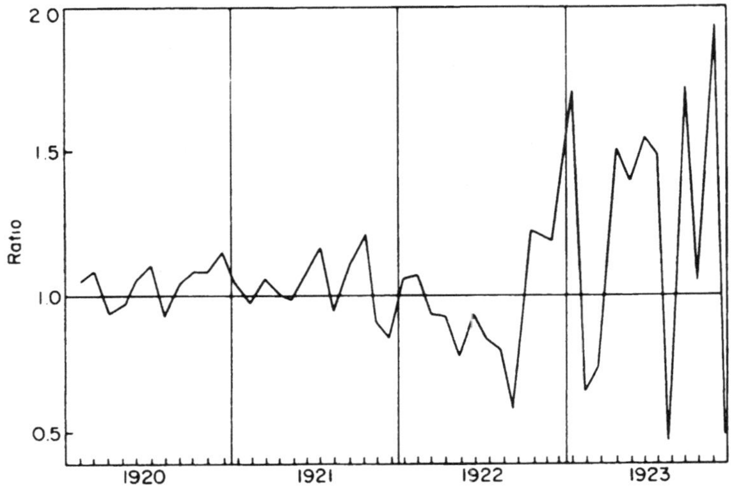

CHART 3. RATIO OF STOCK PRICES TO WAGE RATES FOR GERMANY, 1920–23
Source: C. Bresciani-Turroni, *Economics of Inflation* (London, 1931), pp. 450, 53–54.

price), but also to those between the prices of raw materials and products, or between note issue and prices. Chart 3 shows the relationship between the stock prices and wage rates, both in year-to-year link relatives, during the German inflation after World War I. Chart 4 shows the ratio of the link relative of commodity prices to that of wage rates in Taiwan from 1949–54. Chart 5 shows the relationship between the link relative of stock dividends and that of wage rates in the United States, 1937–57. Charts 3 and 4 show the divergent spiral, and Chart 5, the convergent spiral. Changes in commodity prices, stock prices, or dividends are used to represent changes in profits. I believe that, like the multiplier theory and

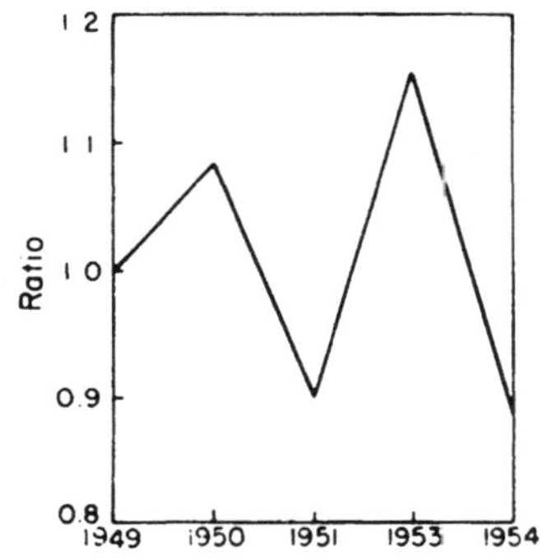

CHART 4. RATIO OF LINK RELATIVE OF COMMODITY PRICES TO THAT OF WAGE RATES FOR TAIWAN, 1949–54

the acceleration principle in theories of business cycles, the mechanics of spiraling process developed in this note can have many important applications in studies of inflation. These mechanics, for instance, may be used to explain the paradoxical phenomenon of acute money supply despite the plethora of note issue during inflation; for this phenomenon is merely a case of the currency expansion lagging behind price increases.

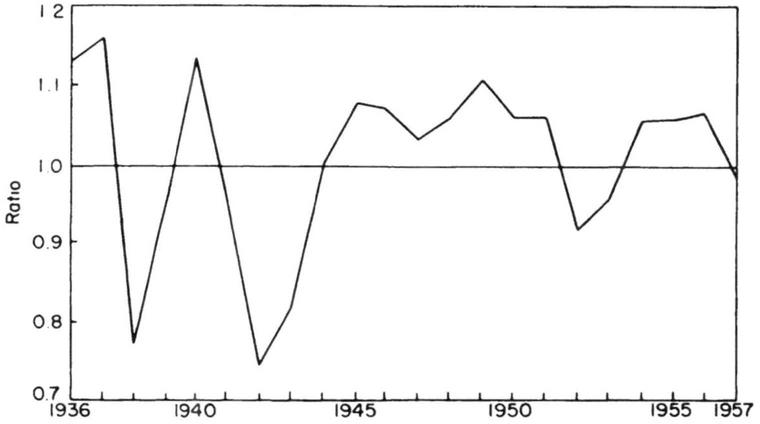

CHART 5. RATIO OF LINK RELATIVE OF STOCK DIVIDENDS TO THAT OF WAGE RATES FOR UNITED STATES, 1936–57

The spiraling mechanism can also be useful in analyzing the redistributional effects of inflation, arising from the lead or lag in income adjustment during inflation. A divergent spiral indicates the accentuation of the inflationary process, and a convergent spiral reflects adjustments toward stabilization.

5. These models demonstrate more effectively the mechanics of the inflation process than do some of the earlier studies. Brown's exposition in *The Great Inflation, 1939–1951* is comprehensive, but it does not have the rigor one finds in some of the presentations using more mathematics than Brown did. Holzman's paper[8] does give a rigorous treatment of the subject, but the models he presents fail to bring out some of the basic features of the inflation spiral, shown in our Charts 1 and 2.

Appendix 2 Statistics of Chinese Government Revenue and Expenditure

The statistics of the Chinese government finance are among the most confused of the Chinese statistics. These statistics are confusing because there are several versions of such statistics, but not all are compatible. These versions include (a) the final budget figures; (b) the statistics compiled by the Department of Statistics of the Ministry of Finance, on the basis of ten-day reports submitted by various revenue and expenditure offices in various parts of the country; (c) the statistics published in the annual report of the Finance Minister; and (d) the statistics of the Central Bank recording actual cash receipts and outlays of the government.

Those under (c) are the most important. These were carefully compiled by the various departments of the government and audited by the government auditors; they were in fact the official and final report of the government accounts. But because of the time consumed in collecting the necessary data from distant corners of the country, because of protracted interdepartmental consultations, and because of the usual "red tape" in government administration, these official compilations for a given fiscal year were usually not completed until months after the calendar conclusion. Moreover, these official statistics were published only for the fiscal years from July, 1928, to June, 1935, and for those from July, 1940, to June, 1944.

Those under (b) are available for the entire span from 1928 through 1948, which covered virtually the entire administration of the Nationalist government in mainland China. These figures were preliminary in nature and were not duly audited. They were crude but useful indicators for policy formulation mainly because of the promptness of their compilation. For the periods where the final report figures were not available at the Ministry of Finance, these statistics were in fact the only official data available.

Those under (a), which usually differ widely from actual receipts and expenditures, are obviously less reliable and useful than the statistics previously mentioned. The budget figures should therefore be used only when better information is not available.

There are important differences between the bank statistics referred to under (d) and those compiled by the Ministry of Finance. In principle, the records of the Central Bank were kept on the basis of actual cash receipts and disbursements. For instance, in the case of expenditures, the records of the Ministry usually considered that an authorization sent to the Central Bank for payment was equivalent to payment, but in the books of the Bank, no payment was recorded until the money was actually disbursed. Similar discrepancies also existed in the case of receipts.

In the present study, the figures for the final report are used whenever available. For the years when they were not published, the data compiled by the Department of Statistics of the Ministry of Finance is used. The budget estimates and the Bank's records are also occasionally used to provide additional information not obtainable from the above-mentioned statistics. Under such conditions it is possible to represent a reasonably accurate picture of the fiscal conditions prevailing in China before and during the inflation.

In passing, it may also be pointed out that the Directorate General (later known as the Ministry) of Budgets, Accounts and Statistics, the official auditor and statistical office of the Nationalist government, did not itself compile any revenue or expenditure statistics which might be considered as an independent source of information. In principle, all the statisticians and accountants in the various government offices (including those of the Ministry of Finance) were the appointees of the Directorate General and were therefore his resident auditors or supervisors in these offices. All the government accounts were prepared and audited by these experts. To that extent, the accounts and statistics released by the Ministry of Finance might also be considered as a joint undertaking of the Ministry and the Directorate. Fiscal statistics available in main official publications of the Directorate were compiled on the basis of the government budget, on the reports of the Ministry of Finance, or from other data supplied by the Ministry. It therefore does not seem justifiable to consider the statistics published in *The Statistical Abstract* and *The Statistical Yearbook* as an independent version of government accounts, preferable to those released by the Ministry of Finance. This seems to be the premise upon which Dr. Douglas S. Pauuw's "Chinese National Expenditure During the Nanking Period," *The Far Eastern Quarterly*, *XII* (November, 1952), 3–26, particularly Appendix A of the article, is based.

Appendix 3 Effects of Inflation on Government Debt in Foreign Currencies

The purpose of this appendix is to show the condition under which the cost of servicing a foreign-currency bond in a given period may exceed the cumulative receipts derived from the bond up to the end of that particular period. For the purpose of this discussion, we assume that both the purchase and servicing of the bond are made in local currency on the basis of the prevailing exchange rates. It is further assumed that the bond is sold by the Central Bank only at the beginning of each year, that the bond matures at the end of n years from the time when it was first issued, that the repayment of its principal in a given year amounts to $\frac{1}{n}$ of the outstanding balance, and that an interest at the rate of i percent on the outstanding balance is paid at the end of each year. The exchange rate is denoted by r and the period is denoted by t ($= 1, 2, 3, \ldots, T \ldots n$). The period under consideration is T. The amount of principal (in units of foreign currency) of the bond sold is P. The weighted average of time periods elapsed between the receipt of principal and the end of period T is $\bar{t}\left(= \frac{\sum_{t=1}^{T} tP_t}{\sum_{t=1}^{T} P_t}\right)$. The weighted average of the exchange rates at which the bonds were sold is $\bar{r}\left(= \frac{\sum_{t=1}^{T} r_tP_t}{\sum_{t=1}^{T} P_t}\right)$. The receipts derived from and the payments made on the bond for various periods are shown in Table 3.

The payment for servicing the bond in a given period (or year) T exceeds (or fall short of) the cumulative receipts derived from that bond through period T, if

$$\frac{r_T i}{n}\left(\sum_{t=1}^{T} P_t\right)(n - T - \bar{t}) - \frac{r_T}{n}\sum_{t=1}^{T} P_t > (\text{or} <) \sum_{t=1}^{T} r_tP_t;$$

or

$$\frac{r_T}{n}(in - iT - i\bar{t} + 1) > (\text{or} <)\ \bar{r},$$

TABLE 3. RECEIPTS FROM AND PAYMENTS ON FOREIGN-CURRENCY BONDS

Period	*Principal received at beginning of period*	*Interest payable at end of period*	*Principal repayable at end of period*
1	r_1P_1	r_1iP_1	$\frac{r_1}{n}(P_1)$
2	r_2P_2	$r_2i\left\{\left(\frac{n-1}{n}\right)P_1 + P_2\right\}$	$\frac{r_2}{n}(P_1 + P_2)$
3	r_3P_3	$r_3i\left\{\left(\frac{n-2}{n}\right)P_1 + \left(\frac{n-3}{n}\right)P_2 + P_3\right\}$	$\frac{r_3}{n}(P_1 + P_2 + P_3)$
4	r_4P_4	$r_4i\left\{\left(\frac{n-3}{n}\right)P_1 + \left(\frac{n-2}{n}\right)P_2 + \left(\frac{n-1}{n}\right)P_3 + P_4\right\}$	$\frac{r_4}{n}(P_1 + P_2 + P_3 + P_4)$
T	r_TP_T	$r_Ti\left\{\left(\frac{n-T+1}{n}\right)P_1 + \left(\frac{n-T+2}{n}\right)P_2 + \left(\frac{n-T+3}{n}\right)P_3 + \cdots + \left(\frac{n-1}{n}\right)P_{T-1} + P_T\right\}$ $= \frac{r_Ti}{n}\left(\sum_{t=1}^{T} P_t\right)(n - T - \bar{i})$	$\frac{r_T}{n}(P_1 + P_2 + P_3 + \cdots + P_T) = \frac{r_T}{n}\sum_{t=1}^{T} P_t$
Total for T periods	$\sum_{t=1}^{T} r_tP_t$		

$$\text{where} \quad \bar{r} = \frac{\sum_{t=1}^{T} r_t P_t}{\sum_{t=1}^{T} P_t}; \text{ or } \left(i - \frac{iT - il - 1}{n}\right) > (\text{or} <) \frac{\bar{r}}{r_T}.$$

If $n = 10$, $i = .05$ per annum, $T = 6$, and $l = 3$ (a situation quite close to one under which some of the Chinese bonds were issued during the inflation), then the term on the left side of the inequality has a value of .135. Thus the ratio $\bar{r}/r_T$ has a value greater than .135, if the receipts are to exceed the payments, and vice versa. Under the condition of a runaway inflation with the external value of local currency depreciating rapidly, it is quite possible to have the value of this ratio fall below .135, reflecting the excess of the servicing payments over the cumulative receipts.

The inequality also shows that the higher the interest rate and the shorter the life of the bond, the greater the likelihood for the payments to exceed the receipts.

Appendix 4 Effects of Inflation on Income Tax

Let p denote the price index, y, the money income, and the subscript i ($= 1, 2, 3, \ldots$), the month, then $\sum_{i=1}^{12} y_i$ = the money income actually received during the twelve-month period without allowing for changes in prices; $p_{12} \sum_{i=1}^{12} \left(\frac{y_i}{p_i}\right)$ = the twelve-month income expressed in terms of prices as of the twelfth month; and $p_{15} \sum_{i=4}^{15} \left(\frac{y_i}{p_i}\right)$ = the income for the twelve-month period extending from the fourth through the fifteenth month, expressed in terms of the prices of the fifteenth month. Consider then two cases.

In the first case, assume that the income remains constant at the level of unity and that the price index is doubled in each month. In the second case assume that both income and the price index double in each month. In both cases, the tax is assessed on the basis of the money income actually received and is collected at the end of the fifteenth month. The amounts of the incomes (with and without the price adjustments) and the burden of taxation are shown in Table 4.

In the first case, the twelve-month income in current yuan (without allowing for price changes) is 12 yuan. The incomes expressed in terms of the price of the twelfth month and the fifteenth month amount to 4,095 and 32,760 yuan respectively. Thus an assessment based on the unadjusted income taxes only $\frac{1}{341}$ of the income expressed in the price of the twelfth month, or only $\frac{1}{2730}$ of the income expressed in the price of the fifteenth month.

In the second case, the cumulative income actually received in the first twelve months is 4,095 yuan, that in terms of the price of the twelfth month is 24,576 yuan, and that in terms of the price of the fifteenth month remains at 32,760 yuan. Thus a tax assessed on the basis of the income not allowing for price changes taxes only $\frac{1}{6}$ of the income in terms of the price of the twelfth month, or only $\frac{1}{8}$ of the income in terms of the price of the fifteenth month.

It is clear from the previous discussion that inflation does have distorting effects on income tax. This distortion exists regardless of whether the

TABLE 4

	Month[a]	Income in current yuan[b]	Price index[c]	Income in price of 12th month[d]	Income in price of 15th month[e]
Case One: Income remains same; price index doubles each month					
	1	1	1	2,048	16,384
	2	1	2	1,024	8,192
	3	1	4	512	4,096
	...	...	...	...	...
	10	1	512	4	32
	11	1	1,024	2	16
	12	1	2,048	1	8
	...	...	...	...	...
	15	1	16,384		
Total for 12 months		12		4.095	32,767
Case Two: Income and price index double each month					
	1	1	1	2,048	16,384
	2	2	2	2,048	16,384
	3	4	4	2,048	16,384
	...	...	...	...	...
	10	512	512	2,048	16,384
	11	1,024	1,024	2,048	16,384
	12	2,048	2,048	2,048	16,384
	...				
	15				
Total for 12 months		4,095		24,576	196,608

[a] Month $= i$. [b] Income $= y_i$. [c] Price index $= p_i$

[d] Income in terms of price index of 12th month $= p_{12}\left(\frac{y_i}{p_i}\right)$.

[e] Income in terms of price index of 15th month $= p_{15}\left(\frac{y_i}{p_i}\right)$.

monthly income remains constant while prices change, or rises in proportion to the prices. The more the rise of income lags behind that of the prices, the greater are the distortion effects of inflation on income tax. The previous discussion also implies that such distortion effects can be substantially reduced if the system of pay-as-you-earn is used in tax collection. This system of collection however is not applicable to all taxable incomes. It therefore has its limitations as a solution to the tax problems arising from inflation.

Appendix 5 Changes in Private Holdings in Foreign Assets

While the study of the history of the official reserve in foreign assets has to be based on fragmentary data and on guesses to fill in the gaps, the data for the private holdings and their movements are even less satisfactory. Because of the unavailability of information, this study of private capital movements is confined only to the dollar assets and to the period from January, 1946, to March, 1949. In the absence of a better basis, the study is made mainly on the comparison between the records of the Central Bank, which show the government holdings, and the reports published by the United States Treasury Department, which give the position and movement of all Chinese funds in the United States including both private assets and official holdings. An analysis of the differences between the Chinese records and the American reports yields a rough picture of the movements of private capital.

The American data is published in *The Treasury Bulletin* and *The Federal Reserve Bulletin*. These publications give the statistics for (1) the net capital movements between the United States and foreign countries during a given period; and (2) the net short-term liabilities of these countries to or their net claims on the United States at a given point of time. The short-term claims on the United States (i.e., liquid assets of foreign countries) consist mainly of foreign deposits with American banks, the American Treasury bills, the certificate of indebtedness, and commercial papers held in the United States by their foreign owners. The short-term liabilities of foreign countries are represented mainly by loans from American banks to foreign borrowers, and the latter's liabilities on the acceptances made by American banks on their account. The net capital movements for a given period are represented by the sum of (1) net movement in short-term bank funds; (2) changes in brokerage balances; and (3) net purchases or sales of dollar securities. In subsequent discussions, however, the study of China's flow of capital is to be confined only to the movements of the bank funds and security transactions. Changes in the brokerage balances are not included because the amount of these balances in the case of China was insignificant compared with the bank funds or security transactions. In contrast to the Chinese data, which cover only the official reserves in specie and foreign currencies, the United States statistics show in detail the movements of the dollar assets registered under the ownership of Chinese nationals, both official and private, but do not cover Chinese assets held in other foreign countries. After January, 1950, statistics with breakdowns of the short-term dollar assets held by banks and other official institutions of China as well as those held by nonbanking private interests have been published in *The Treasury Bulletin*. After March, 1951, separate statistics for the holding of mainland China and those of Taiwan have been available. These statistics have provided very useful information concerning the movements of Chinese capital in the 1950s.

The statistics of the Chinese foreign-asset holdings of the Chinese government have been discussed at length in Chapter V. After March, 1949, however, the record of the official holdings became so fragmentary that a meaningful comparison of the Chinese and American records is no longer possible.

A comparison of the American and Chinese statistics shows that China's net dollar holdings were strongly influenced by changes in the short-term claims of the American banks on China. When the amount of such claims was high, the amount of the net holdings (i.e., China's total dollar holdings minus U.S. claims), were accordingly reduced, and vice versa (see Chart 2). The claims on China, representing mainly interbank transactions, were usually high when international trade was brisk. This was true at the end of 1946 and during the third quarter of 1947, when the Exchange Equilization Board and its flexible-rate policy came into operation; and during the period from May to August, 1948, when the exchange certificate system was operating successfully. On the other hand, when trading activities receded, as in the months after Shanghai was taken over by the People's Government and in the period before the Shanghai market was formally reopened in 1946, the amount of short-term claims on China was usually low.

If the aberrations resulting from changes in the short-term claims is ignored, it would seem that the amount of "other balances," represented by the difference between the amount of the Chinese holdings reported by the American statistics and the holdings of the Central Bank of China, remained fairly stable during the postwar years under consideration. In general, their amounts ranged between U.S. $150 million to U.S. $190 million during 1946 and the first quarter of 1947, and between U.S. $100 million to U.S. $150 million during most of 1948 and 1949. The abrupt dip during September, 1948, may be attributed partly to the transfer of private funds to the Central Bank as required by the monetary regulations, and partly to trade activities as reflected by the increase in the amount of the short-term claims on China in that particular month.

From the detailed statistics after January, 1950, the following observations may be derived (see Charts 1 and 2):

1. At the beginning of 1951 mainland China still had net dollar holding of about U.S. $45 million, of which about two-thirds belonged to the banks and official institutions, and the remaining third to other private holds. During the entire period of 1951–53, the amount of these institutional holdings, fluctuating within a narrow range from U.S. $27 million to U.S. $30 million, remained fairly stable. Since virtually all the dollar holdings of the Nationalist government and its banks were either exhausted

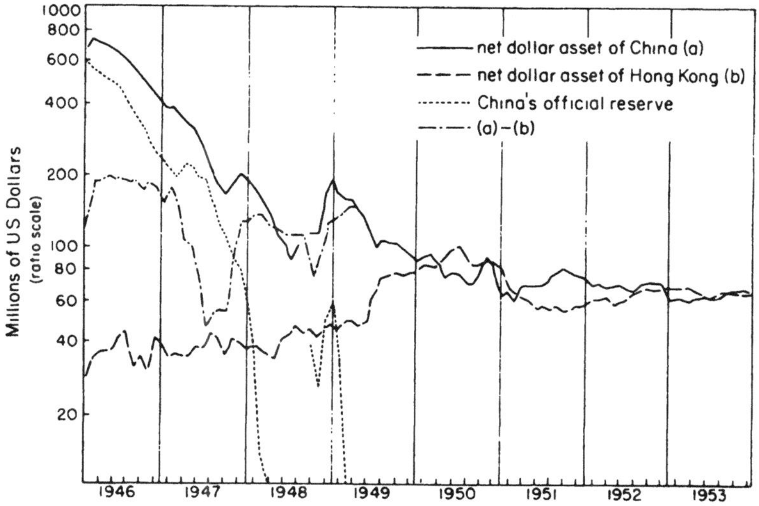

CHART 1. NET SHORT-TERM DOLLAR ASSETS OF CHINA (INCLUDING TAIWAN) AND HONG KONG, 1946–53

or transferred to the account of Taiwan, and in view of the meagre opportunity that the Communist government had to build up a sizable dollar balance in the United States, there was little likelihood that these recent holdings contained any official assets. They may therefore be considered as reflecting mainly the holdings of private banks on the mainland. Since the United States government froze all such assets, the amounts of these bank funds presumably remained stable during the last few years.

2. Nonbanking private holdings on the mainland, on the other hand, clearly showed a downward trend, with the outstanding balance being steadily reduced from about U.S. $17 million in March, 1951, to about U.S. $8.3 million in July, 1953.

Bank balances were not the only dollar assets the Chinese held. Another possible alternative was United States dollar securities, including both bonds and stocks. A review of the statistics shown in the records of the

Central Bank and those published in the *U.S. Treasury Department Bulletin* and the *Federal Reserve Bank Bulletin* indicates the following: (a) During 1943–45 a part of the rapidly accumulated dollar holdings of the Chinese government was invested in American securities. According to the records of the Central Bank, such investments at the end of 1945 amounted to

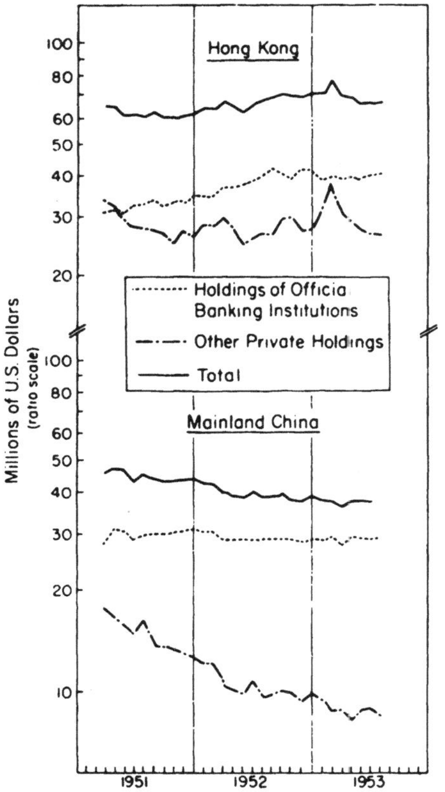

CHART 2. SHORT-TERM DOLLAR ASSETS OF HONG KONG AND MAINLAND CHINA, 1951–53.

U.S. $405 million and consisted mainly of United States bonds and certificates of indebtedness. In the meantime, the American reports showed that United States government bonds and certificates of indebtedness credited to Chinese ownership in the custody of American banks amounted in January, 1946, to U.S. $436.6 million. This sum presumably consisted mainly of the holdings of the Chinese Nationalist government. (b) During the period 1943–45 China made a net purchase in dollar securities of U.S. $192.44 million. During 1946–48, there were total sales of U.S. $267.8 million and total purchases of U.S. $58.8 million, or a net sale of U.S. $209 million. From these statistics, it is obvious that not all the security holdings of the Chinese government liquidated during those postwar years (amounting to U.S. $405 million) were included in the above statistics of security transactions. Moreover, since the amount of the purchases and that of the sales are about equal, there is no definite indication, so far as those statistics are concerned, of the flight of capital from China. (c) Another noteworthy point is the fact that during August and September, 1948, there were unusually heavy sales of American securities by the Chinese—a phenomenon which may be associated with the sudden dwindling of "other balances" during the same period, and which was probably caused by the fear that United States authorities would expose to the Chinese government the Chinese assets held in the United States.

Besides the dollar funds and security transactions mentioned above, some of the Chinese funds and security purchases were carried in the name of individuals or firms of other nationalities, or of the residents in areas outside China. It is difficult of course to trace these transactions. A possible indication of such activities may be found in the changes of dollar funds and securities held in the account of Hong Kong. Because of its geographical proximity to the mainland of China and because of the existence of a free exchange market, Hong Kong during the postwar years provided both a convenient resort for the Chinese capital that escaped from the mainland and a useful channel for funneling such funds to other foreign markets.

According to the American record, the amounts of net short-term dollar assets (i.e., short-term assets minus short-term liabilities) held by Hong Kong residents ranged from U.S. $20.9 million to U.S. $26.6 million during the period 1943–45. At the end of 1945, this balance was U.S. $26.6 million. During 1946, the amount rose steadily, reaching U.S. $39 million by the end of the year. During 1947 and the first half of 1948, the amount of the balance remained fairly stable with monthly totals fluctuating within a range of U.S. $33–44 million. After China's monetary reform in August, 1948, however, there was a marked upward turn. In May, 1949, when Shanghai was taken over by the Communists, the amount of Hong Kong's net short-term assets in the United States reached U.S. $49.3 million. Thereafter, apparently due to the increased inflow of refuge capital from China, the balance climbed to U.S. $64.5 million by the end of June and to U.S. $80.2 by the end of the year when the entire mainland of China fell under the control of the People's Government. If the increase in the dollar assets of Hong Kong is taken as an indicator of the flight of capital from China, the following aspects of the situation emerge.

1. A comparison of the net short-term dollar assets of Hong Kong at the end of 1945 and the end of 1949 shows an increase of U.S. $53.6 million, which may be taken as a rough measure of the magnitude of the

flight of funds from China to America via Hong Kong during those years. The American reports further showed that during the period 1946–49, there was a net capital flow from Hong Kong to America amounting to U.S. $54.9 million, virtually all in the form of bank deposits.

2. The statistics of Hong Kong holdings reflect unmistakably the increased flight of capital from mainland China following the monetary reform in August, 1948, and the control of the mainland by the Communist government in the latter part of 1949. In fact a large part of the increase in the dollar holdings of Hong Kong actually occurred during those months.

3. The net gain in Hong Kong dollar holdings during 1946–49 and the net loss in China's private holdings for the same period (each amounting to U.S. $40–50 million) were nearly in equilibrium.

Since January, 1950, the *Treasury Bulletin* has published gross short-term dollar assets (i.e., with no allowance for short-term liabilities) held by banks and official institutions and by other foreigners. These classified data show that at the beginning of 1951, out of some U.S. $60 million of Hong Kong holdings, about half belonged to the banks and official institutions and half to "other" holders. During 1951–53 while the holdings of the banks and official institutions actually decreased from U.S. $45–50 million at the beginning of 1950 to about U.S. $27 million at the middle of 1953, the trend of other private holdings, fluctuating most of the time between U.S. $30 million and U.S. $40 million, remained fairly stable. There was some reduction during the second part of 1950 and the early months of 1951, but those losses were all restored after the third quarter of 1952. Consequently, during the greater part of 1953 the dollar assets of "other" holders constituted about two-thirds of the total dollar assets of Hong Kong. The predominance of the holdings of nonbanking private interests further substantiates our conviction that to a large extent the expansion of the Hong Kong dollar assets during the postwar years was due to the flight of capital from mainland China. In fact, as there was no central bank in Hong Kong and most of her official holdings were presumably kept in pounds sterling rather than in dollars, the remaining third of the Hong Kong dollar assets should in large part represent the holdings of the Chinese banks operating in the British colony. To some extent the expansion of those holdings in relation to the 1943–45 amount may also arise from the outflow of capital from China.

The statistics for security transactions published in the *Treasury Bulletin* show that the volume of purchase and sale of dollar securities by Hong Kong residents was greatly increased after 1949, and that there were net purchases amounting to U.S. $2.3 million, U.S. $7.0 million, and U.S. $1.3 million during 1950, 1951, and 1952 respectively. During the entire span of 1948–52, there was a net purchase amounting to U.S. $6–7 million.

The movements of capital between Hong Kong and the United States, however, can at best provide only a partial picture of the flow of funds between China and the British colony, as these capital movements may to some extent include the holdings of Hong Kong residents other than those associated with the mainland. Nor do they cover the funds remaining in Hong Kong, which has been an important resort for refugee capital from China during the postwar years.

In this light, the following conclusions may be drawn concerning the movements of capital in China during the inflation.

1. A comparison of the Chinese and American records shows that the private dollar holdings of China amounted to U.S. $150–190 million during the years immediately following V-J Day, to U.S. $100–150 million during 1948 and the early part of 1949, and to U.S. $45–50 million during the latter part of 1949 and 1950.

2. In the published statistics of the United States Treasury there is no indication of an appreciable increase in China's holdings in dollar securities since the war.

3. In view of the steady decline in the amount of private holdings in China and the steady expansion of private dollar holdings in Hong Kong, it is possible that the expansion of Hong Kong holdings resulted in part from the transfer of Chinese funds to the Hong Kong account. Evidence for such transfers was particularly strong after the monetary reform in 1948 and after the Communists' control of mainland China during the latter part of 1949. It is estimated that such transfers would be in the neighborhood of U.S. $40–50 million, including both the increase in the bank deposits and the net purchases of dollar securities.

The above estimates for private dollar holdings during the postwar years do not, of course, cover all the capital transfers from China. For instance, they do not include the transfers retained in Hong Kong, and the amount of such transfers may be even larger than the dollar holdings estimated in our previous discussions. Nor has this study covered the flight of Chinese capital to countries other than the United States and Hong Kong, because of the unavailability of data. However, in view of the exchange restrictions in the sterling countries other than Hong Kong, they could not be attractive havens for refugee capital from China. The lack of close commercial relations between China and countries like Switzerland made the latter less popular as resorts for Chinese capital.

Appendix 6 Supplementary Tables

The first seven tables in this Appendix are supplementary to the text in Chapter II; the last three of the tables are supplementary to the text in Chapter VII.

APPENDIX TABLE 2.1. AMOUNT OF NOTE ISSUE OUTSTANDING
monthly averages

End of Month	*1937*	*1938*	*1939*	*1940*	*1941*	*1942*	*1943*
January	1.31	1.68	2.31	4.45	8.2	16.0	35.7
February	1.36	1.70	2.36	4.67	8.7	16.8	37.9
March	1.37	1.68	2.41	4.69	9.2	17.5	40.4
April	1.39	1.70	2.49	5.22	9.6	18.5	43.7
May	1.41	1.71	2.59	5.60	10.1	20.0	46.5
June	1.41	1.73	2.70	6.06	10.7	24.9	49.9
July	1.45	1.75	3.19	6.25	11.3	27.5	52.5
August	1.51	1.82	3.34	6.65	11.9	26.4	56.3
September	1.55	1.93	3.59	6.84	12.7	27.9	60.5
October	1.56	2.04	3.72	7.07	13.4	29.9	64.4
November	1.60	2.16	3.92	7.49	14.4	31.8	68.9
December	1.64	2.31	4.29	7.87	15.1	34.4	75.4

End of Month	*1944*	*1945*	*1946*	*1947*	*1948*	*1949*
January	81.6	202.0	1,149.9	4,509.5	40,940.9	20,821.56
February	86.6	226.2	1,261.2	4,837.8	53,928.7	59,663.51
March	95.9	246.9	1,345.6	5,744.1	69,682.1	196,959.53
April	104.4	280.8	1,528.1	6,901.1	97,798.9	5,161,240.00
May	113.8	336.5	1,796.0	8,381.3	137,418.8	
June	122.8	397.8	2,112.5	9.935.1	196,520.3	
July	129.1	462.3	2,158.6	11,664.1	374,762.2	
August	137.6	556.9	2,376.6	13,697.3	296.82	
September	150.2	674.2	2,700.6	16,948.1	956.75	
October	161.2	805.9	2,983.9	20,791.2	1,595.39	
November	170.3	901.0	3,296.2	26,878.9	3,204.32	
December	189.5	1,031.9	3,726.1	33,188.5	8,186.33	

Units: in billion fapi yuan for months through July, 1948, or in million Gold Yuan for the months thereafter. Each fapi yuan is equal to 3,000,000 Gold Yuan. The figure for April, 1949, includes only the note issued up to the 27th.

Source: Unpublished official records of the Central Bank of China.

APPENDIX TABLE 2.2. THE INDEX OF NOTE ISSUE
(amount outstanding June 30, 1937 = 1)

Month	*1937*	*1938*	*1939*	*1940*	*1941*	*1942*	*1943*
January	—	1.19	1.64	3.16	5.81	11.34	25.31
February	—	1.20	1.67	3.31	6.17	11.91	26.87
March	—	1.19	1.71	3.33	6.52	12.41	28.65
April	—	1.20	1.77	3.70	6.81	13.12	30.99
May	—	1.21	1.84	3.97	7.16	14.18	32.98
June	—	1.23	1.91	4.30	7.59	17.65	35.39
July	1.03	1.24	2.26	4.43	8.01	19.50	37.23
August	1.07	1.29	2.36	4.71	8.44	18.72	39.93
September	1.10	1.37	2.55	4.85	9.01	19.78	42.90
October	1.10	1.45	2.64	5.01	9.50	21.20	45.67
November	1.13	1.53	2.78	5.31	10.21	22.55	48.86
December	1.16	1.64	3.04	5.58	10.71	24.39	53.47

Month	*1944*	*1945*	*1946*	*1947*	*1948*	*1949*
January	57.85	143.90	815.53	3,198.23	29,036.09	44,301.19 (10^3)
February	61.42	160.42	894.47	3,431.06	38,247.30	126,879.81 (10^3)
March	68.01	175.11	954.33	4,073.83	49,419.92	419,062.83 (10^3)
April	74.04	199.15	1,083.76	4,894.40	69,360.92	10,981.31 (10^6)
May	80.71	238.65	1,273.76	5,944.18	97,460.14	
June	87.09	282.13	1,498.23	7,046.17	139,376.99	
July	91.56	327.87	1,530.92	8,272.41	265.79 (10^3)	
August	97.59	394.96	1,685.53	9,714.40	631.53 (10^3)	
September	106.52	478.16	1,015.32	12,019.93	2,035.64 (10^3)	
October	114.32	571.56	2,116.24	14,745.53	3,394.45 (10^3)	
November	120.78	639.01	2,337.73	19,063.05	6,817.70 (10^3)	
December	134.40	731.84	2,642.62	23,537.94	17,417.72 (10^3)	

The note issue indices were compiled on the basis of the data shown in Appendix Table 2.1. From 1937 through July, 1945, the note issue series represents the fapi and other notes issued by the Nationalist Government. For a few months that followed, however, these currency figures include not only the fapi issued in its own right but also the fapi notes for displacing the currencies issued by the Japanese-sponsored Central Reserve Bank and the Federal Reserve Bank, which are also known as the "puppet" notes. The exchange with the "puppet" notes was made at a ratio of 200 to one fapi yuan. In August, 1948, the fapi was superseded by Gold Yuan at a ratio of 3,000,000 fapi to one Gold Yuan. Indices shown in this table were adjusted for the fapi-Gold Yuan conversion, but not for the conversion from the "puppet" notes to fapi. If the note issue indices are to be compared with the price indices of Shanghai, the former should be adjusted for the conversion between fapi and the "puppet" notes, as well as that between fapi and Gold Yuan. See also the explanatory note for Appendix Table 2.3 for similar adjustments in the indices of Shanghai prices.

Source: Unpublished records of the Central Bank of China. The statistics for the months through July, 1948, are in billion fapi yuan, and those of the subsequent months are in million Gold Yuan. All the listed figures, except those of the first four months of 1949, are monthly averages. The amounts outstanding at the end of each month are used for 1949.

APPENDIX TABLE 2.3. THE WHOLESALE-PRICE INDEX OF SHANGHAI, 1937–49

(average of January–June, 1937 = 1)

Month	*1937*	*1938*	*1939*	*1940*	*1941*	*1942*	*1943*	*1944*
January	1.01	1.27	1.20	3.15	6.78	15.21	58.04	214.40
February	1.01	1.17	1.23	4.13	6.96	17.43	69.49	275.89
March	1.00	1.11	1.28	3.89	8.01	22.83	64.39	341.78
April	.99	1.13	1.28	3.80	8.48	24.22	57.92	328.98
May	1.00	1.10	1.40	4.11	8.85	26.80	64.26	382.67
June	.99	1.09	1.53	4.59	8.91	26.76	73.68	575.74
July	1.02	1.14	1.60	4.74	9.15	29.71	115.32	634.28
August	1.07	1.21	2.10	4.57	10.10	30.69	140.07	618.07
September	1.12	1.17	2.65	5.19	10.50	30.74	125.58	742.18
October	1.08	1.18	2.32	5.51	11.97	32.46	132.91	1,141.50
November	1.15	1.16	2.49	5.58	14.55	42.06	143.75	1,522.79
December	1.24	1.15	3.08	6.53	15.98	49.29	176.02	2,509.71

				1948		*1949*	
Month	*1945*	*1946*	*1947*	*(A)*	*(B)*	*(A)*	*(B)*
January	3,127.71	185,685	1,374 (10^3)	25,495 (10^3)		77 (10^9)	96 (10^9)
February	4,236.50	351,208	2,133 (10^3)	36,511 (10^3)		539 (10^9)	933 (10^9)
March	5,809.38	511,988	2,242 (10^3)	59,012 (10^3)		2,432 (10^9)	5,693 (10^9)
April	6,434.14	516,463	3,696 (10^3)	68,408 (10^3)			151,733 (10^9)
May	8,035.80	761,450	5,691 (10^3)	98,329 (10^3)			
June	38,301.00	744,750	6,691 (10^3)	176,960 (10^3)			
July	41,887	814,364	6,234 (10^3)	521 (10^6)			
August	86,400	857,100	6,596 (10^3)	944 (10^6)	1,117 (10^6)		
September	69,174	1,018 (10^3)	8,651 (10^3)	1,182 (10^6)	1,200 (10^6)		
October	75,724	1,073 (10^3)	11,976 (10^3)	1,322 (10^6)	1,516 (10^6)		
November	198,504	1,063 (10^3)	13,317 (10^3)	15,259 (10^6)	15,463 (10^6)		
December	177,088	1,143 (10^3)	16,759 (10^3)	21,568 (10^6)	36,788 (10^6)		

The price indices are primarily those compiled by the Economic Research Department of the Central Bank of China with, however, the following modifications: The Bank's original indices of September, 1945, and all subsequent months were each multiplied by 200; the Bank's indices for the months from late August, 1948, through April, 1949, were each multiplied by an additional factor of 3,000,000.

For the months after August, 1948, both the monthly average, denoted by (*A*), and the index at the end of each month, denoted by (*B*), are given; because of the intensification of the inflation during these months, there are substantial discrepancies between these two sets of indices. Indices for all other periods are monthly averages. In September, 1948, the Shanghai price index, as originally published by the Central Bank, shows a sharp drop to 199.70 from 42,788 of the previous month, both having January–June, 1937 = 1. The drop was mainly a result of changing the currency unit from the Central Reserve Bank note, which had been used in the Shanghai area during the Japanese occupation, to the fapi yuan, the currency of the Nationalist government, at a ratio of 200 to one fapi yuan. To allow for such a shift, it is necessary to multiply all the Shanghai price indices of September, 1945, and the subsequent months by 200. The unadjusted Shanghai price index compiled by the Bank for the first eighteen days of August, 1948, was 4,927,000 (Jan.–June, 1937 = 1). The index for August 19–31, using the same base period, was 1.64 as a result of the issuance of Gold Yuan on August 19, 1948, at a ratio 3,000,000 to one fapi yuan (see various issues of *The Central Bank Monthly*). To account for this conversion, Bank's indices for all the subsequent months were multiplied by 3,000,000 in addition to the above-mentioned factor of 200, making a total multiplier of 600,000,000.

It is not known why the Central Bank compiled the price indices as it did. Apparently both of the above-mentioned adjustments are necessary in order to make the Shanghai price indices of the postwar months comparable to the earlier indices.

In his book *The Inflationary Spiral*, Mr. Chang Kia-ngau used price indices compiled by the Bureau of Budgets, Accounts, and Statistics for 1938–1947, and the indices of the Central Bank for months of 1948 and 1949, when the Bureau's indices are not available. He took no account of the fact that the coverages and the methods of compilation of these two sets of indices are quite different. Nor did he make any adjustment to allow for the two conversions in 1945 and 1948 mentioned above. Consequently his Shanghai indices for the months from September, 1945, through the first part of August, 1948, represent only $\frac{1}{200}$ of the price increase that had actually occurred, and his indices for all subsequent months show only 1/600,000,000 of the actual increase.

APPENDIX TABLE 2.4. THE WHOLESALE-PRICE INDEX OF CHUNGKING, 1937–49 (average of January–June 1937 = 1)

Month	*1937*	*1938*	*1939*	*1940*	*1941*	*1942*	*1943*
January	—	.98	1.08	1.79	11.08	29.21	58.93
February	—	1.06	1.08	1.93	11.56	31.64	72.53
March	—	1.05	1.10	2.00	11.87	35.15	74.35
April	—	.98	1.12	2.63	13.95	41.18	82.92
May	—	.99	1.17	2.84	17.13	43.56	104.80
June	—	1.03	1.20	3.36	17.26	41.62	112.50
July	.97	.98	1.22	4.20	22.16	39.97	144.70
August	.95	.90	1.26	4.94	22.26	46.08	157.16
September	.96	.93	1.37	6.15	23.36	52.38	159.20
October	1.00	.97	1.46	6.58	24.28	56.07	160.20
November	1.00	.99	1.67	8.90	29.14	58.58	182.91
December	.98	1.04	1.77	10.94	28.48	57.41	200.33

Month	*1944*	*1945*	*1946*	*1947*	*1948*	*1949*
January	218.24	658.60	1,337.12	3,537.08	63 (10^3)	8,422 (10^4)
February	266.05	914.71	1,417.50	4,923.67	81 (10^3)	48,669 (10^4)
March	362.19	1,189.00	1,478.00	4,390.50	137 (10^3)	292,815 (10^4)
April	403.50	1,296.10	1,775.30	5,021.78	167 (10^3)	546,930 (10^4)*
May	483.00	1,480.00	1,878.96	6,400.57	219 (10^3)	
June	544.70	1,553.00	1,716.45	9,253.40	455 (10^3)	
July	497.21	1,645.00	1,555.61	13,535.63	1,325 (10^3)	
August	464.21	1,795.00	1,583.18	14,716.67	1,438 (10^3)	
September	471.80	1,226.00	1,868.91	18,658.26	360 (10^4)	
October	472.25	1,184.17	2,094.40	26,956.00	615 (10^4)	
November	506.80	1,350.85	2,364.06	31,176.00	1,980 (10^4)	
December	548.60	1,404.48	2,687.63	40,107.00	3,048 (10^4)	

* The index for the fifth week is 375.15 (10^9).

Sources: The Central Bank Monthly and unpublished records of the Bank.

APPENDIX TABLE 2.5. AMOUNT AND INDEX OF THE CENTRAL RESERVE BANK NOTE ISSUE

	1941		1942		1943		1944		1945	
Month	*(A)*	*(B)*	*(A)*	*(B)*	*(A)*	*(B)*	*(A)*	*(B)*	*(A)*	*(B)*
January	19	1.00	326	16.93	4,056	210.66	22,964	1,193	164,229	8,530
February	24	1.25	416	21.61	4,404	228.68	23,641	1,228	201,455	10,463
March	30	1.56	636	33.03	4,896	254.23	25,985	1,350	236,229	12,269
April	39	2.03	745	38.69	6,313	327.88	28,842	1,497	305,268	15,855
May	49	2.54	774	40.20	7,740	386.36	33,297	1,729	432,667	22,472
June	71	3.69	1,278	66.38	9,825	510.28	39,344	2,043	715,353	37,153
July	87	4.47	1,485	77.13	10,873	564.7	44,690	2,321	1,306,626	67,863
August	105	5.45	1,655	85.96	11,766	611.1	52,461	2,725	3,159,862	164,115
September	120	6.18	1,864	96.81	12,583	563.5	63,460	3,296	3,882,563	201,650
October	151	7.79	2,218	115.20	13,884	721.1	83,096	4,316		
November	181	9.40	2,960	153.73	15,974	809.6	106,670	5,540		
December	261	13.56	3,696	191.96	20,015	1,039.5	138,191	7,177		

(*A*) denotes amount of note issue in million yuan of the Central Reserve Bank notes, and (*B*) the index with January, 1941 = 1.
Source: The Department of Issue, the Central Bank of China.

APPENDIX TABLE 2.6. THE FRB NOTE ISSUE AND WHOLESALE PRICES OF NORTH CHINA, 1940–44

	1940			*1941*			*1942*			*1943*			*1944*		
	(*A*)	(*B*)	(*C*)	(*A*)	(*B*)	(*C*)	(*A*)	(*B*)	(*C*)	(*A*)	(*B*)	(*C*)	(*A*)	(*B*)	(*C*)
January	.50	1.00	1.00	.74	1.49	1.36	.95	1.91	1.74	1.71	3.45	3.47	4.25	8.58	10.45
February	.50	1.00	1.16	.70	1.41	1.25	.94	1.90	1.81	1.73	3.50	3.87	4.50	9.08	13.90
March	.53	1.06	1.23	.71	1.43	1.37	.92	1.86	1.84	1.79	3.60	4.55	4.80	9.69	15.07
April	.54	1.10	1.27	.69	1.39	1.35	.92	1.85	1.86	1.84	3.71	4.91	5.07	10.22	15.57
May	.55	1.11	1.39	.69	1.39	1.36	.92	1.85	1.88	1.88	3.80	5.10	5.40	10.81	16.44
June	.70	1.21	1.39	.69	1.39	1.38	.95	1.91	1.89	1.95	3.94	4.86	6.05	12.20	17.33
July	.58	1.17	1.30	.68	1.38	1.39	.96	1.93	1.90	2.06	4.16	4.88	6.73	13.57	20.32
August	.57	1.15	1.29	.69	1.39	1.44	.98	1.97	1.94	2.28	4.61	5.40	7.30	14.73	25.49
September	.59	1.19	1.31	.76	1.53	1.47	1.07	2.16	1.95	2.57	5.19	6.19	8.65	17.45	29.10
October	.62	1.26	1.34	.85	1.71	1.51	1.26	2.53	2.03	2.92	5.89	7.48	10.55	21.29	36.65
November	.66	1.32	1.32	.93	1.88	1.60	1.44	2.90	2.07	3.36	6.77	8.10	12.83	25.80	47.79
December	.72	1.44	1.31	.97	1.95	1.66	1.59	3.21	2.17	3.83	7.72	8.87	16.23	32.70	73.34

(*A*) denotes the amount of FRB (Federal Reserve Bank) note issue in billions of yuan.
(*B*) is the index of the note issue (January, 1940 = 1).
(*C*) is the index of wholesale prices of North China (January, 1940 = 1)

Sources: Unpublished records of the Central Bank; Wu Kang, *Historical Materials Relating to the Inflation of Old China*, pp. 44–48; and the Economic Institute of Nankai University, *A Collection of Nankai Indices*, pp. 21–41.

APPENDIX TABLE 2.7. THE NOTE ISSUE AND WHOLESALE PRICES OF MANCHURIA, 1946–48

	Note Issue		*Whole Prices of Mukden*	
	(1) *Amount*	(2) *Link relative*	(3) *Index*	(4) *Link relative*
1946				
Jan.	1.3			
Feb.	2.9	2.17		
Mar.	4.9	1.69		
Apr.	11.2	2.30		
May	25.0	2.23		
June	44.6	1.78	191	
July	60.4	1.35	198	1.04
Aug.	101.3	1.67	229	1.16
Sept.	150.7	1.49	335	1.46
Oct.	188.2	1.25	374	1.12
Nov.	228.8	1.21	371	.99
Dec.	275.3	1.20	399	1.08
1947				
Jan.	362	1.32	492	1.23
Feb.	402	1.11	782	1.59
Mar.	475	1.18	928	1.19
Apr.	559	1.18	1,390	1.50
May	643	1.15	2,007	1.44
June	746	1.16	2,511	1.25
July	880	1.18	3,445	1.37
Aug.	1,024	1.16	3,787	1.10
Sept.	1,146	1.12	4,176	1.10
Oct.	1,520	1.33	6,820	1.63
Nov.	2,109	1.38	9,538	1.40
Dec.	2,773	1.31	21,416	2.25
1948				
Jan.	3,663	1.32	30,493	1.42
Feb.	4,572	1.25	32,806	1.08
Mar.	6,318	1.31	41,919	1.28
Apr.	7,724	1.27	86,486	2.06
May	12,571	1.63	178,920	2.07
June	27,124	1.75	308,599	1.72
July	32,086	1.22	914,987	2.96
Aug.	no data		1,884,410	2.06

Sources: For the note issue: the unpublished records of the Central Bank. For the price index: *The Central Bank Monthly* (various issues) and Wu Kang, *Materials Relating to the Inflation of Old China*, pp. 136–39.

APPENDIX TABLE 7.1. LOANS AND DEPOSIT LIABILITIES OF CHINESE BANKS, 1932–46 (in million yuan)

Year	*Deposits*	*Loans*	*Ratio of Loans to Deposits*
	THE CENTRAL BANKS		
1932	168.5	163.0	96.74%
1933	244.7	220.8	90.23
1934	272.6	166.6	61.12
1935	634.0	383.2	60.44
1936	757.0	962.0	127.21
1937	661.0	698.0	105.60
1938	962.0	1,549.0	161.01
1939	1,282.0	2,594.0	202.34
1940	1,476.0	5,093.0	345.05
1941	2,229.0	9,216.0	413.46
1942	9,564.0	33,141.0	346.51
1943	13,885.0	86,373.0	622.06
1944	54,871.0	234,882.0	428.06
1945	342,583.0	1,362,016.0	397.57
1946	4,277,046.0	7,283,615.0	170.30
	GOVERNMENT BANKS		
1932	771.5	627.9	81.39%
1933	902.2	821.1	91.01
1934	994.9	937.6	94.24
1935	1,472.3	1,333.5	90.57
1936	1,919.4	1,291.7	67.30
1937	1,341.0	1,400.0	104.40
1938	1,774.0	2,259.0	127.34
1939	3,032.0	4,427.0	146.01
1940	3,993.0	6,086.0	152.42
1941	7,599.0	11,476.0	151.01
1942	15,322.0	6,984.0	45.58
1943	9,817.0	9,425.0	96.01
1944	25,299.0	15,957.0	63.25
1945	128,896.0	103,301.0	80.14
1946	754,758.0	758,315.0	100.47
	PRIVATE BANKS		
1932	1,175.5	1,170.7	99.59%
1933	1,447.3	1,274.5	88.06
1934	1,736.3	1,502.1	86.51
1935	1,683.1	3,152.1	187.28
1936	1,874.9	1,552.2	82.79
1937	1,115.0	849.0	76.14
1938	1,166.0	851.0	72.98
1939	1,433.0	1,014.0	70.76
1940	1,831.0	1,102.0	60.19
1941	2,884.0	2,029.0	70.35
1942	3,164.0	3,111.0	98.32
1943	4,656.0	5,140.0	110.40
1944	9,803.0	7,598.0	77.51
1945	10,473.0	16,207.0	154.75
1946	86,368.0	151,754.0	175.70

Source: *The Statistical Yearbook, 1948*, pp. 261–64.

APPENDIX TABLE 7.2. LOANS ASSETS OF CHINESE BANKS

	(1) Central Bank		(2) Government Banks		(3) Sub-Total		(4) Private Banks		(5) Total
End of Year	(A)	(B)	(A)	(B)	(1) + (2) (A)	(B)	(A)	(B)	(1) + (2) + (4) (A)
1932	163.0	8.31	627.9	32.01	790.9	40.32	1,170.7	59.68	1,961.6
1933	220.8	9.53	821.1	35.45	1,041.9	44.98	1,274.5	55.02	2,316.4
1934	166.6	6.39	937.6	35.97	1,104.2	42.36	1,502.1	57.64	2,606.3
1935	383.2	7.87	1,333.5	27.39	1,716.7	35.26	3,152.1	64.74	4,868.8
1936	962.9	25.29	1,291.7	33.93	2,254.6	59.22	1,552.2	40.78	3,806.8
1937	698.0	23.69	1,400.0	47.50	2,098.0	71.19	849.0	28.81	2,947.0
1938	1,549.0	33.24	2,259.0	48.49	3,808.0	81.73	851.0	18.27	4,659.0
1939	2,594.0	33.28	4,427.0	55.10	7,021.0	87.36	1,014.0	12.62	8,035.0
1940	5,093.0	41.47	6,086.0	49.56	11,179.0	91.03	1,102.0	8.97	12,281.0
1941	9,216.0	39.52	12,076.0	51.78	21,292.0	91.30	2,029.0	8.70	23,321.0
1942	33,141.0	76.65	6,984.0	16.15	40,125.0	92.80	3,111.0	7.20	43,236.0
1943	86,373.0	85.57	9,425.0	9.34	95,798.0	94.91	5,140.0	5.09	100,938.0
1944	234,882.0	90.71	10,466.0	6.36	251.348.0	97.07	7,598.0	2.93	258,946.0
1945	1,362,016.0	91.93	103,301.0	6.97	1,465,317.0	98.90	16,207.0	1.10	1,481,524.0
1946	7,283,615.0	88.89	758,315.0	9.25	8,041,930.0	98.14	151,754.0	1.86	8,193,684.0

(*A*) denotes value in billion *yuan*, and (*B*) denotes the percentage in total loans shown in column (5).
Source: Same as Appendix Table 7.3.

APPENDIX TABLE 7.3. DEPOSIT LIABILITIES OF CHINESE BANKS, 1932–48

End of Year or Month	(1) Central Bank (A)	(1) Central Bank (B)	(2) Government Banks (A)	(2) Government Banks (B)	(3) Sub-Total (1) + (2) (A)	(3) Sub-Total (1) + (2) (B)	(4) Private Banks (A)	(4) Private Banks (B)	(5) Total (1) + (2) + (4) (A)
1932	168.5	7.96	771.5	36.47	940.0	44.43	1,175.5	55.56	2,115.5
1933	244.7	9.43	902.2	34.78	1,146.9	44.21	1,447.3	55.78	2,594.2
1934	272.6	9.08	994.9	33.12	1,267.5	42.20	1,736.3	57.80	3,003.0
1935	634.0	16.73	1,472.3	38.85	2,106.3	55.58	1,683.1	44.41	3,789.4
1936	757.0	16.63	1,919.4	42.17	2,676.4	58.80	1,874.9	41.19	4,551.3
1937	661.0	21.21	1,341.0	43.02	2,003	54.23	1,115.0	35.77	3,117.0
1938	962.0	24.65	1,774.0	45.46	2,736	70.11	1,166.0	29.88	3,902.0
1939	1,282.0	22.30	3,032.0	52.75	4,314	75.05	1,433.0	24.93	5,747.0
1940	1,476.0	20.21	3,993.0	54.69	5,469	74.90	1,831.0	25.08	7,300.0
1941	2,229.0	17.53	7,599.0	59.78	9,828	77.31	2,884.0	22.69	12,712.0
1942	9,564.0	34.10	15,322.0	54.62	16,821	88.72	3,164.0	11.28	28,050.0
1943	13,885.0	48.96	9,817.0	34.62	23,702	83.58	4,656.0	16.42	28,358.0
1944	54,871.0	61.03	25,299.0	28.06	80,100	89.09	9,803.0	10.90	89,903.0
1945	342,583.0	71.08	128,896.0	26.74	471,479	97.82	10,473.0	2.17	481,952.0
1946									
Jan.					785.0	91.23	75.5	8.77	860.5
Feb.					880.3	91.46	82.2	8.54	962.5
March					938.9	89.35	111.9	10.65	1,050.8
April					1,474.4	89.03	181.6	10.97	1,656.0
May					1,545.0	88.69	197.0	11.31	1,742.0
June					3,017.3	92.90	230.5	7.10	3,247.8
July					3,898.9	92.71	306.4	7.29	4,205.3
Aug.					3,726.7	91.91	328.2	8.09	4,054.9
Sept.					4,233.8	91.57	389.6	8.43	4,623.4
Oct.					3,265.4	88.59	420.6	11.41	3,686.0
Nov.					4,581.3	90.22	496.8	9.78	5,078.1
Dec.					5,176.5	91.24	497.0	8.76	5,673.5

TABLE 7.3 (*continued*)

End of Year or Month	(1) Central Bank (A)	(1) Central Bank (B)	(2) Government Banks (A)	(2) Government Banks (B)	(3) Sub-Total (1) + (2) (A)	(3) Sub-Total (1) + (2) (B)	(4) Private Banks (A)	(4) Private Banks (B)	(5) Total (1) + (2) + (4) (A)
1947									
Jan.					5,207.4	89.46	613.8	10.54	5,821.2
Feb.					5,076.6	87.07	754.0	12.93	5,830.6
March					5,325.2	82.54	1,126.4	17.46	6,451.6
April					5,067.3	77.22	1,495.1	22.78	6,562.4
May					10,133.3	87.84	1,402.2	12.16	11,535.5
June					11,967.7	89.33	1,429.0	10.67	13,398.7
July					12,441.4	86.41	1,957.0	13.59	14,398.4
Aug.					13,634.1	84.23	2,552.8	15.77	16,186.9
Sept.					17,268.8	85.88	2,838.8	14.12	20,107.6
Oct.					18,540.8	85.84	3,059.5	14.16	21,600.3
Nov.					20,312.0	83.37	4,050.4	16.63	24,362.4
Dec.					24,336.6	83.76	4,719.0	16.24	29,055.6
1948									
Jan.					30,730.0	83.50	6,073.6	16.50	36,803.6
Feb.					40,341.0	81.50	9,155.7	18.50	49,496.7
March					58,124.0	85.91	9,532.0	14.09	67,656.0
April					86,081.0	85.18	14,975.4	14.82	101,056.4
May					126,327.0	84.63	22,936.0	15.37	149,263.0
June					181,129.0	86.81	27,527.1	13.19	208,656.1

(*A*) denotes value in billion yuan, and (*B*) the percentage in total deposit as shown in column (5).
There are no data for spaces left blank in table.
Sources: *The Yearbook for Chinese Banks* (all editions), *The Statistical Abstract of the Republic of China* (Nanking, 1947), p. 70–72, and *The Central Bank Monthly* (in Chinese), various issues.

Notes

INTRODUCTION

1. F. Machlup, "Another View of Cost-Push and Demand-Pull Inflation," *The Review of Economics and Statistics*, XLII (1960), 125–39.

2. B. Hansen, *A Study in the Theory of Inflation* (New York, 1951), Chapter III.

3. United Nations, *The World Economic Survey for 1957* (New York, 1958), pp. 23–33, 71–73, and 87–97.

4. E. Lundberg, *Business Cycles and Economic Policy*, trans. by J. Potter (London, 1957), p. 205.

5. Hansen, *A Study in the Theory of Inflation*, Chapter II.

6. Lundberg, *Business Cycles and Economic Policy*, p. 183.

7. W. S. Salant, "Inflationary Gap," *American Economic Review*, XXXII (1942), 308–14; M. Friedman, "Discussion of the Inflationary Gap," *American Economic Review*, XXXII (1942), 314–20; G. W. Ensley and R. Goode, "Mr. Warburton on the Inflationary Gap," *American Economic Review*, XXXIII (1943), 897–99.

8. J. M. Keynes, *How to Pay for the War* (New York, 1940), Chapter IX.

9. The terms "P-approach" and "Q-approach" were originally used by J. R. Hicks to refer to the analysis based on the adjustment through prices and to that based on the adjustment through quantity of output. J. R. Hicks, "Methods of Dynamic Analysis," *25 Economic Essays in Honor of Erik Lindahl* (Stockholm, 1956), pp. 139–51.

10. For further discussion of this subject, see J. K. Galbraith, "Market Structure and Stabilization Policy," *The Review of Economics and Statistics*, XXIX (1957), 124–33; R. F. Harrod, "The British Boom, 1954–58," *Economic Journal*, LXVI (1956), 1–16; and T. Balogh, "Productivity and Inflation," *Oxford Economic Papers*, X (1958), 222–24.

11. Lundberg, *Business Cycles, and Economic Review*, p. 207.

12. Lundberg, *Business Cycles, and Economic Review*, pp. 176–79.

13. Harrod, "The British Boom, 1954–58," *Economic Journal*, LXVI (1956),1–16.

14. United Nations, *The World Economic Survey for 1957*, pp. 23–33.

15. For detailed discussion of these two types of investment, see E. M. Bernstein and I. G. Patel, "Inflation in Relation to Economic Development," *International Monetary Fund Staff Papers*, II (1952), 363–98.

I. THE PATTERN OF THE CHINESE INFLATION

1. The most comprehensive statistics of various note issues for the period of inflation are found in Wu Kang, *Chiu-chung-kuo t'ung-ho peng-chang shih-liao* (Historical Materials Relating to the inflation in Old China), (Shanghai, 1958), pp. 45–48. 92–96, 122, 136. This is a Communist publication released in 1958. Even then statistics are not complete and have to be supplemented by those taken from the unpublished records of the Central Bank.

2. The Department of Issue kept only those notes that were printed but not yet issued for circulation.

3. *Chung-hua min-kuo tung-ch'i t'so-yao* (The Statistical Abstract of the Republic of China) (Nanking, 1947,) pp. 48–51. Chang Kia-ngau, *The Inflationary Spiral* (New York, 1958), pp. 371–73, uses the statistics of the Ministry of Audit, Accounts, and Statistics for 1938–47, and the statistics of the Central Bank of China for 1948–49 without indicating differences in the coverages and compilation methods of these two indices.

4. For further discussion of the Bank's price indices, see W. Y. Yang and C. S. Tang, "Wu-chia chih-shu pien-chih chi fen-lei wen-ti" (Problems in the Compiiation and Classification of Index Numbers of Commodity Prices), *chung-yang yin-hang yueh-pao* (The Central Bank Monthly), II, No. 11. (1947), 1–16.

5. The average monthly rate of increase is equal to the average link relative minus one. For example, the average month-to-month link relative of note issues for 1937–41 is 1.0393 (see Table 1.1). The monthly rate of increase is therefore 1.0393–1, or about 3.9 percent.

6. These parities are computed from Central Bank indices of 1945.

	Price indices		
	Chungking (based on fapi) 1	*Shanghai (based on CRB notes) 2*	*Price parities (2 ÷ 1)*
Aug.	1,795	86,400	48.1
Sept.	1,226	69,016	56.4
Oct.	1,184	75,724	62.2
Nov.	1,350	198,504	145.6

7. The comparisons, unless otherwise indicated, in this section are made on the basis of monthly averages rather than on end of month indices.

8. For further discussion of the financial conditions in postwar Manchuria, see Shun-hsin Chou, "Chan-hou tung-pei pi-chih chih chêng-li" (Monetary Rehabilitation in Postwar Manchuria), *tung-pei ching-chi* (The Economic Journal of the Northeast), I, No. 1 (1947), 1–3. Except for the section on military scripts issued by the Soviet army during its occupation of Manchuria after V-J Day, the article is reproduced in Wu Kang, *Historical Materials Relating to the Inflation in Old China*, pp. 41–44, 132–34.

II. INFLATIONARY PRESSURES IN THE GOVERNMENT SECTOR: RECEIPT AND EXPENDITURE

1. In this study, the term "revenue" is used to refer to government revenue other than the receipts from borrowing, and the term "receipt" covers both the revenue items and the receipts derived from borrowing. During the years under inflation, the government expenditures were approximately equal to the government receipts (including borrowing) of the corresponding period, because of the unlimited advances of the Central Bank.

2. 16.54 picul = 1 metric ton.

3. For details of the British income tax, see E. E. Spicer and E. C. Pegler, *Income Tax and Profits Tax*, 18th ed., revised by H. A. R. J. Wilson (London, 1948).

4. *Tsai-cheng nien-chien* (The Public Finance Yearbook), (Nanking, 1948), Part IV, p. 59.

5. For further discussion on the measurement of tax graduation, see R. E. Slitor, "The Measurement of Progressivity and Build-in Flexibility," *Quarterly Journal of Economics*, LXII (1948), 124ff; R. A. Musgrave and Tun Thin, "Income Tax Progression," *Journal of Political Economy*, LVI (1948), 498ff; A. C. Pigou, *A Study in Public Finance*, 3rd. ed. (London, 1949) Chapter 2; and Shun-hsin Chou, *The Capital Levy* (New York, 1945) Chapter 3.

6. There are no detailed provisions for depreciation charges or inventory valuation in the income tax laws of 1936 and 1943.

7. *Public Finance Yearbook*, 1948 ed., Part IV, pp. 69–72.

8. E. C. Brown, *Effects of Taxation: Depreciation Adjustment for Price Changes* (Boston, 1952).

9. *Public Finance Yearbook*, 1948 ed., Part IV, pp. 69–72.

10. The relationship between this weighted-average valuation of inventory and the valuation based on the first-in first-out (FIFO) and the last-in first-out (LIFO) methods are shown by the following illustration. Assume that there are eight units of initial inventory at the beginning of a period, purchased at the following order and prices:

Number of units purchased	1	1	1	1	1	1	1	1
Price in dollars	1	2	3	4	5	6	7	8

Of these eight units, four are left in the final inventory at the end of period; thus the values of the initial inventory, the final inventory, and the cost of goods sold computed on the basis of the FIFO, LIFO, and Chinese methods are as follows:

	FIFO	*LIFO*	*Chinese method*
1 Initial inventory	36	36	36
2 Final inventory	26	10	18 (=4 × $4.5)
3 Cost of goods sold (= 1 − 2)	10	26	18 (=4 × $4.5)

11. *tou* = *shih sheng* = 10 liter = 2.270 U.S. gallons (dry).

12. *shih chin* = ½ kilogram.

13. H. P. Wald, "Use of Tax Collection in Kind to Combat Inflation in the Republic of Korea," *Public Finance*, IX, No. 2 (1954), 186n. The estimate was made by Joseph Froomkin in a paper prepared for the Conference on Agricultural Taxation and Economic Development, January 28–February 3, 1954, Cambridge, Massachusetts.

14. Such as the China Steamship Navigation Company, a shipping company which depended heavily on government subsidy in its operation.

15. John F. Due, "Retail Sales Taxation in Theory and Practice," *National Tax Journal*, III (1950), 315–16.

16. Carl S. Shoup, *et al.*, *Report on Japanese Taxation by the Shoup Mission* (Tokyo, 1949), II, 168–70.

17. According to the Chinese law when the volume of transaction could not readily be ascertained, the business tax might be assessed on the basis of invested capital. This method of assessment, however, is not so commonly used as the one based on the gross turnover.

18. Shoup, *Report on Japanese Taxation by the Shoup Mission*, II, 166.

19. The American figures are calculated from the data given in United States Department of Commerce, *National Income* (Washington, D.C., 1954), pp. 165–66 and 172–73; and various issues of *Current Survey of Business*. The figures for other countries are calculated from the data given in various issues of *International Financial Statistics* published by International Monetary Fund.

20. United States Department of State, *United States Relations with China* (Washington, D.C., 1949), p. 1045.

21. Chinese Ministry of Information, *China Handbook 1937–1945* (New York, 1947), pp. 208–09.

22. Excluding those grants for foreign exchange operations during 1939–41.

23. These subscription statistics are compiled from an unpublished report of the Central Bank of China.

24. According to the accounting record of the Central Bank, only U.S. $471,060 out of a total of U.S. $100 million remained unsold.

25. The statistics relating to the debt services are taken from unpublished accounting records of the Central Bank of China.

26. R. Hsia, *Price Control in Communist China* (New York, 1953), pp. 60–62.

27. In my opinion, the phrase "guaranteed purchasing-power" has a broader implication than that of "constant purchasing-power" or that of "stable purchasing-power." For a guaranteed-purchasing-power bond may be defined as a bond with its value either fully or partially guaranteed. Except those redeemable in gold or foreign currency, most of the Chinese bonds reviewed in the section above had an escalator clause that ensured only a partial guarantee of a bond's value. Clark Warburton uses the term

"guaranteed purchasing-power bond." C. Warburton, "A Hedge Against Inflation," *Political Science Quarterly*, LXVII (1952), 1–17.

28. A. Marshall, *Official Papers* (London, 1926), pp. 9–12, 31; J. M. Keynes "Testimony in the Committee on National Debt and Taxation," *Minutes of Evidence* (London, 1927), II, 278, 286–87; G. L. Bach and R. A. Musgrave, "A Stable Purchasing Power Bond," *American Economic Review*, XXXI (1941), 823–35; B. R. Goode, "A Constant Purchasing Power Savings Bond," *National Tax Journal*, IV (1951), 332ff; and C. Warburton, *Political Science Quarterly*, LXVII (1952), 1–17.

29. "Middle Eastern Inflation," *The Economist* (*London*), CXLVIII (1945), 285; and R. F. Mikesell, "Financial Problems of the Middle East," *Journal of Political Economy*, LIII (1945), 164–76.

III. INFLATIONARY PRESSURE IN THE PRIVATE SECTOR: CONSUMPTION AND INVESTMENT

1. *National Income: A Supplement to the Survey of Current Business* (Washington, D.C., 1954), p. 49.

2. According to Ou Pao-san, *Chung-kuo kuo-ming so-to* (The National Income of China) (Shanghai, 1947), I, 171, the percentage distributions of consumption expenditures for various social and racial groups are as follows:

	Farm population	*Nonfarm population*	*Mongolians and Tibetans*	*Total for all groups*
Food	59.8	29.5	61.8	46.8
Clothing	6.8	15.9	6.7	10.7
Housing	3.8	11.3	4.0	7.0
Fuel	10.4	7.3	12.1	9.1
Miscellaneous	19.2	36.0	15.4	26.4
Total	100.0	100.0	100.0	100.0

3. T. H. Shen, *Agricultural Resources of China* (Ithaca, N.Y., 1951); and *Chung-hua min-kuo tung-ch'i t'so-yao* (The Statistical Abstract of the Republic of China) (Nanking, 1947), Table 5.

4. It is unsatisfactory because the division between occupied and free China did not usually conform to the boundaries of the provinces.

5. As represented by the average for 1934–38.

6. Chinese Ministry of Information, *China Handbook, 1937–1945*, p. 369.

7. Yu-kwei Cheng, *Foreign Trade and Industrial Development of China* (Washington, D.C., 1956), p. 265.

8. *Oriental Yearbook*, (Tokyo, 1942), pp. 865–965.

9. Rapseed and peanuts, postwar productions of which exceeded prewar levels, are not major crops of China.

10. *Foreign Commerce Yearbook, 1948* (Washington, D.C., 1950), pp. 442–43.

11. Based on the statistics published in the monthly reports of the Chinese Maritime Customs for 1946 and 1947.

12. *Ibid.*

13. For detailed discussions of these two types of investment, see E. M. Bernstein and I. G. Patel, "Inflation in Relation to Economic Development," *International Monetary Fund Staff Papers*, II, No. 3 (1952), 363–98.

14. *Foreign Commerce Yearbook, 1948*, pp. 442–43.

15. The production statistics for bristle are not available. My observation of decreasing production is based on the fact that the postwar population of hogs in the country declined in comparison with the prewar population.

16. The net gold sales represent the excess of the gross sales over the amount of gold purchased during the inflation by the government from the public.

17. Wu Kang, *Chiu-chung-kuo t'ung-ho peng-chang shih-liao* (Historical Materials Relating to the Inflation in Old China) (Shanghai, 1958), p. 245.

18. *Foreign Commerce Yearbook, 1950* (Washington, D.C., 1952), p. 145; *Annual Reports of the Hong Kong Government* (Hong Kong, 1948–1957).

IV. INFLATIONARY PRESSURES IN THE INTERNATIONAL SECTOR: FOREIGN EXCHANGE AND TRADE POLICY

1. For explanations of these terms, see W. M. Scammel, *International Monetary Policy* (London, 1957), Chapter 4.

2. For comprehensive discussions of China's currency reform of 1935, see W. Y. Lin, *The New Monetary System of China* (Shanghai, 1936); and F. M. Tamagna, *Banking and Finance in China* (New York, 1942), pp. 142–49.

3. The relation between the cross-rates derived from the buying and selling quotations of the Central Bank and the dollar-sterling rate in the foreign market is that wherever the exchange rates are quoted in terms of foreign currency equivalent per yuan, the conditions necessary for a stable market are $\frac{D_s}{S_b} < R < \frac{D_b}{S_s}$. In these inequalities, D_s and D_b represent the Central Bank's selling and buying rates for the dollar, S_s and S_b the selling and buying rates for sterling; R is the dollar-sterling rate prevailing in the foreign market. Similarly, if the exchange rates are in terms of the Chinese currency equivalent per unit of foreign currency, the stability conditions are $\frac{D_b}{S_s} < R < \frac{D_s}{S_b}$. Under conditions like those in China in 1935–36, the above relations between the cross-rate and the relevant exchange rate in the foreign market are applicable to any two foreign currencies in relation to the home currency. Tamagna had a brief reference to this problem of the cross-rate, but failed to show the significance of the problem to the Chinese foreign-exchange policy. Tamagna, *Banking and Finance in China*, pp. 113–14.

4. *Yin-hang chou-pao* (Banker's Weekly), XXIV, No. 3 (1938), 1–10.
5. Tamagna, *Banking and Finance in China*, p. 274.
6. The five members of the Board were Messrs. K. P. Chen (Chairman), Tsu-yee Pei, Tehmei Hsi, A. M. Fox, and E. L. Hall-Patch. They all assumed office upon the inauguration of the Board. Mr. Fox's alternate, Dr. William H. Taylor, took up his office at the same time as Mr. Fox. After Taylor was detained by the Japanese in Hong Kong, Mr. S. Adler was appointed as Taylor's successor. Mr. K. K. Kwok, Mr. Hsi's alternate, and Dr. W. Y. Lin, Mr. Pei's alternate, were appointed on August 12, 1941, and September 21, 1941 respectively. Mr. Hall-patch's alternate, Mr. W. C. Cassels, was introduced to the Board on December 6, 1941. Mr. K. P. Chen's alternate, Dr. Cho-ting Chi, was appointed on March 3, 1942. This information is based on an unpublished report of the Board submitted to the governments of China, the United States, and the United Kingdom.
7. For a detailed discussion of the freezing orders, see Tamagna, *Banking and Finance in China*, pp. 252–60.
8. Based on an unpublished report of the Board.
9. Based on an unpublished report prepared by Mr. Yang Kwei-ho on behalf of Mr. K. P. Chen and made available to the author by Mr. Chen. Data for exchange sales by the Board from November 22, 1941, to the end of 1941 were not available, however.
10. Purchases of Chinese yuan made under the stabilization agreement and financed by United States credit amounted to U.S. $10 million. These were repaid in April, 1943. No detailed breakdown is given for the total. Department of State, *United States Relations with China* (Washington, D.C., 1949), p. 1045.
11. It was often contended that an upward adjustment would usually be followed by a series of similar adjustments in commodity prices, gold quotations and foreign exchange rates in the open market. In such a vicious circle, the official quotations of gold and foreign exchange, like a dog chasing its own tail, would never be able to catch up with the market quotations.
12. Mr Cyril Rogers, who served as chairman of the Stabilization Fund of 1939–41, was also an influential adviser of the Central Bank in 1946.
13. The Fund Committee consisted at first of three members—K. P. Chen, the chairman, Hsu Po-yuan, vice minister of the Ministry of Finance, and H. J. Shen, the general manager of the banking department of the Central Bank. The number of committee members was later increased to five to include, besides the original members, Dr. S. Y. Liu, deputy governor of the Central Bank, and S. W. Kung, a manager and foreign-exchange expert of the Bank of China. Regular members of the technical committee included H. J. Shen of the Fund, R. C. Chen of the Bank of China, T. N. Lee of the Bank of Communications, C. F. Thomas of the National City Bank of New York, G. H. Stacey of the Hong Kong

Shanghai Banking Corporation, and C. Rogers and Arthur Young of the Central Bank.

14. The Central Bank of China, Circular 131, May 7, 1948. This system is very much similar to advanced payments for imports used by Indonesia and other countries in recent years.

15. Including a protest from the United States ambassador. *United States Relations with China*, pp. 1002–03.

16. For a detailed discussion of these export promotion measures, see Chungjen C. Chen, "Additional Facilities for Importation of Raw and Packing Materials to Boost Chinese Exports," *China Trade Monthly*, January, 1947, 1–50.

17. The Central Bank of China, Circular No. 145, June 30, 1948.

18. The Central Bank of China, Circular No. 170, March 1, 1949.

19. According to the Bilateral Agreement between the Chinese and United States governments (and as in the case of the ECA operations in many other countries) a counterpart fund was deposited with the Central Bank for all commodities imported into China. *Economic Aid Agreement Between the Republic of China and the United States of America*, Article V, signed on July 3, 1949.

20. The Central Bank of China, Circular Nos. 170 and 171.

21. For detailed information on the Greek and Peruvian certificate systems, see *International Financial Statistics*, III (1949), 164; and *Eighth Annual Report on Exchange Restrictions*, (1957), pp. 253–55.

22. This author participated in many discussions and studies of the certificate system before it was formally adopted by the Chinese government.

23. The Hong Kong bank notes in circulation at the end of September, 1949, amounted to H.K. $805,625,497, *Far Eastern Economic Review*, VII (1949), 637.

24. There were a few exceptions such as liquor, cigarettes, on which duty was imposed.

25. Such import licenses were sometimes needed to meet the government requirements of the exporting country.

V. INFLATIONARY PRESSURES IN THE INTERNATIONAL SECTOR: TRADE, PAYMENT, AND FOREIGN AID

1. A multiple regression analysis of the Chinese imports of rice and raw cotton with the reference to the degree of overvaluation of the Chinese currency in terms of foreign money, the domestic production in China, and the relevant prices in foreign markets shows these results:

For cotton import	*For rice import*
$b_{cv.pf} = -1.52$	$b_{rv.pf} = -1.42$
$b_{cp.vf} = -1.18$	$b_{rp.vf} = -1.70$
$b_{cf.vp} = -0.40$	$b_{rf.vp} = -1.69$

The *b* is the coefficients regression; *c* denotes the cotton imports; *r*, the rice imports; *v*, the degree of overvaluation of Chinese currency in relation to American dollar; *p*, the index of domestic production of the commodity concerned; and *f*, the price of the corresponding commodity in foreign market.

2. For further discussion of these three terms of trade, see von Haberler, *The Theory of International Trade* (New York, 1937), trans. by A. Stonier and F. Benham; J. Viner, *Studies in the Theory of International Trade* (New York, 1937), pp. 558ff.; C. P. Kindleberger, *Terms of Trade* (New York, 1956).

3. Based on the statistics in United Nations, *Demographic Yearbook*, 1958 (New York, 1958).

4. F. M. Tamagna, *Banking and Finance in China* (New York, 1942), pp. 364–65.

5. *China's Net Specie Import* (+) *and Export* (—), *1936–39*

Year	*Gold*	*Silver*
1936	−12,877	−75,983
1937	−17,261	−17,318
1938	+ 4,157	−15,009
1939	− 406	− 235
Total	−34,701	−208,545

6. Based on statistics published in *Federal Reserve Bulletin*, XXVII (1941), 267. See also Chart 1 of Appendix 5.

7. Department of State, *United States Relations with China* (Washington, D.C., 1949), pp. 1043–44.

8. These figures are derived from the Central Bank's statistics of note issue and the dollar-yuan exchange rate in the free market.

9. UNRRA and BOTRA denote the United Nations Relief and Rehabilitation Administration and the Board of Trustees for Rehabilitation Affairs respectively.

10. Department of State, *United States Relations with China*, pp. 470–512.

11. *Ibid.*, p. 470. See also the discussion of the gold policy in Chapter VI.

12. *Ibid.*, p. 1043; and G. Woodbridge *et al. UNRRA: The History of United Nations Relief and Rehabilitation Administration* (New York, 1950), 2, 378.

13. Compiled from the monthly reports of the Chinese Maritime Customs for 1946 and 1947. UNRRA supplies arrived in China before the end of 1947. Woodbridge, *UNRRA: The History of United Nations Relief and Rehabilitation Administration*, 2, 379.

14. United Nations Relief and Rehabilitation Administration, *Operational Analysis Papers No. 51: Industrial Rehabilitation in China* (Washington, D.C., 1948), p. 2.

15. Woodbridge, *UNRRA: The History of United Nations Relief and Rehabilitation Administration*, 2, 398.

16. Department of State, *United States Relations with China*, p. 1023; and Woodbridge, *UNRRA: The History of United Nations Relief and Rehabilitation Administration*, 2, 409.

17. Based on unpublished records of the Council for United States Aid to China.

18. Department of State, *United States Relations with China*, p. 1049.

19. For a detailed discussion of the food rationing system, see *ibid.*, pp. 1021–24.

20. *Ibid.* p. 1017.

21. *Ibid.* p. 1017.

22. Such as public works projects.

23. Department of State, *United States Relations with China*, p. 1017.

24. Shell Co., Socony Vacum Oil Co., Caltex Co., and Chinese Petroleum Co.

25. Based on unpublished records of the Central Bank of China.

VI. BANK CREDIT, VELOCITY, AND INFLATION

1. Information is taken from *Yin-hang nien-chien* (The Chinese Bank Yearbook) (Shanghai, 1934–37), 1934–37 eds.

2. This administration was also known as the Joint Administration of the Four Government Banks, for at the time of its institution, the membership included only the Central Bank, the Bank of China, the Bank of Communications, and the Farmers Bank. Later on the membership was expanded to include all seven government-owned banks.

3. For a detailed history of China's public treasury system, see the Chinese Ministry of Information, *China Handbook, 1937–1945* (New York, 1947), p. 2047.

4. *Chün-chêng chi-kuan kung-k'uan t'sun-hui pan-fa* (The Rules and Procedures for Handling Government Deposits and Remittances). The full text of these rules and procedures, which were progmulgated by the Nationalist government in July, 1946, is available in Research Department, Central Bank of China, *Chin-jung fa-kwei ta-ch'üan* (Collection of Financial Laws and Regulations) (Shanghai, 1947), pp. 39–40.

5. A struggle for government funds among the banks was not an experience unique to China. Similar developments occurred in Greece. During the early postwar years, about half of the deposits in Greek commercial banks were government funds. In February, 1949, the commercial banks were required to keep a minimum deposit reserve with the Bank of Greece, one equivalent to 22 percent of government deposits and 10 percent of other demand deposits. These ratios were later raised to 25 percent and then to 35 percent for government deposits, and to 12 percent for other deposits. At the end of 1950, all public deposits in commercial banks were required to be transferred to the Bank of Greece, which would in turn redeposit funds with the commercial banks to enable

them to extend credits to private borrowers. E. Ap. Eliades, "Stabilization of the Greek Economy and the 1952 Devaluation of the Drachma," *International Monetary Fund Staff Papers*, IV (1954), 22–72.

6. Percent of Capital Assets to Deposit Liabilities of U.S. Banks

Year	*Percent*	*Year*	*Percent*
1939	12.01	1947	7.38
1941	10.28	1948	7.74
1945	6.37	1949	7.96
1946	7.29	1950	7.89

The statistics are for all banks, including all member and nonmember banks and mutual savings banks, in the United States. Source: *Federal Reserve Bulletin*, XXXVII (1951), 1275.

7. J. M. Keynes, *A Treatise on Money* (London, 1930), Vol. II, Chapter 25; R. M. Goodwin, "The Supply of Bank Money in England and Wales," *Oxford Economic Papers*, IV (1941), pp. 1–29.

8. The American data are for all banks in the United States and the British statistics cover all the clearing banks of London.

9. The study of the relation between deposits and loans can be based on either the combined statements of bank assets and liabilities for 1932–36 and 1946, compiled by the Bank of China and the Central Bank, or on the statistics on bank loans and deposits for the period 1936–46, compiled by the JHOGB. Because of their continuity and wider coverage, the statistical series, rather than the combined statement, is used as the basis of this study.

10. The absurdity of the Ministry's banking policy may be illustrated by this writer's personal experience as an officer in charge of the financial affairs in the Economic Council for Manchuria during 1946–47. During their fifteen-year occupation of the country the Japanese had successfully converted the old financial institutions, mostly archaic and disorganized, into a well-planned modern banking system, headed by the Central Bank of Manchou. The transformation was effected mainly by a process of gradual reorganization and consolidation of small and unstable banking institutions into a few chains of modern banks. To apply the Ministry's policy to Manchuria would have meant to revert from the modern system to the ancient and disorganized financial institutions. Despite the Council's opposition, the Ministry insisted on the extension of its policy to Manchuria, and approved the restoration of some old banks.

11. The reasoning underlying the statements in the text is given as follows: Let M and M' denote respectively the note issue and bank deposits in circulation, and the subscripts represents the period, then

$$\frac{M_2 + M'_2}{M_1 + M'_1} < \frac{M_2}{M_1} \qquad \text{(i)}$$

so long as

$$\frac{M'_2}{M'_1} < \frac{M_2}{M_1} \text{ or } M_1M'_2 < M'_1M_2. \qquad \text{(ii)}$$

If this is true, then the appearance of M'_1 and M'_2 in (i) contributes to reducing, rather than to accentuating, the rate of increase in the volume of money in circulation. The validity of the above claim is proved as follows: (i) may also be written as

$$M_1M_2 + M_1M'_2 < M_1M_2 + M'_1M_2.$$

The above relation is true so long as the relation (ii) holds.

12. Since the usual mechanism of open-market operations was not available to China's central bank, the adjustment of the reserve ratio became particularly important as a mean for draining off the excess reserve.

13. A. J. Brown, *The Great Inflation, 1939–1951* (London, 1955), Chapter VIII.

14. Let M = the volume of note issue, M' = the volume of check or deposit money, P = the price index, T = the physical volume of production, V = the velocity of note issue, V' = the velocity of check or deposit money, a = the ratio M'/M, or $M' = aM$, b = the ratio V'/V, or $V' = bV$. Consider the usual equation of exchange; $PT = MV + M'V' = MV + (aM)(bV) = MV(1 + ab)$. By transposition, we have $V = \frac{T}{1 + ab}\frac{P}{M}$. Thus V varies with the ratio P/M if T, a and b all remain constant.

15. For detailed discussions of the relationship between debits and bank clearings, see G. Garvy, *The Development of Bank Debits and Clearing Statistics and Their Use in Economic Analysis* (Washingtion, D.C., 1952), Chapter IV.

16. R. T. Selden, "Cost-Push Versus Demand-Pull Inflation, 1955–1957," *The Journal of Political Economy*, LXVII (1959), 6.

17. W. L. Smith, "On the Effectiveness of Monetary Policy," *American Economic Review*, LXVI (1956), 588–606.

18. Discussions in this section are based mainly on information in *Ts'ai-cheng nien-chien* (The Public Finance Yearbook) (Nanking, 1945 and 1948), 1945 ed., Part XI; and 1948 ed., Part X; *China Handbook, 1937–1945*, p. 408; Chu Ssu-huang, *Min-kuo ching-chi-shih* (The Economic History of the Republic) (Shanghai, 1948), pp. 425–531; *The Chinese Yearbook, 1944–45* (Shanghai, 1948), pp. 614–15; and unpublished statistics and working papers of the Central Bank of China.

19. Department of State, *United States Relations with China* (Washington, D.C., 1949), p. 1045.

20. This figure was taken from an unpublished report of the Central Bank.

21. I was a member of the committee.

22. H. Feis, *The China Tangle* (Princeton, 1953), pp. 299–303.

23. See the following unsigned articles in the *Economist* (London), "Gold Sales in India," CXLV (1943), 653; "Gold in Egypt," CXLX (1943), 720; "Palestine's Inflation Problems," CLXIII (1953), 848–50; "The Gold Cure," CXLVI (1944), 79; "Middle Eastern Inflation," CXLVIII (1945), 285. See also R. F. Mikesell, "Financial Problems of the Middle East," *Journal of Political Economy*, LIII (1945), 165; and R. F. Mikesell, "Gold Sales as an Anti-Inflationary Device," *Review of Economic Statistics*, XXVIII (1946), 105–08.

VII. THE REDISTRIBUTIONAL EFFECTS OF THE CHINESE INFLATION

1. G. L. Bach and A. Ando, "The Redistributional Effects of Inflation," *The Review of Economics and Statistics*, XXXIX (1957), 1–13.
2. *Ibid.*
3. *Ibid.*; R. A. Kessel, "Inflation-Caused Wealth Redistribution," *American Economic Review*, XLVI (1956), 128–41.
4. The modern textile industry contributed in 1933 about 41 percent of China's factory output. Of a total of 763,000 factory operatives in China, 459,000 were employed in textile factories. Pao-San Ou and Foh-Shen Wang, "Industrial Production and Employment in Prewar China," *Economic Journal*, LIX (1949), 431.
5. The real wage index compiled by the Directorate of Statistics in Nanking for 1946 and 1947 and referred to in a previous discussion was higher than the corresponding index computed from the price and the cost-of-living indices. The upward bias of the former series could be due to the fact that the cost-of-living index, which was used by the Directorate to deflate the money-wage index in order to obtain the real wage index, was too low. As among other data it used the controlled rent (for houses) and the price of rationed food supplies, neither of which was representative of the market conditions then prevailing. In fact, if the cost-of-living index is used (as it was) as a standard of wage payments, then both the supply of cheap food rations to the workers and rent control constitute indirect subsidies to employers.
6. These percentages are derived as shown at top of next page.
7. From 1937 to March, 1949, the price of the common stock of the Wheelock Company, one of the favorable foreign-currency stocks, multiplied by 2,613 (10^9) times, as against a multiplication of 2,432 (10^9) times for the wholesale price index of Shanghai. Similarly during the first eight months of 1948, the index for the prices of foreign-currency stocks multiplied by 10.01 times, as against 7.0 times for the index of the wholesale prices.
8. For further discussions of interest rates, see Chapter VI; and Shun-hsin Chou, "Interest, Velocity, and Price Changes under Hyper-inflation," *The Southern Economic Journal*, XXV (1959), 425–33.

Percent of currency depreciation per month	*Real Income Received* *First month*	*Second month*	*Third month*	*Total*	*Index*	*Loss in Real Income*
0	100	100	100	300	100	0
10	90	81	72.9	243.9	81.3	18.7
20	80	64	51.2	195.2	65.1	34.9
30	70	49	34.3	152.3	51.1	45.9
40	60	36	21.6	117.6	39.5	60.5

9. In computing the real rate of interest, Irving Fisher uses the following formula: $I = i - p'$, where I represents the real rate of interest, i the money rate of interest, and the p' percentage increase of the commodity-price index. Keynes, Hicks and Sraffa, on the other hand, expressed the rate of real interest in the following terms: $I = \frac{1 - p'}{1 - i} - 1$, which may also be written as $(i - p')/(1 - p')$. In other words, the Fisher formula expresses the rate of real interest by the difference between the rate of money interest and the percentage increase in the price index of the corresponding period. The second formula, on the other hand, requires the multiplication of the result obtained from the first formula by an additional factor of $1/(1 - p')$.

Under normal economic conditions, in which the price index remains fairly stable, the factor $1/(1 - p')$ is essential if the undue upward bias caused by the wide price fluctuations is to be avoided. For this reason, the Keynes-Hicks-Sraffa formula will be used as the main basis in our discussion of real interest, although Fisher's method will also be occasionally brought in for comparison. See I. Fisher, *Theory of Interest* (New York, 1930), Chapter XIX; P. Sraffa, "Dr. Hayek on Money and Capital," *Economic Journal*, XLII (1932), 50; M. J. Keynes, *The General Theory of Employment, Interest and Money* (New York, 1936), pp. 222–24; and J. R. Hicks, *Value and Capital* (London, 1946), Chapter XI.

10. This definition was advocated in, United Nations, *Inflationary and Deflationary Tendencies, 1946–48* (New York, 1949), pp. 13–14, 48–50.

11. This statement is less applicable to the borrowers of cheap loans from the government banks than to those who borrowed at realistic rates of interest.

12. For a comprehensive report of the situation, see *Chung-yang yin-hang yueh-pao* (The Central Bank Monthly), I, No. 1 (1946), 56–58.

13. The full Chinese text of the regulation is available in *Min-kuo ching-chi-shih* (Economic History of the Republic) (Shanghai, 1948), p. 697.

14. "Kuan-yu chieh-fang-chien yin-chien-yeh wei-ching-chang ts'un-k'uan kei-fu pan-fa" (The Regulations Relating to the Repayment of the

Preliberation Deposits with Banking Institutions), *Hsin-hua yueh-pao* (The Hsin-hwa Monthly), January 20, 1953.

15. J. M. Keynes, *A Treatise on Money* (London, 1930) II, 174; and J. M. Keynes, *How to pay for the War* (New York, 1940), pp. 64–65.

16. For a detailed exposition of this thesis, see J. Robinson's review of C. Bresciani-Turroni, *The Economics of Inflation*, *Economic Journal*, XLVIII (1938), 510–11.

VIII. A COMPARISON OF THE CHINESE AND OTHER INFLATIONS

1. The review in this section is based mainly on the statistical data and historical summaries of foreign-exchange experiences of various countries published in various issues of the Bank of International Settlements, *Annual Report*, and the International Monetary Fund, *International Financial Statistics* and the *Report on Exchange Restrictions*.

2. The selling rate was 119.30 per U.S. dollar.

3. For a detailed study of the French monetary experience after the World War II, see P. Dieterlen, *The Monetary Problem of France* (New York, 1948).

4. J. J. Polak and T. C. Chang, "Effects of Exchange Depreciation on a Country's Export Price Level." *International Monetary Fund Staff papers*, I (1950), 63–66. In the article, the relation between the relative changes in the price parity and in the exchange rate was measured by "the effectiveness of depreciation," which was defined as "the percentage change in the ratio of the export prices of two countries (prices in both being expressed in the same currency) which is associated with a percent change in their exchange rate."

5. F. D. Graham, *Exchange, Prices and Production in Hyperinflation: Germany, 1920–1923* (Princeton, N.J., 1930), pp. 117–26, 155–59; C. Bresciani-Turroni, *The Economics of Inflation* (London, 1937), pp. 225–52; J. Robinson's review of C. Bresciani-Turroni's *The Economics of Inflation* in *Economic Journal*, XLVIII (1938), 507–13.

6. Graham, *Exchange, Prices and Production in Hyperinflation: Germany, 1920–1923.*

7. F. A. Southard, Jr., *Some European Currency and Exchange Experience: 1943–1946* (Princeton, N.J., 1946), p. 10; and Dieterlen, *The Monetary Problem of France*, pp. 55–57.

8. United Nations, *Inflationary and Deflationary Tendencies, 1946–1948* (New York, 1949), p. 48.

APPENDIX 1. MECHANICS OF INFLATIONARY SPIRAL

1. A. J. Brown, *The Great Inflation, 1939–1951* (London, 1955), Chapters 4–6; J. Duesenberry, "The Mechanics of Inflation," *The Review of*

Economics and Statistics, XXXII (1950), 144–50; F. Holzman, "Income Determination in Open Inflation," *The Review of Economics and Statistics*, XXXII (1950), 150–58; T. Koopmans, "The Dynamics of Inflation," *The Review of Economics and Statistics*, XXIV (1942), 53–64; R. Turvey, "Period Analysis and Inflation," *Economica*, XVI (1949), 18–28; and R. Turvey "Some Aspects of the Theory of Inflation in a Closed Economy," *The Economic Journal*, LXI (1951), 531–43.

2. P. A. Samuelson, "Dynamic Process Analysis," *A Survey of Contemporary Economics*, ed. by H. S. Ellis (Homewood, Illinois, 1956), Chapter 10.

3. J. C. R. Dow, "Analysis of the Generation of Price Inflation. A Study of Cost and Price Changes in the United Kingdom, 1946–54." *Oxford Economic Papers*, VIII, New series (1956), 252–301.

4. The rationale of this equation is as follows: During the inflation, the basic trend of money wage multiplies at a constant rate of α per year (or each period). Thus, if the wage (or wage index) is 1 for period O, then it is α for period 1, α^2 for period 2, α^3 for period 3, and so forth. Because of the possible lag in wage adjustments, however, actual wage increases do not keep abreast of those of price or profit. Consequently, the wage of a given period t deviates from its basic trend, and this deviation is denoted by the factor $(-\beta)^t(Q_1 - Q)$. Here $(Q_1 - Q)$ denotes the "shock," which starts a process of adjustment represented by the series $(-\beta)(Q_1 - Q)$, $(-\beta)^2(Q_1 - Q)$, $(-\beta)^3(Q_1 - Q)$ . . . for period 1, 2, 3, . . . , respectively.

5. It should be noted that α and β, though not unrelated, are by no means identical, especially when profit and wage rates are changing from period to period.

6. Equation (2.5) is derived as follows: According to equation (2.3), $P_t = \alpha^t P$. Substituting equations (2.1) and (2.2) in equation (2.3),

$$\eta Q_t + (1 - \eta) W_t = \alpha^t[\eta Q + (1 - \eta) W],$$

or

$$Q_t = \alpha^t Q + \frac{\alpha^t(1 - \eta)}{\eta} W - \frac{(1 - \eta)}{\eta} W_t,$$

which gives (2.3).

7. Since equation (2.8) is concerned only with absolute numbers, the minus sign attached to the entire term $(-\beta)^t(Q_1 - Q)$ and that of β have no longer any significance for our result. These signs are therefore ignored in relation (2.8).

8. Holzman, *Review of Economics and Statistics*, XXXII (1950), 150–58. The defect of Holzman's models is shown by plotting the period-to-period link relatives, the ratio of wage (W) to income (Y) and ratio of profit (Q) to income (Y). All these relatives and ratios are derived from

the numerical illustrations given in Table 4 of Holzman's article. None of these diagrams demonstrates adequately the spiral mechanisms shown in Charts 1 and 2.

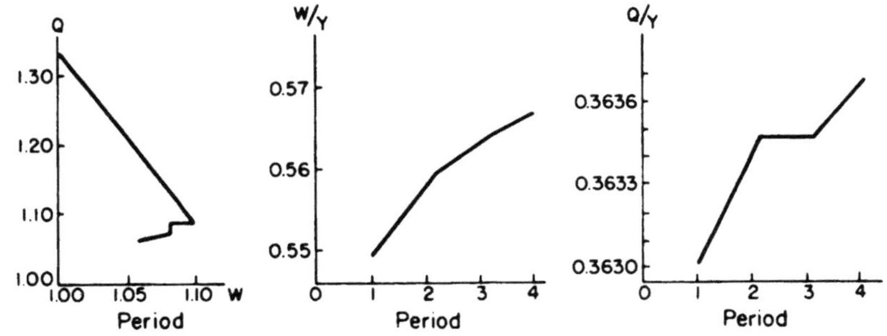

Index

Agricultural economy, 5–6
Agricultural income, 243
Agricultural production, 90–94, 96

Bankers' Association and Native Bankers Guild: Joint Reserve Board, 192
Bank of China, 116, 121, 126–127, 133, 163, 187–88, 190, 191, 206
Bank of Communications, 116, 121, 126–127, 133, 187–88
Bankruptcies, 254
Banks: assets, 198–208; clearings, 191, 221–23; deposit redemption, 255–56; deposit reserves, 194–96, 199–200; deposits, 107, 211–16, 222; foreign, 189; government funds in, 197–98; government, 187–89, 190 *et passim*; interest rates, 233–35, 250–54, 270–71; investment portfolios, 200–1; liabilities, 198–208; loan repayments, 255–56; loans, 108–12, 196–97, 201–8, 213–14, 233; market operations, 193–94; modern, 189–90; native, 163, 189; number, 208–9; private, 163, 187–90, 194–95, 197–98, 199 *et passim*; rediscount policy, 192–93
Bank withdrawals, restrictions on, 118–19
Board of Trustees for Rehabilitation Affairs, 173–74

Central Bank of China, 25, 82, 83, 120, 165, 187; Department of Issue, 18; foreign exchange policy of, 117, 119, 124–25, 126, 128–29, 131, 132–34, 135, 136, 137, 140, 141, 143–53, 156, 167–72, 181–82; functions of, 77, 81, 85, 166, 187 *et passim*; loan policy of, 112, 113, 144, 253; monetary policy, 14–15; note issues of, 44, 116; records of, 74; regulations of, 38, 60, 131; Research Department, 19; statistics of, 28, 237
Central Bank of Manchou notes, 1–2
Central Cooperative Bank, 188
Central Reserve Bank notes, 1, 14, 23, 24, 25, 28–29, 220
Central Trust, 188
Chang Chun, 140
Chang Kia-ngau, 139, 140
Chartered Bank of India, Australia, and China, 121
Chiang Ching Kuo, 26
Chiang Kai-shek, 172
China Air Transport, 177
China Merchant Steamship Navigation Company, 60
China Relief Program, 178–80
China Textile Industries, Incorporated, 60, 108, 193–94
China Waterway Transport, 177
Commodity tax, 40–41, 42, 47, 48, 61–64
Consolidated Bonds, 245, 249
Consolidated tax, *see* Commodity tax
Consumer expenditures, 90–95, 113
Consumer goods, 94–97, 101–2
Corn, 96
Cost-push inflation, 6–7
Cotton, 94, 96, 97–98, 107
Currency: areas, 1–3, 5, 14; effect of supply on inflation, 13–15; *see also* Notes
Customs, revenue from, 40–41, 43–46, 61–64
Customs Gold Unit, 44–45

Debt service, 41–42, 70, 74, 75, 78–87
Defense, expenditure for, 41–42, 70–71, 74, 75
Demand-pull inflation, 6–7
Directorate General of Budgets, Accounts, and Statistics, 237
Dollar assets, post-war Chinese, 293–99
Dollar notes (Hong Kong), *see* Hong Kong dollars

Economic Coordination Administration, 147, 177–78, 180–82
Education abroad, expenditure for, 74–75
Ewo Breweries, 245
Ewo Cotton Mill, 245
Exchange Control Commission, 124–25
Executive Yuan, 140
Expenditure, governmental, *see* Government expenditure
Export-Import Board, 143
Export-Import Link System, 139–40
Export-Import ratio, 158–59
Exports, 95–96, 103, 104–5, 106, 141–42, 150–52, 159–62

Fapi currency area, 1, 3, 5, 14
Fapi notes, 18, 21–23, 28–31, 116, 120–22, 126, 130, 214, 217, 218, 220, 225, 261; converision rates, 24, 25, 31, 33–39
Farmers Bank of China, 188
Farm income, *see* Agricultural income
Federal Reserve Bank of China notes, 1, 28–29, 120, 220
Fiscal system, 40–42, 61–62, 87–88
Food Supply Commission of Shanghai, 134
Foreign aid, 173–84
Foreign-currency bond, servicing cost, 288–90
Foreign exchange, 44–46, 69–71, 73–78, 88, 97, 105, 115–57, 166–72, 191–94; deposit certificate system, 151–55, 169; France, 267–68; Germany, 268; Greece, 148–49, 267; Peru, 149
Foreign Exchange Clearance Certificate System, 146–48
Foreign Exchange Stabilization Fund Committee, 132–39
Foreign Exchange Surrender Certificate System, 139, 144–46
Foreign Relief Program, 178–80
Foreign service, expenditure, 74, 78
Franc, conversion rate, 267

Gold, 105–7, 166, 170–72, 219, 224–32, 245–49
Government banks, 187–89
Government bonds, 81–87
Government expenditure: China, 40–42, 62–64, 67–78, 269–70; Germany, 269–70
Government income: China, 40–67, 71–73, 269–70; Germany, 269–70; *see also* Customs, revenue from, Income tax, Land tax, Monopolies, etc.
Gross barter terms of trade, 160–61
Gross national product, 73

Hansen, B., quoted, 7, 8–9
Hong Kong dollars, 107, 149–51, 164, 172
Hong Kong Shanghai Banking Corporation, 121, 133, 189

Import duties, *see* Customs, revenue from
Imports, 97–99, 151–52, 159–62; cost of, 76–77; expenditure for, 74; Free China, 94–95; Occupied China, 95; quota system, 127, 141–44; restrictions, 131, 133
Income tax, 41, 50–55, 291–92
Income terms of trade, 160–62
Industrial economy, 5–6
Inflation in China: causes, 11–16; characteristics, 1–15; social implications of, 15
Investment, expenditures for, 99–107
Investment for ownership-benefit, 105–7, 113–14
Investment for use-benefit, 101–5, 113–14
Investments, financing of, 108–13

Japanese currency areas, 1–2
Joint Administration of Government Banks, 188–89
Joint Head Office of Government Banks, 192–93; 196–97, 233

Keynes, J. M.: cited, 9; quoted, 257

Land tax, 55–57
Lundberg, E.: formula for inflationary gap, 8; quoted, 10

Machlup, F., quoted, 7
Manchurian note area, 2, 14
Manchurian notes, 2, 31; conversion rate, 31, 38–39
Mayar Silk, 245
Military expenditure, *see* Defense, expenditure for
Monetary areas, *see* Currency areas
Monetary reform, 25–28, 116
Monetary Reform Act, 227
Money shops, *see* Banks, native
Monopolies, as government revenue, 47–48

National City Bank of New York, 133
National Highway Transport, 177
National income, 71–73
National Resources Commission, 108
National Treasury Act, 197

Native Bankers Guild, 192
Net terms of trade, 160–62
Nickel currency, 150
Note issues: authority for, 190–91; China, 260–66; expenditure for, 74–76; Germany, 260–66; Greece, 260–66; Hungary, 260–66; statistics of, 18, 20, 21–22, 24, 27, 28, 30, 32, 36, 212, 215, 216, 218–19
Notes: Central Bank of China, 44, 116; Central Bank of Manchou, 1–2; Central Reserve Bank, 1, 14, 23, 24, 25, 28–29, 220; Fapi, 18, 21–23, 24–25, 28–31, 33–39, 116, 120–22, 126, 130, 214, 217, 218, 220, 225, 261; Federal Reserve Bank of China, 1, 28–29, 120, 220; Hong Kong dollars, 107, 149–51, 164, 172; Manchurian, 1–2, 31, 38–39; Taipi, 32–37; Yuan, 1, 4, 25–27, 28, 44–45, 69, 77, 83, 116–18, 122, 126–27, 131–37, 141, 146, 149–50, 153, 156–57, 171, 220, 225, 226, 261; *see also* Currency

Official reserves, 165–72
Overseas Chinese Banking Corporation of Singapore, 163
Overseas remittances, *see* Remittances

Pei Tsu-yee, 132
Postal Remittances and Savings Bank, 188
Price-index bond, 85–86
Price indices: Canton, 19; Chungking, 19–29; Kunming, 19; Manchuria, 30–31; Shanghai, 19–29, 32, 34; Taipei, 32, 34; Taiwan, 32; Tientsin, 28–29
Prices: agricultural, 243; Chungking, 21–23, 28, 214–15, 218, 219, 232–40, 253, 255; Germany, 260–66, 270–71; Greece, 260–66; Hungary, 260–66; Shanghai, 21–22, 28, 214, 216, 218–19, 240–43, 245–50, 253, 255, 260–66; Tientsin, 28
Producer goods, 101–2

Regulation for Controlling Private Banks, 194
Remittances, 36, 37–38, 162–65, 188
Revenue, governmental, *see* Government income
Rice, 91–94
Russian military currency, 2

Salt tax, 40–41, 61–64
Shanghai Dock Yard, 245
Shanghai Security Exchange, 85, 228
Shao, Albert, 149
Shoup Mission Report, quoted, 67
Silver, 116, 150, 166, 170–72, 225, 227
Sino-American-British Stabilization Board, 123–130, 167, 168, 185, 189, 192; Shanghai policy: 125–26
Sino-British Stabilization Fund, 120–22, 127, 129, 167, 185, 189, 192
Smuggling, 40, 61, 150, 153
Standard Shirts, 245
Statistics, sources, 16–17, 18–19, 107, 165, 166, 167, 168, 221, 237, 245, 286–87, 293, 294, 296, 298
Stocks, 245, 247, 249–50
Surplus property, 57–61, 63, 173

Taipi notes, conversion rate, 32–37
Taiwan currency, 1–2
Taiwan Paper Mill, 60
Taiwan Sugar Company, 60
Taxes, *see* Income tax, Land tax, Salt tax, etc.
Temporary Banking Regulation for the Emergency Period, 210
Textile Control Commission, 134
Tobacco, 97–98
Trade policy, 123–24, 127–30, 131–36, 139–44, 151–62
Transportation industries, 103–4

United Nations Relief and Rehabilitation Administration, 173–78
United States Dollar Bond, 82
United States Dollar Savings Certificate, 83
United States Dollar Short-Term Treasury Notes, 84–86
United States Dollar Victory Bond, 83
United States Treasury Credit of 1942, 174

Wages, 68–69, 71; Chungking, 237–40; professional and civil workers, 244–45
Wei-wah check system, 119
Wheat, 94, 96–98
Wheelock Company, 245, 313*n*7
Wing-on Textiles, 245, 249

Yen, conversion rate, 266
Yuan notes: conversion rate, 44–45, 69, 77, 83, 116–18, 122, 126–27, 131–37, 141, 146, 156–57, 171, 225, 226, 249, 261; gold, 1, 4, 25–27, 149–50, 153, 220; silver, 1, 4, 27–28, 150
Yui, O. K., 140

Bei Fragen zur Produktsicherheit wenden Sie sich bitte an:
If you have any questions regarding product safety, please contact:

Walter de Gruyter GmbH
Genthiner Straße 13
10785 Berlin
productsafety@degruyterbrill.com